From
Civilization
to
Segregation

From Civilization to Segregation

SOCIAL IDEALS AND SOCIAL CONTROL
IN SOUTHERN RHODESIA, 1890–1934

Carol Summers

OHIO UNIVERSITY PRESS

ATHENS

Ohio University Press, Athens, Ohio 45701
© 1994 by Carol Summers
Printed in the United States of America
All rights reserved
98 97 96 95 94   5 4 3 2 1

Ohio University Press books are printed on acid-free paper ∞

Library of Congress Cataloging-in-Publication Data

Summers, Carol, 1964–
    From civilization to segregation : social ideals and social
control in southern Rhodesia, 1890–1934 / Carol Summers.
        p.   cm.
    Includes bibliographical references and index.
    ISBN 0-8214-1074-1
    1. Zimbabwe—History—1890–1965.   2. Zimbabwe—Social
conditions—1890–1965.   3. Zimbabwe—Race relations.   I. Title.
DT2959.S86   1994
968.91—dc20
                                                                    94-196
                                                                    CIP

CONTENTS

ABBREVIATIONS

ABC	American Board of Commissioners for Foreign Missions. Also known as the American Board.
BSAC	British South Africa Company. Also known as the Company.
BSAP	British South Africa Police
CBMS/IMC	Council of British Missionary Societies/International Missionary Congress. An interdenominational protestant missionary umbrella organization.
CNC	Chief Native Commissioner. Until 1913, there were two in Southern Rhodesia: the CNC Mashonaland and the CNC Matabeleland. Thereafter the jobs were combined.
CO	Colonial Office, Great Britain
CWM	Council for World Missions. Holds records for the LMS.
DRC	Dutch Reformed Church
GP	Government Printer of Southern Rhodesia
ICU	Industrial and Commercial Workers' Union
HC	High Commissioner. Representative of the Colonial Office at the Cape.
HMSO	His/Her Majesty's Stationary Office
JAH	Jesuit Archives, Harare. British Society of Jesus (Catholic) records, stored in Mount Pleasant, Harare, Zimbabwe.
JT	Jeanes Teacher, a type of extension, supervising treacher, supported by the Carnegie Corporation.
LMS	London Missionary Society. Archival references are to CWM.

MMS	Wesleyan Methodist Missionary Society. The British Methodists, also known as WMMS.
MQ	*Mashonaland Quarterly.* Southern Rhodesian Church of England missionary magazine (same as SRQ).
NACE	Native Affairs Committee of Enquiry (1911)
NAD	Native Affairs Department. Also known as the Native Department, headed by the chief native commissioner.
NADA	*Native Affairs Department Annual.* A periodical published by the NAD, but for a popular audience—advertised to settlers as the thing to read if you wanted to known more about your workers and the world of Southern Rhodesia.
NAZ	National Archives of Zimbabwe, Borrowdale, Harare, Zimbabwe.
NC	Native Commissioner. Frequently combined with the name of the region to specify the responsible official e.g., NC Belingwe, NC Gutu, NC Goromonzi).
NDD	Native Development Department. Also known as the Department of Native Education or Department of Native Development, headed by the Director of Native Education or the Director of Native Development.
PSRMC	*Proceedings of the Southern Rhodesian Missionary Conference.* A meeting of the white missionaries of the region, held every two years.
RAU	Rhodesian Agricultural Union, an organization of white farmers.
RNLB	Rhodesian Native Labour Board
RC	Resident Commissioner. Representative of the CO in Southern Rhodesia.
SANAC	Southern Africa Native Affairs Commission
SoN	Superintendent of Natives. Ranks below CNC, and above NC.
SPG	Society for the Propagation of the Gospel. Also USPG, Church of England.
SR	Southern Rhodesia
SRMC	Southern Rhodesia Missionary Conference. Inter-

denominational organization of white missionaries in Southern Rhodesia.

SRQ   *Southern Rhodesian Quarterly.* Church of England parish magazine (same as MQ).

USPG   United Society for the Propagation of the gospel, Church of England

WMMS   Wesleyan Methodist Missionary Society. Also MMS, British Methodists.

ZMR   *Zambesi Mission Record.* The Catholic missionary magazine for Southern Rhodesia.

A NOTE ON TERMINOLOGY

Almost all the words available to discuss social change in southern Africa carry either pejorative or problematic associations and implications. This makes writing without insulting or misleading the reader into an extremely complex task, made even more difficult by the focus of this work on how contemporaries viewed the dynamics and problematics of social change. The words used in this work are therefore the results of expediency and compromises rather like the processes they describe, though, I hope, less malignant.

I have chosen the word *European* to designate those of European ancestry. *Europeans* includes a diverse group of people, born everywhere from the Americas, through the British Empire, to England and Europe itself. I have continued to use this as a term to refer to those people of European ancestry born in Southern Rhodesia or South Africa, as the term *Rhodesian,* frequently used in the early twentieth century to refer exclusively to those of European ancestry born in the region, seems excessively misleading.

I have used the word *African* to refer to anyone or any group with African ancestry. In doing so, I am attempting to bypass current debates over the origins of Shona identity and the nature of Ndebele society. I therefore use *Shona* and *Ndebele* only when such distinctions are immediately relevant. And I only refer to such subgroups as Manyika, Kalanga, Karanga, and so on when my sources have made such distinctions relevant to my argument. More problematically, I have also used the term *African* to designate both permanent African immigrants to the region, such as the Mfengu ("Fingoes") and the mass of workers referred to by colonial officials as "non-indigenous Natives," who came from throughout the Southern African region. I have rejected the term *Zimbabwean* to describe the African inhabitants of Southern Rhodesia as excessively anachronistic. And I have generally refrained from the use of *Black* and *White* as, for much of this period, the debates may carry racist implications, but are about culture and mutability, rather than about racial absolutes.

I have chosen to refer to cultural and racial communities. This is an attempt to force the reader, through the use of terminology from an earlier period, to understand the processes the terminology was used to describe, and the connotation of not merely interests, but also values, that affected contemporaries' logic and actions. Contemporaries discussed communities, and their redefinition, from cultural to racial entities, is one of the major transitions described in this study. The term "community" also carries relevant connotations of social comprehension and construction within debates over race, ethnicity, and nationalism evoked by Benedict Anderson's work *Imagined Communities*.

Discussing government, administration, or the state in Southern Rhodesia is made more complicated by changes in the structure and nature of that state. The British South Africa Company ruled until 1923, subject to an imperial charter and a sometimes myopic process of imperial oversight. In 1923, the British parliament granted Southern Rhodesia "responsible government," which consisted of a government elected by voters within the territory, according to a restricted but formally nonracial franchise, overseeing an administration that remained subject to imperial reservations in, significantly, the area of Native Policy. The Company paid for the Native Department's expenses until 1923, but Native Department officials could only be appointed with approval from the Colonial Office, and the department as a whole was formally responsible to the imperial Colonial Office, not the Company. All aspects of the Company's administration were subject to the decrees of a Legislative Council that included increasing numbers of nonofficial members elected by European settlers. After 1923 the administration continued, with few changes in personnel, but under the new authority of a government in the classic parliamentary sense—a premier and his cabinet, later to become a prime minister and cabinet. Amid these changes, I have attempted to distinguish between the Company (an economic enterprise), the administration (a bureaucracy), the state (structural frameworks, including the bureaucracy), and the government (the political leadership). The differences are important, as they provide complexity to the social debates occurring in the twentieth century.

Despite my attempts to be careful, many dubious terms nevertheless appear within this study. The adjective *Native,* referring to Native Education and Native Development programs, projects a possibly pejorative, but necessary, implication of distance from any common European core of values, culture, or economic development. It is also a contemporary term, used so extensively that to put it consistently into quotation marks would prove excessively tedious. The terms *chief, induna, headman,* or *paramount* are used only when invoked by contemporary records, or when the status is one defined or imposed by the colonial government. I have, however, had to use the concept of *elders* to discuss gerontocratic divisions within the African community.

Even more difficult than the words describing people, though, are the words for processes. *Progress* and *development* are both intensely problematic concepts, constantly redefined, which should be subjects of enquiry rather than convenient labels for defined processes. This work is about the many efforts made to redefine them. I have chosen to use the word *civilization,* with a carefully circumscribed definition, both because there is no other concise satisfactory term for the bundle of concepts it contains, and as a way of bringing the language of the past to the present-day reader.

Regardless of this care, in this discussion of the mutability of concepts used to understand and control change, many terms will remain problematic, best defined by the context within which they are used by my sources or myself. I have not attempted to tidy up the pejorative—sometimes directly abusive—language of my sources. Instead, I have presented it because, unlike any bowdlerized version, it allows the reader to understand contemporary argumentation directly.

ACKNOWLEDGMENTS

My research for this work was funded by a dissertation research fellowship from the Social Science Research Council, and by graduate support from the Johns Hopkins University, including a Richard J. Owen Fellowship, and Department of History Fellowships, teaching assistantships, and grants. The Faculty Research Committee of the University of Richmond (Virginia) also funded a productive trip to Zimbabwe and England during 1992.

This project feels as though it has taken forever, but many people have tried to help the process along. Philip Curtin, my primary dissertation advisor, read and remained encouraging. Sara Berry read the whole dissertation and made suggestions. David Cohen offered suggestions and support during the process. The students of the African and Comparative History seminars at Johns Hopkins read chapter after chapter, without too much groaning, providing me with the useful illusion that someone was interested in what I was writing. The other members of my dissertation committee—Norma Kriger, Gillian Feely-Harnick, and Ashraf Ghani—also asked good questions and made interesting suggestions. Marcia Summers also read the whole work in draft form and suggested ways to make it more comprehensible. More recently, Kenneth Vickery has provided a useful reading and set of suggestions, and Louis Tremaine has commented on a portion of the manuscript. Unfortunately, I cannot claim to have taken everyone's suggestions. Some will have to wait for future papers and projects.

This work has only been possible because of the existence and helpfulness of libraries, archives, and their staffs in the United States, England, and Zimbabwe. I enjoyed my time in the archives tremendously, with the possible exception of the hours crouched over microfilmed newspapers, and I look forward to returning, as I know there is inevitably more fascinating material.

INTRODUCTION

Between the invasion of Mashonaland by the British South Africa Company's pioneer column during 1890 and the election of the explicitly segregationist Huggins government in the general elections of 1933, life in Southern Rhodesia changed dramatically as residents struggled, often unsuccessfully, for prosperity. The construction of Southern Rhodesia as a settler colony, though, was more than just an economic or political process. It also involved the construction, management, and deployment of new systems of understanding and knowledge. The administration, settlers, missionaries, and Africans sought to profit from, induce, or control social change in both African society and the dominant European community. To do so, they worked to develop and use images, ideas, and concepts of their neighbors and their environment, of what was unlikely, possible, probable, or inevitable, and then use that knowledge, along with economic, military, political, and other resources, to remold themselves, and other inhabitants of the region into the building blocks of order, development, and change. Southern Rhodesia's society was not built through the attempts of a single coherent group, be it settlers, missionaries, or Africans. Its plans were not drawn by any particular Native Affairs Commission, or imposed through successful governmental interventions. One crisis after another, a stingy administration, and a multiplicity of individuals and interests, built a Southern Rhodesia that had dreams, and nightmares, of unity but a reality of tension and conflict.

Searching for ways to comprehend and control social change, the inhabitants of Southern Rhodesia struggled and experimented. In 1890 the pioneer column of the British South Africa Company marched through Matabeleland, the kingdom in the southwest of present-day Zimbabwe, and occupied the region known as Mashonaland, establishing forts and land claims centered on Fort Victoria (Gweru), Salisbury (Harare), and Umtali (Mutare). The pioneer column and early prospectors both used violence and believed in violence as a way of legitimizing European rule and extracting gold, cattle, and labor from the Africans of the territory. In 1893 the settlers and Company successfully provoked the Matabele war, opening Matabeleland to European occupation, and attacking the Matabele state. But during 1896 and 1897, the Risings, sometimes known as the first Chimurenga, broke out as Africans fought, threatening European profits and control, and proving that Africans could also use violence. European faith in violence faltered, despite the Company's eventual bloody military victory. Violence alone, while temporarily useful as a way of raiding a marginal frontier region, proved an expensive and uncertain way to achieve order or profits. The Risings taught both Europeans and Africans that they could not afford the costs of unrestrained violence.

In the aftermath of the war, Africans, missionaries, officials, and settlers sought a more secure basis for order and profits, and began to develop an image and rhetoric of "civilization" as a strategy for social change. In Southern Rhodesia, ideas of civilization did state societal values. But the values were not static. Instead, the ideas and rhetoric of civilization provided a way to discuss policies designed to promote social change. The Southern Rhodesian idea of civilization had three major policy implications. It called for a cultivation of individualism among Africans. It suggested that conflict between Africans and Europeans could be blocked if Africans learned European culture, whether literacy, English, work discipline, or Christianity. And, finally, this idea of civilization placed an emphasis on the newly liberated individual's acceptance of the economic logic of market capitalism and participation in market-oriented economic activity, as a seller of goods or labor.

Ideas of civilization, though, proved an awkward fit with the economic needs of the region. Employers, nearly all settlers within the region, demanded cheap labor, coerced if necessary—labor for prospecting, for mining, for farming, and for all forms of commercial, governmental, and domestic service. In the aftermath of the South African war, Southern Rhodesia's economy sought to struggle to its feet. The mining sector became increasingly credible as settlers established hundreds of small mines that, requiring little capital and paying paltry wages, produced profits from the small quantities of gold they did mine, and, upon proving their success, could sell out to larger concerns. Market agriculture developed as well as Africans and Europeans turned toward the extensive cultivation of maize, experimented with tobacco, and fought for access not merely to domestic markets, but also to regional and international markets. Much of the expansion of the European-directed economy, though, was carried on with labor from "nonindigenous natives"—men from Mozambique, Nyasaland, Northern Rhodesia, and even South Africa. And these labor migrants, and the indigenous Africans as well, learned to work the system, selecting jobs, pursuing education, and protesting difficulties—sometimes, thanks to experience on the job or in a school, protesting in English.

The assimilationist values and policy implications of the idea of civilization began to lose their appeal to many factions of the Southern Rhodesian population as assimilation appeared to be working all too quickly and all too well, to the point where, in the eyes of nervous Europeans—if not in reality—civilized Africans were threatening European dominance. As the missionary-influenced imperial government and the distinctly rapacious British South Africa Company were increasingly marginalized by a gradual settler takeover of the state which culminated in the establishment of settler "responsible government" in 1923, a new key image, the idea of discipline, began to emerge from debates over social control and to grow into a new theory for guided and controlled social change. The idea of civilization had embodied an image of social change in which 'progress' or development' would grow organically from a mass of African individuals. But by the 1920s, the inhabitants of Southern Rhodesia were attempting to intervene, making 'development' less organic than architectural, an enterprise that, far from proceeding fluidly as a natural process, had to be planned and implemented. Attempts to plan for change and to control its results were explicit in the governmental, settler, and missionary debates and intervention in education, and the association, during the late 1920s, of "Native Education" with "Native Development" in an explicit attempt to promote a separate African culture, society, and economy and, indeed, an African civilization removed from rather than assimilated to that of the European settlers.

The new ideas of the 1920s, in conjunction with the very real economic changes and economic crisis of the Depression, led to the segregationist initiatives of the late 1920s and the 1930s. Both Africans and Europeans shifted from a logic of individuals and individual opportunity to one in which the racial community provided the fundamental unit of social analysis. In doing so, they sought to prevent the blurring of social lines by 'progressive' or 'degenerate' individuals, whether African or European, and added a substantial measure of inertia to an otherwise volatile process of individual cultural learning and identification. The idea of communal solidarity ran directly counter to the very real diversification that had taken place in both the African and European communities of Southern Rhodesia, whether through the prosperity of a few African commercial farmers or the impoverishment of unskilled European laborers. But by making policy for the average African or European and by using state power to reinforce social boundaries, the distinctly shaky state graduated from social engineering policies designed to prepare people for a specific future to using the image of segregation to direct intervention in the social structure of a contemporary society threatened by economic collapse and social contradictions.

The inhabitants of Southern Rhodesia, throughout the period in question, had a variety of interests, values, and perspectives on social change and social control. The key images, types of knowledge, and ideologies that they built reflected this variety, and contained internal contradictions which prevented an easy, stable system of domination from evolving. Instead of providing an ideological framework capable of shaping the hearts and minds of Europeans or Africans within the region, these ideas and images provided words and a rapidly changing language through which individuals and groups could comprehend, communicate, and contend with each other in a complex process of negotiation on the terms of a new society.

The difficult work of creating knowledge and communicating the elements of social ideologies between the social groups, economic sectors and geographical regions was not always coherent or instantaneous. This study examines how knowledge and communication were used, changing over time even as the social, economic, and political context changed. But while it is possible to assign specific dates of political transition—such as the 1923 transfer of administrative authority from the British South Africa Company to the Responsible Government of the settlers' state—such precision is impossible with knowledge and ideological concepts. Both are attached to people, who may continue to hold them long after they have gone out of fashion. Both are connected to specific institutions within society which, though rising and falling in prominence within the regional debates, may continue to exist long after their moment of influence. This study therefore periodizes ideological change not by looking at sharp boundaries or critical breaks, but by finding clusters of discourse—clusters that frequently overlap and blend in to each other. The ideas of civilization, for example, did not vanish after 1906, though they did, at least temporarily, lose their dominant place in political and social debates. And useful ideas are rarely ever lost entirely: though beyond the chronological scope of this work, Timothy Burke has argued that ideas of civilization made a comeback after World War II,[1] and demands for discipline can be seen in the letters to the editor printed by the *Herald* during the student unrest of recent years at the University of Zimbabwe.

This work is a history of public opinion—of common knowledge, assumptions, and issues—rather than a history that concentrates on the details of what happened in Southern Rhodesia during its formative period. The historiography of Southern Rhodesia, and of today's Zimbabwe, is full of discussions of what happened. Early historians such as Lewis Gann, Colin Leys, and, to some extent, Philip Mason, provided histories that focused on the development of the settler state of Southern Rhodesia and its power over the far larger African population. These historians' willingness to analyze the state and the European community as though the African majority was irrelevant limits their usefulness today. They used a very narrow definition of politics, focusing on electoral politics and formal interest groups rather than contemplating the political implications of daily life or wider social issues. Indeed, it is almost unthinkable that a present-day scholar could begin a study of political history in Southern Rhodesia by asserting, as Leys did, that the African population "was mostly too inexperienced to play much part in politics, even if it had been permitted to do so."[2] These histories, even when acknowledging shortcomings of the European community, as Gann did repeatedly over issues ranging from the formation of reserves to the technologies of European farming, tended to accept European domination of a society divided between Europeans and Africans as natural or legitimate.[3] The early historians did, however, take questions of consciousness seriously, at least in discussing the European population. And they and such careful studies as D. J. Murray's *Governmental Systems of Southern Rhodesia* and Claire Palley's *Constitutional History of Southern Rhodesia* provide formal analyses of the European-dominated state and the settler community that discuss structures, institutions, and laws critical to an understanding of how debate was structured within the region.[4]

Fortunately, from the mid-1970s, revisionist studies of Southern Rhodesia—studies that use a wider definition of politics and consider Africans as actors in the region's economy, politics, and society—have proliferated, exploring the past both by sector of the economy, as Charles van Onselen's *Chibaro* and Robin Palmer's *Land and Racial Domination* have done for mining and agriculture respectively, and by region.[5] This study could not have been written without the background of these and other works. Debates, ideas, plans, and fears acquire meaning from their physical, economic, social, and political contexts—not solely from the texts that provide the sources for my research.

Southern Rhodesia as a whole, however, provides a coherent unit of analysis for more than just structural depictions of the administration. Despite the differences between the opinions and knowledge of miners and farmers, or between the perspectives of Belingwe or Gutu, there were aspects of Southern Rhodesian public opinion and public knowledge which affected the region as a whole, and which call for a synthetic approach. Southern Rhodesia was under a single idiosyncratic and constantly changing administration. Its inhabitants, particularly its European inhabitants, organized on a national level, reading the same newspapers and electing representatives to the same assembly. The region's native policy was also increasingly unified from region to region as Mashonaland and Matabeleland were put under a single chief native commissioner, tax policy was standardized from region to region, the judicial decisions of native commissioners were subjected to a colony-wide appeal process that eliminated appeals to local differences or community standards, and legislation differentiated the Africans of the region not into Shona, Ndebele, or other ethnic or regional subgroup, but into only two categories: "indigenous Natives" and "non-indigenous Natives."

Just as the existence of Southern Rhodesia-wide laws, administration, media, and organization make the region reasonably coherent internally for an examination of ideas of social change, several sharp differences between Southern Rhodesia and its neighbors make it important that its history be examined carefully, rather than merely incorporated into a larger regional history of Southern Africa. Despite extensive debate until at least the 1920s over the possibility of the union of Southern Rhodesia with the Union of South Africa, the population, society, and economy of Southern Rhodesia differed significantly from those of the Union. The European population of Southern Rhodesia was far smaller, both absolutely and as a percentage of the total, than that of any region of the Union, and had arrived more recently. It was predominantly English-speaking, with a Dutch-speaking minority small enough to be politically isolated even within European electoral politics. And at the beginning of the twentieth century, the sections of the population who formed the middle of the Union's social pyramid were nearly missing from Southern Rhodesia. Asians, "Coloureds," and even educated and skilled Africans were scarce in Southern Rhodesia before the 1930s. "Native Police," "boss boys," clerks, and even qualified mission teachers and evangelists were often immigrants from South Africa. Until at least the 1930s, there were no Southern Rhodesian equivalents for the institutions—such as Lovedale, Fort Hare, or even Tiger Kloof—that provided higher education for a few South African Blacks and shaped South African debates over "civilization" and Native Education.[6] Economically, too, Southern Rhodesia lacked the strength and complexity of any region of the Union. Its mining could not compare to that of Kimberly or the Rand. Its industry and commerce were woefully underdeveloped. And even its agriculture was rudimentary compared to that of Natal or the Cape. During the period before the 1930s, the structure and stratification of Southern Rhodesia was direct and abrupt, an order of magnitude removed from the complexities of South Africa proper. These differences preclude any wholesale importation from South Africa of explanations for Southern Rhodesian Native Policy, Native Education policies, Native Development initiatives, or segregation as a whole.

Yet while its newness and marginality distinguished Southern Rhodesia from the Union, its status as a settler colony rather than a protectorate distinguished it from other British-dominated neighbors such as Bechuanaland (Botswana) and Nyasaland (Malawi) and even, to some degree, from Northern Rhodesia (Zambia). The local European community was substantial enough to override or modify general imperial ideologies or policies. While protectorate officials frequently voiced paternalistic ideals or appealed to theories of indirect rule in favor of enlightened or traditional African leadership, Southern Rhodesian Europeans explicitly and firmly reminded policymakers that settlers' interests came first. The existence and power of the settler state and economy differentiated Southern Rhodesia sharply from its nearest neighbors.

Recently, Ian Phimister has made a new attempt at a national history, using the region of Southern Rhodesia as his unit of analysis and taking the new revisionist, heavily materialistic, research into account. His *Economic and Social History of Zimbabwe* is an eminently useful book, laying down coherent descriptions of the economic and social changes Southern Rhodesia experienced from conquest to 1948.[7] Even more than the more specialized materialistic studies, though, it leaves the reader asking questions—questions about who knew what, when, questions about whether people made choices, and if they did, on what basis, and questions about meaning (What was the significance to various members of the society of changes in capitalism, economic development, or state formation?). My work, in its focus on perception, interpretations, subjective knowledge and choices, is an attempt at a constructive antithesis to Phimister's work.

Recently, as the political situation in Southern Africa has become increasingly complex, yet another type of analysis of domination and accomodation has begun to emerge from works such as Dane Kennedy's *Islands of White,* which uses anthropological theories of the creation and maintenence of cultural boundaries to attempt to understand the dynamics of separation and power, and Jean and John Comaroff's *Of Revelation and Revolution,* which asks how that domination was understood and mediated through cultural knowledge.[8] Neither of those works focuses exclusively on Southern Rhodesia, as Kennedy's compares settler communities in Southern Rhodesia and Kenya, and the Comaroffs' work centers on a Tswana region of South Africa. Yet both studies, though entirely different in methodology and theoretical perspectives, work to reintroduce culture, and questions of cultural engineering, into Southern African studies.

This study, using the background of earlier political, economic, and cultural studies, examines the dynamics of social change in a region marginal both economically and politically to the larger world on which it was increasingly dependent. Others have looked at economic or political change. Instead of repeating or directly challenging that work in a reexamination of events through current notions of how economies develop or societies change, this study selects specific issues which the historical actors themselves considered potentially decisive for the future of the region, and debated vigorously—issues such as Native Policy, Native Education, Native Development, and segregation. These debates ranged across economic sectors, and up and down the social hierarchy and were broad enough to occasionally incorporate smaller more focused controversies over such issues as family law, criminality, health policy, or even conservation. The arguments actors used in these society-wide controversies, and the policies that were debated or implemented, help to uncover both how those actors perceived change, believing it could be induced, shaped, or controlled, and the communities' patterns of logic and values. These were not peripheral debates. Issues such as native policy, education, and development were perceived by the inhabitants of Southern Rhodesia as issues that mattered. These debates were not merely rhetorical. Ideas were constantly challenged by economic realities. Statements of how the world should work were upset by the actions of those who had other ideas. And not all of the opinions which shaped policies were set down in words on paper. Many were expressed by African men who left Southern Rhodesia in search of higher pay on the Rand or at Kimberly, African women who moved to cities or missions and stayed, African children who made difficult choices between herding and school, and those Europeans who ignored the admonitions of their community's leaders and gravitated toward the African community either to live within it or to prey on it.

This, then, is a study of social discourse in the sense that it examines what was said about a society and how that society defined itself. But it incorporates to some degree an examination of social praxis, as the ways in which ideas and policy changed during implementation provide clues to the nonverbal statements of a social debate that was not confined within the European community. In the Southern Rhodesian context, Ian Phimister has objected to examinations of discourse, dismissing a notable attempt to understand the logic of ideas about conservation and development by arguing that "by its very nature, discourse's signification does not admit of external appeal," and asserting that without that possibility of "external appeal"—or context—such studies are not history.[9] This study attempts to retain its links to history through an aggressive contextualisation of discourse, an understanding of discourse as characterized by internal debate and struggle rather than timeless hegemony, and a steady awareness that rhetorical systems change over time, responding to both pressures from their contexts, and to their own internal contradictions.[10] Throughout this integration of social thought and social policy, the focus remains on change rather than continuity, and on struggles, and the failure of containment, rather than on an ideal construction of effective systems of social control.

Source limitations have restricted this analysis of ideology and policy primarily to a discussion of European ideas, conflicts, and strategies. It is also, substantially, restricted to public sources—either published or widely circulated—rather than drawing on private internal communications of the administration, settler organizations, or the African community, though I did gain access to the holdings of the National Archives of Zimbabwe during the final stages of the revision process. The sources I have used in this study are sources emerging from and contributing to contention. None are neutral. The most staid perspectives I have encountered emerged from official documents of the administration of the region. Mission materials, either unpublished or public propaganda, have been invaluable as sources of both details and arguments. Settler perspectives have been readily available, often in vitriolic form, through Legislative Council (or Legislative Assembly) debates, personal memoirs or reminiscences, and the newspapers, which conveyed not merely reports of public meetings, but editorials discussing varieties of settler opinion, and letters to the editor, reflecting some of the more extreme viewpoints held by individual settlers. All of these sources, in addition to providing insights into their authors, can be sifted for the opinions, knowledge, and hopes of other groups within the region. In a society that, however antagonistic, was never as wholly separated into racial or cultural communities as many of its inhabitants wished, commentary on others was constant. No analysis even of settler ideology, let alone the debates that went on in official or missionary circles, would be complete without some understanding of the many ways in which Africans' actions, and Africans' understanding, shaped the sets of possibilities invoked by articulate debaters within the colonial context.

Through an analysis of the key images used to understand society, and a discussion of the many threads woven into the social debates of the colony, this study attempts to evoke and understand the hopes, plans, fears, and decisions of those who lived in Southern Rhodesia from the turn of the century to the early 1930s, emphasizing that the society was not static, monolithic, or even, for many of its participants, immediately and permanently comprehensible.

NOTES

1. Timothy Burke, "Lifebuoy Men, Lux Women: Commodification, Consumption and Cleanliness in Colonial Zimbabwe" (Ph.D. Dissertation, Johns Hopkins University, 1992) especially chapter 7.

2. Colin Leys, *European Politics in Southern Rhodesia* (Oxford: Clarendon Press, 1959) 1. See also L. H. Gann, *A History of Southern Rhodesia: Early Days to 1934* (New York: Humanities Press, 1965) and Philip Mason, *The Birth of a Dilemma: The Conquest and Settlement of Rhodesia* (London: Oxford University Press, 1958).

3. Gann described the multi-racial society as rather like a slice of Neapolitan ice-cream—clearly in contact, distinct when intact, but capable of melting into a mess about the edges. Gann, *A History of Southern Rhodesia,* 172.

4. D. J. Murray, *The Governmental System in Southern Rhodesia* (Oxford: Clarendon Press, 1970) and Claire Palley, *The Constitutional History and Law of Southern Rhodesia 1888-1965* (Oxford: Clarendon Press, 1966). Another, notably weaker, book from this period of research was William J. Barber, *The Economy of British Central Africa* (London: Oxford University Press, 1961).

5. Charles van Onselen, *Chibaro* (London: Pluto Press, 1976) and Robin Palmer, *Land and Racial Domination in Rhodesia* (Berkeley: U. of California Press, 1977). For examples of regional studies, see Per Zachrisson, *An African Area in Change: Belingwe 1894-1946* (Gothenburg: U. of Gothenburg Press, 1978); Benjamin Davis and Wolfgang Doepcke, "Survival and Accumulation in Gutu" *Journal of Southern African Studies* 14 (October 1987) 64-98 and Terence Ranger's work on the Makoni District. Currently, a popular approach is to use a specific region as a basis for a discussion of a specific topic within Southern Rhodesia as a whole. See, for example, Elizabeth Schmidt's work on Goromonzi district, "Ideology, Economics and the Role of Shona Women in Southern Rhodesia, 1850–1939" (Ph.D. in History, U. of Wisconsin, Madison, 1987).

6. See C. T. Loram, *The Education of the South African Native* (London: Longmans, Green, 1917); E. H. Brookes, *The History of Native Policy in South Africa* 2d edition (Pretoria: van Schaik, 1922, 1927) and E. H. Brookes, *Native Education in South Africa* (Pretoria: J. L. van Schaik, 1930). For a secondary discussion, see Saul Dubow, *Racial Segregation and the Origins of Apartheid in South Africa, 1919-36* (New York: St. Martin's 1989). Both Loram and Brookes were influential in discussing the meaning of education, but the specific issues under discussion, ranging from practical training to ideas of civilization, acquired different contexts, and thus both different constituencies and different implications, as they were moved north.

7. Ian Phimister, *An Economic and Social History of Zimbabwe,*

1890-1948: Capital Accumulation and Class Struggle (London: Longman, 1988).

8. Dane Kennedy, *Islands of White* (Durham, NC: Duke University Press, 1987) and Jean Comaroff and John Comaroff, *Of Revelation and Revolution: Christianity, Colonialism and Consciousness in South Africa* v. 1 (Chicago: University of Chicago Press, 1991).

9. Phimister is referring to William Beinart, "Soil Erosion, Conservationism and Ideas about Development" *Journal of Southern African Studies* 11:1 (October 1984) 52-83. Ian Phimister, "Discourse and the Discipline of Historical Context" *Journal of Southern African Studies,* 12:2 (April 1986) 263-275, esp. 275.

10. Thus, my understanding of consciousness and knowledge in Southern Rhodesia differs markedly from the Comaroffs' understanding of consciousness in the Southern Tswana regions of South Africa. While for them, the principal element of consciousness seems to be the question of cultural identity and ultimately the creation of an ideological hegemony through contacts between missionaries and Tswana, the central issue of consciousness which I see in Southern Rhodesia is cultural change—the possibilities of training and learning, education, progress, and development. This difference between the Comaroffs' work and my own has three probable sources: first, our differences in theoretical perspective and attitudes toward time, second, substantial differences between the sources we have drawn on, and third, a difference in the power of the dominant states and classes of South Africa and Southern Rhodesia.

CHAPTER ONE

Perception and Conquest

VIOLENCE IN MASHONALAND AND MATABELELAND, 1890–1896

In 1890, when the British South Africa Company's pioneer column marched through Matabeleland into Mashonaland, that column was an unambiguously military organization, designed by its imperial sponsors to use both the threat and the practice of violence to establish Company authority over the land and people of the region. Missionaries, traders and hunters who had previously traveled the region provided the Company with some information about the new territory. That information, though, was inconsistent and haphazard, incapable of providing a coherent image of the land and people to be conquered. It had been provided by people who had sought to find niches within African societies, rather than to destroy or to exploit systematically. The pioneer column and the initial European establishment in Southern Rhodesia lacked a coherent worldview or ideology capable of integrating the scattered images of the local realities and the facts of military domination into a history or ideology capable of justifying the incursion and occupation to the various relevant constituencies of imperialism: the British government and mission and humanitarian organizations back in Britain; Europeans setting out to scramble for a profit in the new land; and, most importantly, the Africans who were the objects of this incursion, whose social, political, and economic systems had to be transformed in order for the imperial initiative to succeed. The Company, and the settlers it led into the region, lacked any strategy

other than violence for dealing with Africans. Without a strategy for
civilization and uplift, a "Native Policy," or even a grand design for
development, the company relied on blunt, undisguised force.

Early Images

Europeans in Matabeleland and Mashonaland before 1890 sent
home stories of the people they had dealt with that emphasized the
differences between Ndebele and Shona, and optimistically provided support for the missionary, explorer, or company scout's
presence and prospects.

From the beginnings of missionary incursions into the region,
missionaries drew local life in images of cruelty and despotism that
justified, or even demanded, intervention. Robert Moffat's description of the Ndebele between 1829 and 1835, before they had
crossed the Limpopo into the region that became Southern Rhodesia, emphasized that the Ndebele were essentially good—people
capable of kindness and intelligence—but that under Mzilikazi's
rule the kingdom was characterized by

> the warriors [who] though living amid the bewildering mazes
> of ignorance and superstition, debased, dejected and oppressed
> under the iron scepter of a monarch addicted to shedding
> blood, possessed noble minds, but alas! whose only source of
> joy was to conquer or die in the ranks of the sovereign.[1]

Moffat, a missionary of the London Missionary Society (LMS), starkly
declared Mzilikazi's rule "the very essence of despotism. The per-
sons of the people, as well as their possessions, were the property
of their monarch."[2] And this situation of oppression and the waste
of human potential showed no signs of abating. In 1855 Moffat emphasized that "every man of the Matabele is a soldier ready to grasp
his weapon at a moment's notice," and that the king ruled this as-
semblage of soldiers with such a firm hand that "to harbour the
idea that there was a God greater than Moselekatse, would be
viewed as the veriest madness and expose one to the danger of being hung up by the neck."[3] In an 1860 visit, Moffat stated the image
of a power-drunk warrior state even more emphatically, arguing
that in Matabeleland,

> Their government is their despotism—there is only one great
> man in the nation, whose word is law. He holds no council,

> hears no suggestion, for no one dares be wiser than he, or to suggest what may be a better plan. Whatever he orders to be done, however outrageous to humanity and to common sense, is received, even by those to whom he confides important matters, with expressions of the profoundest admiration, however differently they may think. . . . Everyone executes his orders to the fullest extent, fearing lest anyone should find occasion to whisper in the king's presence that he had failed in fulfilling any iota of the orders given. Each dreads his neighbors. Each is careful of the words which drop from his lips. All are terrified at the very idea of being suspected of not loving and fearing him above everyone else, which accounts for the outrageous nonsense called praise, which is poured into his ear from morn til night.[4]

Moffat portrayed the Ndebele as a people of soldiers, militant to an extent that violated common sense. This command of force enslaved them, binding them into a despotic system where, however powerful the group might be, individuals lacked free will and could only use power for the benefit of, or in the service of, the king.

Moffat's emphasis on the effectiveness and completeness of the military despotism he described both justified his pressure for the introduction of Christianity as a new enlightening ideology and explained why he had been able to make so little progress. When permission was, on occasion, granted for his preaching, he declared, "Never in my life did I witness such rivetted attention and astounded countenance. . . ." The Gospel of Salvation, he went on to assert, was something radically new to his listeners.[5] Moffat's enthusiastic denunciation of Ndebele society as militaristic and cruel proved that Mzilikazi was perhaps wise in his reluctance to let his subjects pay too much attention to this rogue propagandist. But the subjects themselves, after the initial entertainment value of the new cult preacher wore off, may also have been increasingly uninterested in a faith which went out of its way to draw their society as one of cruelty and abject subjugation.

The members of the London Missionary Society who established themselves as permanent missionaries in Matabeleland believed that fear of the king made people reluctant to learn. The local people clearly viewed the message of the missionaries as subversive, and many were unwilling to align themselves with the missionaries. But this reluctance may have been based in apathy rather than in fear—an apathy that would be highly inconsistent with the totally mobilized society that Moffat sought to portray. Sykes complained,

> I have tried times without number during the past year to in-
> duce people to learn to read, and have spent hours, again and
> again, in explaining to them the advantages of being able to
> read and write. Some have said they would learn to read at
> once, but when they found that it would require weeks, per-
> haps months, their resolution vanished. They have said they
> would learn if I would give them something for learning, which
> I always decline to do.[6]

This immediate agreement, followed by a slow falling off when the
learners discovered how much work was involved in acquiring literacy, was congruent with an explanation based in apathy rather
than in fear of the rulers. In the existing society, literacy and the
Christian culture promoted by the missions provided no clear advantage.

During this early period, Moffat's portrayal of the Ndebele nation
was not accepted uncritically, even by European visitors. Frederick
Selous, who hunted and traded extensively in the region from 1882
to 1887 and observed Ndebele military action close up, provided a
more ambivalent portrayal of the nation:

> . . . the country had . . . been thickly populated. . . . Every
> cluster of rocks had been the site of a Mashuna village. . . .
> But the ever-present fear of invasion by the cruel and blood-
> thirsty Matabili had caused the natives of this rich and fertile
> tract of country to desert the homes of their forefathers and
> retreat towards the east and north.[7]

But he described a Ndebele raid as "a very bold enterprise" that
was "only partially successful." In all, the first expedition against
the "Batauwani" was "a singularly bloodless one."[8] And the second
expedition Lobengula sent against these people was "a most disas-
trous one," in which it was mostly the Ndebele who were shot in
battle, drowned in a trap, or starved in the desert during an ignominious retreat.[9]

Selous's descriptions emphasized relations between the Ndebele
and their neighbors rather than domestic politics and, although he
agreed with the missionaries regarding the cruelty of the Ndebele,
he did not particularly seek to justify British intervention. His descriptions diverged sharply from the image of the invincible state
offered by the LMS contingent. Where the missionaries depicted a
totalitarian tyrant able to control his subjects' very thoughts, Selous

sketched a limited military structure that was occasionally beaten by organized resistance.

From the late 1880s, another important perspective on the region came from the agents of the British South Africa Company who sought concessions from Lobengula for their prospective ventures into the region. The LMS missionary David Carnegie commented on the effect of the scheming that surrounded the concession hunting by noting to his superiors that Matabeleland was politically "somewhat unhinged at present."[10] And beyond the region itself, Company activity sent rumors flying. W. H. Brown, a just-off-the-boat would-be explorer, stated that from these sponsored rumors, he understood that

> in the neighborhood of the Zambesi River lay a country, healthful, rich in mineral deposits . . . in the hands of a savage potentate, called Lo Bengula. This unclaimed territory covered an area almost equal in extent to the combined countries of Germany and France. To the westward lay Portuguese Angola, and the recently acquired German territory of Damaraland. The Congo Free State formed the northern boundary of this vast expanse, while Portuguese East Africa separated it from the Indian Ocean. On its southern border was the South African Republic (Transvaal) and British Bechuanaland . . . .[11]

Company-sponsored rumor throughout South Africa, Brown noted, listed Lobengula as "King of Matabeleland, Mashonaland, and other adjoining territories."[12] The emphasis in the Company's reports was on the extent of the territory and its potential riches. Furthermore, while the Company did not purport to like Lobengula, neither did it portray him in terms as grim as those used by the early mission literature. Instead, his majesty was emphasized, and, as he was the head of his state and his government, the Company was fully willing to supply him with large quantities of military equipment in part payment for his concessions.[13] The Company was not overly worried by any martial qualities the Ndebele kingdom might possess.

The descriptions of the Ndebele kingdom and the Ndebele differed according to the interests of the observer, but certain elements of militarism were agreed on by all. Pre-1890 descriptions of the Shona, though, are rare and more diffuse.[14] The Ndebele state does appear to have circumscribed missionaries' access to Shona regions, much to the frustration of some missionaries, such as

Francois Coillard, who went into the region from 1878 to 1880. He had proposed work there around what is today Masvingo and had been allowed in to make a preliminary survey before Lobengula declared the region closed to evangelization. While regretting vehemently his inability to evangelize that field, his descriptions of the Shona he met were far from flattering. Coillard wrote that they

> have few wants; a bit of calico or a bead necklace is all they need. Nevertheless, if we refused to buy their sky-blue milk or the siftings of their flour, we could not escape violent altercations. . . . The chief Chibi nearly murdered me. . . . And with all that, what cowards they were! Did but the shadow of a Matabele darken the horizon, cries of terror resounded on all sides. A general stampede took place. . . .[15]

This hair-trigger tenseness provided Coillard with a reason to follow Lobengula's injunction and seek his converts elsewhere.

Nonevangelical European observers of the Shona and Shona regions were likewise scarce, and for many of the same reasons. Frederick Selous appeared to have seen the Shona primarily through their relationship with the Ndebele. Like Coillard, he saw the Shona as a people under constant military threat. Shona villagers, he explained, were so prepared to flee Ndebele attack that he, in order to approach a Shona village, sent people in advance to assure them of his friendly intentions, since "otherwise, as I knew from experience, every man, woman, and child would have bolted, and I should not have been able to obtain from them the provisions I needed."[16] Other than their proficiency at fleeing, though, the Shona made little impression on Selous. They were reasonably prosperous, willing to sell him supplies, and occasionally helpful as scouts when he hunted in their territory, but in his descriptions nothing caught his attention or that of his readers. For Selous, the Shona were a mere feature of the landscape, there to be exploited. Selous, in his dual role as adventurer and scout for the BSAC, provided an innocuous image of a people who were fundamentally timid and who, when tamed, could become a resource for the Company even as the land they farmed did.

During this early period of settlement, the few Europeans who wrote the descriptions that formed the basis for European ideas of the Ndebele and Shona peoples had generally experienced enough of the Ndebele court, or of Shona villages, to allow some ambiguity to enter their narratives. Even Moffat's description of despotism did not exclude humanity entirely: Mzilikazi, during the 1855 visit, was considerate enough to inquire into why Moffat looked so morose, and, on being told it was because Moffat pined for opportunities to preach, promptly arranged an impressive opportunity with a command audience.[17] And in his storytelling, Selous acknowledged that within Matabeleland justice was not arbitrary when he wrote of a three-day trial of himself and three other white traders and hunters on the charge of having shot hippopotami without royal permission. The trial was before not just Lobengula, but a council of headmen, and, after a careful examination of the evidence, the court imposed fines of varying degrees of severity according to who had shot the most hippos.[18]

As long as the European presence was marginal, and the uses of European solidarity minimal, ideology played little practical role in the business of trading, hunting, negotiation, or evangelization. Each European observer maneuvered within an African world as necessary, and then wrote home about it in a fashion designed to secure the maximum possible benefit for himself: the missionaries explaining their lack of converts; the traders and hunters justifying their casual attitude toward local authorities; and the forerunners of the Company emphasizing the extensiveness of Ndebele domination with the intent of taking as much as possible of that territory for themselves.

Company Violence

When the British South Africa Company gained its charter, though, based on a dubious concession that was repudiated by Lobengula even before the paperwork could be processed in England, the Company put itself into a precarious position with regard to each of its potential constituencies.[19] It had to sell a policy of Company-dominated imperialist expansion to a heterogeneous external constituency back in Britain comprised of the Colonial Office, the British government, parliament, the stock exchange, and even missionary-influenced public opinion. The Company also had to satisfy or subdue objections from an even more divided internal constituency containing mining, trading, and agricultural settlers, missionaries, and Africans. Unlike previous missionaries, traders, prospectors, or hunters who had acknowledged the Ndebele king's authority over Matabeleland, and had been careful to avoid unnecessary offense even in Mashonaland, the BSAC came into the region with the intention of taking control. According to oral tradition, the Africans who observed the pioneer column's activity were shocked by the contrast between earlier visitors and the Pioneers. The Europeans who visited earlier, had been "human, polite and considerate, and taken nothing that they had no right to take." With the Pioneers and afterwards, though, came settlers who "disregarded all the good manners and common decencies that the VaShawasha and their Shona countrymen had mistakenly thought were the common heritage of all human beings."[20] The Company sought a firm control which would make politeness irrelevant. Initially, this assumption of political and economic control was limited to Mashonaland as a separate region, in theory held under the suzerainty of the Ndebele kingdom. This relationship proved uncomfortable for both the Ndebele and the Company, and came to an end after the brief Matabele war of 1893. After that time, the Company ruled in Southern Rhodesia, arguing that it held Mashonaland by right of concession, and Matabeleland by right of conquest, and that its military triumph would usher in a new age of prosperity.

During the period from 1890 to 1896, new European views of the region began to emerge as the various factions sought to take advantage of the opportunities inherent in a newly "opened" region. As documented history held little to constrain the newcomers in their interpretations of the local past and the local people, a situation of interpretive anarchy existed, in which actors translated their interests directly into impressions, observations, and descriptions of the conditions under which they sought profits.

The Company's external constituency was complex. The head offices of the Company in London, and the board of directors, were interested less in what happened on the ground and in the mines of Southern Rhodesia than they were in what sold on the stock market and for how much. But as a royally chartered monopoly company, the BSAC was more than just a commercial concern outside Southern Rhodesia, even as within it. It was a cheap imperial venture, extending the area in Southern Africa claimed by the British and excluding the Portuguese or any other group that, the government feared, might otherwise claim the region to the detriment of future British interests.[21] The BSAC's charter was written for and approved by the British government.[22] Thus, the 1889 version contained several important clauses designed to make Company rule palatable to a British public potentially dubious over the privatization of imperialism. There was a provision for a veto by a secretary of state should the British government disapprove of the Company's rule, and there were a few guidelines inserted to suggest how the BSAC should govern, including clauses that prescribed a minimalistic approach to any development of law and government for the Africans of the region:

> The Company as such, or its officers as such, shall not in any way interfere with the religion of any class or tribe of the peoples of the territories aforesaid or of any of the inhabitants thereof, except so far as may be necessary in the interests of humanity. . . .
>
> In the administration of justice to the said peoples or inhabitants, careful regard shall always be had to the customs and laws of the class or tribe or nation to which the parties respectively belong . . . but subject to any British laws which may be in force in any of the territories aforesaid, and applicable to the people or inhabitants thereof.[23]

These clauses ultimately affected how the Company chose, in subsequent years, to portray the people it ruled. The important facts were less the constraints (noninterference and careful regard) than the escape clauses (the "interests of humanity" and the "constraints of British laws"). These encouraged the Company to portray African culture as contrary to the "interests of humanity." And the language meant that should the Company want to develop a policy to define the position of Africans in the region, it would need to justify its proposals either as reinforcements of African tradition or as parts of a British law that applied to all in the region, regardless of race. Along with a specific clause precluding slavery, these provisions limited the Company's choices and pushed it to explore images of Africans and the relation of African custom to the "interests of humanity" in order to seek a profit while working within the constraints of the charter. To satisfy its British constituency, the BSAC needed the appearance of benevolent paternalism.

This external constituency, of the British government and all the organizations that could influence it in Britain, was enough to interest the Company in developing a history of the Shona and Ndebele that made its own administration look benevolent. This interest in the appearance of benevolence became increasingly pronounced during the decade as the Company suffered a series of incidents that produced bad press in Britain, including the Matabeleland War of 1893, and then the involvement of the administrator of Southern

Rhodesia, Dr. Leander Starr Jameson, in a notorious and poorly planned attempt to conquer the Transvaal goldfields.

British oversight was not, during this early period, a serious problem for the Company. The Colonial Office found interference discouragingly expensive and, up to the serious Risings of 1896–97, its concern appears to have been limited to cases where the Company had not merely overstepped, but cost Britain either money or imperial prestige. In 1889 the British government approved the charter through this indifference, listening to neither Lobengula's repudiation of the treaty terms, nor his repeated assertion that the Company had taken far more than anyone in the region had contemplated selling, or indeed had a right to sell. But the Matabele War of 1893, which involved troops from the imperial Bechuanaland Border Police in addition to the local volunteers paid by the Company in promises of land and minerals claims, interrupted that indifference. After the war, the Colonial Office and the BSAC negotiated a new agreement to supplement the charter and provide for the establishment of an actual administration to rule the expanded territory. But, though a few words changed, there was little new in the agreement regarding how Africans should be ruled. The agreement directed the administration to respect African civil law except where it was "repugnant to principles of morality, or to any law or ordinance in force in the said territories," and prohibited "any exceptional [race-specific] legislation save as regards liquor, arms, and ammunition and as regards the title to and occupation of land."[24] Those provisions, however, did nothing to restrict the raiding by BSAC officials who saw the new order in council as an institutionalization of their pattern of predatory rule. And after the war, the Company's seizures, labor policies, and taxes hit Matabeleland, an area that had previously had some ability to protect itself from such depredation.[25]

The Colonial Office's indifference to this administrative violence continued despite occasional missionary protests concerning various atrocities or violations. Rev. Eva, a Methodist who could give an eyewitness account of how the police murdered three indunas (Ndebele councilors or leaders) in Lomagundi, saw his protests go nowhere even though John White, a fellow missionary, asserted that it was the duty of the home branch of the Wesleyan Missionary Society to put pressure on the BSAC back in Britain.[26] Such actions occurred throughout the area controlled by the Company, without provoking the Colonial Office or the government.[27] Missions and missionaries could and did engage in a sporadic oversight, and did win a few local victories, but they could neither change the Company's business tactics nor mobilize imperial intervention. British oversight remained such a nebulous concept that it deterred neither the initially illegal imposition of a hut tax on Africans in 1893 nor Company involvement in the notorious Jameson Raid in 1895, which explicitly violated the letter of the 1894 agreement, which had finally legalized the hut tax but spelled out distinct territorial limits for BSAC activity.[28]

Instead of reform, the Company offered the British government, its stockholders, and the public, an increasingly coherent set of key images growing from stories of African violence. The "interests of humanity" in all likelihood had little to do with the Matabele War, for example, which was, instead, closely related to the BSAC's realization that Mashonaland was not as rich as speculators had hoped and that Matabeleland promised new opportunities for wealth.[29] Despite these practical reasons, though, the Company explained its war rather differently. In its stockholder's report, the BSAC told how "the quarrel that then broke out [in 1893] was forced upon the Company by the attempt of the Matabele to enforce their claim to murder or carry off the Mashona men, women and children to slavery."[30] The Company—which showed few other signs of compassion for Africans whom it ignored, bullied, recruited, and punished—declared its war of expansion a war of compassion with a suffering people, surely not something mission or humanitarian interests in England could object to, and a display of force within the constraints of the charter's loophole that legitimated action for the "interests of humanity." In the aftermath of the 1893 war, the Company began to develop for British consumption a view of the region's history that painted the BSAC's actions in a beneficent light by demonizing the Ndebele and portraying the Shona as Ndebele human cattle. Within this Company-created context, even Company atrocities could not outrage British public opinion, as these violations represented an administration which, despite its flaws, appeared less barbaric than its predecessors.

Any appearance by the Company as a benevolent organization, paternalistic in its attitude toward Africans, would not, however, please the European members of its internal constituency, most of whom were intent on acquiring windfall profits from the development of a new imperial dependency. These prospectors, adventurers, traders, and farmers feared any interference in their harsh management of African labor or resources. These early settlers, contemplating the prospects before them of trading, mining, or farming, could easily believe they had been promised prosperity, not just by the rumors of mineral riches that had reached South Africa, but also by the concrete promise the Company gave to the members of the pioneer column that each was to be entitled to fifteen gold claims and a 3000-acre farm.[31]

Most of the early settlers came to Mashonaland expecting to find gold; misleading stories and explorers' yarns had popularized the region as the land of King Solomon's mines.[32] The mining faction of Europeans in Southern Rhodesia was interested in profits and rumors of profits, not in satisfying British public opinion that imperialism was being pursued in a paternalistic fashion. The prospectors' British audience was the same set of speculators on mining stocks that funded the Company itself, but without the direct Colonial Office oversight that occasionally brought the BSAC into a semblance of circumspection. Within the region, the mining constituency was interested in the necessities of day-to-day prospecting and exploitation of resources. Its primary concern was with garnering the resources necessary to pursue that exploitation. Miners needed labor to find, stake, explore, and develop their claims. Labor, therefore, no matter how it was recruited, was much more important to prospective miners than charter stipulations regarding the honoring of African traditions or the "interests of humanity." But labor was not the only requirement for the establishment of successful mines. Employers also needed some degree of monetization of the local economy. They could recruit labor more easily when potential workers saw a use or a need for the wages they might earn. Furthermore, prospectors needed to be able to buy food for their workers and themselves. These linked interests, in labor and monetization, meant that the prospectors' interests ran directly contrary to the protections written into the charter and could best be served by organized, Company-led domination. Using a rhetoric of conquest, Europeans pulled people away from customary responsibilities in the local economy and society, and attempted to realign both to produce a labor force.

Like the prospectors, the European farmers of Southern Rhodesia were more concerned with the immediate local requirements of their enterprises than they were with the distant demands of public opinion in Britain. Most, indeed, had some prospecting interests in addition to their farms. Labor was as much a concern for the farm as for the mine. Land was important, but land on the scale of the claims being staked in Southern Rhodesia was worthless for purposes other than speculation unless a labor supply was available. Settlers were not staking claim to small family farms. Instead, the Company offered 3000-acre claims for military service in the pioneer column or the Matabele War, and some claims were even bigger. W. H. Brown refers, apparently without sarcasm, to his frustration at finding his claim limited by the speculative claims of land companies to "a paltry twelve thousand acres," rather than the hundred thousand he had initially set out to acquire.[33] Some settlers used their farms for cattle rearing, a relatively non-labor-intensive form of farming, but one that would nevertheless require some nonfamily workers. But agriculture in Mashonaland was not limited to pastoral herding. With prices of food and of commodities such as tobacco scandalously high (when they could be bought at all), farmers had a substantial incentive to initiate truck or tobacco gardening, extremely labor-intensive forms of agriculture, and to put as much soil under cultivation as they had labor to work. That strategy was complicated by the reluctance of Africans to work for wages, either because they were capable of farming on their own and marketing their own produce to miners and traders, or because they were unwilling to tolerate employers who were rude and violent.[34] Miners found their profits limited by their capital and by what they found, or rather, did not find, in terms of mineral deposits. For farmers, the linkage with labor was more direct. Those who could acquire labor, through whatever means, could make money.

These mining and farming settlers did not see the Matabeleland War as arising from a mere humanistic desire to protect the Shona from Ndebele predation. By 1893 the settler community was frustrated. Gold had proved to be far more difficult to acquire than the optimists had expected, and most of the gold that had been found lay in the remains of old mines that had been nearly exhausted through precolonial mining. Furthermore, prospects for gold in Mashonaland in the future were dimming rapidly. By 1893 various mining engineers were coming to the conclusion, in reports censored by the Company, that Mashonaland would never be a major gold producer and that the boom had been built on little but dreams.[35] Prospectors, already disappointed by the failure of those dreams, were even more disillusioned when they considered the fine print in their claim contracts, which granted half of their returns, or half the stock of any company formed to exploit mineral finds, to the BSAC.[36] Farming also fell short of settlers' dreams of a path to quick wealth. It was hard work, requiring knowledge of local climactic and soil conditions, careful coordination of labor, and canny planning of marketing. Worse, settlers already frustrated by their mediocre fortunes found themselves contending with appallingly high food and commodities prices.[37] Settlers needed the spoils of conquest, cattle, labor, and food, for their economic survival.

That frustration laid the groundwork for the settlers' militant response to Ndebele attempts to reassert Ndebele authority in 1893. In the tentative and new economy of Company-controlled Mashonaland, labor was crucial. What prosperity did exist depended on the availability of a steady supply of "Maholis," workers who came from regions where they had been subject to the Ndebele. Employers viewed these people as good workers, willing to work for low wages in mines or on farms. When the Ndebele sought to reestablish tributary relationships and a pattern of Ndebele raiding developed in the Victoria region, these workers showed signs of fleeing. Settlers, concerned to maintain their labor supply, demanded a military response to quell the Ndebele once and for all.[38] Ndebele authority, they emphasized, was bad for business.[39] Settlers expected the war to break that authority and establish the foundations for their ideal, settler-dominated, society. Their hopes, fears, and expectations regarding the war indicate quite clearly how they wanted the administration's policy toward Africans to evolve.

Settlers in Mashonaland hoped the war would address two sources of their irritation: the BSAC and the Ndebele kingdom. When settlers held public meetings in Salisbury and Victoria to demand that the Company go to war, they were acting in part defensively, out of fear that Company equivocation and compromise with the Ndebele had made the British community of the region appear weak, and an appropriate target for Ndebele action. Contemporary notions of psychology asserted that Africans would take advantage of anyone who appeared less than strong, but that an appearance of strength was all that was needed for a successful bluff. Settlers felt that in failing to put forward this appearance of strength in the face of the provocation of Ndebele raids on their workers, the Company had positioned them as weak targets. They argued that it had no right to do so. Policy decisions should, they contended, be made by those who would have to live by them.[40] But settlers were not motivated solely by a desire to make themselves safe. They were also acting offensively to strengthen their position relative to that of the BSAC. The public meetings demanding action represented settlers' attempts to achieve some local political control of their community. The private meetings held later, Brown contended, sought to take advantage of the BSAC's need to recruit troops for military action from the settler population to renegotiate the terms of BSAC authority, particularly the half share the Company claimed in all gold mines.[41]

Settlers did not, however, threaten the Company with violence. That they saved for their other target, the Ndebele and the Ndebele kingdom. After an Ndebele raid, it was difficult for the settlers to persuade their employees to stay. One settler complained that not only were the workers "paralyzed with fear," but their fear was with cause, for European assurances were nearly meaningless. The workers, he said, asserted, "When you white men came into Mashonaland, you promised that if we worked for you, you would prevent the Matabeli from raiding us. Here we are working for you, and here are the Matabeli killing our wives and children, and raiding our homes."[42] This awareness by Africans that Europeans had broken a security agreement did not merely "paralyze" the workforce, it "put a stop to all mining development work in the country . . . [and] brought every other description of industry and enterprise to a standstill."[43] In the face of this economic shutdown, initiated by military action, settlers were impatient to respond in kind, "to take the matter into their own hands and themselves avenge their losses."[44]

Settlers analyzed the reasons for this difficulty in ways that gradually became embedded in local European concepts of what it meant to be African. W. H. Brown's narrative emphasized the culpability of the Shona in provoking an Ndebele military response:

> . . . Mashonas . . . had exhibited signs of insolence. . . . Owing to the advent of the white men, who assumed to be the protectors of the oppressed aborigines, the latter, true to their racial idiosyncrasies, had begun prematurely to exult over the emancipation from their thraldom by the exhibition of defiant disdain toward . . . the Matabele king. . . .[45]

"Racial idiosyncrasies" and "insolence," characteristics of the victims, were thus, in this analysis, to blame for the victims' problems. But the Ndebele did not escape Brown's censure. Even as the Shona began to emerge in his description as the craven beings of later stereotypes, the Ndebele were animalized as predators who sought "freedom of action in their human hunting preserves."[46] With this description of Africans as guilty prey or sadistic predators, he laid out images that became central to an image of the nature of Africans that justified European hegemony.

This settler response, voiced in public meetings in Victoria and Salisbury, rose out of frustration and fear: frustration with the economic conditions of the country, and fear that if the workforce could be killed, eventually the European settlers would also become targets. But the themes settlers raised in the call for action, and the remedies they proposed for the threatened labor crisis, became the fundamental elements of settler attitudes toward Africans and toward the management of Africans. In protesting an initial Company policy of conciliation and in demanding military action, the settlers began their assertion that policy toward Africans should be made by those with local knowledge, who had to live with the results of that policy, rather than by the imperial government, or even the London office of the Company. In asserting that a threat to the labor supply justified military action, they showed signs of what eventually became a customary belligerence—a willingness to do anything to ensure a labor supply, and an acceptance of a logic in which the best way to justify any policy was through an argument that it promoted labor. And in demanding the destruction of the Ndebele state, rather than some system of compromise and border recognition, the settlers declared their opposition to power sharing with any African powers and their demand that the government of the region be European. Backing this demand,

> capitalists openly spoke of withdrawing capital. Farmers and traders threatened to trek out of the country, and a very strongly worded address was presented to Dr. Jameson . . . to the effect that, unless the Company settled this question, once and for all, . . . by breaking up the Matabeli power, they were determined to . . . leave the country, or—undertake the settlement of the question themselves.[47]

And, in 1893, Jameson, speaking for the Company in Mashonaland, eventually backed the settler demands, defining and defending a settler-Company alliance.[48]

Flexibility

Selous argued not only that the Matabele War was necessary, but that every European in the region agreed on that necessity, apart from one: Douglas Pelly, a newly arrived Church of England missionary. Selous attributed Pelly's objections to ignorance of the two factors settlers used to justify the war: the character of the Ndebele, and the deleterious effects of Ndebele actions on the efforts of the colonists.[49] Pelly, however, was unlikely to have been quite as ignorant as Selous suggested. His opposition was most likely based in a different set of priorities from those held by the settler community. The "character of the Ndebele" was, for missionaries, perceived as mutable, something that could be altered through education and changes in the state and society. And the effect of Ndebele actions on the efforts of the colonists would take second place as a missionary concern to the effects of settler retaliation on the Africans who must be encouraged, pressured, and taught to change. Missionaries were not ignorant. Their differences with the dominant European perspective on the question of the justice of the Matabele War could be more accurately traced to the ideas of various missionaries regarding change and how it could best be brought about.

Missionary logic diverged in several important ways from the dominant settler values of Europeans in Southern Rhodesia. Initially, the goals of settlers in the region involved a desire to get rich quick. Development, guided change, civilization, or the transformation of the local population were nonissues to them, except insofar as they affected the labor supply, land, and the prospector's ability to find and extract gold. Missionaries were rather different. Their primary interests, from the first expedition Moffat made to the Ndebele Court, revolved around change. Thus, while they might describe the Ndebele as a people enmeshed in a cruel and despotic state, they did not seek to characterize the people themselves into some fixed ideal. They did not see the "nature" or "character" of the Africans they worked with as a fixed, immutable, or definable thing. Static characterizations could only limit their work. Thus, while a frustrated missionary might declare, as Thomas did, "the people are afraid to think for themselves and have no confidence in one another," that timidity was analyzed as a characteristic of their social situation rather than of their souls.[50] Individual Africans were perceived by missionaries as normal, rational people, not as subhumans existing only to serve.[51]

Long-term missionaries in Matabeleland, those from the LMS and the Society of Jesus, saved their antagonism and frustration for the state. Father Prestage, a Jesuit priest, declared it impossible to do mission work under the eyes of Lobengula's state.[52] And the LMS was equally frustrated.[53] Given that sense of frustration, after years in Matabeleland with nothing to show in terms of social change or even individual conversions, many missionaries were initially enthusiastic when the Company marched into the country in 1890, beginning to establish a dominance that the missionaries hoped would eventually form a countervailing power to the Ndebele state. The Jesuits and the LMS saw a hope of greener pastures in Mashonaland under the Company. Carnegie, an LMS missionary, speculated hopefully about the Mashona as a people "given to . . . self improvement" among whom a new Lovedale-style industrial training institution could be built.[54] The Jesuits moved quickly to peg out and establish the Chishawasha Mission station, near the new headquarters of Salisbury. And gradually, other missionary societies began to come to the region. One of the earliest was the Church of England, one of whose representatives, Pelly, was described by Selous as the war's sole local white critic.

Thus, instead of emphasizing an ideal nature of an individual African in their descriptions, the missionaries emphasized the formative power of state and society. And missionary strategy and tactics were designed to facilitate the remolding of African individuals into a new, more ideal society. Missionary societies did differ among themselves in the details of tactics and organization, but their commonalities tended to be more substantial than their differences. Each missionary society, as it came into the region, began its progression through the various stages of missionary enterprise. Initially, mission activity was limited to the simple evangelization that could be accomplished in an itineration through the region. Moffat's missions represented this stage for the LMS, the Jesuits performed several swings before settling down, and Bishop G. W. H. Knight-Bruce and others made similar evangelical trips for the societies that sought to establish themselves in Mashonaland after the Company began to rule. Such trips were designed to provide missionaries with contacts in the region, and some basic knowledge about the conditions with which they would have to contend. But they were not mere intelligence-gathering missions. They were also, through widespread preaching and singing, to begin the dissemination of Christian religious ideas and idioms that might, on further swings, or after the establishment of a station, be brought together into something approaching a conventional faith. Once evangelized, the Africans could be relied on to discuss the messages of the missionaries with each other, gradually developing terms in which to understand the missionary religious discourse, regardless of whether or not they subscribed to it.[55] And the evangelical swings had one other important purpose as well. They were intended to arouse the interest of the population in the missionaries and to secure at least tacit agreement by the authorities for the extension of mission work. No missionary could expect to establish himself or herself in totally hostile territory. Thus, the agreements with local leaders were crucial for missions hoping to proceed on to the next level of mission development.[56]

Once itinerant missionaries and evangelists had succeeded in developing a religious language and acquiring the acceptance of local leaders, they sought to establish mission stations. Those stations varied little from denomination to denomination. They consisted of a farm, worked by Africans, which, ideally, grew the missionaries' food and provided a small source of income for the mission. In addition to the portion of the farm that the missionaries supervised and farmed with hired labor, there was also land on which African communities continued business as usual, farming land that had technically become part of the mission. And these communities provided the core population for intensive evangelization. Before the arrival of the BSAC, missionaries from the LMS had acquired such a farm from Lobengula at Inyati, and the Jesuits had been granted Empandeni. After the BSAC arrived, it was responsible for land grants, which the missionaries seized eagerly.[57] But mission stations were more than just farms. To be effective, they needed to be schools as well. In theory, the farms merely provided the economic base for the evangelizing schools which would provide the religious justification for the mission. These schools and the educational activities they implied were crude, generally only a small step up from the fireside group teaching of the evangelical on itineration. But they were the first priority of all mission stations, regardless of denomination, and only when the missionary in charge could write to his sponsors that a school had been started could the mission station truly be said to have been founded.[58]

Missionaries needed schools to teach the system and scripture of standard Christianity. In the Rhodesian context, Christianity had two major components: discipline and faith. Ideally, missionaries expected the two to go together. They therefore wound the institutions designed to produce each as close together as possible. The farm was to teach discipline, and the school faith. But the schools were sometimes, in the earliest period of a mission station, comprised almost exclusively of the missionaries' farm employees. And the schools, with their emphasis on teaching people to be quiet, listen to authority, and memorize instructions, sought to teach discipline as a prerequisite to any religious faith. The mission station, with its school, paralleled the settler's farm or mining settlement in its emphasis on discipline, but it diverged sharply in its attempts, from the beginning of its establishment, to teach faith, specifically a faith of the book, one which required literacy and the ability to communicate with a larger world.

In the early 1890s, no mission society had effectively passed from the initial stages of the mission station into the later stage of the establishment of communities where at least some of the social bonds ran through the Christian faith, and where that faith had been to some degree adapted to local needs. Nor had they reached the final stage, at which the proselytization finally began to add up and, with generational change, children grew up in the church to become adults and then elders, transforming the nature of the community at all levels. Missionary ideologies of the local people had not yet had time to evolve. Dissent within the small mission community over the war was therefore almost inevitable, as some missionaries saw it as a holy war in which missionaries should take an active part,[59] some viewed it as salvation in the form of the sweeping away of a frustrating and possibly evil state,[60] some feared the expansion of settlers who would reduce the Africans to slavery,[61] and some, such as Bishop Knight-Bruce, merely commented that while war was the fastest way to open up a mission field, it was not likely to produce the most solid reception.[62]

In the early 1890s, missionaries in Mashonaland and Matabeleland were uninterested in images of Africans that would make their work or fundraising more difficult. They sought instead to portray the people as clay that, with a bit of pressure, could be molded into a new society based in Christianity. But within the region, they had to contend with two factions potentially able to destroy that image: the European settlers and the African communities. The missionaries feared that the settlers, through their employment practices and bad example, risked destroying the willingness of Africans to listen and change in the ways the missionaries sought. Missionaries disliked the Boers and their labor practices. "The Boer," one missionary asserted, "looks upon the native African as he does upon his oxen. They must work, under the lash if need be. . . ."[63] The image of Africans as oxen damaged their potential as valuable human converts, and the reality that it reflected—farmers who forced workers into laboring in settler farms for nine months of the year—threatened the economic and cultural survival of the communities the missionaries sought to christianize. And missionaries did not merely argue that overwork caused problems. They also felt that all too many of the Europeans of the region were examples not of civilization or Christianity, but of coarseness and barbarism.[64] The clay, they implied, was being shaped into an inferior form.

But the missionaries realized that not all the distortions of their program were emanating from the white settlers. The second force capable of altering missionary plans was that of African communities and individuals who, through their actions and choices, demanded a voice in their own future. Until the Matabele war, the African communities of the region appear to have been genuinely ambivalent about the European expansion. Within Matabeleland, at an elite level, the European incursions, initially in the form of innocuous traders able to offer arms and goods, were useful, though the kings quite easily recognized the possible dangers, and Lobengula became extremely wary during the late 1880s when conducting negotiations with concession hunters. Even then, however, the dispute was not over economic benefits, but over questions of authority and culture. The LMS missionary Bowen Rees declared in 1890 that Lobengula was "dead against civilising influences coming into his country."[65] At a nonelite level, though, both in Matabeleland and Mashonaland, European incursions offered new economic opportunities, and through them, access to goods and freedoms from customary authorities that earlier generations might have dreamed of, but not achieved. In 1869 Matabeleland, LMS missionaries away from Lobengula's court described the local hunger for consumer goods. For beads, cloth, or other items, people were willing to go to school or work, or even to loiter about the mission looking for the opportunity of earning goods.[66] And even in 1890, the local population could be glad to see a missionary because of the market he offered for their surplus grain.[67] In Mashonaland people were also eager to sell their agricultural surplus and gain goods. Opportunities were pursued energetically or even militantly, before the Company takeover, as they were too rare to let pass.[68]

After the BSAC arrived, it developed a market for labor as well as goods, increasing social tensions within the African societies from which the labor came. Despite the settlers' concerns that labor was scarce, or likely to evaporate in the face of military threats from the Ndebele, Ndebele labor for Europeans increased steadily from 1891 to 1893, as young men sought to earn money for guns and to acquire resources outside the lineage structure.[69] This independence represented a problem for the leadership of the state and lineages as it threatened both the state's command of military labor and the spoils of war, and the lineage's control over the resources of reproductive labor, as men acquired alternative sources of income for their livelihood and potentially their payment of brideprices.[70]

The Company's provision of a market for goods and services was, however, not enough to satisfy the African members of its internal constituency as it rapidly became apparent that the Company suffered from limitless wants. Instead of, like early traders and missionaries, settling itself into a low profile position as a useful diplomatic and economic link with the wider world, the Company undermined the Ndebele state from the time it arrived in the region, both through prominent actions in taking control of Mashonaland and ordering the Ndebele not to raid or seek tribute from that region, and through the economic destabilization caused by the increased independence of young men. Furthermore, Lobengula and his indunas were quickly forced to realize that BSAC actions were not mere negotiable mistakes. They were part of a policy. And when Lobengula and his council had to face the Company's refusal to accept their repudiation of the Rudd concession, its unwillingness to accept any limits on the nature of its exploitation of Mashonaland, and its consistent encroachments and lack of deference, they realized that the Ndebele state's survival was threatened. By the late nineteenth century, the balance of power between the Ndebele and the Shona may have already begun to shift in favor of the Shona.[71] As leaders of a regional power unwilling to lose its authority, the indunas of Matabeleland could not look calmly at successful Shona cattle raids into formally Ndebele territory. They demanded action. By 1893 the Ndebele had rejected the attempts of the BSAC to peacefully render them subjects, and the Company proceeded to use force. The Company won the Matabele War without too much difficulty, but the war did not entirely crush the Ndebele state.[72] And the war had little effect on most Shona regions, far from the conflict and insulated by distance from BSAC activity. When, after the war, the Africans found Company rule multiplying the pressures of economic change by instituting a hut tax, enforcing labor, and seizing cattle, thus undermining the local economy and society, they did not make their peace with the new system and act as clay to Company or missionary remodeling. Neither Company nor missionary ideologies had succeeded in reaching and reshaping the local people into subjects of the administration.

Communication

By 1896, when the Africans of Southern Rhodesia made their dissatisfaction with Company rule abundantly clear, speaking in the common tongue of violence, the various factions and groups of the region had begun the long process of laying out images of their neighbors and the region's history. But the images were fragmentary and sometimes inconsistent rather than parts of an integrated ideology, terminology, or language of imperial domination. They were fragments that reflected the interests of each individual group or faction rather than comprehensive compromise ideologies capable of mediating between groups and melding them into ruling coalitions or resisting alliances. Before the 1896 Risings, Southern Rhodesia was ruled through force, and justified through force, rather than through an effective ideology. The Company explained to its external constituency that its military maneuvers in the Matabele War constituted a benevolent defensive response. The BSAC was a force, and it justified itself through an image of the Ndebele as a force. The settlers used and demanded force with even fewer efforts at justification. The Africans, who found themselves subject to force and struggled to respond to it, discovered that without violence, their protestations had little effect on the new rulers.

NOTES

1. Robert Moffat, *Missionary Labours and Scenes in Southern Africa* (London, 1842), 538–43.
2. Moffat, *Missionary Labours,* 543.
3. Moffat to LMS, 7 February 1855, CWM 1/1/A/5.
4. Moffat to LMS, 2 October 1860, CWM 1/1/C/11.
5. Moffat to LMS, 7 February 1855, CWM 1/1/A/5.

6. Sykes to LMS 3 August 1863, CWM 1/2/B/34.

7. Frederick C. Selous, *Travel and Adventure in Southeast Africa* (London: Rowland Ward, 1893; reprint, New York: Arno Press, 1967), 48.

8. Selous, *Travel and Adventure,* 101.

9. Selous, *Travel and Adventure,* 102-3.

10. Carnegie to LMS, 17 June 1887, CWM 2/3/C.

11. W. H. Brown, *South African Frontier* (London, 1899; reprint, New York: Negro Universities Press, 1970), 43.

12. W. H. Brown, *South African Frontier,* 44.

13. W. H. Brown, *South African Frontier,* 44.

14. Early Portuguese descriptions do exist, and are used extensively in studies of precolonial history, such as S. I. G. Mudenge, *A Political History of Munhumutapa* (Harare: Zimbabwe Publishing House, 1988) or D. N. Beach, *The Shona and Zimbabwe, 900-1850* (Gweru, Zimbabwe: Mambo Press, 1980). The Portuguese sources do not, however, appear to have had much influence on the early British, Dutch, German, American, or French observers of the region.

15. Francois Coillard, *On the Threshold of Central Africa;* 3d ed., (London: Frank Cass, 1897, 1971), 31-32.

16. Selous, *Travel and Adventure,* 48.

17. Moffat to LMS, 7 February 1855, CWM 1/1/A/5.

18. Selous, *Travel and Adventure,* 136-38.

19. Philip Mason, *The Birth of a Dilemma* (London: Oxford University Press, 1958), 131-45.

20. Lawrence Vambe provides, in *An Ill-Fated People: Zimbabwe before and after Rhodes* (London: Heinemann, 1972), 99, a telling of some of the oral traditions he learned from his family as he grew up on the Chishawasha mission station.

21. J. S. Galbraith, *Crown and Charter: The Early Years of the British South Africa Company* (Berkeley: U of California Press, 1974), 107-10.

22. For a detailed analysis of the issues and power struggles within the imperial (British) and subimperial (Cape) communities during the extension of British influence and Company rule in Southern Africa, see D. M. Schreuder, *The Scramble for Southern Africa, 1877-1895* (Cambridge: Cambridge University Press, 1980), esp. 203-end.

23. "Charter of the British South Africa Company" in "Papers relating to the administration of Matabeleland and Mashonaland" (London: HMSO [C7383], 1894). Charter dated 19 December 1889.

24. Agreement signed by High Commissioner Henry B. Loch and the BSAC directors Abercorn and Fife, 23 May 1894. Quoted in W. A. Wills and L. T. Collingridge, eds., *The Downfall of Lobengula* (London, New York, 1894, 1969), 316.

25. For example, see Julian R. D. Cobbing, "The Ndebele under the Khumalos, 1820-1896" (Ph.D. thesis, U. of Lancaster, 1976), 367.

26. Eva, Report of Police Visit on Hartley Station, October 1894, WMMS 333/2; John White 5 February 1895, WMMS 333/3. The head of the mission, Isaac Shimmin, summed up the situation in a letter of 9 September 1895, (WMMS 333/3) by writing it off after a private talk with Dr. Jameson (BSAC Administrator), arguing that the conditions in the region made it imperative for the Society to remain on Rhodes' good side, or fail. The investigation was apparently allowed to drop.

27. For example, Wilder to American Board of Commissioners for Foreign Missions (ABC), 27 April 1894, ABC 15.4, vol. 20, item 277; Wilder to ABC, 1 January 1895, ABC 15.4, vol. 20, item 280.

28. Agreement signed by High Commissioner Henry B. Loch and the BSAC directors Abercorn and Fife, 23 May 1894. Quoted in W. A. Wills and L. T. Collingridge, eds., *The Downfall of Lobengula*, 313–19.

29. Galbraith, *Crown and Charter*, 267, 287–291.

30. British South Africa Company, report to stockholders, for 1892–1894 (London: 1895), 17.

31. Mason, *Birth of a Dilemma*, 143.

32. Hugh Marshall Hole, *The Making of Rhodesia*, (London: Macmillan, 1926), 2–4, describes the effect on settlers of explorers' accounts of riches. And would-be adventurers could also read a newly published novel on the subject. H. Rider Haggard, *King Solomon's Mines:* (London, 1885).

33. Brown, *On the South African Frontier*, 307.

34. T. O. Ranger, *Peasant Consciousness and Guerilla War in Zimbabwe* (London: James Currey, 1985) 26–32, notes that when it was possible to market produce rather than labor, Africans did so, engaging in "self-peasantization" rather than accepting even a modified form of proletarianization. And even NCs complained of men with short tempers, who sought work discipline through a sjambok, and then boasted about the floggings "as if they had accomplished a wonderful feat." Meredith (NC Salisbury) to CNC, 12 February 1895, NAZ N1/2/2.

35. Galbraith, *Crown and Charter*, 282–86.

36. Galbraith, *Crown and Charter*, 289.

37. Brown, *South African Frontier*, 162–63.

38. Arthur Keppel-Jones, *Rhodes and Rhodesia, The White Conquest of Zimbabwe, 1884–1902*, (Kingston: McGill-Queen's University Press, 1983), 232.

39. For example: ". . . the war was an absolute necessity, and the crushing of the Matabeli power at any cost the only possible means of maintaining the supremacy of our race on the plateau of Central South Africa . . . In Mashonaland there has never been but one opinion on the subject, an opinion . . . held by every white man who had gone to the country with a view to bettering his condition in life . . ." F. C. Selous, in W. A. Wills and L. T. Collingridge, eds. *The Downfall of Lobengula*, 2–3.

40. Galbraith, *Crown and Charter*, 293.

41. Brown, *South African Frontier,* 270.

42. Quoted in P. B. S. Wrey, in Wills and Collingridge, *Downfall of Lobengula,* 58-59.

43. Selous, in Wills and Colleridge, *Downfall of Lobengula,* 6.

44. Hole, *Making of Rhodesia,* 295.

45. Brown, *South African Frontier,* 266-67.

46. Brown, *South African Frontier,* 267.

47. Wrey, in Wills and Collingridge, *Downfall of Lobengula,* 62.

48. High Commissioner (Cape Town) to Jameson (BSAC Administrator), Victoria, 24 July 1893, CO879/39/454.

49. Selous, in Wills and Collingridge, *Downfall of Lobengula,* 3.

50. T. Thomas to LMS, 27 November 1868, CWM 1/2/B/3b.

51. For example, Sykes to LMS 1 March 1867, CWM 1/2/C/45 (discusses people making decisions about schooling versus working in their gardens); Joseph Cockin to LMS, May 1879, CWM 1/3/B/77 (discusses conversion and influence by missionaries).

52. A. J. Dachs and W. F. Rea, *The Catholic Church and Zimbabwe, 1879-1979* (Gwelo: Mambo Press, 1979), 28.

53. Joseph Cockin to LMS, May 1879, CWM 1/3/B/77.

54. D. Carnegie to LMS, 14 February 1890, CWM 2/4/A.

55. For example, Douglas Pelly, Letters, *Mashonaland Quarterly* 4 (April 1893): 6-8, in which he discusses the importance of African oral culture to missionary dissemination of information.

56. For example, D. Pelly, Letter (dated 2 October 1892), *Mashonaland Paper* 3 (January 1893), in which he discusses his early contract with Umtasa.

57. For example, "The Mashonaland Mission" (undated prospectus for a Church of England Mission) attached to the *Mashonaland Paper* June 1892, which asserts that the availability of mission farms makes the extension of evangelical opportunity too good to pass up.

58. For example, LMS: Sykes to LMS 3 August 1863, CWM 1/2/B/34; American Board: Gilson to ABC, 25 February 1891, ABC 15.4, vol. 20, item 4 and F. R. Bunker to ABC, 13 November 1893, ABC 15.4, vol. 19, item 190; Anglican: D. R. Pelly, Letter (dated 2 October 1892), *Mashonaland Paper* 3 (January 1893).

59. "Not to act in the present crisis would deserve the execration of the whole civilised world." Shimmin, 3 August 1893, MMS 333/2.

60. Bowen Rees to LMS, 8 February 1892, CWM 1/5/A/114, asserts no progress will be made until "the power of this chief is broken and until we are clothed with more power from on high." See also "Observations to Propaganda Fideii," October 1893, box 49, Jesuit Archives, Harare.

61. Wilder to ABC, 26 February 1894, ABC 15.4, vol. 20, item 276.

62. Knight-Bruce, 19 November 1893, USPG/CLR 142.

63. Wilder to ABC, 26 February 1894, ABC 15.4, vol. 20, item 276.

64. G. W. H. Knight-Bruce, *Journals of the Mashonaland Mission 1888 to 1892* (London: USPG, 1892); John White to MMS, 16 June 1894, MMS 333/2; Wilder to ABC, 27 April 1894, ABC 15.4, vol. 20, item 277.

65. Rees to LMS 15 December 1890, CWM 2/4/A.

66. Sykes to LMS 1 March 1867, CWM 1/2/C/45.

67. Rees to LMS 15 December 1890, CWM 2/4/A.

68. Francois Coillard, *Threshold of Central Africa,* 31–32.

69. Cobbing, "Ndebele under the Khumalos, 1820–1896," 218–19.

70. Cobbing, "Ndebele under the Khumalos," 1, 181, 219.

71. D. N. Beach, *War and Politics in Zimbabwe, 1840–1900* (Gweru, Zimbabwe: Mambo Press, 1986), 33–37.

72. Cobbing, "Ndebele under the Khumalos," 366.

CHAPTER TWO

Violence and Comprehension

Making Authority, 1894–1898

When the BSAC declared victory in the Matabele War it, and most European observers of the war, saw the victory as completing the conquest of Southern Rhodesia. With the contemporary faith in the destruction of the Ndebele state and the cowardice of the Shona, these observers in Britain and in Southern Rhodesia expected the BSAC to institutionalize its rule as a predatory administration promoting the exploitation of the region. They were not disappointed. The Company quickly opened Matabeleland for prospectors and settlers, engaged in massive cattle raiding, and attempted to impress its governance further on the Africans by instituting a hut tax, administered by official hut tax collectors. In the context of this European security, the 1896 uprisings in Matabeleland and Mashonaland were a grave shock. Through them, Africans became audible to a deaf European public, by speaking in the European languages of force and military threat. In objecting forcibly to the Company and settlers' systematic patterns of brutalization, raiding, and displacement, the Ndebele set limits to European exploitation. And in risings that opposed the imperial transformation of their people into abject vassals, the Shona sought to prevent European characterizations of their people from becoming true.

Between contemporary comments, rueful post-1896 reflections on the causes of the Risings, and recent studies of the BSAC's tactics, it is clear that Company rule in the period from 1893 to 1896 was abusive. The Company and nearly all the European inhabitants of Matabeleland and Mashonaland were enthusiastic enough about their future prospects to avoid worrying about the implications of their methods. Each economic, political, or social difficulty, therefore, tended to be met by European attempts to push Africans harder.

The BSAC set the stage for such an attitude in its looting and expropriations after the Matabele War. It attempted to make a quick profit in Matabeleland through land seizures, gold claims, cattle looting, and impressment of labor.[1] This looting made resources available for the European community, encouraging settlers to see Matabeleland as a place of promised prosperity, probably in gold, certainly in cattle. Matabeleland boomed. By March 1895, nine months after its founding, the new European Bulawayo had a European population of 1,537—a spectacular growth compared to Salisbury's relative stagnation at 493 Europeans after more than four years.[2]

The boom's victims were Africans. Settlers often pegged out ranches without occupying them, but enough land was claimed for the Ndebele to realize their danger of expropriation.[3] And the dangers of the other European tactics were difficult to ignore. In an economy where much of the accumulation of wealth took the form of cattle herds, the Company's claim to all the cattle of Matabeleland—to be divided between the Company and the settlers who took part in the war—hurt. As the seizures went on, month after month, year after year, they caused social disruption and economic dislocation and provided a graphic illustration of the Company's intentions.[4] Forced labor, in various forms, was also disruptive, as it extracted young male labor, exposed young men to market goods, and encouraged those men—potential warriors—in disrespect for their elders. Women, too, were subject to seizure by the Company, its agents, or the settlers.[5]

The BSAC built the post-1893 economy of the region on an increasingly institutionalized victimization of Africans; it responded to a slowing of the loot-fueled boom by using Africans' resources to address Company economic and political problems. Africans provided mining capital, labor for expanding enterprises, and a reason for Company prestige among settlers after the Company administrator was embroiled in the Jameson raid. The Company's enthusiasm overwhelmed any sense of moderation. Three related initiatives sought to intensify the extractions from the African economy: the levying of a hut tax, the development of a forced labor regimen, and the institutionalization of an enforcement mechanism through the hut tax collectors—who were soon designated as native commissioners (NCs)—and their armed messengers (or "native policemen").

The BSAC was constantly in need of money, and it petitioned the imperial government for permission to levy a hut tax in Mashonaland even before the Matabele War was over. The hut tax was supposed to finance the Company's administration over Africans, who, it claimed, "have benefitted largely by the establishment of a settled order of white government,"[6] which provided safety and efficient markets. No sooner had the Matabele war ended than the Company sought to extend the tax to Matabeleland.[7] The cash-starved Company wanted the revenue from the tax, but a far more important aim was to promote labor force participation. Some taxation advocates actually advocated that the tax be imposed only on those adult African men who did not go out to work for Europeans.[8] The BSAC request to the Colonial Office stated as platitudes that

> one of the principal difficulties found in dealing with African races is that of teaching the habits of settled industry, and . . . in Mashonaland, with a considerable demand for native labour, the necessity of paying this small annual tax will to a certain extent furnish an incentive to labour which might otherwise be wanting, and experience shows that those who have once been induced to work are more likely to work again than those who have not worked are to begin working.[9]

These goals were sufficiently important that, under Jameson, hut tax collection began at least fifteen months before imperial approval arrived in 1894, with returns substantial enough to promote speculation in BSAC shares.[10]

The BSAC intended the hut tax not just to provide funds for a capital-poor company, but also to promote the monetization of the African economy, and thus increase the dependence of Africans on Europeans for trade goods and opportunities for wage labor. Unlike cattle raiding or random looting, it was supposed to be the instrument of extraction by an administration committed to law and order. It gained widespread European approval within the region when it proceeded peaceably; Father A. M. Hartmann, a Catholic priest, endorsed it willingly enough in his comments for the BSAC report by noting that where it was enforced in Mashonaland or Matabeleland, the "country is settling down peaceably."[11] But the tax collection did not always occur peaceably and, in the face of resistance, its collection could all too easily be merely a new opportunity for looting. At least one farmer complained of NC Brabant's collection tactics, which involved seizing the cattle of whoever happened to have them, without regard to who held what tax liability. "How," he asked, "would an Englishman; settled in his castle at Home, like to see the Government come down and take away his goods . . . because the people in the nearest town could not meet their taxes. . . ."[12] The hut tax did not immediately become a part of an established state. It was merely a form of extraction to make ends meet. And the tax obstructed the Company's own stated goals of encouraging Africans to seek peace, and to go to work for wages, as tax collectors accepted payment in kind, not always insisting on money, and raided for cattle when other collection tactics failed.

The hut tax was not the BSAC's sole method of extracting economic resources from Africans on a continuing basis. The Company was short not merely of the capital necessary to finance the region's development, but also of willing African labor. To solve this problem, it resorted to forced labor. After the 1896 Risings, the imperial government investigated the administration of the region and concluded that compulsory labor had undoubtedly existed.[13] Unofficially, its presence was unmistakable. The *Rhodesia Herald* commented obliquely that during the seasonal labor crunch, "the Government has done all it possibly can,"[14] though it refrained from making explicit the government's policy of aggressive labor recruitment. Others, though, saw no need to equivocate. Many native commissioners openly advocated forced labor for a certain period each year, and some went so far as to argue that whole African communities should be moved into locations to ease government oversight and the extraction of labor.[15] H. Marshall Hole, a later Company notable, remembered how

> the officials . . . send their black police into the districts for recruiting purposes. The latter, dressed in a little brief authority, abused their powers and strutted through the villages, ordering the young men to come and work and sometimes compelling them by physical force.[16]

The LMS missionary Cullen Reed characterized the tactics as "slave raiding with limitations."[17] And even a casual observer after the Risings mentioned how the local administration of the BSAC worked in the rural areas to "boss things up."[18] Faced with a formal inquiry, some NCs equivocated on the tactics they had used to recruit labor, but many admitted openly to the use of force, seeing it as fully justified if the labor was needed and not voluntarily forthcoming.[19]

Workers were forcibly recruited not merely for the occasional governmental jobs such as road building and porterage for native commissioners on itinerations, but for private employers. Even years later, officials continued to assert that it was only reasonable to require local inhabitants to carry the NC's supplies on tour, or to order them to make roads for administrative purposes.[20] Officials did not pay such occasional, local workers. When they wrote of recruiting labor, they were discussing recruitment for mines and farms, which might or might not even be near the laborer's home.[21]

Forced labor was important to the administration not merely as a source of unwilling labor, but as a means of mobilizing a cheap labor force. Company officials and other European employers in the region were unwilling to allow the demand for scarce labor to determine its price. Employers who paid more than the going rate, one emphasized, were acting antisocially, not only impoverishing themselves, but depriving the entire country of the economic advantages to be gained from cheap African labor.[22] Perhaps realizing the destructive effects of its cattle-seizing hut tax raids on the productive capacity of African communities, Company officials shifted from raiding for cattle to raiding for labor. Those who did not pay their hut taxes were personally liable for two months of labor, for a wage of 10 shillings, which would be devoted to their tax arrears.[23]

Seizures, whether of cattle or labor, were not likely to endear the BSAC to the imperial government. And by the end of 1895, when the territory's administrator, Dr. Jameson, had become the central character in the embarrassingly unsuccessful Jameson raid, improving relations with the imperial government had become crucial. The Company needed respectability. The Jameson raid, an illegal military intervention in a region outside the BSAC's territory, was bad enough, but it was only one of the many examples critics of Company rule could point to in illustrating Company-sponsored anarchy. A corps of hut tax collectors, later called native commissioners could, in this atmosphere, help improve the Company's relations with the British government by reducing the appearance of administrative anarchy, while keeping up extractive pressure on the African economy.[24]

Anarchy was a major concern because the BSAC did not, in the period from 1893 to 1896, have a monopoly on the exercise of force within its territory. Complaints regarding the prevalence of violence came not just from Africans but, for various reasons, from many sectors of the European community. One farmer objected that whenever a farmer lost something, it was all too common for him to go into the local kraal and seize whatever he wished in recompense, a fact that made labor recruiting more difficult than necessary as potential workers feared the repercussions of an angry employer more than they wanted the goods they could earn.[25] Some missionaries objected to violence by settlers both because it was counterproductive and because it outraged their sense of human dignity. Bishop Knight-Bruce, who confessed that the Africans he dealt with had made him long to thrash them, nevertheless emphasized that temptation must be avoided and that real progress could only be made through educating Africans into good work habits, rather than "terrifying them with a stick into running about spasmodically for a month."[26] George Wilder, a missionary with the American Board of Commissioners for Foreign Missions (American Board), argued that settlers' tendency to whip Africans was dehumanizing, a reduction of the African to an ox.[27] Others, however, discussed unofficial violence only obliquely, as Reed of the LMS did when he noted that the station was making progress for the first time because the local people, worried about "villainous white men," were willing to move onto the mission station, where they "could get the benefit of a European's protective influence" as a protection against other Europeans and the native police.[28]

During this early period, the Company could invoke few social sanctions against this potentially counterproductive nonofficial violence. It relied too heavily on violence itself to effectively oppose its use by others. The Native Department, at least prior to 1896, had no distinct philosophy of Africans or African behavior. The Company designed that department as a military structure to rule over an occupied people through the threat—and, when necessary, the use—of force. Its officials were young, mobile, and generally able to speak some African language with at least rudimentary competence. Some got caught engaging in questionable practices, such as the native commissioner who evidently sent his policemen to a kraal with threats of burning it and thrashing the "chief" unless he procured a woman for the native commissioner to rape,[29] or the resident magistrate and native commissioner who were involved in the seizure and imprisonment of a newly installed "chief" for hut tax delinquency.[30] But, without any ideological tools to modify its rule or make its violence one aspect of an integrated strategy of rule, the Company could not help but appear hypocritical on those rare occasions when it objected to unofficial violence.

The institutionalization of the Company through hut taxes, forced labor, and the officials designated to mobilize them did not represent any ideological shift on the part of the Company from the speculative raiding of its early years. Its goals, and to a large extent its tactics, remained the same. To the Africans who felt the impact of institutionalization firsthand, however, and had either experienced conquest or watched their neighbors suffer it, this institutionalization brought an intensification and regularization of an already uncomfortable domination. Reporting the murder of three leaders of the Lomagundi community, the MMS missionary Weavind remarked that "Many of them [the Africans] are even now saying that their lot was more bearable under the Matabele than it is under the white men."[31] The administration's defense in the Lomagundi incident, Weavind reported, was that such things were necessary for the establishment of permanent order.[32] Africans, after the Matabele War, faced the realization that the Company was not merely passing through. It intended to stay.[33]

Alternatives

By 1896, missionaries within Southern Rhodesia were beginning to develop a policy and an ideology that would integrate their ideas of what Africans were with mechanisms to make them achieve what the missionaries felt they could be. Seeking an alternative to Company-sponsored violence, they sought to "civilize" the Africans. Civilizing Africans meant more than just teaching literacy. It meant teaching them about European cultural beliefs and practices. The itinerant preaching of the earliest missionaries gradually gave way to the establishment of stations containing farms and schools, through which missionaries sought to inculcate not just an abstract ideology of Christianity, but a concrete pattern of labor and the vital skill of literacy. Missionaries from groups as diverse as the Jesuits and the American Board believed that Africans would learn by practicing skills and observing the example of the missionaries.

The Jesuits, who were slow to object to any Company activity and generally defended the administration even in the face of well-founded charges, asserted that "a just and paternal administration which protects the Mashonas against unfair and harsh treatment will advance the civilization of a whole nation of natives."[34] The paternal treatment the Jesuits advocated could involve a substantial measure of strictness and did not imply that they were training Africans into equality with Europeans.[35] Chishawasha, for years the only substantial Catholic mission station in Mashonaland, sought to remove children from their homes, discipline them into patterns of intensive labor, and teach them rudimentary literacy.[36] But the Fathers successfully integrated their harshness with their ideology of proselytising and improvement. Unlike other large-scale employers, they did not have difficulty recruiting willing, and initially unpaid, laborer-students to work for between five and eight hours of industrial work and four to five hours of "literary work" daily.[37]

A missionary integration of work and learning developed in the early years of the missions not to satisfy administration requirements or settler objections, but because the most accessible Africans for schooling were children or young people employed on the mission station. In the early years of the LMS mission, Sykes sought to acquire pupils from among the thirty to forty young people he employed to do his gardening by refusing to pay them until after the daily lesson.[38] And even after the Company's conquest, similar practices were common. Pelly's first excursion into teaching involved the renting of boys from Chief Umtasa at the rate of five pounds per ten boys per month. After teaching them for two to three hours a day, he planned to sublet their labor out in the town to defray expenses.[39]

In the mission stations, the intersection between work and learning was vital because the stations were farms with substantial labor requirements. The emphasis of all the missionaries, with the possible exception of those at Chishawasha, was on the New Testament, rather than the "Gospel of Work."[40] It was galling for missionaries to admit to home audiences that employment played a major role in the collection of students and the retention of readers to the stage of baptism. But in 1889 Bowen Rees, an LMS missionary, argued that "There is no chance of teaching them unless they work and stay with us."[41] And the other societies found much the same problem even far from Matabeleland. Wilder, of the American Board down at Mt. Silinda, in Melsetter, commented in 1894 that his only regular students were his farm employees.[42] Hiring students, whether the jobs were perceived as part of the students' tuition or whether the school was perceived as part of the workers' jobs, was one way for early missionaries to gain concentrated access to and authority over young Africans.[43]

Given the mission farm nexus of education and labor, settler complaints that the missionaries were "the cause of all the wrong relationship between the white men and the black"[44] and spoiled the "raw native" for real work[45] could be dismissed by missionaries as mere grumbling by individuals who needed scapegoats for their lack of success. Missions, missionaries emphasized, believed in combining work with study, training the whole person in a way that would teach without making the pupil either servile or haughty. But it was precisely this complete education to which many settlers objected. European employers were not interested in work and study. They were interested only in study that improved the African's ability to work for European employers, study that was rudimentary to the extent that it was usually described more accurately as training, a training primarily in deference and discipline rather than in any mental or manual skills. Whenever an African failed to defer, these settlers saw this lack of deference as evidence that the missions had failed.

The goal of those who would govern or manage Africans, announced a local 1895 editorial, should be "to instil into the native mind that civilisation means industry, peace and justice." The writer cautioned that "so far, nothing worthy of the name has been done to educate the native of this land . . . to stem without demoralisation the wave of civilisation which is now advancing on the country."[46] Civilization, which the missionaries sought to promote, was, in itself, a threat for the settler community, which relied on often brutal force. Settlers responded that civilization was also a danger to Africans. The African, they declared, was not yet ready. He was "not a man and a brother . . . [but] a child and a very distant cousin."[47] Thus, even though settlers were willing to acknowledge that an African could probably learn "differential calculus, or the merits and demerits of bimetallism" with relative ease, true education, appropriate to the situation, would have nothing to do with abstruse intellectual issues, but would "drill him gradually into healthy civilised habits, beginning with that of industry."[48]

In 1895 W. H. Brown stopped an African on a Salisbury street, and asked him if he knew anything about some hatchets that had allegedly gone missing. According to a settler who reported the incident,

> the boy, strong in the faith planted in his breast by many black missionaries, retorted in a manner calculated to irritate a saint, . . . and went on jabbering with the gratuitous insolence acquired to perfection only by a native who has received not less than two years mission training.

The confrontation rapidly became serious when Brown got out his sjambok (whip) and hit a few people, whose cries attracted a crowd, armed with assorted weaponry, from a nearby beer-drink.[49] The most important message of the incident for this correspondent was the missionary responsibility; his explicit assumption was that the missionaries had subverted a potential employers' Eden of submissive workers. When Brown later commented on the incident, which had brought him before a magistrate for assault on an African, he commented only, "I was not aware at the time . . . that striking a kaffir for insolence was a criminal offense."[50] Many of the settlers of the period after 1893 and before 1896 felt themselves invincible. They were essentially uninterested in notions of what the Africans of the region could become as skilled workers, intelligent decision makers, or even moral Christians. They wanted crude labor and deference. Nothing more, lest the laborers make explicit demands on their employers. They were, by and large, willing to tolerate the rapacious behavior of the BSAC, seeing it as a far less threatening strategy for managing Africans than any missionary-influenced educational tactics would be.

War

But in 1896 the illusion the BSAC shared with the settlers, that they could rule by force and make what use they wished of the majority of the country's inhabitants, cracked. At the end of March 1896 the *Rhodesia Herald* reported that a "calamity has fallen upon the land . . . unsuspected and unforseen . . . tragic and grave."[51] In a later account, a settler described how reports filtered in to Bulawayo of native policemen and settlers being killed, stories which were lurid in their details of mutilations and of the deaths of women and children.[52] These reports set off a flurry of activity, as Europeans from all over Matabeleland attempted to get to the laagers, and the Company sought to mobilize a military force to fight and sent messages out of the territory pleading for imperial troops and for permission to issue arms to the Europeans clamoring for weapons at the Bulawayo laager.[53]

The initial local European reaction was one of outrage.[54] But even as the European and European-affiliated population of Bulawayo crowded into the laager and began to prepare for a war, individuals in both Matabeleland and Mashonaland were beginning to analyze the situation, finding scapegoats and reexamining their ideas concerning the Africans and how Africans were likely to behave. In his letter of 10 April, the LMS missionary Reed described growing animosity in Bulawayo directed at the Company. There was, he wrote, talk of lynching the acting administrator, and it was a common belief that the Company was stopping the post to conceal the severity of the situation. Reed clearly perceived the rising as a response, by a people who had never been fully conquered, to intolerable conditions imposed on them by the Company's cattle raiding, compulsory labor, and malpractice both in permitting individual traders and native policemen to harass the population and then in withdrawing its military force for the Jameson raid in a maneuver that made the administration seem weak. Most disquietingly, Reed reported that apart from a few laagers, "the country is in the hands of the Matabeles and there seems every probability that it will remain so for a good many months to come." The Africans were fighting "with accuracy and determination."[55] In Mashonaland, not yet the subject of its own risings, even nonmissionary sources offered criticism of the Company's administration, which not only had been too unintelligent to discern earlier what was happening, but which bore some of the responsibility for the Rising. The BSAC had, according to the writer's opinion, either exercised too much leniency toward Africans reluctant to work,[56] or neglected to "put down with a stern hand the treatment of the natives received from some of the first prospectors and police," ignoring its responsibility for "laying solid foundations in native policy."[57] When the Rising broke out in Matabeleland, Mashonaland's major newspaper commented that Mashonalanders must not panic at the difficulties of Europeans in Matabeleland as "we are not in their danger. . . ."[58] Europeans in Mashonaland were complacent, secure in their belief that the Shona were not only a nonwarlike people, but probably grateful for European protection from the Ndebele anyhow. But that complacency was shattered by the middle of June, when those Shona took up arms and began their own version of a rising. The concept of a Shona rising was so unlikely to the Europeans of Salisbury that they initially met it with disbelief. "We do not see sufficient evidence in the murders and the attitude of the natives," reported the *Herald,* "to conclude that anything like a general, or even a partial, rising is contemplated. But the known facts certainly give rise to anxiety. . . ."[59] And when the rumors solidified into the reality of a Shona rising, the news "fell upon us like a thunderbolt, for no one had ever dreamed that the Mashonas . . . were capable of rising and committing horrible atrocities."[60]

The Company claimed to believe that the Africans who rebelled were acting out of superstitions involving witchcraft and magic, spells and prophecy.[61] In an influential 1967 study, T. O. Ranger sought to make sense of the reports of African mobilization and organization by accepting Company reports of a cult-led movement and valorizing them as a protonational resistance movement.[62] Later research has cast doubts on the idea that the Risings were coordinated by religious leaders. The Ndebele, Julian Cobbing argued, organized their rising around a state that had survived the 1893 war damaged, but still capable of organizing a response to the intolerable conditions of BSAC colonialism.[63] D. N. Beach's studies of the Shona have likewise cast doubt on the role of mediums and priests, emphasizing instead the pressure on the Shona economy both from Company maladministration and from natural disaster. Beach has seen the Rising as growing from smaller incidents as far back as 1894 and culminating not through magical coordination, but through a distinctly uncoordinated ripple effect. Furthermore, he has insisted that any successful explanation must discuss not merely why some Shona rose, but why some remained calm or even sent military aid to the Company, and he has found his answers in the internal linkages and tensions of Shona politics.[64] All descriptions and analyses of Africans' views on the Risings agree, however, that they did not represent a fundamental disjuncture in the African worldview. They responded directly to the threat represented by the BSAC and settler administration using methods that appeared to the Africans who had the initiative in this military endeavor as natural, methods growing out of the experiences of the years under the BSAC and from the strategies of survival perfected in years before that. For Africans, the revolutionary intellectual and ideological implications of the Risings did not emerge until they found themselves losing and were forced to develop new strategies of survival as individuals and communities.

After their initial emphatic beginnings, the Risings stretched into the repeated military confrontations of a guerrilla war. In the tension of the conflict and afterward, Africans considered "the weakness of their forces and the strength of the enemy, the Europeans, " and found themselves contemplating "human savagery, misery, injustice, blood and death."[65] The Company forces responded to the Risings with an all-out war. They sought to destroy the economic base of the African forces by pursuing a scorched earth policy, burning kraals and destroying grain stores.[66] The European army dynamited the caves of Mashonaland—which were both military fortifications and the homes of villages who had taken refuge in them—killing men, women, children and any remaining livestock, and destroying food stores.[67] The Africans of the region found it impossible to be safe in the atmosphere of the Europeans' total warfare against anyone who was not white. Drunk European troops fired on "friendlies" [Africans fighting against the Risings].[68] Sober officers ordered the shooting of noncombatant women and had no qualms about killing children.[69] Occasional hotheads even engaged in hunting down and assassinating African allies.[70]

After the initial attacks and killings, Europeans experienced less violence than they dealt out. The laagers were effective, though cramped and unpleasant. Combatants, however, a high proportion of European men in Southern Rhodesia, experienced skirmishes in which the Ndebele fought with "accuracy and determination,"[71] as the African forces had quickly "commenced to learn . . . and showed every sign of putting . . . knowledge to practical use." The inference was unavoidable: "The Matabele is no fool; his preconceived notions of how to fight the white man have long since been discarded."[72] The realization was disquieting, as it potentially meant a long campaign. But the Europeans had long seen the Ndebele as a "martial race." The initial military successes of the Ndebele, and the difficulty European forces found in defeating them, dismayed Company officials, who were wary of the cost,[73] but settlers or soldiers could understand that their foes were the martial representatives of a nation that had never really been defeated.[74]

Fighting the Shona, however, proved a far more disorienting experience for European forces. The common perception of the Shona had been as a "scattered and disunited people, who from a fighting point of view were contemptible."[75] And yet they were not only fighting, they were proving difficult for a European force to beat. Their tactics were "baffling," as they fought from the shelter of their rock forts or effectively fortified villages or caves.[76] Settlers were slow to modify their belief in Shona cowardice and disorganization. Even when the Shona fought effectively, the Europeans perceived the successes as examples of "the strength of a weak people when they unite for a common purpose,"[77] rather than a sign that the European evaluation of the people had been wrong. The tactics, far from being admired, were regarded by some Europeans as further examples of Shona cravenness.[78]

The experiences of each force during the Risings affected the making of a peace. The economic warfare hurt Africans throughout the region, regardless of whether they were fighters. The Rising in Matabeleland had emerged, among other causes, out of a frustration with locusts and cattle disease that had threatened the livelihood of the community even without the additional burdens of the Company. When the Company burned food stocks during the Rising, it was destroying a portion of what little food remained in the region. The Ndebele, facing the prospect of not merely individual, but communal starvation, were willing, after a few months of fighting, to negotiate. The Company was, by that time, equally willing to negotiate with the Ndebele. The Shona Rising had rendered its economic and military position extremely tenuous. The fighting disrupted production and transportation, rapidly destroying any hope of profit from mining or agriculture, and the Rising in Mashonaland increased the Company's direct military costs substantially.[79] Furthermore, the Company was having its own difficulties with supplies.[80] The road to the Cape was open, but should the Risings continue, Africans who had remained neutral or sided with the Company could decide to close it, making resupply even more difficult than it was.[81] And if the Company could not demonstrate its ability to hold land, the imperial troops that were temporarily assisting the BSAC could easily become the vanguard of an imperial takeover of Company responsibilities, leading to a revocation of the charter.[82] With each side interested in a quick settlement, Cecil Rhodes and the BSAC, in a series of meetings with some of the Ndebele leaders, negotiated an end to the Ndebele Rising.[83] At the indabas [meetings], the indunas explained to Rhodes and the other negotiators the Ndebele view of the events of the previous six years. Somabula discussed the Matabele War and Jameson's broken promises. Sikombo spoke of the abuses by the native police, who as young men set above their elders were socially disruptive, and he explained that the native commissioners, who were raiding their kraals and seizing their cattle and women, were intolerable. Rhodes accepted these complaints, and together the Ndebele leaders and the BSAC officials began to negotiate the details of reserve land and grain supplies.[84] In a series of meetings, the indunas and the officials constructed a settlement complete with perks for the Ndebele leaders and promises of a more intelligent native policy.[85]

The Shona rising, though, did not end so quickly. In December the Salisbury newspaper was still cautioning European residents of the region about their danger. They could not, it informed them, consider the area "as safe as Picadilly." Overconfidence was dangerous.

> Times without number have the Mashonas been described as timid, abject creatures who were incapable of showing fight, and within a few weeks of the actual outbreak the same was said. The Mashonas rise? The idea was too absurd! . . . It is now a matter of history that they *did* rise, and, what was even worse, could fight, in their own peculiar way, far better than the Matabele.[86]

The Company and the European community, no longer trusting their own knowledge or judgment regarding the Shona, wanted to crush them, not to negotiate a settlement. The Company justified its pursuit of war rather than settlement by arguing that unlike the Ndebele, who had a coherent state system with leaders who could speak for their people in a negotiated settlement, the Shona were divided. The divided people, the Company believed, were held together by a system of prophets and religious leaders. Those leaders, however, were never accessible for discussion, as it was the secular leaders who fought the battles. This divided leadership undermined the ability of any one individual or category of leaders, (e.g., "petty chiefs") to negotiate. Unlike the Ndebele leaders, who were presumed to have sufficient control over their forces to be able to guarantee their side of a bargain, the division of power among leaders, and among a secular and religious leadership, added an uncertainty to any negotiations and undermined any possibility of a settlement. The Company also realized that its expectations of Shona passivity had proven egregiously incorrect. Theories of Shona "nature" allowed for the possibility that the Rising occurred because the Shona had never been forced to realize European strength. If that was the case, trouncing the Shona unmercifully was the only way to gain their respect for the future. That might have been enough to slow

Company willingness to negotiate a settlement. But worse yet was the realization that possibly a mistake had been made in the early analysis of Shona "nature." And if that was the case, the Company would have to accept uncertainty not only in the organizational categories of who ruled the Shona, but also in the analytic categories it used to predict Shona behavior. These ideological and analytic uncertainties, combined with the very real uncertainty most of the population of Mashonaland seems to have experienced over who, exactly, was winning the prolonged struggle, was enough to prevent the Company from making overtures to the Shona combatants.

Settlers shared the Company's reluctance to negotiate, agreeing emphatically with many of its reasons.[87] While, in Matabeleland, settlers and prospectors were reported to have headed out to their claims and farms even before the formal settlement was complete, the Europeans of Mashonaland, shocked once, were somewhat shyer of returning to their previous casualness.[88] They wanted a decisive military victory, not pleas to negotiate. Settlers demanded that the Company compel surrender rather than request it.[89] And they were not convinced that any victory was in sight. The *Rhodesia Herald* cynically observed at the beginning of 1897 that the rebellion was far from broken. In fact,

> we . . . are not only unable to effectually cope with them, but are practically unable to do anything for ourselves or for the country. . . . In spite of our forts, our Maxims, and all other modern implements of warfare, the natives will continue to resist us . . . until their power as a nation is utterly broken.[90]

Local European sentiment against a negotiated settlement appears to have been strong enough to provide substantial popular support for officers who, acting contrary to orders, shot leaders who might (depending on which sources were believed) have surrendered on terms.[91] Such actions made any Shona initiatives toward settlement difficult as they not only endangered potential negotiators, but also cast doubt on the Europeans' reliability in promising anything.[92] The Shona Rising, therefore, sputtered on as European tactics emphasized the destruction of growing crops, the burning of villages, and the dynamiting of caves. Only at the end of September 1897 did the European campaign end, and the last trials of Shona leaders dragged on until April 1898.[93]

Policies

In both Matabeleland and Mashonaland, the end of the Risings signaled the beginning of a search for a Native Policy. A new context of danger and expense surrounded the settler communities after the Risings had shown the Europeans their vulnerability and encouraged them to see the African population as a problem rather than as a resource. And in that atmosphere, an effective Native Policy became vital to all the Europeans of the region.

The definition of this Native Policy, though, took some time. Europeans in Southern Rhodesia viewed it primarily in functional terms: a successful native policy would be a system of managing Africans that kept them passive and compliant, providing security and labor to the Europeans of the region. As a system for securing passivity and compliance, the pre-Rising native policy could be said to be one of force, force that provided European security through police forces and an armed European citizenry, and force which recruited labor for European-directed economic enterprise through hut tax collectors, native commissioners, and their messengers. The Risings, however, showed conclusively that those who lived by the sword—in this case the forcible coercion of others—had to face the possibility of dying by the sword when the coerced fought back.[94] In this context, both the Company and the settlers began to seek a Native Policy as an aspect of a larger Native Question, a question that had to be managed ideologically as well as economically and militarily, lest it undermine the cognitive and ideological assumptions of European superiority along with the physical and economic security of the settler community.

In emphasizing the Native Question, developing a Native Policy, and institutionalizing a native administration, the European community was defining Africans. Specifically, it was seeking to define and delimit Africans as individuals and communities existing in specified relationships to the European administration and economy. The various ideas of the "nature" of Africans that different groups had held before the Risings had been too closely related to individual or factional interests to be able to define the limits of legitimate perception and discussion. Even within distinct social groups, such as missionaries and Company officials, consensus was limited. Furthermore, the vague concepts of the "nature of the African" lacked the ability of later ideological formations to interpret all of African life through a discussion of Africans' relationships to Europeans. The analyses of the Africans had discussed African usefulness, or lack thereof, but they had also left room for a separate African culture and had not attempted to discipline the whole of African life to European needs.

The common European interpretation of the 1896–97 uprisings as the outcome of a lack of comprehension, discipline, or management spelled the end of this laissez faire approach to Africans. Henceforth, concepts of the Native Question provided Europeans with a developing analytic framework within which to perceive and comprehend Africans. In this framework, Africans' visibility and comprehensibility were tied to the Africans' relationship to the European-sponsored society and economy of the region. The format of a Native Policy, administered by an increasingly professionalized Native Department, was to contain the troublesome issues of discipline and management. The Native Policy, like the analytic containment of the Native Question, foregrounded the relationships between Africans and Europeans, using that set of relationships to define Africans and determine how African economies and societies should be administered.

Unsurprisingly, the ideological containment represented by the concept of the Native Question and the administrative containment of the Native Department did not materialize instantly in post-Rising Southern Rhodesia merely because the settlers, the Company, and the colony's imperial sponsors had realized a need for change. The strategies had to be developed during a scattered, ideologically and administratively transitional period from the end of the Risings until the renewal of imperial attention as the Anglo-Boer War ended. And the working out of strategies, structures, and ideologies was a process in which all the parties of Southern Rhodesian society participated: the Company in its guiding role, the settlers with their concerns for the social and economic viability of a European settler society, the missionaries in their niche as intermediaries between Africans and European culture, and, vitally, the Africans as the vast majority of the region, a fissured majority that set forth the conditions and possibilities of social transformation.

The BSAC and the settlers began the process of reconstructing settler society around a new Native Policy as soon as the indabas that ended the Rising in Matabeleland began to look as though they would succeed. The BSAC had, by that time, given thought to what elementary structural changes it could make in the organization of the African population to prevent a recurrence of the Risings. Its first priority was the destruction of the Ndebele state. The BSAC sought no African allies for a policy of indirect rule. It sought authority arising from a relationship between an African and a European. Not only did it refrain from discussing the peace with Nyamanda, Lobengula's newly installed heir to the throne, it made its peace with lesser leaders at the expense of more prominent ones, and sought to develop, through the introduction of a salary system,[95] the lesser leaders as holders of power in their capacity as appointees of the Company. It further limited African leaders through a resettlement scheme designed to bring the African population out of its military strongholds.[96] The resettlement, which would place Africans under the control of European officials rather than Africans, and transfer the allocation of land from African arbitration to the Native Department, was discussed from the first indaba on and was crucial to the European concept of a lasting peace.[97]

Under imperial pressure, the BSAC sought to develop a strategy that would go beyond the mere conciliation Rhodes had offered at the indabas. It began to recruit new native commissioners for its new Native Department, replacing the individuals the Ndebele leaders had objected to and attempting to create a systematic net of administration to replace the haphazard appointments of the earlier period.[98] It sought to develop an intelligence network which, operating through the Native Department, would provide the Company with early warning of any potential future unrest.[99] And, to some degree, it deferred to imperial demands that it desist in requiring forced labor, and work instead to acquire labor through voluntary recruitment.[100]

After the Risings, the BSAC took the issue of administration seriously, seeking to govern as well as to exploit, lest it lose its ability to do either. Many of the initiatives it put forward, though, were the product of imperial demands. As a company chartered in Britain, with a statutory relationship to the British government, it had no choice but to at least listen courteously to the Colonial Office or, more to the point, the high commissioner, or resident commissioner, the local representatives of imperial power, when they demanded that the Company either develop an administration capable of governing its territory or risk losing the administrative mandate. In the aftermath of the Risings and the reports on the conditions that had precipitated them, the BSAC found itself bound into accepting more imperial oversight, oversight that became codified in the 1898 agreement.

Settlers, who lacked that close relationship to the imperial power but possessed a vital interest in the position of the European population of the region, put forward a series of substantial demands that pushed the Company in directions counter to the imperial efforts. Many of the issues settlers raised during this reconstruction period were similar to the issues they had raised in their efforts to provoke the Matabele War. Prominently, and more vociferously than on previous occasions, settlers demanded political reforms to give settlers more control over the territory. Public meetings during June 1897 in Bulawayo and Salisbury called for popular representation in the government of the region. The popular representation notion was specifically seen as a way of preventing imperial proposals from moving toward any native policy that the local European community would regard as weak. Rhodes acknowledged this situation, and the value of the settlers as a pressure group opposed to the imperial government, commenting that the imperial government might "bully the Company . . . but they won't dare to bully a representative Council."[101] The *Rhodesia Herald* chose to discuss the issue in terms not of the imperial government, but of "Exeter Hall," the bogey composed of humanitarian organizations such as the Aborigine Protection Society, which was capable of pushing in Britain for a new attitude toward Africans.[102] Settlers, as during the mobilization for the Matabele War, demanded that native policy be made by those Europeans who knew the country, and activists kept the risks fully in the public mind through allusions to Africans' ability to murder.[103]

Labor was another theme of the Matabele War that settlers again relied on, enshrining it as a crucial ingredient to any native policy satisfactory to them. They did not want to lose access to force as a method of acquiring laborers. But the rhetoric surrounding that force changed. Instead of the 1893 plea that labor was vital to develop the country, settlers in 1897 declared that labor was necessary to improve Africans. In an editorial that objected to Exeter Hall initiatives as likely provokers of plunder and murder, the settlers conceptualized labor as a power for redemption, capable of resurrecting a society out of the ruins of the Risings. The *Herald* forcefully declared,

> Could our natives, by any arts of persuasion, be induced to
> work for us, then to compel them to do so would decidedly be
> wrong. Persuasion has hitherto utterly failed, and, therefore,
> compulsion becomes an imperative duty—a duty which we
> owe both to ourselves and to the natives. So long as the natives
> are led to believe that it is not incumbent on them to work for
> the white man, so long will they continue to remain in their
> present low condition. Until they are taught to work for the
> white man, they will continue to plunder and murder him.
> . . . To . . . encourage the native in his habits of idleness is
> to encourage him to rob and murder his white neighbour.[104]

Indeed, the only aspect of the previous administration worth nostalgia was the ancien régime's attitude toward work; then, "natives were often made to study the dignity of labour by being made to do it."[105] Some settlers were willing to set forth their demand for labor in even starker terms. W. H. Brown, comparing the experience of the African in Southern Rhodesia to the experience of the African-American, declared

> Through an apprenticeship of bondage, the [American] negro
> has been removed from a state of barbarism and superstition
> . . . forcibly weaned from his benighted associations, taught to
> labor, and kept under the influence of an energetic people, he
> has reached a point on the high road of progress that his brother in Africa probably will not attain in a thousand years. . . .[106]

Brown, and many of the settlers, believed that only with a labor policy including coercion could Africans be transformed from their casual labor practices to something more systematic and "advanced."

In the aftermath of the Risings, the issue of European security and control over Africans also gained a new prominence and urgency. Settlers finally recognized that the forcible tactics of the Native Department were insufficient to control the African population or provide adequate security for the white population. Settlers offered no particularly new ideas to ensure security or control. A system of reserves appealed to some, particularly if Africans were restricted to the reserves, unable to leave without labor passes.[107] The idea of a "strong, well paid and judiciously selected police force" also appealed to settlers as a way of preventing future Risings.[108] But reserves had been discussed earlier, and a police system had existed since the invasion. In the absence of new ideas, settlers asked for administrative structures that worked. The settlers recognized that the Ndebele, or even the Shona, might possibly rise again if egregiously mismanaged. Thus, a "complex . . . wise native policy" rather than "stupid official optimism" was crucial to the settlers' peace of mind and to the region's prosperity.[109]

All these issues—local authority, labor, and security—had been raised as problems when the settlers demanded BSAC military intervention against the Ndebele in 1893. But with the Risings, which had put initiative in interracial relations into African hands, worried settlers added a new item to their agenda: the transformation of the African. None of the earlier pressures from the settlers had sought to change Africans in any fundamental way. The emphasis on local control was part of a struggle with imperial power, not against local rivals. The labor question was seen in terms of providing easy access to a standard unit of unskilled labor, rather than in terms of shaping the laborer into an increasingly productive worker. And the security issue was phrased defensively, attempting to shut the Africans out, away from a core European settler community made uneasy by the power of the people from whom they had taken so much.

Early settler notions of the transformations they wished to see in Africans were vague, well expressed by a resolution "to improve that which is good in them and eradicate that which is bad." Yet settlers did tend to agree on what was good and what was bad. Among the improvements the writer suggested was "impressing upon them the wholesome fact that they are our inferiors morally, socially and mentally, and can never hope to be otherwise."[110] The intent was not to civilize the Africans, which would be a hopeless or counterproductive task, but to improve their deference and, ultimately, their usefulness.[111]

Settlers' complaints about Africans who lacked deference were common from the original incursions into the region. The BSAC complained that the Matabele War was the result of Ndebele who did not know their place and exerted a right they believed they had to raid into Company territory.[112] And, on a more personal level, the Brown incident in 1895, when Brown responded to an African's "insolent" speech with a sjambok, putting himself in danger before an incensed group of Africans who felt no need to defer before his high-handed behavior, was characterized by a European perception that Africans were insufficiently deferential.[113] Not only were the Risings a military expression of communal "insolence," or lack of deference, but Europeans fighting in them frequently found African individuals, on whichever side of the conflict, to be highly provoking.[114]

Deference, however, as Brown learned to his grief, required change not only in the Africans, but in their European rulers. In 1897, at Bishop Gaul's request, a Zulu priest preached a sermon to the English congregation of settlers that included the injunction that settlers must realize that Africans were observing them, "and drawing conclusions; they are, in fact, measuring us by our own bushel of the Gospel, and testing us by its standard." Settlers had two options toward Africans: "either training and refining them into a nobler, purer manhood, or degrading them until they become the dregs and drainage of humanity."[115] To acquire deference from thinking Africans, settlers were told, and indeed began to learn, they needed to cease to be exemplars of "the dregs and drainage of humanity."

After the Risings, some Europeans began to recognize that they would have to change their techniques if they were to extract deference from the Africans. The professionalization of the Native Department was one such step, and linked to that change were calls for improvements in the police.[116] And even settler demands for forced labor were modulated by an increasing awareness that labor had to be recruited on terms "satisfactory to the heathen intelligence of the late rebels," and that African communities should be protected from being the "prey of people . . . whose influence is of the worst" sort.[117] The protection supported was coercive: a compound system and a formal structure of labor recruitment, bringing gangs from the Native Reserves to the compounds. Nevertheless, such sentiments did begin to inform settlers that there were limits beyond which they should not go in their dealings with Africans. Settlers were seeking to differentiate themselves from their African neighbors as people worthy of deference through the beginnings of an ideology of paternal knowledge and management designed to inculcate into Africans the notion that Europeans were superior not merely militarily, but in a holistic way that incorporated intellect, mores, culture, and economy. Insofar as this new ideology began to transform the settler community, it truly had a transformative effect on the culture, economy, and society of Southern Rhodesia, even if its stated purpose, the inculcation of deference into Africans, was never particularly successful.

The new, transformative interests of the settlers were not linked to mere abstract notions of African deference to Europeans. That deference was to serve a purpose: the development of Africans as workers within the European-sponsored economy of the region. Before the Risings, Europeans had been content to rely on a wholly unskilled and uncommitted labor forcibly recruited for extremely short terms of employment; in the aftermath of a European victory, however, the settlers began to demand that Africans be not only forced to work, but taught to do so.

In justifying such a change, settlers began to develop an extensive, frequently repeated, view of an African past in which African men had done no work. Historically, the validity of such notions of male idleness is dubious. Before the Risings, Father A. M. Hartmann wrote for the BSAC that Mashona men worked at agriculture, not leaving it all to the women.[118] And other observers also indicated that one of the consistent problems in recruiting African labor or African learners was that that labor was already employed on African farms.[119] Recent evaluations of late-nineteenth-century participation of African men in agricultural labor in Matabeleland and Mashonaland are mixed. The general consensus appears to be that they did some work, in fairly specific tasks, though scholars such as Julian Cobbing, on Matabeleland, and Elizabeth Schmidt, on Mashonaland, emphasize that women were the most important element of the African agricultural labor force in the precolonial and early colonial period.[120]

Settlers' post-1896 argument that African societies lived exclusively off the labor of women was not based in a balanced analytic view, but in a strategic reinterpretation of the information at hand, to justify the transfer of male labor from the African economy to the European economy. Before the Risings, employers had been fairly understanding of the demands of local agriculture on the time of their employees. As the settler demand for labor increased, though, Europeans became less tolerant of male employees' insistence that it was time to go home and dig. Would-be employers and recruiters asserted that it was the women who did the digging and that an African man was "the worst labourer on the face of the earth," willing to work only a short time for a specific purpose, usually "to amass enough to buy wives and retire into life-long indolence. Honest labour as a man's duty on earth he does not understand. The Kaffir is a gentleman: labour is for his wives to do."[121]

One of the first initiatives of the new settler representatives on the Legislative Council was to attempt to change this. The *Rhodesia*

Herald and the settlers' representative, Col. Raleigh Grey, asserted emphatically that "the kafir must be taught to live by the sweat of his brow," since with so many potential employees in the land, there was no justification for the "monstrous" scale of wages that was in force.[122] Settlers called for every measure possible to "infuse activity into the normally lazy kaffir."[123] The measures settlers suggested were not particularly new or effective. During the campaign, Grey, a winning candidate, proposed a substantially increased hut tax, to applause from a Farmers' Association meeting.[124] Editorials suggested compulsory labor laws modeled on English vagrancy laws and lauded the possibilities of "the forces of starvation" as potential levers to push Africans into wage labor.[125]

The emphasis of all the proposals, however, was on the importance of inculcating a work ethic into African men. Settlers were unhappy when they had to resort to "high" wages to attract workers, both because they disliked the expense, and because they believed that "high" wages would shrink rather than increase the labor supply. Workers with limited wants, they feared, would cease work as soon as they had earned enough to satisfy those rudimentary goals. For the settlers, everything from corporal punishment to guarded compounds, regular wages, economic pressure, and emphatic preaching by native commissioners, was a potential part of the dissemination of this new work ethic.

Challenges

As the dominant groups of Southern Rhodesia, the Company and the settlers were the factions most seriously challenged by the Risings. Their physical (military) domination was challenged, but more importantly their concepts of how to rule were challenged by Africans who, through violence, were able to make themselves heard. In the aftermath of the Risings, the BSAC and settlers each sought to develop a Southern Rhodesian society and economy in their own interests, but each was also forced to reevaluate what those interests were and how they could be integrated into other factions' interests for the sake of a ruling coalition. No coalition emerged automatically; the BSAC, with its British audience, and the settlers, with their primarily economic agenda, did indeed possess conflicting interests even with each other, to say nothing of the conflict inherent in the relations between them and the missionaries and Africans. But with reevaluation, both the BSAC and the settlers began to develop an interest in transformational change. The valorization of change, and the active searching for possibilities that it produced, provided an important precondition for the development of useful Southern Rhodesian images of culture and race, images that sought to contain the conflict of the earliest colonial contacts within ideological formations capable of structuring European perceptions, analysis, and initiatives into a dominant ideology of difference. As the Company emphasized the destruction of former African authorities and assumed administrative responsibility for the territory, and the settlers began to voice demands concerning their interests in a language of change and a debate concerning civilization, they began the modulations that would ultimately allow them to form useful, though tense, coalitions among themselves, with the missionaries, and with selected Africans.

NOTES

1. Julian R. D. Cobbing, "The Ndebele under the Khumalos, 1820–1896" (Ph.D. thesis, University of Lancaster, 1976), 10, 367–79.

2. Arthur Keppel-Jones, *Rhodes and Rhodesia: The White Conquest of Zimbabwe, 1884–1902* (Kingston. McGill-Queen's University Press, 1983), 360.

3. Frank W. Sykes, *With Plumer in Matabeleland* (New York: 1897; reprint ed., 1969) notes how, in the negotiations between Rhodes and the Ndebele leaders at the close of the Ndebele rising, Sikombo asked for a location, and Rhodes informed them that the area Sikombo wanted, on the Umzingwane River, was taken up by the white men.

4. Imperial policy opposed the seizure of all Ndebele cattle, arguing that some should be left to supply the basic needs of the people. J. S. Galbraith, *Crown and Charter: The Early Years of the British South Africa Company* (Berkeley: University of California Press, 1974), 338. But the Company spent years attempting to acquire as many cattle as possible, on some occasions even seizing them back from the Shona who had taken them as recompense for the damage of raids. Keppel-Jones, *Rhodes and Rhodesia,* 374–75.

5. Many sources describe the ways in which young male labor was extracted—whether rounded up by the native commissioner, or by a local farmer—and some describe the treatment of African women as a griev-

ance set forward by the leaders after the war during the peace talks. In Olive Schreiner's novel *Trooper Peter Halket of Mashonaland* (London: J. Fisher Unwin, 1897) the narrator describes both his attitudes toward the African workers, how he would make the Africans work for him (p. 29), and toward the African women who he has forced to work for him as his concubines and gardeners: "all for the nigger gals" who can support themselves, and can be disposed of (p. 55).

6. BSAC to CO, 7 July 1893, CO 879/39/454.

7. Galbraith, *Crown and Charter,* 323-25.

8. Several NCs suggested making labor mandatory for a specified period each year. Africans who failed to work for Europeans could then, one NC, argued, be taxed five shillings for each month they fell short. NC Hartley to CNC, 30 November 1895 and NC Umtali to CNC Salisbury, 3 November 1895, NAZ N1/2/2.

9. BSAC to CO, 7 July 1893, CO 879/39/454.

10. Galbraith, *Crown and Charter,* 325.

11. Father A. M. Hartmann, S.J., "Native Races," in BSAC, *Report to Shareholders for 1892-1894* (London: 1895).

12. "A Farmer" to the Editor, *Rhodesia Herald,* 1 February 1895.

13. Sir R. E. R. Martin, ed., *Report on the Native Administration of the British South Africa Company* (London: HMSO [C8547], 1897).

14. "Native Labour," *Rhodesia Herald,* 16 October 1895.

15. Edwards (NC Marondellas) to CNC, 29 November 1895, backed the removal of African communities. Other NCs consulted on the labor question, notably Mooney (NC Hartley) and the NC Umtali also backed firm control and mandatory labor. NAZ N1/2/2.

16. Hugh Marshall Hole, *The Making of Rhodesia* (London: Macmillan, 1926, 1967), 349.

17. Reed to LMS, 10 April 1896, CWM 1/5/C/135.

18. Sykes, *Plumer in Matabeleland,* 5.

19. Keppel-Jones, *Rhodes and Rhodesia,* 401-7.

20. "Report of the Commission of Enquiry . . . into alleged administrative abuses by NC Belingwe . . . , 1907" and J. W. Posselt's description of his time (before 1906) in Belingwe, NAZ A3/18/14.

21. CNC to Admin, 28 January 1918 NAZ A3/18-27, describes how an NC Gutu offered those without tax money a choice. They could "let the law take its course" and go to a prison term that might include hard labor, or "voluntarily" go to work at local farms, or at the asbestos mine. During one year, the NC Gutu supplied more than 250 laborers through this strategy.

22. "Native Labour Question," *Rhodesia Herald,* 22 February 1895.

23. "Another Farmer" to editor, *Rhodesia Herald,* 8 March 1895.

24. J. J. Taylor, "The Emergence and Development of the Native Department in Southern Rhodesia, 1894-1914" (Ph.D. thesis, University of

London, 1979), 2, sees the origins of the Native Department in the BSAC's attempts to circumvent imperial authority.

25. "Another Farmer" to editor, *Rhodesia Herald,* 8 March 1895.

26. G. W. H. Knight-Bruce, *Journals of the Mashonaland Mission 1888 to 1892* (London: USPG, 1892), 45; also Knight-Bruce to USPG, 19 November 1893, USPG/CLR 142: Mashonaland, Letters Received.

27. Wilder to ABC, 26 February 1894, ABC 15.4, vol. 20, item 276.

28. "villainous white men": John White (MMS) to MMS, 16 June 1894, MMS 333/2; quotation: C. Reed to LMS, 20 October 1895, CWM 1/5/B/178.

29. White to MMS, 22 November 1895, MMS 333/3: White reported that the incident occurred in a kraal in Hartley where he was spending the night, otherwise he would never have found out about the incident. Nothing, he noted, was unusual about this case, except that a missionary was on the scene to complain.

30. Wilder to ABC, 27 October 1895, ABC 15.4, vol. 20, item 282. Wilder was worried that he would lose his credibility with the people, as he had been required to serve as interpreter in this transaction. He was, however, able to report not only that his position appeared undamaged, but that the resident magistrate involved was removed, the second BSAC official that the American Board mission had gotten rid of.

31. Weavind to MMS, 27 October 1894, MMS 333/2. After the Shona Rising had broken out, Shimmin reported that in previous years, "the Mashonas often said that they preferred the Matabele to the white men, because the former came only once in three or four years . . . but the white man was always with them. There is no doubt that in many cases the native felt that he had now no rights whatever and that even a rude justice was denied him." In the same report, Shimmin noted that few whites survived long enough to flee Lomagundi, the site of one of the most notable outrages against an African community. Shimmin, "The Mashona Rebellion," 10 August 1896, MMS 333/3.

32. Weavind to MMS, 27 October 1894, MMS 333/2.

33. W. H. Brown, *On the South African Frontier* (London, 1899; reprint ed., New York: Negro Universities Press, 1970), 201–2, describes how, in 1892, his hostesses in a Shona village still viewed the Europeans' presence as temporary. They wanted to know "how soon they would have enough" gold, and return to South Africa. And they warned him that Europeans should not stay too long, or they would be killed. On the change of attitude following the Matabele war, see Keppel-Jones, *Rhodes and Rhodesia,* 414.

34. Father A. M. Hartmann, S. J., "Native Races," BSAC, *Report to Shareholders for 1892–1894* (London: 1895), 84.

35. The local opinion of the different priests varied, according to the tradition Vambe reports, but some, specifically Father Biehler, were perceived as excessively strict and high-handed. Father Richartz received a

more popular rating, as incomprehensible, but extremely kind. Lawrence Vambe, *An Ill-Fated People: Zimbabwe before and after Rhodes* (London, Heinemann: 1972), 126-27.

36. Col. F. Rhodes from Chishawasha to BSAC, 14 January 1895, box 98, Jesuit Archives, Harare provides a glowing description of the station. Richartz to N. C. Cambell (Duplicate book), 9 October 1897, discusses from the priests' point of view the practice of removing children from their homes and trying to break their family ties. "Chief Chivero," undated typescript autobiographical narrative, box 328, describes his memory of leaving his mother for the mission, and eventually being baptized around 1895. Details of the mission's actual achievements can be read in later sources when visitors were disappointed in what they found (e.g., schoolwork and theology: Ignatius Gartlau, "Notes on Visitations, Chishawasha," September 1907, box 98 JAH; industrial training: Ignatius Gartlau, "Notes on Visitations, Chishawasha," August 1908, JAH, box 98.

37. Richartz Letter Box, Richartz to Inspector of Schools, 12 June 1902, box 356 JAH. The students were also given several months off each year to go help with work at home.

38. Sykes to LMS, 1 March 1867, CWM 1/2/C/45. The experiment failed, though, in the face of worker opposition and Sykes's own qualms about paying students.

39. D. R. Pelly, Letters, *Mashonaland Paper* 3 (January 1893).

40. Chishawasha is a potentially tricky case because the only extended description I have encountered of the mission's early stages was written by Col. F. Rhodes, who was not only not a missionary, but was directly affiliated with the Company. He wrote to the BSAC on 14 January 1895 that "The Fathers have adopted a system which, while providing for a moderate amount of school work, recognises the great importance of an industrial training; the boys are therefore taught the usefulness of labour" (box 98, JAH). This communication could indicate that the Jesuits had an anachronistic sense of the importance of labor. It could also indicate that, knowing his affiliations, they had emphasized to him, and he emphasized to his audience, the aspect of the training that was of the most immediate concern: training for labor. Nothing, however, would seem to indicate that in 1895 Chishawasha was, in the later sense of the term, an Industrial Institute.

41. Bowen Rees to LMS, 9 September 1889, CWM 2/3/D.

42. Wilder to ABC, 27 April 1894, ABC 15.4, vol. 20, item 277.

43. In other words, this was not a systematic system of industrial education of the American Hampton-Tuskegee model. James D. Anderson, *The Education of Blacks in the South, 1860–1935* (Chapel Hill: University of North Carolina Press, 1988), 35, discusses the various models of industrial training available to educators in the late nineteenth century. The early mission schools in Southern Rhodesia were distinguished from

the Hampton model by the fact that, as Anderson puts it, "simple manual training was not a basic part of the instructional program; at Hampton, manual labor formed the core. . . ."

44. A missionary reporting on what he had been accused of being, "General Notes," *Mashonaland Quarterly* 4 (April 1893): 6-8.

45. G. W. H. Knight-Bruce, *Journals of the Mashonaland Mission 1888 to 1892* (London: USPG, 1892), 9.

46. "Native Education," *Rhodesia Herald,* 3 May 1895.

47. "The Everlasting Native," *Rhodesia Herald,* 10 July 1895.

48. "Native Education," *Rhodesia Herald,* 3 May 1895.

49. "Makunta Muka" (white, pseudonym) to editor, *Rhodesia Herald,* 5 April 1895.

50. W. Harvey Brown to editor, *Rhodesia Herald,* 19 April 1895.

51. "The Matabele Revolt," *Rhodesia Herald,* 1 April 1896.

52. Hole, *Making of Rhodesia,* 356-57.

53. After the Jameson raid, arms were not supposed to be issued without the permission of the high commissioner. This took time to arrive. Keppel-Jones, *Rhodes and Rhodesia,* 445.

54. Reed, an LMS missionary, reported that the Rising "played into the hands of those . . . who have . . . urged that the best thing for the country would be to kill them all and so leave the whole country for the white man. Whereas before such an opinion was only expressed casually and occasionally, since these massacres it is almost universal [among whites]." Reed to LMS, 10 April 1896, CWM 1/5/C/135.

55. Reed to LMS, 10 April 1896, CWM 1/5/C/135.

56. Brown, *South African Frontier,* 322.

57. "The Matabele Revolt," *Rhodesia Herald,* 1 April 1896; "Some Side Lights," *Rhodesia Herald,* 8 April 1896.

58. "The Matabele Revolt," *Rhodesia Herald,* 1 April 1896.

59. "Our Native Troubles," *Rhodesia Herald,* 17 June 1896.

60. Brown, *South African Frontier,* 344.

61. For example, Robinson to Chamberlain, CO 879/520/8338.

62. T. O. Ranger, *Revolt in Southern Rhodesia 1896–1897: A Study in African Resistance* (Evanston: Northwestern University Press, 1967). Ranger emphasized the roots in African history of the movement, tracing it to a semimythical Rozwi empire (p. 9), and to the leadership and coordination of ritual leaders (pp. 142ff.). He emphasized that while the colonial pressures were acute, they did not automatically lead to a systematic and coordinated response: the customary Mwari-Mlimo cult leaders, and the mediums, did. And he argued that "through all these risings there ran a strain of repudiation of the white man's way of life and of his goods; of prophetic warning against their seduction" (p. 353). His conclusions were politically significant in the context of the second "chimurenga" for majority rule.

63. Cobbing, "The Ndebele under the Khumalos," 252–53.

64. D. N. Beach, *War and Politics in Zimbabwe, 1840–1900* (Gweru, Zimbabwe: Mambo Press, 1986), 119–47. H. H. K. Bhila, *Trade and Politics in a Shona Kingdom* (Harare: Longman, 1982), 246, argues that in Manyikaland, the failure of Mutasa's people to fight can be explained through an examination of the economic devastation and political chaos that struggles between the BSAC and the Portuguese had produced, dismissing the notion that political rivalries between Mutasa and Makoni (a notable rebel leader) might have precluded military cooperation. If Bhila is accurate, the Manyika represent an extreme example of Beach's ripple-effect Rising, in which they fought years before the Chimurenga proper. A less inspiring, but more convincing reading, however, would indicate that the Manyika stayed neutral because they did not see the Rising as a single unifying opportunity for opposition, and therefore, amid economic difficulties, paid attention to old political rivalries.

65. Vambe, *An Ill-Fated People,* 22–23.

66. Sykes, *Plumer in Matabeleland,* 97. For a fictional, melodramatic account, see Schreiner, *Trooper Peter Halket,* 39.

67. For example, CO 879/520/18875 or White to MMS, 12 August 1897, MMS 333/4.

68. For example, Administrator to HC 18 September 1896, CO 879/520/21065.

69. For example, J. A. C. Gibbs to Chief Staff Officer, 4 August 1896, CO 879/520/20173.

70. Keppel-Jones, *Rhodes and Rhodesia,* 458–59, discusses the murder of Jubane Hlabangana, who had sought to keep the Mangwe road open.

71. Reed to LMS, 10 April 1896, CWM 1/5/C/135.

72. Sykes, *Plumer in Matabeleland,* 174. Sykes described how in many situations the Ndebele warrior was just as effective as the white soldier, possibly more so, and how Ndebele tactics of using the landscape and sheltering from gunfire were both intelligent and effective. The sole dissident on the question of Ndebele intelligence as fighters was R. S. S. Baden-Powell, who emerges from his own narrative (*The Matabele Campaign* [London, West Port, Conn.: Negro Universities Press 1897, 1970]) as an obnoxious self-promotor. He appears to have represented no consensus, and indeed was only present in Matabeleland for a short period of time.

73. See Keppel-Jones, *Rhodes and Rhodesia,* 453.

74. Sykes, *Plumer in Matabeleland,* 4: ". . . the Matabele were not conquered . . . neither did they in the smallest degree consider themselves so. . . ."; see also Reed's discussion for the LMS, 10 April 1896, CWM 1/5/C/135.

75. Shimmin, "The Mashona Rebellion," 10 August 1896, MMS 333/3.

76. Hole, *Making of Rhodesia,* 376–77.

77. Shimmin, "The Mashona Rebellion," 10 August 1896, MMS 333/3.

78. Brown, *South African Frontier,* provides a sample of the hard-line settler position. He argues that the Shona rose out of fear of the Ndebele (p. 349).

79. Ranger, *Revolt in Southern Rhodesia,* 227–28.

80. For example, Sykes, *Plumer in Matabeleland,* 215. Sykes also describes the inadequacy of rations for the troopers, and the scurvy that became a serious problem (p. 107).

81. Beach, *War and Politics,* 144.

82. Ranger, *Revolt in Southern Rhodesia,* 227–28.

83. Cobbing notes that, significantly, Rhodes's Indaba was not with the most senior or elevated members of the Ndebele nation, and that Nyamanda, the designated king, was specifically excluded for fear of future political implications. This was, according to Cobbing, the beginning of Native Department policy of elevating minor leaders, and ignoring major ones. "Ndebele under the Khumalos," 432.

84. Sykes's account of the first indaba, in *Plumer in Matabeleland,* 222–26, is fairly detailed.

85. Hole, *Making of Rhodesia,* 375–76.

86. (Emphasis in original) "The Native Problem," *Rhodesia Herald,* 9 December 1896.

87. Knowledge, for example, was vital to the reestablishment of settler confidence. "In trying to arrive at a satisfactory solution of the native question, it is necessary to obtain a thorough knowledge of the natives with whom we have to deal. . . ." "The Native Question," *Rhodesia Herald,* 2 December 1896.

88. Hole, *Making of Rhodesia,* 375. Compare the certainty of the Europeans he describes in Matabeleland to the persisting uncertainty of Mashonaland, where, even after the conflict was officially closed, "at this present moment in Mashonaland, outside a fifty-mile radius of Salisbury, the natives have the ball at their feet, and their gun robberies down the Umtali Road conclusively prove that the natives have an excellent notion as to the facts." Editorial, *Rhodesia Herald,* 4 May 1898.

89. "The Native Question," *Rhodesia Herald,* 2 December 1896.

90. *Rhodesia Herald,* 27 January 1897.

91. Major Watts had Makoni shot; Baden Powell supervised the shooting of Mvini. Both were courtmartial offenses, directly counter to orders. Both officers remained on duty while the charges were pending. Neither prosecution was carried far. CO 879/520.

92. See, for example, White to MMS, 12 August 1897, MMS 333/4: ". . . they have an absurd notion in their heads that the Government intends to shoot all the adult males amongst them." Pelly, *Mashonaland Quarterly,* 18 (November 1896): 9–16, confirms that this fear had its

roots in European actions earlier in the campaign when "many men . . . are seriously wishing to kill *everything* with a black skin—friends and enemies alike." (emphasis in original).

93. Hole, *Making of Rhodesia,* 378–79.

94. Dane Kennedy, *Islands of White* (Durham, N.C.: Duke University Press, 1987), 18, estimates that approximately 10 percent (370 individuals) of the European population was killed in the Risings.

95. Cobbing, "Ndebele under the Khumalos," 419, 432. On the specific policy of providing indunas with salaries, see Administrator, Bulawayo, to HC, Capetown, 12 October 1896, who indicated that the Company was in the process of developing a system "which will make it to the interest of the principal Indunas to be loyal to the Government." CO 879/520.

96. Keppel-Jones, *Rhodes and Rhodesia,* 526.

97. For example, Sykes, *Plumer in Matabeleland,* 225, 226.

98. This would not be easy. Baden-Powell, *Matabele Campaign,* 463–64, reported that finding native commissioners with the proper character had been a chronic problem for the Company in the past, a problem he directly linked to the Rising. See also Administrator, Bulawayo, to HC, Capetown, 12 October 1896, CO 879/520. One of the first tasks of the new Executive Council, founded in 1898, was to approve a list of Native Department officials. Executive Council of Southern Rhodesia, Minutes 1898, 21 December 1898, CO603/1.

99. Administrator, Bulawayo, to HC, Capetown, 12 October 1896, CO 879/520.

100. Settlers complained that under the new system, "the most good-for-nothing Mashona can as little be compelled to work against his will as . . . the editor of this paper." "Native Labour," *Rhodesia Herald,* 22 September 1897.

101. Rhodes, quoted by Milner, in Keppel-Jones, *Rhodes and Rhodesia,* 554–55.

102. For example, "Native Labour," *Rhodesia Herald,* 22 September 1897.

103. For example, "Our Duty to Ourselves," *Rhodesia Herald,* 7 October 1896. Apprehension regarding any possibility of renewed rebellion persisted. The next acute episode was in November 1899, when the Executive Council responded by declaring martial law in six districts of Matabeleland (23 November 1899), and then extending to the five more districts (30 December 1899) Executive Council of Southern Rhodesia, Minutes 1898, CO603/1.

104. "Our Native Question," *Rhodesia Herald,* 21 April 1897.

105. "Native Labour," *Rhodesia Herald,* 22 September 1897.

106. Brown, *South African Frontier,* 391.

107. "The Native Revolt: The Situation," *Rhodesia Herald,* 11 November 1896.

108. "Our duty to Ourselves," *Rhodesia Herald,* 7 October 1896.

109. "The Natives, Again," *Rhodesia Herald,* 2 March 1898.

110. "The Native Question," *Rhodesia Herald,* 2 December 1896.

111. For example, ". . . the semi-civilised native is a far more despicable and contemptible creature than his more barbarous brother." "The Native Question," *Rhodesia Herald,* 2 December 1896.

112. BSAC, *Report to Shareholders for 1892–1894* (London: 1895), 17.

113. "Makunta Minta" (white, pseudonym) to editor, *Rhodesia Herald,* 5 April 1895; W. Harvey Brown to editor, *Rhodesia Herald,* 19 April 1895.

114. See, for example, the story told by Brown, *South African Frontier,* 402, of a sergeant and his servant. And European observers were particularly upset by the defection of Native Police—employees of the BSAC who, though trained and armed with BSAC equipment, showed their contempt for their employers by fighting for the rebels. For example, Duncan (acting administrator) to BSAC Board, 3 April 1896, CO 879/520/10086.

115. "Extracts from a sermon preached by our native [Zulu] priest at my request for an English Congregation here." Bishop Gaul to SPG, 13 March 1897, USPG/CLR 142.

116. "The Natives Again," *Rhodesia Herald,* 2 March 1898.

117. "Mashona Labour," *Rhodesia Herald,* 6 April 1898; "The Protection of Labour," *Rhodesia Herald,* 29 November 1898.

118. Father A. M. Hartmann, "Native Races," in BSAC, *Report for 1892–1894* (London, 1895).

119. For example, Sykes to LMS, 1 March 1867, CWM 1/2/C/45—and note that Sykes was writing of Matabeleland when he wrote of the competition of African agricultural work.

120. Cobbing, "Ndebele under the Khumalos," 153, 181; Elizabeth Schmidt, "Farmers, Hunters and Gold Washers: A Reevaluation of Women's Roles in Precolonial and Colonial Zimbabwe," *African Economic History* 17 (1988); and Elizabeth S. Schmidt, "Ideology, Economics, and the Role of Shona Women in Southern Rhodesia, 1850–1939" (Ph.D. Dissertation, University of Wisconsin, Madison, 1987), 5–6, 156, 170–73.

121. "Natives and Labour," *Rhodesia Herald,* 28 February 1899.

122. "The Black Tribes of Rhodesia," *Rhodesia Herald,* 30 May 1899.

123. Description of issues of campaign, *Rhodesia Herald,* 23 May 1899.

124. *Rhodesia Herald,* 28 March 1899.

125. "Natives and Labour," *Rhodesia Herald,* 28 February 1899.

CHAPTER THREE

"Civilization" and Social Planning

Native Policy, 1898–1906

In 1905, after taking evidence throughout Southern Africa, including Southern Rhodesia, the South African Native Affairs Commission (SANAC) concluded

> that the advent of civilisation has . . . tended to loosen tribal ties, to undermine wholesome patriarchal control, and has let loose in the midst of the resultant disorganisation all the temptations and vices which dog the steps of civilised advance. But where it has destroyed it will again construct; the great powers of Christianity and education are at work. There has been and there continues a great struggle between the powers of good and evil, of light and darkness, of enlightenment and ignorance, of progress and tradition, of Christianity and heathenism. Is it, therefore, surprising that much of what was picturesque, attractive, and even admirable in the Native when untouched by European influences has been swept away? The final outcome of a righteous war is not to be judged by the devastations of opposing armies or by the scenes of slaughter and bloodshed on the field of battle. No less fallacious would be the attempt to gage the eventual issue of the civilisation of the Natives by the many unfortunate features of the struggle which still prevail.[1]

The SANAC report was a massive compilation of written and oral evidence, seeking to enquire into the views of all sectors of society regarding the problematic realities of life for Africans and the Europeans with whom they came into contact. When the evidence was gathered in Rhodesia, in 1904, it represented settler, native administration, and missionary views during a period when approval of efforts to "civilize" Africans was at an all-time high. In this context, the idea of civilization as a process of change and as a characteristic of superiority provided Africans, missionaries, administration and Native Department officials, and settlers with a set of linked concepts through which they could interpret and seek to shape the changes they were suffering, surviving, promoting, or blocking.

A definition of civilization was embedded within the volumes of the SANAC evidence, a definition used and understood by all factions of the European community of Southern Rhodesia. It had three vital elements. First, civilization in the Southern Rhodesian context implied a sort of individualism, as opposed to the communalism that Europeans tended to assume had been the previous or "primitive" state of Africans.[2] Second, civilization implied some degree of affiliation with European culture. In its most basic sense, this meant a rudimentary acquaintance with the English language, literacy, or Christianity. This aspect of the definition emphasized that the individual, "free" from customary communal ties, entered into communication with and comprehension of the European community.[3] The third aspect of civilization was the economic concomitant of this cultural disassociation and reassociation: the individual's development of a newly vital relationship with capitalistic market economics, as a seller of labor and a buyer of consumer goods.[4] Various factions of the African and European communities chose carefully which aspects of the ideology of civilization to emphasize. All the Europeans, in the aftermath of the communally organized violence of the Risings, emphasized the individual's disassociation; the missionaries emphasized the importance of cultural change; and the administration concentrated on the economic implications of developing individualism. But, as the SANAC report concluded, despite the drawbacks some aspects of the ideology had for individual factions, it came as a unit. The "undermining of wholesome patriarchal control" was vital to the recruitment of individuals as students in mission stations and laborers in the European-owned economy. And both mission and commercial sources acknowledged that the questions of cultural and economic change were linked.

Civilization, even in Southern Rhodesia, was a classically liberal ideology, emphasizing the individual's cultural and economic decision-making ability. It was aimed directly at young African men, who were the individuals assumed to have the greatest intellectual and economic flexibility, to be the most important potential converts or workers, and to be the most potentially dangerous opponents. In that context, with the implications of the individual's transformation into an inhabitant of a European world, civilization represented the sort of fundamental disjunction with the African past that would have been unthinkable prior to the Risings. But the devastation of the Risings forced Africans to struggle for survival in a transformed world in which the European presence was a fact that could no longer be ignored. With the establishment of European native commissioners as real authorities with power over African lives, and with the deaths, defeats, and compromises African authorities suffered in the Risings and their aftermath, European pressure on young African men became acute.

The new society and economy confronted young African men with hut or poll taxes and settlers' demands for their labor. They found themselves forced into decisions regarding obedience to their elders, education and conformance to European cultural ideas, and labor as a potential source of funds for taxes, goods, and bridewealth. In response, some acted in ways that diverged from the paths their elders had followed. The chief native commissioner (CNC) of Matabeleland observed this divergence in 1904 when he noted that "the younger generation have considerably improved their status and industrial habits."[5] Their decisions were the immediate cause of the "undermined patriarchal control" that the commission saw. "The fathers have no authority over their children," complained one missionary, and another missionary reported visible disintegration: "The father scolds a boy for something he had done and wants to thrash him, but the boy runs on to an ant heap and talks back to him, and when the father tries to get at him he runs away."[6] Sikombo, one of the Ndebele leaders interviewed by the commission, implied the same point when he complained that the people over whom he had nominal authority could roam the entire region, beyond his control.[7] The sons used this freedom of movement, and the necessity of earning enough for their hut tax payments, to change the balance of authority between elders and juniors within the African community.

The freedom of movement and exposure to European-directed workplaces and culture also shifted the generational balance of knowledge. "The younger Natives of Rhodesia," observed one native commissioner, "show a surprising thirst for knowledge, and a determination to get it by some means or other. . . . I know many adult males who have, with very little assistance, acquired a knowledge of reading and writing, and whose every spare moment is spent with a book."[8] Some of these highly motivated students may well have been studying with itinerant, unaffiliated African teachers, who were paid by their students outside of any missionary structure.[9] Thoughtful leaders understood this hunger for knowledge. When the commission inquired into his attitude toward the education of African children, Gambo commented, "As we have to live with the white man, I think it is as well we should be educated. We would then understand the white man and his laws better."[10] Mawoko was even more directly pragmatic in his specific request for a school,

> not . . . that he had any keen desire for instruction himself, but . . . he thought it was wise to move with the times . . . [saying] 'if I do not have a church here, I know that all my boys and young men will leave me, and then who will pay my taxes for me?'[11]

Elders' attempts to maneuver within a European world which they found increasingly difficult to comprehend had consisted of one failure after another: Lobengula's concessions had permitted the occupation, and the leaders had produced military defeat and a dubious peace. Their attempts to discover their rights, if any, had in at least one case met with an ignominious disciplining when the Executive Council of Southern Rhodesia deposed and fined Umjaan, an Ndebele leader, for convening a meeting of Ndebele leaders with a British solicitor.[12] Some African leaders, therefore, saw education as vital for the salvation of the people, regardless of its effects on their personal authority. Like Gambo, Sikombo recognized that when he responded to a leading question by proclaiming, "No man would like to be kept down and be only the size of a rabbit, when he might be made into a big man. We would like to progress."[13]

While leaders and elders often felt threatened by education, even when they regarded it as a necessity in a changed world, many young men perceived it more purely as an opportunity.[14] The period after the Risings was marked for the mission societies by a demand-led expansion of their educational system, which strained the limited resources they had available for their schools. By 1904 Archdeacon Frederick Beaven, reporting financial crisis, wrote that "Penhalanga [the leading Church of England school] has no room for the many that clamour to enter," and the school instituted an entry fee of £3 per student. Students still came, producing an enrollment of over 100 boys and young men.[15] Similar conditions characterized the work of the other societies.[16]

When young men sought out the closest equivalent to higher education available to Africans in that time and place, they were pursuing not just economic rewards—as the unpaid or underpaid work required in a mission station in return for education could require a substantial sacrifice in comparison to farm or mine wages—but cultural understanding and an ability to command respect within the new European-dominated world.[17] Kraal schools, which proliferated under the LMS, the Church of England, and other mission societies, offered some rudimentary education and, along with itinerant teachers, provided the bulk of the education accessible to Africans. With pathetically low quality and a chronic lack of organization, however, African-run peripheral schools provided no credentials for Africans seeking advancement within the European-dominated economy.[18] But those Africans entering various central schools during the first decade of the century were an ambitious and upwardly mobile minority. The small elite of students who paid £3 for entry into Penhalanga, or the £8 yearly fee at the new Methodist school at Nengubo, were adults, who had previously worked for Europeans.[19] The LMS industrial institute, for example, taught only 29 pupils in the course of the ten years before 1909. Those pupils demanded and received recognition of their superior skills from prospective employers.[20] And at a more substantial school, Rev. G. A. Wilder explained to the commission that "when the Native starts here, he becomes . . . more independent, more cheeky for that matter, takes on new ideas."[21] Those "new ideas" were important for Wilder, the missionary community, and the European community of Southern Rhodesia in efforts to "civilize" Africans. And they were crucial to those Africans who saw civilization, or at least comprehension, as an alternative to degradation.

The formal education of the missionary sector was not, however, the only transformative contact between Africans and Europeans in the post-Rising period. Hut taxes created an urgent need for money, and young men frequently found that money through wage labor for Europeans. The restrictions on economic resources after the decline in the cattle population from war and rinderpest, and the restriction of farmland through the relocations, also reduced the economic opportunities young men could find within their own communities. Those factors pushed young men into the new economy. Their decisions regarding labor were, however, real. Young men made them not merely because they were pushed, but also because the new economy did offer opportunities.[22] Wage labor offered not merely money to pay taxes, but money obtained outside the customary structures of authority, money that could be used as the wage-earner chose. Goods such as clothes and blankets were attractive.[23] And the money could also, to some extent, be converted to status within the African community as a young man paid bridewealth, became the first in his community to own a plow, or supplied the cash for family members' taxes. The new economy also pulled Africans because positions such as native policeman, messenger, or mission-trained teacher were new sources of authority.[24]

For young men, shut out of positions of authority and economic power within their own communities through a lack of seniority, the combination of push factors and pull factors could be quite powerful in encouraging at least a part-time movement into the European-owned economy. Wage work for Europeans, though, particularly mine labor, was not an attractive option. In 1903, for example, of 7500 workers recruited for mine labor in Southern Rhodesia, all but 700 came from outside the territory.[25]

Several factors combined to make Africans doubt the benefits of participation in the new economy. Perhaps most prominent was the inadequate wage structure. The rewards offered by wages of 5 to 20 shillings a month were simply inadequate return for the labor demanded, and the annual wages of £20 to £40 that some employers complained of were all but nonexistent.[26] Even positions requiring education did not offer much in terms of wage rewards. The American Board, in 1905, raised the wages of married Shona teachers to 25 shillings a month, a sum the mission committee soon acknowledged was too low to live and pay taxes on.[27]

Young men also found other, less tangible, problems with wage work. It might offer a way beyond the war-damaged resources of the African economy, but it did not offer opportunities to organize production, make production decisions, and enjoy, or profit from, the rewards of successful endeavors.[28] Charles van Onselen, discussing mine labor in Southern Rhodesia, emphasized the competition that mines in the region faced from the attractions of peasant agriculture or the higher wages of South Africa.[29] For young men with limited resources, the most attractive proposal within this context would be a limited stint of labor at the highest possible wage to provide capital and connections necessary for establishment as a peasant farmer with a wife, a garden, and the time to enjoy them.[30] When employers demanded consistent and long-term labor, they were negating the advantages wages could offer, as they broke into the time their sometime employees needed to cultivate their families' fields, enjoy the rewards of their work, and prepare themselves to earn more.

There was a more central problem as well: deference. The wages implied in economic strategies of civilization might free young men from the need to defer to elders who controlled access to the means of production and reproduction. The deference demanded in customary society, though, was limited in time and by stage of the life cycle. Some day, the youth would himself be an elder. Working for Europeans, however, African employees were expected to defer, were punished if they did not, and were offered little if any hope that they themselves might achieve the positions of authority the Europeans occupied within the new economy as officials, miners, traders, or large-scale farmers.[31] Therefore, except as a temporary strategy or in connection with a position implying authority within the African community, such as teacher or policeman, proletarianized wage labor offered young men a mirage of emancipation from a temporary subordination in return for the acceptance of a permanent one. Given this situation, Africans' reluctance to abandon links with home communities and customary sources of status was plainly rational.[32]

While they did not flock to European dreams of economic civilization, Africans did not reject the civilization policy in its entirety. It offered too many possibilities to young men—a group vulnerable to the attraction of altering the balance of authority, knowledge, and economic power within African communities.[33] And, through the combination of the educational with the economic aspects of civilization, some young men sought to escape the frustrations inherent for them in the settler view of civilization. By seeking education and the knowledge necessary to communicate with the new economic world of capitalist markets and surplus production, these men sought to serve their period of subordination and then emerge as important actors in an integrated economy in which they would, as the controllers of peasant production, control their own work of themselves and that of their families, and, as educated men, command authority and respect both within the African communities and in the new, mixed society. They were, in Sikombo's phrase, seeking to be "big men" rather than "rabbits."

Mission Perspectives

Missionaries approved of the ideology of civilization because it provided support for many of their methods and goals. Using the ideology, they conceptualized Africans as children capable of being cultivated and civilized into a true adulthood. This metaphor of childhood underlay missionaries' demands for obedience, discipline, work, and scholarship—demands that had to be justified to two important constituencies: the Africans the missionaries sought to recruit to their schools and farms, and the settlers whose society they functioned within. Through obedience, discipline, work, and study, they implied, Africans could grow to adulthood as responsible members of a civilized, Christian citizenry.

Africans found the missionaries demanding masters. In 1899 the Anglican St. Augustine's School reported that of the nineteen boys who had attended the school during the term, ten "found the discipline too hard."[34] And the attrition continued to be substantial. The next term, four of eleven students left, and in the years that followed, students continued to leave, whether because an individual "did not like being at school, as he was unable to drink beer there" or because a group protested additional work assignments of cooking or housework.[35] Nor was such conflict restricted to the Anglican missions. The liberal American Board mission had similar problems, and the stricter Catholic missions at Chishawasha and Empandeni extracted seven to eight hours a day of labor from senior pupils only through rigorous surveillance.[36]

Africans accepted the conditions of labor and deference only when they could see a use for them. But the metaphor of African young people as children, maturing through work and study into responsible adults, was a powerful one. The American Board mission responded, successfully, to students objecting to the discipline, by emphasizing that discipline was only a stage on the way to excellence and, possibly, to a theological school in Natal.[37] And Lawrence Vambe, writing of the oral tradition of the Chishawasha mission's African communities, asserts that they recognized that the mission, in providing education, came closer than most Europeans to seeing

Africans as "children of the same God who had created all humanity."[38] Even Father Biehler, famous for brutal disciplinary tactics, was tolerated because the methods made advancement possible and eventually helped graduates to break down some racial barriers by taking positions as skilled craftsmen.[39]

Many missionaries recognized a possibility of racial convergence and, ultimately, assimilation, and responded with comments ranging from acceptance to acute ambivalence. Asked whether he "would turn the black man into a white man," the American Board missionary, Rev. Wilder, responded, "I should practically do that, and turn him into the most useful individual that could be made for the benefit of the country, and that can best be done by civilising him."[40] Wilder argued that the concept of a chief must be discredited and his power broken by the institution of individual land tenure. With social and economic fragmentation, and compulsory education, each individual "must be independent of everybody else, and then he will begin to think and do something for himself."[41] When faced with his interrogators' incredulity, he backpedaled slightly, emphasizing that this would not happen rapidly but through an inexorable process of evolution, and if Africans were not brought to the point of being able to respect themselves and be respected by Europeans, the European community would be drawn down to their level.[42]

Wilder certainly shocked the commission in his willingness to accept all the implications of a policy of civilization. Most of the other missionaries chose to follow policies of civilization and assimilation, while refraining from speaking too clearly about the logical implications of their actions. At the 1906 synod, the Anglican church was faced with a sharp split between missionary and settler opinions on issues of education and civilization.[43] Bishop Gaul, overseeing the Church of England missions while retaining pastoral responsibility for the European community, had observed with ambivalence noted in 1900 how one thing led to another when, after visiting St. Columba's School, he wrote,

> Civilization produces funny puzzles. Having taught the natives to wear clothes (personally I wish clothes were unnecessary) we must teach them to *wash* them. Then the [European-employed] men get used in farms to properly cooked meat, and baked bread and potatoes, and even puddings . . . natives *will* wear shoes as they get into touch with modern . . . *notions*. . . . We must patiently train them to take their proper

place in the industrial life of the country, then will come property and civil rights in due course.[44]

Gaul and other Anglicans worried about the expectations and intercommunal tensions involved in this historical drift, seeking to emphasize an ideology of Christian obedience as a way of defusing pressures by Africans for independence, decreased labor requirements, and equality.[45] Bishop Gaul, though, read and approved of W. E. B. Dubois and advocated racial evolution to equal citizenship,[46] writing to a settler audience,

> it is our bounden duty to look upon the natives of the country . . . as a solemn trust committed to us. We have no right, even if we had the power, to stunt, starve, dwarf or destroy life. No one but an idiot, a maniac, or a devil could think we had that right. We find ourselves here for many reasons, but . . . one purpose . . . and that is to develop ourselves by developing the earth and all around us.[47]

The Conference of Anglican Mashonaland Clergy responded to tension between the missionaries and the European lay community by passing resolutions in 1902 that may have been deliberately unclear in asserting that "while accepting loyally the consequences of Christ's identification of Himself with universal humanity, [the Christian faith] recognises the inequalities existing in individuals and races, arising from the fact that neither individuals nor races are born with equal faculties or opportunities." Another resolution, though, spelled out Gaul's position more clearly, stating, "We believe that the final object of all true statesmanship must be the development of responsible citizenship."[48] These were the conclusions Gaul's church found difficult to accept. Gaul resorted to hope and faith that the Native Question would, through the uplift of Africans, answer itself as Africans developed into a responsible citizenry. By 1904, though, facing the commission, the sole Anglican clergyman interviewed was already disassociating himself from the resolutions.[49]

Missionaries in close day-to-day contact with Africans were precisely the ones most likely to find problems with the idea that individuation, education, and economic transformation could produce Africans fully able to take places in a new community as equal Christians. Part of their doubt arose out of concern for settler attitudes. Wilkerson, the LMS industrial specialist, occasionally despaired of getting jobs for the students he trained, since "white men will not allow a native skilled though he should be to work with them. Contracts have been made in which the clause is inserted. No skilled black labor to be used."[50] This settler resistance to skilled African workers persisted, and even intensified, affecting even the early graduates of the government industrial schools in the 1920s and 1930s and eventually leading to a formal color bar in the 1930s.

But missionary worries about the realization of their educational hopes were not limited to concern about settler acceptance of "civilized," educated, or skilled Africans. They also worried about the attitude of African communities toward the neophyte Christians. Missionaries were doubtful that African individuals, no matter how well taught, would be able to maintain their new standards when they found themselves in contact with their families and communities and were forced to function in an African world that had not yet been wholly transformed. The education of African children into Christian adults did not necessarily give those adults the ability to withstand pressure or temptation from a dubious community. Initially, missionaries working closely with Africans attempted to address this concern in various ways.

The most ambitious strategy was Chishawasha's effort to remove African children from their families, raise them to adulthood on the mission, and keep them there, in Christian villages, permanently held apart from African culture and the temptations of family and the African community. Africans, the Jesuits noted, had "to give up a great deal" in becoming Christians:

> In many points, the freedom of action which he has previously enjoyed is now to be taken away, or at least much restricted; and obligations of which he has not hitherto dreamt are to be imposed and cheerfully submitted to. . . . In Mashonaland, . . . on account of the depravity of the unregenerate native, it is impossible to baptise anyone who does not promise to leave his former pagan surroundings, settle in the Christian village, and remain under the influence of the Fathers. . . . Those who are thoroughly acquainted with the kind of life which the heathen Mashonas live in the kraals or villages, the gross superstition in which they are sunk, and oftentimes the disregard of the laws of morality which prevails among them, see plainly that there could be no possible hope of the neophytes living as Christians should, were they permitted to return to their old homes.[51]

And Jesuit protectiveness was not limited to saving converts from African culture. Father Richartz was also wary of the effects of town life and sought to prevent his charges from going off to work even at the cost of lending them money for brideprice payments.[52]

No other mission society went so far in protective efforts; even the Jesuits found the approach too costly to use at Empandeni and began phasing the system out at Chishawasha by 1908.[53] But the sentiments expressed by missionaries unsure how their followers would respond under pressure were common, as common as the family pressure that called students home, restricting their schooling, or the economic pressure that forced Africans into wage work. Family and community pressures affected the attendance patterns of students at both central boarding institutions and local kraal schools. H. Juliette Gilson, who headed Mt. Silinda school for the ABC, characterized her students as "fickle," promising to remain for at least a year, but leaving when "a message comes from home that they are needed to drive the birds from the grain."[54] And the pressures on students at kraal schools, away from the boarding institutions, were even more severe. Mission schools in Matabeleland often had enrollments above a hundred, but attendance tended to be highly irregular as work or (the missionaries implied) whim kept children away.[55]

Missionaries worried over the implications of encouraging children and young people, particularly girls, to disobey their parents and turn to the mission as the source of community, culture, and education. One of the Brothers at St. Augustine's solemnly assured a leader of the neighboring kraal that his curriculum included "obedience to *chief* and *parents*."[56] Archdeacon J. H. Upcher emphasized obedience further, trying to encourage parents to exert authority because "if they [students] cannot obey parents, how shall they obey their Heavenly Father?"[57] The Bishop expressed concern that women might run from their husbands to the mission station, emphasizing that "this we cannot allow, as we must uphold the duties of wives to their husbands, even in polygamy. We must not handicap the Church's discipline in the future."[58] And even the Jesuits worried about the results of removing students entirely from their parents and community, and about the willfulness of girls and women.[59]

Thus, mission policy toward students' families remained tense, pulled between missionaries' wishes to extract students from "pagan" households, their inability to fund such a removal, their concern over the destruction of patriarchal authority, and their knowledge that removal merely postponed or distanced temptation rather than teaching young people to live with it and reach an accommodation between filial obedience and independent Christianity.

Mission attitudes toward work were, likewise, problematic. Work was an important part of the discipline of a mission station, and the expansion of wants and exposure to European material culture was a vital part of a mission education.[60] But many missionaries dreaded the prospect of their charges leaving them for the wage work of the towns, settler farms, or mines, fearing the pressures and influences individuals would experience in such settings, cut loose, however temporarily, from their communities. Worried about the prospect of contamination, missionaries fought hard against the 1901 proposal to raise the poll tax to £2, with taxation beginning at age fourteen and no exemptions for students.

Father Richartz was the tax's most vocal critic, willing to confront the Mashonaland Farmers' Association itself with his objections.[61] Richartz accepted the popular characterization of Africans as lazy with that laziness reinforced by the African community.[62] The proposed tax, however, would destroy his plans to create civilized Christian communities apart from the European towns or the African villages by forcing men to seek wage labor to finance their taxes. Those who supported the tax, he argued, did so not from a desire to promote civilization, but out of ignorance, brutality, and hatred of Africans. In the face of such pressure, Europeans had, he asserted,

> the duty . . . to do what is in our power to meliorate those natives and to make them law-abiding, useful citizens in their own way, subject to the higher educated population, we have a sacred duty to teach them obedience towards God and Government, to be content with their state, but it is a crime to throw them away and deal with them as if they were less than slaves.[63]

Richartz's objections were seconded by John White of the English Methodists, who emphasized that the tax would cause hardship, unsettle the Africans, and fill them with enmity for His Majesty's Government.[64] Implicitly, White was threatening another rebellion by the African communities, citing the precise problems that had, in the imperial government's view, led to the 1896 Risings. Both implicitly admitted that Africans had not yet begun to respond to economic pressures as civilized capitalistic workers. Under pressure, they implied, their African pupils would reject mission notions of civilization and turn to their own communities and culture for solutions.

Missionaries found the ideology of civilization useful in canvassing for donations back in England, through forums such as the *Mashonaland Quarterly,* the *Zambesi Mission Record,* and other missionary publications. But on the ground in Southern Rhodesia, only an occasional, newly arrived, missionary would describe the mission station as one big happy family following parental directives to adulthood.[65] Others recognized missionary methods as a stern, physical discipline, and the situation as one of inherent conflict. Occasional missionaries responded to Africans with punishments and coercion that differed from the tactics used by settlers only in their imaginative variety. And in their defensiveness regarding settlers' complaints of "mission boys" and their willingness to see Africans as willful, misbehaving children even after years of training, missionaries exhibited a notable doubt as to the success of the civilization process.

Worse yet, mission educators faced acute funding problems. Before 1907, only four schools ever received administration grants-in-aid for African education—grants that, together, comprised between two and five percent of administration spending on education.[66] And mission societies that perpetually operated in need of funds found the demands of financing a regional educational system to be excessive.[67] Successful civilization would, missionaries emphasized to impatient constituencies of foreign sponsors, local administrative officials, settlers, and Africans, be slow.

In emphasizing the necessity of slow progress, missionaries sought to change the temporal dimensions of a Native Policy of civilization. While Wilder shocked the SANAC by acquiescing to the characterization of the American Board's work as an attempt "to turn the black man into a white man" through civilization, he modified his position substantially when asked, "Does it appeal to you as a thing which is possible under the laws of nature to transfer a creature from one sphere to another so rapidly?" He responded, "I did not say rapidly."[68] Wilder did not, in fact, offer any suggestion as to how long transformation would take. Another American missionary, J. M. Springer, seconding Wilder's sentiments, advocated eventual "absolute political equality between black and white." But such an explicit declaration required an equally elaborate attempt to place such an event far, far in the future, and Springer emphasized that not only was the franchise unthinkable at the time, but education itself must be gradual, not merely for the individual, but with a slow advance from generation to generation. "I do not," he stated, "believe in carrying it too far in any one generation."[69]

And despite reporting substantial changes (as C. D. Helm, a long-time LMS missionary, did in informing the commission that the Ndebele he knew had improved their moral condition remarkably and "taken . . . wonderfully to labor . . . for wages"),[70] missionaries clearly evaluated the progress against their images of the African past rather than the eventual ultimate standard of European civilization. When the commission's questions changed the standard back from a relativistic yardstick to a direct discussion of equality with Europeans, Helm was willing to defend his mission's efforts by stating, "If it ever comes to this, that the Native gets superior to the white man, why should not he have the benefit of his superiority? But I do not think there is a chance of it."[71]

Even the most progressive missionaries implied that the assimilationist goal of an equal Christian African citizenry was so far away in time as to be useful in theory, but nearly unthinkable in practice. In practice, missions were daunted by their perceptions of European opposition, African ambivalence, and missionaries' doubt regarding the ability of a policy of individualism to overcome a historical experience, a communal background, and an economic logic distinct from that of the European civilization being taught. In the near term, missionaries chose to emphasize obedience and the education of Africans as subaltern functionaries within the new European-controlled society and economy. When asked to comment on the changes the LMS's decades of activity had brought to Matabeleland, Baleni, an LMS African preacher, responded that "in former days there were men who had been taught, and who were Christians, just as there are now; there may possibly be a few more now than there were then, but the change has not been great."[72] In his lifetime, which included the dramatic upheavals of wars and Risings, the mission's pressure for transformation, and settlers' increasing concern over educated Africans, he had seen no substantive progress toward equality, assimilation, or civilization.

Official Perspectives

In the immediate aftermath of the 1896–97 Risings, Earl Grey, the administrator of the BSAC, had assured the Martin Commission,

> The aim of the Administration is to initiate a sound native policy, calculated in time to produce . . . those industrious habits which are so essential to civilization, without interfering more than is absolutely necessary with the customs and habits of the natives themselves. . . . the Administration hopes to secure the country against a recurrence of disorder, to safeguard the interests of the natives, to promote their civilization, and also to meet the reasonable requirements of the white population.[73]

By 1904, when the SANAC was accumulating evidence regarding that Native Policy, it had become obvious to everyone in the administration that not all those goals were achievable simultaneously, at least not without creative definitions of industry, safeguarding customs, security, civilization, and the interests of the European population.

The Company's first concern continued to be security, as it sought to prevent another Rising and to assert control over the territory it had conquered. This control was not automatic or absolute: the Executive Council declared martial law in at least eleven districts during 1899, amid rumors of Risings, and during each subsequent year, the principal item of interest in the annual reports of the chief native commissioners and the opening speech of the administrator to the Legislative Council was the assurance that the "attitude of the natives was satisfactory."[74] Another Rising was a real possibility; the Native Department treated Mapondera's resistance as a true threat and remained worried by potential remnants of an Ndebele state.[75] Cautious reports of unrest, such as Taberer's discussion of "vague feelings of unrest" among the Shona during 1903 and 1904 were enough to provoke panic, unless hedged around by assurances that "at present everything is quiet, and everything points to the fact that the natives are thoroughly contented."[76] And when a settler reported witnessing African policemen being taught to shoot, public meetings restated European fears that another Rising could break out and Europeans would again be surprised: "We never know at any moment how small a matter may start a big rising of natives."[77]

The Company's native commissioners tended to attribute threats to the security of the region in terms of African leaders' distrust of civilizing advances. Taberer attributed the 1903 unease to "the amount of solid civilization the native had to assimilate in the past 18 months," though he acknowledged that the scarcity of food might also have contributed to the unrest.[78] Individual NCs objected to possible policy initiatives regarding polygyny, the mobility of young men, and education as dangerous policies that, attempting to impose civilization, would lead to serious unrest. The acting NC at Mtoko characterized attempts to discourage polygyny as attempts to "create a social revolution," and he went on to point out that young men were moving about, able to "give an immense amount of trouble . . . [and] openly defy the local [African] authority." And some of these men were even uncontrollable by Europeans, as young men with Christian training were "more independent, and inclined to approach the level of the white man, which in some cases almost amounts to impertinence."[79] The dangers, he implied, were obvious. Other NCs seconded him, complaining of demoralization, Bible training, and the destruction of Africans' "natural honesty and simplicity."[80]

Yet in the early years of the Native Department, few of the native commissioners were willing to write off strategies of civilization because they violated the goal of safeguarding African customs and ran the risk of provoking defensive violence. Instead, the Native Department officials emphasized the need to manage change and civilization in ways that would eventually solve the security problem by luring Africans away from the dangerous authority of African elders into a European-directed mixed society. Taberer emphasized that "as civilization increases, the native chiefs become discontented while their people realise the benefits. . . ."[81] The security problems of civilization were, in other words, a temporary problem of transition. The Native Department in the early years was willing to let African customs and the customary African leadership become, in the imagery of the SANAC, a casualty of the slaughter and bloodshed of the righteous war for civilization.[82]

The Native Department, and the administration as a whole, followed the same logic that led Africans and missionaries to the ideology of civilization. The primary functions of the Native Department were to provide security for the white population of the region and to induce as many African men as possible to work for Europeans. Civilization, as an ideology that emphasized the disaggregation of African societies into individuals pursuing personal rather than communal interests, decreased the danger that those individuals would suddenly and surprisingly rise up in communally organized rebellions. The CNC of Matabeleland wrote in his 1901 report that "there is absolutely no cohesion amongst the natives, and thus each little tribe, as it were from mutual jealousy and opposition, has become a little kingdom in itself," and discussed how he had encouraged "this harmless rivalry" as "the most politic form of governing the natives."[83] In Mashonaland, such policies had had such an effect that by the time of the SANAC's visit, the administrator could argue that, in all of Mashonaland, "there were no Natives of sufficient importance who could with advantage be called" to testify.[84]

Accepting the Africans' new affiliations with European culture, particularly Christianity, was more worrisome for the NCs. W. S. Taberer explained to the SANAC that

> I have met many natives who have been to schools, and I have always found the raw Native the better Native to deal with . . . . it is so undoubtedly. . . . [The Christian or educated Native is] not so get-at-able as the ordinary Native. . . . Once a Native leaves his Location and goes to a mission school . . . he at once looks to the particular mission people as his immediate guardians, and he will not recognise the Native Commissioner.[85]

Taberer went on to agree with his interrogator's suggestion that educated Africans were more independent, more likely to assert their rights, less law abiding, and less inclined to work. Substantially, however, what worried him was the prospect of Africans who did not submit automatically to control by the administration.[86] Other native commissioners voiced more specific worries. Already in 1899, the urban NC Bulawayo, Lanning was objecting to education and what was "generally termed Christianising" as developing Africans into "unmitigated scoundrels." The process, he emphasized, "thoroughly encourage[d] laziness."[87] Even so, the administration had a substantial security interest in preventing Africans from organizing oppositional activity, whether through customary authorities—as Umjaan and his committee may have attempted in 1899, Chilimanzi in 1902, and Maduna in 1906 and 1907[88]—or through the prophetic system, which was the Company's official explanation of the 1896 Risings.[89] Together with the sheer convenience of African employees who could be told what to do even by a settler unable to speak a local language,[90] this was a powerful argument for the cultural changes implied in the ideology of civilization.

Supreme even above security interests, though, was the Company's interest in, and desperate need for, economic change in African societies, particularly for the promotion of African wage labor. The Company's profitability demanded not merely the security to exploit the region's mineral and agricultural resources, but the inexpensive African labor to make that exploitation possible. In his study of the Native Department's bureaucratic maneuverings, J. J. Taylor has argued that it was this need for labor that provided the department's dominance in the administrative hierarchy, and that the entire Native Problem was, from the perspective of the Company, rarely more than an attempt to acquire and control an African labor force.[91]

During the period immediately after the Risings, though, imperial attention was at an all-time high, encouraging officials to be careful of the methods they used to recruit labor.[92] The Native Department issued various circulars ordering NCs to be careful about their recruiting practices. In 1895 the CNC had ordered NCs to "make a point of instilling into the minds of the Natives the idea that . . . it would be for the good of the Natives themselves and of their Districts that they should earn by labour the money with which to pay their Tax."[93] But by 1897 the CNC was obliged to order, bluntly, "Under no consideration whatever is any compulsion to be exercised in obtaining natives for labour."[94] That, and subsequent circulars, went on to suggest that NCs should attempt to help labor recruitors by making known the opportunity to work. But the Native Department messengers were ordered not to coerce, merely to inform the various chiefs. Individual NCs might boast, as one did in 1899, that the Africans in his region had "worked exceedingly well during the year . . . not of their own accord but because they have been constantly called out by me."[95] But the CNC restated his orders in a general circular in 1901, ordering NCs to obey "to the letter" the instruction that

> no influence either direct or indirect may be used to induce or cause Natives to seek work. The duties of Native Commissioners which are not in the slightest particulars to be exceeded are simply to register *Natives offering for work* and guide them to places where labour is required; and to assist Natives

> in obtaining fair treatment and observance of contracts. It
> must be repeated that Native Commissioners *are under no
> circumstances to enter into contracts or to interest themselves
> on behalf of any employer* . . . . contravention of the terms
> of this instruction will be regarded as a serious offence and
> dealt with accordingly.[96]

In 1902 the acting CNC again cautioned NCs, ordering them not to accept capitation fees for assisting in recruitment for specific mines or enterprises.[97] By 1902 at least one NC actually was disciplined for such recruitment, though he argued that his recruitment had followed Taberer's argument that labor "has got to be done some how or the mines will have to close down."[98] The repeated statements from the CNC might indicate that the initial orders against coercion and recruitment were not taken very seriously, but gradually, with prosecution and cautioning of specific offenders, the new regulations did restrict forcible labor recruitment by NCs. Under such imperial pressure, the calling out of labor was increasingly limited to specific work carried on for the NC or the NC's station, at least until the acute labor shortages of 1911.[99]

Such limitations left the NCs and the Native Department with three tools for the extraction of labor: the direct economic pressure of taxes, the ideology of labor as a strategy for personal betterment, and the cultivation of consumer materialism, or "wants," capable of pressuring Africans into the workforce. All of these strategies could easily be integrated into an ideological structure of civilization. Taxes, transformed from hut taxes levied on communities into poll taxes aimed at individuals as the price of citizenship, promoted tensions within African communities—tensions capable of dividing young men from old and sending the young men as individuals out into the workplace. The ideology of labor was part of concepts of civilized citizenship, a path to individual progress. NCs wanted African young men to learn "the dignity of labor and a just sense of duty" as a step toward "an equality which only worthiness in a native can command from a white man."[100] That aim was somewhat different from the mission strategy of acculturating their students to European culture through education, as it emphasized compulsory work and obedience with no communal reward.

Strategies for promoting wants were rather vague. The Native Department, though, seized upon a concept of increasing wants as an important facet of the economic transformation from Africans' limited wants as members of African communities to unlimited wants as individual consumers in a materialistic society. Customary Africans, CNC Taberer argued,

> have no desire to become rich. Their one idea is to obtain the necessary money to pay the tax . . . and then return to their homes, and loll about in idleness, drinking beer. . . . it will be necessary to introduce a higher standard of living at the kraals, and the natives, while at work, must be educated to higher wants and ambitions, so that when they return to their kraals, their friends may regard them with envy, inducing rivalry.[101]

The Native Department's strategy for extracting labor could be seen as one of shattering African communities, attempting to co-opt useful young men, and seeking to use the basest available emotions, such as envy and rivalry, to create a mass of useful workers.

The Native Department, and the administration in general, expected certain characteristics of the ideal African worker. He—women were not viewed as prospective employees until the 1920s—should be an individual whose ties with family and community were loose or nonexistent. In other words, he should not be married, because married men were less willing to engage in wage labor than unmarried men, since their labor was needed at home, and they could rely on their wives' labor and the income from the family's peasant production for subsistence and taxes.[102] But, in addition to questions of willingness to work, NCs also worried about the logistics of married men's work. If the wives remained at home, they might escape their absent husbands' supervision, damaging men's position as head of the family. If, however, they came to the urban townships or the mining compounds, they would be unable to farm and would be under pressure to improve their incomes through participation in the illegal service industries that provided workers with beer or sex—industries that threatened patriarchal control.[103]

The Native Department's ideal African worker was not merely detached from any African family or community, he was also acculturated to at least some aspects of European society. Europeans did not want to hire skilled workers, but they did expect some acquaintance with European culture and European-style work discipline. Africans could find that familiarity difficult to acquire or accept. One European observer complained that

> It took a long time for a savage, unused to tableware, brushes
> and crockery . . . to grasp the different uses of the multitude
> of strange utensils . . . to realize that a sock . . . should not
> be employed as a coffee-strainer and that it is an offence against
> good taste to clean out the inside of a saucepan with [a] . . .
> hairbrush.[104]

And Vambe, recording the oral tradition he grew up with, recalled that the elders of the Chishawasha community valued work, but despised European notions of work discipline, with new ideas of paid labor for work by the day or hour, "work that went on from sunrise to sunset, from Monday to Saturday, season to season and from year to year. Such a mode of existence was singularly barren and reduced human beings to the level of cattle or donkeys."[105] Yet "habits of industry," as the NCs tended to refer to them, were crucial to Europeans when they needed Africans able to operate within European work norms. An acquaintance with the tasks of the wage laborer could also be useful, particularly in the building trades. Employers, in any case, became frustrated when faced with workers who lacked the common European basis of knowledge concerning how to get things done.[106] Communication skills were important as well, not necessarily in English, but in "Kitchen Kaffir" or Fanakalo, its industrial variant.[107] The Native Department's ideal African worker would also be impressed by the material sights of European-directed society, sufficiently impressed to want to emulate the consumption patterns of Europeans, spending his wages as he earned them, making his stay in the compound or town a long one and his return certain.

Such ideal workers would not necessarily be pleasant people, either in their home communities or their European-owned workplaces. But they would fill the economic requirements of an expanding settler economy admirably, doing so in response to "civilizing" pressures rather than physical force. And however much individual native commissioners might despise or dislike Africans who had been in contact with European individualism, culture, and economic materialism, the policy of the department was to cultivate such civilizing tendencies, accepting as inevitable that Africans would, in the words of an often-repeated cliché, assimilate the vices of civilization more readily than the virtues.[108]

Despite regretful comments by underlings, the chief native commissioners of Mashonaland and Matabeleland made clear through years of annual reports their support for civilization as a tactic of social and economic change. Taberer, the CNC Mashonaland, who had informed the SANAC of his dislike of educated Africans, felt that Africans left alone, away from the stimuli of civilization, were a serious problem. In 1901 he reported that "they appear to want little, and procure that little without any trouble." They worried about nothing, he asserted, and he blamed even their occasional health problems on that lack of motivation.[109] In 1904, despairing of his ability to extract voluntary labor from the Shona communities, he emphasized that that was the first year in which the Africans had truly felt pressure from their new, civilized government, and he hoped that this pressure would encourage Africans to go into European-dominated areas to work and would inspire change through envy and rivalry.[110] Government pressure, he acknowledged in 1906, was not enough to extract the quantity of labor the European-controlled economy needed, and he advocated restricting the size of the reserves, to force Africans "despite themselves, to travel the road of progress . . . into direct contact with civilization."[111] Despite his assertions that he had "always found the raw Native the better Native to deal with,"[112] and the implication in his annual reports that "raw Natives" were inert, making "civilizing" change far from inevitable, he chose to promote that "raw Native's" transformation as part of an integrated strategy of social and economic management and change.

H. J. Taylor, the CNC Matabeleland, differed from Taberer in his impression of the inevitability of change. Matabeleland was, economically, much more active in mining than Mashonaland, and the reserves smaller,[113] not merely forcing Africans and Europeans into closer contact, but encouraging Africans to seek prosperity through change.[114] Africans, Taylor emphasized, accepted the idea of change, and merely needed guidance as to the direction of that change. In any case, given that change was already underway, "a good beginning of the means adopted to lift the native from savage life to enlightenment must prove beneficial to the country in the end, and so long as this policy is maintained, I do not anticipate any serious discontent from the natives."[115]

Despite philosophical differences on the nature of Africans, Taberer and Taylor were agreed on the need for a policy of contact and civilization. For Taberer, civilization was a strategy of desperation, designed to knock a comfortable African population from its secure niche in peasant production into the fray of the labor market. For Taylor, civilization was a way of controlling the shape of the changes and transformations already occurring, changes that, unless shaped, might undermine the region's economic and social viability and threaten the settlers' security.

The Native Department tended to use the tax revenues it collected from Africans as a standard of its success at civilizing Africans. When the NC of Sebungwe described his people as uncivilized, he emphasized the difficulties of collecting taxes and offered, as supporting evidence, his observations that "the people [were] wildly suspicious, and with a strong desire . . . to place obstacles in the way of and passively resist all outside interference with themselves and their country."[116] Taberer, discussing popular ambivalence regarding civilization, indicated that the hut tax was one of the most important initiatives in making people realize they were "under a civilised Government."[117] And when Taylor wished to emphasize the progress civilization had made in Matabeleland, he wrote about the Ndebele response to an increase in taxes, and their general obedience and compliance. "Ready compliance with legislation" and "rapid progress in the appreciation of their relations to the Government" indicated that Africans were participating in "the rapid march of civilization in this Protectorate."[118] This standard, more than any other aspect of the administrative attitude toward civilization, emphasized that, to the Company and the Native Department, civilization was a strategy for the establishment of an effective system of European rule, rather than a paternalistic concept of eventual equality.

The Native Department and administration shared with some young African men and with missionaries a concept of the future of Southern Rhodesia as a civilized region where cognitive, cultural, and economic convergence between Africans and Europeans had produced a new, advanced society, centered around cities, mines, and capitalistic agriculture. But where the Africans who participated in this vision viewed the change as one of Africans' progress as educated individuals able to achieve positions of respect and prosperity within the individual's lifetime, and missionaries hoped for the slow cultivation of that equality through generational change, the Native Department and the BSAC administration viewed civilization as a strategy for maximizing Africans' usefulness to Europe.

Settler Perspectives

The settler community shared the Native Department's and the BSAC administration's notions of civilization as a strategy for promoting African disaggregation, labor, and familiarity with European material culture. But settlers, while demanding a native policy and offering frequent comments on it and labor, taxes, and education, rarely used the language of civilization to describe Africans or the process of change overtaking the African communities of the region. They were interested in the needs of their own community.

While Africans sought through education and economic change to acquire respect and power, missionaries looked to some idea of eventual civilized citizenship, and the native administration sought to use the ideology of civilization to shape a useful, ideologically based obedience to contain African social and economic changes, settlers identified themselves with civilization, the Africans with barbarism, and attempts to bring Africans into a civilized context in any posture other than abject subjugation as threats to economic excellence, higher culture, and moral integrity. Settlers used the language of civilization to express their own communally conservative sense of threat and endangerment, and to oppose change rather than to promote or shape it.

Near the beginning of the first session of the Legislative Council to include elected members from the settler community, one of those members opened a debate on native administration in Southern Africa. "The natives," Grey declared, "were sufficiently protected by the Charter and by several Orders in Council to secure their rights against interference. *Their* status was defined, and it only remained to put in force a workable law for their government and control. . . ."[119] Grey emphasized that the settlers felt ill-used, their status undefined, and their community shut out of the management of its subject population. This theme continued to dominate settler pronouncements on Africans. "All they asked in this country," a later spokesman declared,

> was that they should be allowed to manage the natives justly and rightly. The natives must be made to understand that they cannot claim the same privileges as the white people enjoyed after 2000 years—that they cannot attain that in one generation. . . . [The settlers] were a small community and it was necessary that the small intelligent and enlightened community should control.[120]

Settlers were even more emphatic when writing to each other in the medium of the *Rhodesia Herald,* the *Bulawayo Chronicle,* or the *Rhodesia Advertiser.* One article declared, "The ignorant mob [the Aborigine Protection Society in league with the imperial government] that persists in venerating an ideal of the kafir races is set to ride colonists to their destruction. The alternative is for the latter to refuse to play the patient ass."[121] And that extreme declaration was far from unusual. At the beginning of the twentieth century, settlers portrayed themselves as a community—a civilized community—under threat by the barbarian masses.

This terror of change emerged, with increasingly emotional arguments, in settler discussions of three issues: labor and the taxes designed to procure it, education and the implications of literate or skilled Africans, and the "black peril" scares that reflected Europeans' fears that they had lost control not merely over their economic position and cultural knowledge, but also over the sexual security of their bodies and those of their family members.[122]

Labor was the ultimate make-or-break economic issue for the viability of the settler economy. When, in 1901, native commissioners were reminded that their duty no longer included the recruitment of labor, settlers viewed the effects of that interference with alarm. Addressing a Farmers' Association meeting, one pointed out that

> they had been used to getting their supplies of labor through the native commissioners. All at once an order came from 6,000 miles away, telling them to cancel this arrangement. By a stroke of the pen . . . the farmers were brought to a standstill.[123]

Infuriated by imperial pressure, settler representatives in the Legislative Council demanded local control over native policy and emphasized how devastating restrictions were to the European population of the region. Twisting statistics quite creatively, one representative argued that "the native did not pay an equitable share of taxation."[124] To the SANAC, H. J. Deary, a Salisbury merchant, explained that higher taxes were important to the economic viability of the settler economy. NCs, he argued, should be allowed to act as labor recruiters, as "more labor could be obtained from the natives in this country under different conditions," but, to some extent, taxes could provide an alternative strategy for the extraction of labor, because "if the native is sufficiently taxed, he will work for that tax." The absence of increased taxation, he indicated, had a negative effect, as "the Native mind has been sufficiently educated up to the fact that he does not pay sufficiently."[125]

Settlers' inability to raise taxes, therefore, undermined the revenue base of their administrative structure, the labor base of their economy, and the authority to control African-European contact, which settlers viewed as a crucial issue of prestige.[126] In this version of events, Africans, in alliance with imperial pressure, were "taking advantage" of "the privileges of good administration," without paying for that administration.[127] Furthermore, in the absence of settler control over a labor supply, crops were rotting in the fields while Africans laughed at their would-be employers. Through this nexus of issues, the settlers argued that the economic basis of their dominance was threatened. Settlers described imperial threats as initiatives by a "childish,"[128] "ignorant mob"[129] of "mulish people" who threatened to crush "a young and struggling country."[130]

Labor and taxation issues addressed the question of whether the settler society would be able to maintain its economic dominance. But its dominance was not merely economic, it also involved knowledge and access to a dominant culture that used such tools as technology, literacy, and formal education. African demands for education threatened that cultural monopoly, and here, too, settlers conceptualized the relations between communities in terms of the threat of convergence. The merchant Deary, speaking to the SANAC, argued that Africans should not be given too much education even if they requested it and offered to pay for it. "It would be a mistake in the present state of the country to think of educating the Native," he emphasized, since "the raw Native . . . has very few ideas of civilization, and we have to protect ourselves in this country in this way, that we have hordes of Natives round us, and we have to keep them under control." As long as the African population was so much larger than the European, "We, as white people in this country, have to protect ourselves."[131] Deary did not specify carefully what the threat posed by educated Africans would be, but within his discussion with the commission, and comments by other settlers, there were several candidates.

The first threat was the clear danger of economic competition. Deary pointed out earlier that "if the native is trained to become a mechanic he comes in conflict with the white man."[132] The topic made him uneasy, and he refused to discuss it further. Others were less reticent. William Napier, a Matabeleland farmer and a sometime member of the Legislative Council, argued that the idea of teaching Africans industrial work was a bad one because it promoted equality or competition, and "I should always have the Native as an unskilled labourer as far as I possibly could."[133] Artisans and other Europeans who relied on wages were even more directly threatened by the construction workers missionaries trained because the wages of even skilled Africans were far below those of European craftsmen.[134]

Educated, skilled Africans, as potential economic competitors, threatened mainly working-class Europeans. Even elite Europeans, though, felt threatened when in early-twentieth-century Southern Rhodesia an educated African could be self-employed, removing himself from the pool of potential laborers, competing with Europeans as a market-oriented peasant farmer or itinerant mechanic, or even going from area to area as a teacher, spreading knowledge of how to maneuver within the new system even as settlers sought to extract labor from the local population by limiting knowledge of available options.[135] This indirect economic threat, of an African rejection of participation in the European-directed economy or of a redefinition of the terms of that participation, worried settlers.

Education did not, however, merely undermine the economic superiority of the Europeans. It also undermined their ability to extract deference from Africans who, educated, "thought they were on an equality with the white men."[136] Such an equality threatened the automatic assumption of European superiority on which the culture of the settlers was based. Settlers argued that they had

> come into this country . . . had redeemed it from savagery, and had given the natives laws under which they were equal with the white man. But they could not be so fatuous as to extend the doctrine to its utmost limit and thereby bring upon them the contempt of the native.[137]

Without automatic deference, settlers both felt uncomfortable and feared for their ability to direct the economy and society of the region. The danger was not merely that some elite Africans might know more than some lowly Europeans, though such a prospect did worry observers of the educational deficiencies of the region's European children.[138] The real problem was that the Africans might *feel* equal—or deserving of equality—and, rejecting deference, be extremely difficult to manage or control, posing a threat to business as usual or even to the administration's control.

Such fears of direct and indirect economic competition, and of the demise of deference, worried settlers faced with the possibility of African education. But the fear was expressed in racial terms because settlers did not believe in the missionary concept of the transformative effects of civilization. For settlers, the polish that education could provide was dangerous precisely because it provided a basis for deception and distortion, the manipulation of what settlers viewed as a fundamental difference of culture, gained through millennia of historical experience. Thus, education and civilization could decrease the cultural differences between Africans and Europeans, but not eliminate a fundamental qualitative difference. The settlers responded to this narrowing of the cultural gap between Africans and Europeans through several sorts of anxiety. Napier argued for restrictions on Africans using footpaths in towns.[139] The Salisbury town council contemplated regulations preventing Africans from bicycling in town.[140] The *Bulawayo Chronicle* was vitriolic on the subject of Africans who showed up for work better dressed than their employers.[141] Settlers deplored prisons where Africans and Europeans served their sentences of hard labor on the same work gangs.[142]

The clearest expressions of anxiety, however, surrounded the Black Peril scares which intermittently energized the European communities, and which may have, in the form of chronic worry, shaped popular European attitudes toward Africans in European homes, Africans with European educations, or Africans who appeared civilized. Black Peril, the European fear that European women were in danger of rape from African men, was the crystallization of the entire European community's sentiment that it was civilized, and Africans, however they might on the surface appear, were barbarians or beasts. Settler representatives in the Legislative Council argued for the death penalty for *attempted* rape of an European woman by an African man. Specific cases invoked indicate clearly that an African man could trigger a European woman's fears of rape through mere social contact, or through the unhappy chance of there being a scared woman present in the house he chose to burgle.[143]

The crime was conceptualized by settler representatives as one of the individual African against the European community. Holland argued for the death penalty on the grounds that attempted rape was usually by

> a so-called Christian Kafir. It was not the raw Matabele or
> Mashona that attempted to rape white women, as they had

> some lingering respect for the superior race. . . . Today the
> native laughed at them; he thought they were a parcel of fools,
> and so they were . . . he must be made to recognise that by
> no stretch of the imagination could the white and black man
> ever be on the same plane.[144]

And another representative described Black Peril offenses as "crimes on the part of barbarians and savages" that damaged the entire European civilized community. They were not merely crimes against women, he argued, because

> of the wounded feelings of others. No nation would allow the
> weaker sex to be trampled upon by savages. . . . The native
> was no better . . . than a brute. . . . It was very little better
> than bestiality, and no woman who had been ravished . . . by
> a native was likely to admit in any court of law that the crime
> had been accomplished upon her. . . . There was very little
> difference between the attempt at a crime and the accom-
> plishment of it. . . . It was necessary, to maintain their su-
> premacy, to treat the natives with sternness.[145]

The Black Peril scares were settler arguments that "civilized" Africans were not, indeed, civilized, but capable of "barbarous" assaults.

The settlers, constrained by Company and imperial power and by their own fears of Africans and need for African labor, maintained their own interests, their own sense of community, and their own definition of themselves as the nucleus of civilization amid a mass of barbarians. Through their initiatives on labor and tax policies, African education, and Black Peril, settlers sought to modulate the ideology of civilization into a key far removed from the tones of Africans, missionaries, and even the Native Department and BSAC administration. Settlers sought to use ideas of civilization to exploit and exclude Africans and to bind the Europeans of the settler community together.

Contention

Civilization was not a simple ideology. It performed more than a single task and served more than one faction of an increasingly complex and contentious society. As a conceptual focus for many communities, and many interests, it suggested possibilities, promoted comprehension, and above all else, offered a language for communication. In a rapidly changing region, in the aftermath of conquest, the throes of a neighboring war and the social disruption and dislocation that accompanies economic development, the ideology of civilization served Africans, missionaries, officials, and even settlers as a framework around which to construct their worldviews and to plan strategies and possibilities for the future. In raising issues of individuation, acculturation, and economic transformation, and fitting them together into a comprehensible package, advocates of civilization sought to promote, comprehend, and cope with challenges to the communities, authorities, and economies of earlier days, and to direct a transformation.

Notes

1. *Report of the South African Native Affairs Commission* (SANAC) (Capetown: 1905) 1: 52. The SANAC collected evidence throughout southern Africa from 1903 through 1905, and published conclusions and evidence in five large volumes. Volumes 1, 4, and 5 discuss Southern Rhodesia. Volume 1 contains conclusions, 4 transcribed oral testimony, and 5 printed written responses to the commission's queries.

2. All three of these elements had South African roots stretching further back into the nineteenth century. For a discussion of the South African debates over individualism and communalism, see D. M. Schreuder, "The Cultural Factor in Victorian Imperialism: A Case Study of the British 'Civilising' Mission," *Journal of Imperial and Commonwealth History* 4 (May 1976): 283-317, esp. 289-98.

3. For examples, see Schreuder, "Victorian Imperialism," 294-300.

4. For discussions with reference to South Africa, see Schreuder, "Victorian Imperialism," 300-303, and R. L. Cope, "C. W. de Kiewiet, the Imperial Factor, and South African 'Native Policy,'" *Journal of Southern African Studies* 15 (April 1989): 486-505.

5. H. J. Taylor, *SANAC Report,* 4:149.

6. John White (Methodist Missionary Society [MMS]), *SANAC Report* 4:84-85; W. H. Brown, *SANAC Report* 4:112.

7. Sikombo (NC Carbutt, interpreter) to *SANAC Report* 4:161.

8. H. M. Jackson (then NC Fort Usher), *SANAC Report* 5:340-43. Jackson was one of the only NCs who did not react with automatic vitriol to African studiousness. "Hewers of wood and drawers of water they must be, as a race, to the end of the chapter," he wrote, but "it is to our advan-

tage and theirs that they should become more intelligent hewers of wood and drawers of water." This hunger for education worried most settlers. See, for example, "The Native Problem," *Bulawayo Chronicle,* 17 September 1904 and "Natives and Education," *Bulawayo Chronicle,* 24 September 1904.

9. R. J. Challiss, "The Foundation of the Racially Segregated Educational System in Southern Rhodesia, 1890–1923, with special reference to the education of Africans" (Ph.D. dissertation, University of Zimbabwe, 1982), 70–71.

10. Gambo, *SANAC Report* 4:161.

11. Etheridge, *Mashonaland Quarterly* 62 (November 1907): 10–11.

12. Executive Council of Southern Rhodesia, Minutes, 8 February 1899, CO603/1.

13. Sikombo, *SANAC Report* 4:161.

14. See, for example, the report of school-opening negotiations between the Church of England mission and Mchena, "Brotherhood Diary," *Mashonaland Quarterly* 35 (February 1901): 19–20.

15. Archdeacon Beaven to Bishop, 19 December 1904, USPG/CLR 142; Etheridge, *Mashonaland Quarterly* 49 (May 1904): 7–8.

16. For examples, see Walton to MMS, 7 November 1904, MMS 825/6; Cullen Reed to LMS, 18 February 1903, CWM 62/1.

17. An example of the required sacrifices can be extracted from the description of a "kind of strike" by students at the Anglican Penhalanga station. Brotherhood Diary, *Mashonaland Quarterly* 37 (August, 1901): 15–20. Duthie's assertions that Africans wanted education solely for the purpose of increasing their wages, and went to mission stations only because there they had "a very pleasant time" were typical of the administration's position, but bore little relationship to the observed facts. Duthie spoke to his prejudices. He had been in Southern Rhodesia for three years as an administrator of European education. He knew no African languages, and cared little for African schools during this period. George Duthie, director of education for Southern Rhodesia, *SANAC Report* 4:141.

18. Until Section D of the Education Ordinance of 1907, the administration did not even acknowledge the existence of education when the teaching was done by Africans rather than Europeans.

19. Walton to MMS, 7 November 1904, MMS 825/6. And the Penhalonga fee had risen to £5 by 1907. Etheridge, *Mashonaland Quarterly* 61 (August 1907): 12–13.

20. Wilkerson, annual report for the Industrial Institute (1909), CWM 4/2.

21. Rev. G. A. Wilder (American Board Mission), *SANAC Report* 4:3.

22. S. Jackson (then NC Hartley) even argued that work was sought as a source of education by Africans who "neglect their work and rush off on

the slightest pretext to some teacher or friend for educational instruction. When supposed to be performing their duties they may frequently be found in their huts studying some book or scrawling on some scrap of paper" (*SANAC Report* 5:344–46). Jackson was, however, unusual in arguing that Africans saw educational opportunity as a reason to enter the job market.

23. Arthur Keppel-Jones, *Rhodes and Rhodesia: The White Conquest of Zimbabwe, 1884–1902* (Kingston and Montreal: McGill-Queen's University Press, 1983), 541.

24. E. J. Parker, *Mashonaland Quarterly* 56 (May 1906): 9–11.

25. BSAC, *Report for 1900–1902* (London, 1903); *Bulawayo Chronicle,* 18 May 1903: out of a male population between the ages of eighteen and forty estimated at 105,000. Some Africans from Southern Rhodesia, however, migrated independently or through the Witwatersrand Native Labor Bureau (WNLB) down to the Rand. See "Rand Native Labour," *Bulawayo Chronicle,* 18 April 1903 and "Native Labour," *Bulawayo Chronicle,* 11 November 1905. Charles van Onselen's discussion of regional labor migration patterns, and his emphasis that for many migrant workers, Rhodesia was a stopping off point rather than a destination is valuable on this issue (*Chibaro: African Mine Labour in Southern Rhodesia, 1900–1933* [London: Pluto Press, 1976] 227–44).

26. Earl Grey to BSAC in London, *Rhodesia Herald,* 11 January 1902, alleged that an African could earn £20 to £40, in addition to food, during a year's worth of employment. That statement appears rather grossly overstated when contrasted to statements made at a Farmers' Association meeting, Salisbury (*Rhodesia Herald,* 16 March 1901) indicating that labor board prices for labor (not all of which would be passed on to the employee) were 12s 6d/month (£15/year if, through some unlikely chance, the employee worked a full year and got paid the full labor board price)—and considered ridiculously high. Mashona labor, Dr. Stewart alleged, was only worth about 2s 6d./month plus food.

27. ABC Minutes (June 1905?); and 18–20 December 1905, ABC 15.4, vol. 21, items 51, 54.

28. Keppel-Jones, *Rhodes and Rhodesia,* 541, notes that wages were used to buy cattle to recoup war losses.

29. Van Onselen, *Chibaro,* 74ff. For an example of the arguments he is drawing from, see settler discussions of the affluence of Africans. Examples include: "the fact of the matter is that the natives are too well off," which referred to ownership of livestock, and was offered as an explanation for Africans' reluctance to accept wage work. "BSAC Report 1900–1902," *Bulawayo Chronicle,* 18 May 1903.

30. For Africans in the region, the highest available wages were not even in Southern Rhodesia, but on the Rand or in South Africa generally.

Labor was recruited within Southern Rhodesia for the Rand, in addition to the Africans who made their own way south. See, for example, the Rhodesian Native Labour Bureau (RNLB) controversy, *Bulawayo Chronicle,* 2 September 1905. See Colin Murray, *Families Divided: The Impact of Migrant Labour in Lesotho* (Cambridge: Cambridge University Press, 1981), for an analysis of the ways in which wages could prove vital to peasant, or even subsistence agriculture within an economy and society dependent on migrant labor. Southern Rhodesia had not, by 1900, reached the stage of necessity and impoverishment Murray describes, but the war damage, the destruction of capital through the seizure of cattle and the rinderpest, and the dislocations of land expropriation did have an effect. Murray's conclusions, however, challenge van Onselen's assumption that peasant and proletarian production were alternative models, suggesting an analysis based on life cycle and family history.

31. Racism was real, and unmistakably obvious when it came to filling these leading roles. Furthermore, social segregation and the maintenance of distinctions and difference was a principal function of many of the prosaic bits of legislation regarding daily life. European communities sponsored what can only be considered sumptuary legislation—seeking, for example, to prevent Africans from using the footpaths in the towns. Napier, *Legislative Council Debates* (1904), 20.

32. Note, however, that even Africans in "professions" (e.g., teachers, preachers, catechists) farmed. The only exceptions to this situation were young students, often twelve to fifteen years old, who taught in their school holidays, or as part of their training. Like Africans engaged in industrial work, adult teachers resisted proletarianization.

33. And, incidentally, it offered nothing to senior men but insubordination and problems. Even should they wish to do so, they could not enter mission stations for education, as many of the men were polygynous, an inhibiting factor given the missions' opposition to polygyny, and mission stations preferred to concentrate their limited resources on the young. And as for wage labor, younger men were preferred, both as stronger, and because they were perceived as more adaptable. No man over thirty-five, the resident commissioner (Sir Marshall Clarke), argued in 1903, would be able to earn more than a subsistence wage. (RC to HC, 20 March 1903, Correspondence related to the Hut Tax Ordinance, 1903, CO 603/5.)

34. Brotherhood Diary, *Mashonaland Quarterly* 29 (August 1899): 10–11.

35. Brotherhood Diary, *Mashonaland Quarterly* 30 (November 1899): 15–19; Brotherhood Diary, *Mashonaland Quarterly* 31 (February 1900): 11–13; Brotherhood Diary, *Mashonaland Quarterly* 37 (August 1901): 15–20.

36. Laura Bates to ABC, 17 May 1898, ABC 15.4, vol. 19, item 124; Rich-

artz to Inspector of Schools, 12 June 1902, Richartz Letter Book, box 356, JAH; *Zambesi Mission Record,* 2 (1903): 295.

37. Laura Bates to ABC, 17 May 1898, ABC 15.4, vol. 19, item 124.

38. Lawrence Vambe, *An Ill-Fated People: Zimbabwe before and after Rhodes* (London, Pittsburgh: 1972), 126–27.

39. Vambe, *Ill-Fated People,* 145–46. "Indeed, the Fathers unwittingly gave their boys and girls the impression that they would be as good as white people once they had been trained to use their heads, hands and hearts. . . ."

40. G. A. Wilder, *SANAC Report* 4:5.

41. Wilder, *SANAC Report* 4:9, 18, 25. Wilder went so far as to advocate that Rhodesia should "allow the best of them to attain to the political franchise, I think nothing less would be sufficient."

42. *SANAC Report* 4:6–7. Wilder advocated *compulsory* education for Africans up to Standard IV (unheard of even twenty years later) and quoted Frederick Douglas to the effect that unless both Africans and Europeans acted in a civilized fashion, "the problem of the black man will be answered by the licentiousness of the white man."

43. "Educating the Native," *Bulawayo Chronicle,* 21 July 1906; "Church of England Synod," *Bulawayo Chronicle,* 21 July 1906; "Native Education," *Bulawayo Chronicle,* 21 July 1906.

44. Bishop Gaul, *Mashonaland Quarterly* 34 (November 1900): 3–5.

45. The description of the 1901 Penhalonga strike is relevant here, as well as the discussions with Mchena. The Brotherhood Diary, recording events at the boys' school of Penhalonga, is rich in its emphasis on the teaching of obedience. See also Upcher, *Mashonaland Quarterly* 40 (May 1902): 7–9.

46. Gaul, *Mashonaland Quarterly* 57 (August 1906): 6; Gaul, *Mashonaland Quarterly* 48 (May 1904): 3–5.

47. Bishop of Mashonaland to editor, *Rhodesia Herald,* 27 April 1901.

48. "Resolutions Passed at a Conference of Mashonaland Clergy, on the Native Question," *Mashonaland Quarterly* 42 (November 1902).

49. Rev. J. W. Leary (Church of England, in Southern Rhodesia since 1898), *SANAC Report* 4:217–18.

50. Wilkerson to LMS, 29 March 1906, CWM 67/3. Wilkerson reported similar sentiments as early as 1900, when he wrote, "Skilled native labor is not liked in Bulawayo. I am told natives are not allowed to use tools. . . ." Wilkerson, Industrial Institution, Hope Fountain Annual Report for 1900, CWM 3/1.

51. Editorial, *Zambesi Mission Record* 1 (1899): 180.

52. Fr. Richartz to Fr. Superior, 12 December 1901, JAH, box 26.

53. The cost of the Chishawasha system was discussed from at least 1901, with Sykes questioning whether it was the best "value for money" (Sykes to Moreau, 17 April 1901, JAH box 12). And even as the school

was peaking in 1906, its demands were causing the mission superiors concern (Propaganda Fideii Report, 1906, JAH box 49). By 1908 the additional conflict between German and English staff members resulted in Fr. Schmitz's observation that "the whole existence of Chishawasha is here in question" (Schmitz to Fr. Superior, 27 May 1908, JAH box 100/3). By 1909 the order was in the process of converting the school to a day school (Gartlau to Barthelemy, 6 October 1909, JAH box 100/3).

54. Gilson to ABC, 21 May 1898, ABC 15.4, vol. 20, item 46.

55. For example, Empandeni, *Zambesi Mission Record* 1 (1901): 362-63, 384-85, 437; Carnegie to LMS, Centenary Annual Report, 1903, CWM 3/1—more than 300 names on school register, with average attendance of 160. In Mashonaland, the education boom was a bit slower to take off.

56. Emphasis in original. Brotherhood Diary, *Mashonaland Quarterly* 35 (February 1901): 18-20.

57. Upcher, *Mashonaland Quarterly* 40 (May 1902): 7-9.

58. Bishop to SPG, 28 June 1899, USPG/CLR 142.

59. *Zambesi Mission Record* 2 (1902): 92-93, 151; Fr. Richartz, *Zambesi Mission Record,* 2 (1904): 338.

60. This economic agenda was not specific to Southern Rhodesia. See Christine Bolt, *Victorian Attitudes toward Race* (London: Routledge and Kegan Paul, 1971), 129.

61. Fr. Richartz to Secretary of the Mashonaland Farmers' Association, Salisbury, 1 March 1902, Richartz Letter Book, JAH box 356.

62. Fr. Richartz to Administrator, *Rhodesia Herald,* 1 March 1902.

63. Father F. J. Richartz to Resident Commissioner, 15 July 1903. Correspondence related to the Hut Tax Ordinance, 1903, CO 603/5.

64. J. White to RC, 23 July 1903, Correspondence related to the Hut Tax Ordinance, 1903, CO 603/5.

65. Kerr (at Gwenda) to MMS, 2 September 1902, MMS 825/4. And even Kerr's comment was restricted to a specific outstation, the furthest from the central mission, which he thought was doing an impressive job "with all the degrading influences of heathenism," considering that "there is little to cheer and uplift them beyond the periodic visit of the missionary." Kerr's comment, in other words, is more self-serving than analytic.

66. The 5 percent high was in 1901. From 1903 to 1906 spending on African education was 2 to 3 percent of the Education budget. The schools funded were St. Columba's (Church of England, Bulawayo), Chishawasha (Jesuit), Mt. Silinda (American Board), and St. Augustine's Penhalonga (Church of England). Penhalonga received its first governmental grant in 1902. St. Columba's declined substantially in 1903 and 1904, and dropped from the list in 1905. The actual sums involved were, in any case, pathetic. In 1902, for example, Penhalonga received £21, St. Columba's £44, Chishawasha £28, and Mt. Selinda £40, out of a total education budget for

Southern Rhodesia (European and African) of £3,195. Reports of the Inspector of Schools, 1901–1907, Sessional Papers, Southern Rhodesia, CO 603/3 and onward. Even this pittance was begrudged. See "Natives of Rhodesia," *Bulawayo Chronicle,* 4 June 1904.

67. Apart from the Catholics, whose budgets are difficult to untangle because of the ambiguity over staff wages when the staff was in holy orders, the most important items facing the missionary budget were salaries, houses, and traveling expenses for the European staff, not salaries and schools for poorly paid African teachers.

68. Rev. G. A. Wilder (American Board Missionary, Melsetter), *SANAC Report* 4:5–7.

69. J. M. Springer (American Methodist Episcopal missionary, Old Umtali), *SANAC Report* 4:122, 129, 134.

70. C. D. Helm (LMS missionary, Matabeleland), *SANAC Report* 4:170–72.

71. Helm, *SANAC Report* 4:184.

72. Baleni (LMS employed preacher), *SANAC Report* 4:205.

73. Earl Grey, enclosure 9 in no. 3, *Report on the Native Administration of the BSAC* (London: HMSO, 1897) (C8547).

74. Executive Council of Southern Rhodesia, Minutes, 23 November 1899 and 30 December 1899, CO 603/1. For example, in 1901 the magic words are present in the openings of the speeches of the administrator, the CNC of Mashonaland, and the CNC of Matabeleland, who varied the formula by stating that the Ndebele were in "a state of placid contentment, unbroken by any unrest or dissatisfaction with the Government." See Minutes of the Legislative Council of Southern Rhodesia, CO 603/2; H. M. Taberer, Report of CNC, Mashonaland, for year ending 31 March 1901, CO 603/3; H. J. Taylor, Report of CNC, Matabeleland, for year ending 31 March 1901, CO 603/3.

75. "Mpondera," *Bulawayo Chronicle,* 27 February 1904. For a secondary treatment of resistance, see T. O. Ranger, *The African Voice in Southern Rhodesia, 1898–1930* (London: Heinemann, 1970), 1–45.

76. Taberer, Report of the CNC, Mashonaland, for the year ending 31 March 1904, CO 603/5. In the Legislative Council, one representative mocked this touchiness saying: ". . . unless the natives were fools—which he did not think they were—they must have come to the conclusion that whenever an Ordinance was proposed affecting them, to which they took exception, they had only to make a certain amount of trouble to have the Ordinance promptly withdrawn." Holland, *Legislative Council Debates,* 1904:48.

77. Haddon, "Saturday's Meeting," *Bulawayo Chronicle,* 25 November 1905.

78. W. Taberer, Report of the CNC, Mashonaland, for the year ending 31 March 1904, CO 603/5.

79. F. Rochfort Byron (Acting NC, Mtoko, Mashonaland), *SANAC Report* 5:309-13.

80. S. Jackson (NC Hartley), *SANAC Report* 5:344-46; W. Edwards (NC Mrewas), *SANAC Report* 5:323-27; F. G. Elliot (NC Selukwe), *SANAC Report* 5:327-30; L. C. Meredith (NC Melsetter), *SANAC Report* 5:349-50; J. W. Posselt (NC Charter), *SANAC Report* 5:351-53. These opinions represented a consensus among the NCs who submitted statements to the commission.

81. Taberer, Report of the CNC, Mashonaland, for the year ending 31 March 1904, (CO 603/5).

82. *SANAC Report,* Conclusions, 1:52.

83. H. J. Taylor, Report of the CNC, Matabeleland, for the year ending 31 March 1901, CO 603/3.

84. Sir Thomas Scanlan, *SANAC Report* 1:appendix B, b30.

85. W. S. Taberer (Acting CNC Mashonaland), *SANAC Report* 4:29-43.

86. Taberer, *SANAC Report* 4:42. And he clearly had something to worry about, given the tendency of missionaries to act as legal authorities on their own stations. See, for example, a later correspondence between the Dutch Reformed Missionaries at Gutu and Alheit, and the Native Department, NAZ NVG 3/2/1.

87. Lanning, NC Bulawayo, Native Commissioners (Matabeleland) yearly reports, 1899, NAZ NB 6/1/2.

88. Umjaan was deposed in 1899, Chilimanzi was allowed, after a scolding, to resume his position as chief. Executive Council of Southern Rhodesia, Minutes, 8 February 1899, 20 February 1902, CO 603/1. Maduna was blamed for an enquiry that led to the removal of the NC Belingwe (de Laessoe), who he had accused of extreme cruelty. NAZ A3/18/14.

89. See Julian Cobbing, "The Ndebele under the Khumalos 1820-1896," (Ph.D. thesis, University of Lancaster, 1976) or D. N. Beach, *War and Politics in Zimbabwe, 1840-1900* (Gweru, Zimbabwe: Mambo Press, 1986), 68-156.

90. Dr. George Duthie (director of education), *SANAC Report* 4:139, emphasized that his department had "laid down . . . that one of the first things is for them [the mission schools] to teach the Natives to speak and understand the English language. That is . . . we do not necessarily wish them to learn to read the English language, or to write it, but merely for the purpose of communication with the whites, so as to do away with as much misunderstanding as possible between the Natives and the Europeans. . . ." He also had to report that the missionaries had resisted this demand.

91. J. J. Taylor, "The Emergence and Development of the Native Department in Southern Rhodesia, 1894-1914" (Ph.D. dissertation, University of London, 1979), 98, 120-25, 196, 292.

92. Taylor, "Native Department," 325. He focussed on the role of Sir

Marshall Clarke, who, he argues was probably the only effective resident commissioner ever to occupy the post (p. 307).

93. H. M. Taberer to all NCs, 12 November 1895, NAZ N4/1/1.

94. H. M. Taberer to all NCs, 26 May 1897, NAZ N4/1/1.

95. ANC South Gwanda, annual report for the year ending 31 March 1899, NAZ NB 6/1/2. Africans would not, he emphasized, work of their own volition as "they see work as an unnecessary evil fit to be ranked with sickness, death. . . ."

96. H. M. Taberer (CNC), 17 October 1901, NAZ N4/1/1.

97. Hulley (acting CNC) to NCs, 17 December 1902, NAZ N4/1/1.

98. J. H. Williams, Deposition, 3 December 1902, CO 417/371. Taberer defended Williams, asserting that Williams was basically a good NC despite episodes of flogging and forcible recruitment. W. W. Taberer to Administrator, 10 September 1902, CO 417/371. The administrator accepted the resident commissioner's arguments that Williams must go, but, he argued, "Mr. Williams has undoubtedly rendered good service in the past, and his districts have always been found in good order. . . . I believe . . . that he acted in what he considered to be the interests of the natives. . . ." Administrator Milton to HC, 24 December 1902, CO 417/371.

99. See, for example, settlers' complaints regarding restrictions on NCs recruitment of labor, "The Passing Show," *Rhodesia Herald,* 26 October 1901, or "Exeter Hall Rampant," *Rhodesia Advertiser,* 7 November 1901. In 1911, though, settlers mobilized for labor (*Bulawayo Chronicle,* 29 September 1911) and in response, missionaries preached labor, and native commissioners "must have invoked the name of the government in a much more pointed manner than in the past" (*Bulawayo Chronicle,* 13 October 1911). Despite restrictions on recruiting for settlers, NCs continued to regard it as legitimate to force local people to carry their baggage on itineration, or to work on making district roads: "The Indunas and Chiefs were informed that they ought not to consider it a hardship for the people to be called upon occasionally to assist the NC on his travels from kraal to kraal, seeing that no other means of transport is available. On the subject of roads . . . the people had not been called out to work on the 'white man's roads' but only on roads leading from kraal to kraal." See the "Report of enquiry into alledged abuses by the NC Belingwe" (de Laessoe), 1907 NAZ A3/18/14.

100. W. E. Thomas (NC Bulilima-Mangwe), Annual Reports, 1899, NAZ NB 6/1/2.

101. Taberer, Report of the CNC, Mashonaland, for the year ending 31 March 1904, CO 603/5.

102. For example, S. Jackson (NC Hartley), *SANAC Report* 5:344–46. The extreme expression of this view came from settlers who objected to marriage, and even more to polygyny on the grounds that it forced "slave

wives" to do all the real productive work (e.g., "Labor in Rhodesia: Mr. E. A. Begbie's Views," *Bulawayo Chronicle,* 27 August 1904).

103. See the *Legislative Council Debates* of 1904 (on new Pass Legislation), 38. Meikle, for example, emphasized that African women did not belong in town or on the mines.

104. H. Marshall Hole, *Old Rhodesian Days* (London: Frank Cass and Co., 1928, 1968), 46.

105. Vambe, *Ill-Fated People,* 43, 100.

106. Dr. Stewart, of the Mashonaland Farmers' Association, emphasized his frustration at needing to teach basic discipline and unskilled tasks year after year to employees who worked for a month or two and then moved on. "Ten years incessant teaching," he noted, "had begun to pall. . . ." *Rhodesia Herald,* 16 March 1901.

107. Both Duthie (Director of Education, SR), *SANAC Report* 4:139, and Kerr (merchant), *SANAC Report* 4:212, advocate English. English, however, was not universally used. "Kitchen Kaffir" and Fanakalo were sometimes preferred by settlers. Dane Kennedy, *Islands of White* (Durham N.C.: Duke University Press, 1987), 155–160; van Onselen, *Chibaro,* 152.

108. Or, in the more wordy formulation of the *SANAC Report,* with the removal of customary restraints, "civilization, particularly in the larger towns, brings the Native under the influence of a social system of which he too often sees and assimilates the worst side only." *SANAC Report* 1:55.

109. "The dysentery is doubtless caused by eating roots and drinking beer in excess, and pneumonia is the outcome of self-neglect and being insufficiently clad." Taberer, Report of the CNC, Mashonaland, for the year ending 31 March 1901, CO 603/3. He persisted in this theory of African unconcern, writing in 1902 that many workers on railways or mines got pneumonia and died: "Anyone with a knowledge of the native of this country can see the utterly careless manner in which they look after themselves." Taberer, Report of the CNC, Mashonaland, 31 March 1902, CO 603/5.

110. Taberer, Report of the CNC, Mashonaland, 31 March 1904, CO 603/5.

111. Taberer, Report of the CNC, Mashonaland, 31 March 1906, CO 603/7.

112. Taberer, *SANAC Report* 4:35.

113. Sikombo noted the problem of reserves in Matabeleland when he was interviewed by the SANAC (*SANAC Report* 4:160). Already in 1904, before the expropriations of the Lands Commission, he was able to say, "I cannot find a Government Reserve. . . . It appears that all the country is occupied by farmers . . . whatever land they have pointed out to me has been unsuitable. . . ."

114. Taylor, Report of the CNC, Matabeleland, 1905, CO 603/7.

115. Taylor, Report of the CNC, Matabeleland, 1906, CO 603/7.

116. NC Sebungwe, Annual Report, 1899, NAZ NB 6/1/2. Part of the suspicion arose from the history of traders passing themselves off as government officials and extorting goods and services as "taxes."

117. Taberer, Report of the CNC, Mashonaland, 31 March 1904, CO 603/5.

118. Taylor, Report of the CNC, Matabeleland, 1905, CO 603/5.

119. Col. Grey, *Legislative Council Debates,* 1899:6; emphasis added.

120. P. R. Frames, *Legislative Council Debates,* 1902:113. Note that Legislative debates are recorded in a form which purports to be verbatim, but moves all statements from the first to the third person. Thus, the transcripts elided the *I* and *we* that settlers' representatives must have used constantly.

121. "The Passing Show," *Rhodesia Herald,* 26 October 1901.

122. *Black Peril* was a term commonly used for a white minority population's hysterical fear of rape or even voluntary sexual relationships between African men and European women. Most discussion of the issue, though, was not by women afraid of rape, but by men afraid for their wives and daughters. See Kennedy, *Islands of White.*

123. Haupt, Farmers' Association Meeting on the Native Question, *Rhodesia Herald,* 7 December 1901.

124. Napier, *Legislative Council Debates,* 1904:20. The most creative aspect of this argument was charging the expenses of the police force—a standing army—to the Africans' account, while not giving them credit for paying tariffs and other indirect taxes. When such accounting tricks were discounted, Africans were clearly being taxed at a level which more than supported the administrative structure that governed them. The tax was designed not merely to procure the revenue the administration needed, but also to force Africans into the labor market. When the BSAC treasurer, Newton, stated in a 1903 Legislative Council debate that the proposed "increase of taxation was . . . not on account of any labor considerations. There was no benevolent idea of impressing upon the natives anything in the way of dignity of labor or of inducing them to the mines. . . . The object of the legislation was a revenue one" (183), he was lying.

125. Henry James Deary (merchant, representative of Salisbury Chamber of Commerce, twelve years in Rhodesia), *SANAC Report* 4:50–51, 55.

126. Restrictions on labor recruitment, W. H. Brown asserted, were unwise because Africans "will interpret such policy as actuated by weakness and dictated by the fear of consequences." Mashonaland Farmers' Association Meeting, *Rhodesia Advertiser,* 7 November 1901.

127. Newton, *Legislative Council Debates,* 1903:183. Again, this is the settlers' version, not the historical reality.

128. "The inhabitants of this country will not, we imagine, tamely submit to such childish restrictions in the management of their local af-

fairs." "Exeter Hall Rampant," *Rhodesia Advertiser,* 7 November 1901.

129. "The ignorant mob that persists in venerating an ideal of the kafir races is set to ride colonists to their destruction." "The Passing Show," *Rhodesia Herald,* 26 October 1901.

130. "No amount of explanation, refutation, or any form of argument has any force with these mulish people. . . . Squash one and a dozen take his place . . . wilfully blind, as to commit themselves to such stupendous folly. . . ." Editorial, *Rhodesia Advertiser,* 7 November 1901.

131. H. J. Deary, *SANAC Report* 4:60. Deary's statement was fully in accord with the concept of the Native Question as put forward by the *Bulawayo Chronicle.* See, for example, "Natives and Education," *Bulawayo Chronicle,* 24 September 1904.

132. Deary, *SANAC Report* 4:53–54.

133. Napier, *SANAC Report* 4:168.

134. Wilkerson, (LMS) Industrial Institution, Hope Fountain Annual Report for 1900, CWM 3/1. He noted that his African students had completed a building at half the cost of the architect's estimate. "Skilled [African] labour is not liked in Bulawayo. . . . Natives are not allowed to use tools. Their place is to do the unskilled work." Wilkerson taught bound apprentices through a three-year training course. He did not claim to train master artisans, but "good, reliable, punctual, tidy working lads"—complete with tools.

135. For example, Napier (*SANAC Report* 4:167) mentioned two or three unaffiliated African teachers on his land alone, teachers who may have been one source of the widespread knowledge of the law and its limitations that settlers report on sporadically during these years. For example, Grey (*Legislative Council Debates,* December 1907:18) argued for revision of Native Department codes on the basis that NCs lacked the power to "compel the native to attend," and was therefore often ignored, as their subjects realized their threats were meaningless.

136. Napier, *Legislative Council Debates,* 1904:20.

137. Holland, *Legislative Council Debates,* 1904:21.

138. W. H. Brown was one of the first to pronounce on this subject when, in 1902, he declared that it was "nothing short of criminal to spend money and waste good talent on the education of blacks so long as one white child in Rhodesia is left without a means of education." Farmers' Association meeting, *Rhodesia Herald,* 10 May 1901. Duthie, the administration's director of education, was particularly worried about some cases in Melsetter, where rural European children of Dutch ancestry were growing up illiterate, among the highest concentration of effective mission schools in the region. ". . . we found the very extraordinary circumstance," he reported, "that sometimes whites appealed to Natives to read their letters for them." Duthie, *SANAC Report* 4:141.

139. Napier, *Legislative Council Debates,* 1904:20.

140. *Rhodesia Herald,* 4 January 1902.

141. "Educating the Native," *Bulawayo Chronicle,* 21 July 1906.

142. For example, editorial, *Rhodesia Advertiser,* 13 March 1902.

143. Kennedy, *Islands of White,* 142–44. "In one case, an African man and a European woman collided on a dark Umtali street at night; in the other, an ex-servant broke into the home of a lone white woman to . . . steal food."

144. Holland, *Legislative Council Debates,* 1902:115.

145. P. R. Frames, *Legislative Council Debates,* 1902:113.

CHAPTER FOUR

Disciplining Change

NATIVE POLICY AND NATIVE EDUCATION, 1903–1915

By 1907 some settlers and company officials were arguing that the policy of civilization had failed, and that Southern Rhodesia's laws—based in the formally race-blind codes of the Cape colony—would be inadequate until they distinguished Africans from Europeans, and developed into a distinct Native Policy.[1] In 1909 a vocal settler extended that argument, asserting that the European community should not blithely assume that progress was inevitable. In Southern Rhodesia, he asserted, the Native Department's native commissioners had "adopted the system of letting [the Africans] alone." But Africans were not becoming civilized employees and subjects of Europeans. They had been freed from a rule of tyranny, he contended, but instead of moving toward civilization, appeared to be staggering about aimlessly in a useless anarchy.[2]

Only a few years earlier, the SANAC report had resoundingly endorsed a policy of civilization and a concept of a future in which progress grew naturally from the harrowed field of a conquered Southern Africa. But Southern Rhodesians quickly found untenable such notions of natural progress. Change, they argued, was complex. Unconstrained by a coherent European-directed policy of control, African societies changed in unpredictable and disconcerting ways, becoming "useless and idle" rather than "disciplined" and "civilized."

Within the rapidly changing society and economy of Southern Rhodesia at the beginning of the twentieth century, any dominant ideal of social control or social planning would succeed only to the extent that it was able to cope with change. But as officials and settlers—whose theories of civilization and social change had postulated what Africans might become through a slow transformation over several thousand years—looked at the townships and settlements near them, they recognized that change was happening at a far greater speed than their theories of gradual civilization allowed for. The European sector of the economy was expanding and finally becoming at least marginally profitable as small mines proliferated, using capital more efficiently and pushing their workers hard, and settlers expanded their agricultural activities from cattle raising to maize and tobacco cultivation.[3] This expansion was accomplished by tripling the number of Africans employed by Europeans between 1904 and 1911.[4] In some areas, work for Europeans was becoming a common part of growing up. In others, African families were becoming major peasant producers of everything from maize to beer and chickens, which they sold at mining compounds and in towns, for cash.

As young men went off to work, women brewed beer for money, and families worked as economic firms, using the labor of women and girls to maximize cash crop production, officials feared that the social changes promoted by the policy of civilization were destroying the fabric of African society faster than new structures of control and discipline could be built. Settlers worried that systematic race-based social and economic differences, which they had sought to reinforce through a classification of whites as civilized and Africans as barbarians, were eroding into a messy Native Question posed by European "degeneration" and African "advances."[5] Missionaries who had put the time of equality safely into the distant future in their statements before the South African Native Affairs Commission of 1903–5 suddenly found themselves confronted with African demands for education in Manicaland and some areas of Matabeleland. Headmen requested that schools be opened for their children, and children and young men flocked to overcrowded and understaffed schools in a mass movement which looked capable of spreading to other regions and transforming a substantial fraction of the upcoming generation in decades, or even years, rather than centuries.

In the aftermath of the 1896–97 Risings, European discussions of civilization had conceptualized change as an inevitable, unilinear process. But when that change became imminent rather than a nebulous future prospect, worried Europeans began to reevaluate the inevitability of change and civilization and to ask whether official policies should promote it, manage and direct it, or slow and contain it. The process of civilization, with an ideal of individualism and a theoretical possibility that Africans could learn European culture, enter a formally race-blind power structure, and gain access to wages, capital, and markets, had policy implications intolerable to many Europeans. Within this rapidly changing society, the transformative ideal of civilization proved to be a liberal thesis of individual progress provoking a conservative antithesis of discipline and the preservation of communities. Concepts of civilization had provided useful cognitive frameworks for the Africans, missionaries, officials, and settlers who sought to organize their perceptions and discussions of the region and its possibilities. But the policy implications of these ideas lost favor as Europeans increasingly saw the promotion of "progress" or civilization as the policy equivalent of turning on a fan to provide winds of social change in the midst of a hurricane of social destabilization and reconstruction.

By 1911 ideas of civilization, and the new opportunities they had offered for individual Africans to learn European culture, and participate in the European sector of the economy, threatened the cohesion of the African society and the tidy line settlers had sought to draw between the civilization of the Europeans and the savagery or barbarism of the African masses. The relations between Africans and Europeans were a political flashpoint for the Native Department, which was still haunted by the 1896–97 Risings and had been reminded of potential problems by the 1906 unrest in Natal, to which education and the strength of mission communities may have been a contributing factor.[6] In this atmosphere of threat, officials, settlers, and eventually even missionaries questioned the ideology of civilization and began to seek a model of directed, modulated change opposed to previous unilinear models of social progress toward the heights of civilization. Facing an African population increasingly able to move from region to region, to learn, and, potentially, to vote, Europeans began to develop a multilinear model of social change in which a directive Native Policy, a state-controlled system of Native Education, and an officially promoted policy for the "development" of Native Reserves would offer policy mechanisms through which the social architecture of social planning and social control could be designed and implemented.

The Official Order

In the early years of the twentieth century, the Native Department ruled abruptly, choosing to break down African authorities to make way for European-led change rather than to work toward indirect rule. The department's primary concerns were preventing resistance, maintaining order, collecting taxes, and extracting labor and agricultural resources. Its officials initially worried more about results than methods. Native Department officials during the early years argued that demands and violence were the only languages Africans expected from their rulers. Occasionally, imperial oversight forced officials to moderate their activities, but restraint was more controversial than excess. In 1903, after an assistant native commissioner, J. H. Williams, was fired for "lawlessness combined with personal violence,"[7] his superiors in the Native Department and the administration defended his actions. Williams had combined arbitrary judicial intervention, for which he lacked any legal authority, with floggings, forcible labor recruiting, and massive illegal cattle dealing. He also admitted to frequently "reprimanding" Gutu, a paramount chief, for "not behaving as a paramount should."[8] The charges were basically true, admitted the chief native commissioner for Mashonaland, but "Mr. Williams has hitherto performed his duties to my entire satisfaction. . . ."[9] The BSAC administrator echoed this sentiment, noting that, in the past, "Williams has undoubtedly rendered good service . . . and his districts have always been found in good order." The administrator believed "that he [Williams] acted in what he considered to be the interests of the natives."[10] The administrator agreed to Williams' dismissal only with reluctance. Williams had done violence to individuals, through beatings, but his actions expressed more than contempt for Africans as individuals. In setting himself, a junior employee of the Native Department, above established leaders such as Gutu, a "paramount chief," he did violence to the fabric of an African social order in which the young were expected to defer to their elders. But in disciplining Gutu, Williams was unexceptional. In 1906, when the NC Insiza reported disturbing allegations against his neighbor the NC Belingwe, of cruelty and maladministration, the NC Belingwe, de Laessoe, defended himself by arguing that while it was true that he had, illegally, used corporal punishment, so had every other native commissioner in Southern Rhodesia.[11] He had been sent to that troublesome district, he and his supporters argued, because the local chief, Maduna, had been troublesome, and the CNC of Matabeleland had felt a firm hand advisable.[12] He had given that firm hand, successfully enough that the European residents of the region petitioned the department in his defense, and the attorney general, even after hearing the evidence, argued that while de Laessoe "has undoubtedly transgressed the limits of recognised methods of administration," he was nevertheless "a thoroughly conscientous and painstaking official, a man of intelligence and attainments quite beyond the ordinary and a man who has the interests of the country and its people thoroughly at heart . . . assuming an interest in the general progress of the territory quite beyond the average official. He is a man, I think, who could ill be spared."[13] Maduna, feeling the erosion of his power as de Laessoe seized control, had, according to de Laessoe's defenders, framed the NC by encouraging false charges.[14]

The Native Department actively laid down rules for the customary leadership: it informed indunas in Matabeleland of their duties as subgovernmental officials and it maneuvered the administrative structures of the Mashonaland Native Department to curb, direct, and supersede African leaders.[15]

Education, like the Native Department's administrative policy, functioned in those early years as a wrecking ball swung at the structure of customary society—notable for its existence rather than its content. Before the 1907 Education Ordinance, Education Department officials, though technically responsible for African education as well as the education of Europeans, paid little attention to the activities of mission schools for Africans.[16] And when the Native Department officials commented on the spread of education, they were not observing schooling, but an unofficial, amorphous, and acephalous social movement. Officials saw education as a component of the spread of civilization—a natural outcome of any sort of contact between Africans and Europeans. Schooling was a luxury. Experience as a paid laborer, which taught deference, time discipline and only rudimentary skills, educated an African quite satisfactorily, from the point of view of the Native Department.[17] The laws in effect before 1907 reflected that perception of education as a social process rather than an organized activity affected by administrative policy. Schools for Africans were operated by missionaries or Africans, not by the administration.[18] And though government grants for education existed for schools that educated Africans, the grants were prohibitively difficult to qualify for. In the year before the new rules went into effect, only three schools for Africans received any governmental funding whatsoever: Chishawasha (Jesuit), Mt. Silinda (American Board), and St. Augustine's, Penhalonga (Church of England).[19] To qualify for those minimal grants, schools for Africans had to meet standards of consistent attendance, systematic industrial education, the teaching of English, and numbers of students. Meeting such standards was expensive. Consistent attendance proved achievable only through boarding schools. Industrial education required equipment and trained teachers beyond the means of an underfunded mission.[20] And English-language training required European or Black South African teachers since during these early years few if any Shona or Ndebele teachers had enough knowledge of English to teach it, and, except for nuns, few European missionaries were willing to get involved in detailed classroom work except by supervising teachers.[21] None of these requirements was easy for a small school to meet. Thus small schools, such as those of the Seventh Day Adventists or the London Missionary Society, could not qualify for grants even for the students who boarded at the mission, were subject to industrial training, and were educated in English.[22] The Department of Education strenuously ignored African education, refusing to send inspectors to schools that probably met the conditions of the 1899 ordinance, and visiting none of the schools for Africans for months at a time, despite massive expansions at St. Augustine's and the American Board's schools and a proliferation of smaller day schools throughout much of the region.[23]

Native Department officials took little more notice of these schools than Education Department inspectors had. NCs reported on education as a movement that affected social relations and political authority within the regions they supervised. But they did not try to follow the rapid change of educational opportunities as teachers itinerated, schools flourished or folded, and education became a popular demand among young Africans.[24] The ephemeral schools and the spreading movement to education were not under control by officials of the Education Department or the Native Department, who merely observed, bemused, as Africans taught each other what they had gleaned from their contacts with European culture. Hymns and Bible stories featured prominently in these descriptions—as prominently as literacy, numeracy, or English comprehension. One native commissioner mocked the itinerant teachers' retelling of Bible stories, and another observed that Africans have made up their minds to be educated. They do not quite know what education is, but they have made up their minds to become the same as the white people. For instance, you never hear such a thing as a Kaffir song sung; it is always a Kafir hymn, not because of there being something sacred in the hymn, but because they think that is a step nearer. Their next step is to get a book. Nearly every young Native in the whole country has some sort of book, and they acquire a lot of very useless knowledge; the tonic sol-fa system, and that sort of thing, but nothing can stop their thirst for knowledge. . . ."[25]

The curriculum of the early schools was eclectic rather than systematic, and officials might complain or mock, but they took no action.

Regardless of the actual usefulness or attractiveness of the curriculum—and some of the students making up the large enrollments at Chishawasha or Mt. Silinda were secured through compulsory education rules, rather than voluntary enrollment by interested students—education provided young men and women with an additional source of knowledge independent of the elders within the African community who would once have taught the young about the world. This new curriculum emphasized European concepts of individualism and civilization and trained students in the basics of a world which had changed in the years since their parents' education. In 1904, J. W. Posselt, a thoughtful native commissioner, was already asking,

> what is the ultimate fate of a Mashona educated beyond his sphere? His kraal traditions and points of view have been cut from under him; he heartily despises such of his own kith and kin as have not attained his level of civilization; and yet, betwixt him and the white man there continues to be a great gulf fixed . . . can it then be wondered at that the inevitable result of such education is evil rather than good?[26]

Dissention, Posselt and others began to suspect, was the outcome of a civilizing education in a society that was cut through by a color bar and characterized by cultural differences. Young men used their knowledge of the changing world, and the wages they could earn, to challenge parental authority.[27] Young women rejected marriages intended to cement social ties or facilitate the repayment of loans, justifying their actions with mission-sponsored ideas of individual autonomy and choice, and taking shelter with missionaries.[28] Young men offered their labor outside the community during their most productive years, acquiring the resources for bridewealth without help from their fathers. Neither phenomenon was, in 1907, very significant in numbers. But with such decisions, these young people challenged the controls over reproduction and production built into the institutions of customary society.

The movement toward education provided both the schools that were the physical sites of conflict and the ideas and values that exacerbated tensions between generations. Decisions to found or attend schools were not matters that affected only individuals. They involved communities, and could be hard fought. Observing the conflicts over the establishment of a Seventh Day Adventist school near Gweru, an NC pointed out that "Educational establishments are not regarded with favour by the chiefs, headmen and elders, who consider they gain nothing by their children going to school. Native youths themselves are, as a rule, very fond of learning to read and write."[29] As schooling spread, more and more native commissioners found schools in their districts, multiplying social conflict and complicating the Native Department's responsibilities for order, tax collection, the extraction of labor and agricultural resources, and the prevention of resistance. Social stability was not automatic; it had to be produced and reproduced. Watching the conflicts surrounding education proliferate, officials ended their lack of involvement in education. Social anarchy would make profitable administration difficult.[30]

By 1908 the administration was no longer cavalier toward Native Policy or education. The chief native commissioners began to see hazards in the challenges the earlier promotion of social change had made to customary authorities, as those authorities increasingly lost their ability to supervise or control the young men and women of the region. The first signs of the new attitude emerged in Matabeleland, the region experiencing the most rapid social and economic change. In 1907 CNC Taylor reported an alarming increase in syphilis among Africans near mines and a weakening of parental authority as children defied their parents and flocked to schools.[31] Furthermore, the mobility of men made tax assessment difficult, and the mobility of women threatened the reproductive and agricultural economies.[32]

By the end of 1907, Taylor was seeking ways to shape the rapid changes in his territory. Progress and change were uneven and potentially destabilizing: rapid in some areas, but not always "on legitimate lines." Tentatively, he began to call for a rethinking of Native Policy. With Taberer, the Chief Native Commissioner of Mashonaland, Taylor's Native Department put official emphasis on designing the future by strengthening native commissioners, allying the department with the customary leadership, and striving to discipline the upcoming generation into more amenable subjects. Taylor believed that the time had come for an active "guiding hand of a sympathetic and paternal Government."[33]

The Native Department sought to expand the power of native commissioners, giving them a magistrate's ability to judge and punish.[34] Ideally, this would improve the image of native commissioners among those Africans and Europeans worried about order and administration by giving them something solid to do other than collect taxes. Real powers to supervise and control—as opposed to the nebulous powers and duties they held as the designated representatives of a paternalistic imperial government—should make them relevant local authorities.[35] Intensifying the government of Africans required more than just the empowerment of native commissioners, though. Taylor proposed a new strategic alliance between the Native Department and the customary leadership. The chiefs, he argued, had proven worthy of trust and could therefore be safely given new responsibilities, improving the efficiency of the native administration.[36] The Native Affairs Committee of Enquiry of 1910 approved this scheme, echoing its witnesses in a new support for some form of "tribal control" as

> the system is a considerable aid to administration in the investigation of crime, the maintaining of order, and the collection of revenue: and . . . in fact, without the assistance at present rendered by chiefs and headmen, it would be necessary considerably to increase the police force of the territory . . . the authority of the chiefs and headmen [should] be fully recognised as a necessary element in administration, and all chiefs [should] be subsidised, in order to fix definitely their status and responsibilities.[37]

The Native Affairs Report even suggested that the Shona system for inheritance of chiefship (collateral succession) be modified to a Ndebele variant of primogeniture to permit younger, more vigorous inheritors rather than the often elderly brothers of the deceased chief.[38] Seeing disintegration, the 1910 committee backed the Native Department's efforts to develop a Native Policy that cultivated order by yoking firmly allied and bureaucratized African leaders to the increasing power of the native commissioners.[39]

In their 1907 reports, both Taylor and the CNC Mashonaland, Taberer, wrote of Europeans as the primary agents of change, but by 1909 both saw change as acquiring a new momentum from what Tayor described as a lack of authority within African societies as the structures that had promoted order disintegrated, opening up local societies to the pressures of the region's developing economy. This new dynamic of change offered the imminent threat of anarchy, endangering orderly and disciplined progress. Taylor emphasized that

> the transition of the native from barbarism to civilization is becoming more rapid every year. . . . The time has now arrived when we should adopt a more forward policy in our administration of the natives—a policy embracing prudence and moderation.[40]

A policy of prudence and moderation was, for both Taylor and Taberer, a policy of guided, controlled change antithetical to earlier wholesale attempts to promote civilization by ordering African authorities around. Instead of promoting challengers to customary authority, or encouraging young people to flee from the reserves to the compounds, the Native Department increasingly sought to ensure order through reforms in Native Policy, and to rephrase the language of civilization into a language of discipline.

Nowhere was the emphasis on supervision and discipline stronger than in discussions of education. Education could be dangerous, Taylor emphasized. He reported that Africans sought education avidly,

> and I have been approached on several occasions by chiefs asking that assistance might be afforded them by sending teachers to their kraals. [But] I do not think it is possible for the raw native to understand the object and effect of education. He is liable to take a mistaken view of it, and I am inclined to think it is the duty of the Government to guide the native in the right direction. This can best be accomplished by state supervision, and by making it compulsory for all native schools . . . to comply with . . . the Education Ordinance and to include industrial training in their curriculum.[41]

"Raw natives," Taylor implied, did not understand the dangers to their own communities of raising up a young generation educated in dubious directions. Achieving new heights of paternalism, the Native Department began to take a conservationist's interest in the maintenance of hierarchical social relations within African communities.

And in asking for education, Africans were not merely endangering their own communities; they also challenged the hierarchical relationship between communities. Taylor's worst fear was of the schools operated by the African Methodist Episcopal Church, a denomination that was "known to confuse political propaganda with religious teaching, and is a dangerous influence on the good relations existing between the Europeans and natives."[42]

The Education Ordinance of 1907 established a new level of administrative supervision and control over schools for Africans.[43] The administration wanted European oversight and trained teachers to enforce its ideals of orderly classrooms and the industrial virtues of consistent attendance and cleanliness. In response to these demands, the Education Department, which had previously devoted itself almost exclusively to the education of European children, developed a policy for African education, and the beginnings of the inspection force that would attempt to ensure that the social movement of Africans to education would train Africans in the disciplines of the workplace.[44]

The administration's decision to move toward enforcing regulations requiring industrial education and to promote the development of a trained force of teachers did not, however, translate instantly into a reality. Industrial education remained expensive, and was made more so for the missions through the Education Department's insistence that it be taught by certified European teachers, expensive despite the department's partial salary grants. And providing teachers for the schools became a major problem. Though the Education Department consistently suggested to mission stations that they expand their European teaching force, staffing at all mission stations was sparse, and European teachers were far too expensive.

Most of the teaching was, inevitably, done by African teachers, and it took the mission societies years to develop even marginally adequate teacher training programs.[45] And while the Education Department deplored the standards of this teaching, the Native

Department worried about the possibility that teachers might form an educated, white-collar African elite. Taylor asserted that teachers who would "ultimately have in their charge a large number of native children" should be trained to avoid "the acknowledged mistakes in the training of native teachers in other Colonies." They should spend "a considerable proportion of time" in industrial training, not just academic work.[46] Ideally, they would learn enough to teach, but remain uncritical enough to be obedient to mission school superintendents, Education Department school inspectors, chiefs, and native commissioners. Taylor's model was the industrially disciplined but academically inferior teacher training of the American Hampton-Tuskegee model.[47] Teachers, avoiding the "acknowledged mistakes," would be trained in humility. And the administration wanted those humble teachers to teach the African children of Southern Rhodesia obedience rather than innovation.

Without administrative supervision, the movement toward education might have treated Africans as individuals—capable, like untutored European children, of learning the knowledge and skills to comprehend the European culture and economy and to move within the European sphere as equals. Some early schools were racially integrated, and others put forward highly progressive curricula.[48] But schooling of the sort proposed by the ordinance focused not on knowledge, but on discipline: the temporal discipline of attendance, the bodily discipline of cleanliness and labor, and the intellectual discipline of rote learning and automatic obedience.[49] Missionaries were informed that they should train (not educate) teachers, establish them in proper schools, and inspect them frequently enough to ensure that the teaching remained orthodox and the students disciplined. Under the ordinance, schools were divided into three types: first-class schools, which were boarding schools with European teachers, with at least two hours a day of industrial training, and some rudimentary instruction in English within a total school day of at least four hours (including the industrial time); second-class schools, which were day schools with European teachers and the standards of first-class schools; and third-class, or kraal, schools. Kraal schools gave would-be inspectors the most difficulty, as they were by definition located away from mission stations, and run by African teachers who taught a rudimentary curriculum and little, if any, industrial education.[50] The regulation of education, however, was not oriented to ensuring academic training. No regulations spelled out how many hours were to be spent on reading, or testing standards for basic arithmetic. The standards were disciplinary, specifying numbers of hours of industrial training, necessary levels of attendance, and "discipline and cleanliness." The intent was to train Africans into obedience and reliability as subjects of the settler state and employees of a European-directed economy.

Official concern over the perceived disintegration of African society increased from 1907, when the Legislative Council passed the new Education Ordinance, through the high commissioner's visit in 1909, to 1910, when the Native Affairs Committee of Enquiry (NACE) was set to work on its report. In 1907, official commentary on social disintegration had been limited to the Native Department. But when Ndebele leaders protested the Native Department and the government of Southern Rhodesia in 1909, turning high commissioner Lord Selborne's indaba with Ndebele leaders into a symbolic fiasco for the Native Department, the Ndebele delegation focused the attention of the entire European community, official and settler alike, on the vexed question of Native Policy, and the maintenance of order amid social change. Lord Selborne's indaba with leaders of the Ndebele community was held in Bulawayo in November 1909 as a part of his formal visit to Southern Rhodesia. In meeting with the leaders, he was to some degree reenacting the Rhodes indaba, which ended in a cease fire for the Ndebele in 1896, but more significantly, he was holding a practical meeting, seeking to assert the alliance between the African leadership and the government of the region and to give the African leadership the opportunity to affirm its loyalty to British overlordship. Unlike some colonial displays, this meeting was not a carefully scripted ceremonial, and it provided the opportunity for Ndebele leaders to show precisely how dissatisfied they were with the protection of the Native Department and the imperial government. With Sikombo, a prominent leader, doing much of the talking, the Ndebele leaders put forward both sociopolitical and economic grievances.

The sociopolitical grievances revolved around the colonial destabilization of the Ndebele state and Ndebele society. Sikombo asked that the son of Lobengula be returned to the region as the head of the Ndebele people. He emphasized that the pass laws made it impossible to carry on normal social interactions, as it was not possible to go out of the home kraal without being stopped by a policeman. And another induna argued that the leaders were being restricted to the point of powerlessness, unable even to "chastise their wives" as "on the slightest provocation, the [wives] hurried off to the nearest police office!"[51] Furthermore, the leaders argued, the economic base of their authority was being eroded by European encroachment just as severely as was their sociopolitical authority. Their cattle were impounded, and the land crisis was acute. With the relocations as European farmers forced Africans off the land, these leaders feared that the only thing left for them to do was starve, as they were destitute.[52] Seeing a crisis too severe for mere platitudes, one of the spokesmen stated that "they were all very pleased to see his excellency, but they would continue to die, nonetheless."[53] The rhetorical alliance between the African leadership and the European authorities, they emphasized, needed to be backed by action.

Lord Selborne listened, but refused every request. Acutely tactless, he then demanded the royal salute which would have been a statement by the Ndebele leaders that they approved British rule. They refused to provide that salute, explaining that the high commissioner, as the representative of the British crown, was not entitled to it. He was not a member of the royal lineage, Kumalo, and was not acting as the head of the Ndebele. Within an increasingly tense atmosphere, it took a threat from the high commissioner, several speeches by officials, and the intervention of a "town boy," before the leaders could be persuaded, half an hour later, to offer the royal salute, "Bayete." Later, some of the older leaders visited the CNC and expressed "contrition at what had occurred," blaming the protest action on the young men.[54]

The incident showed just how uncomfortable Africans' unified protest—even peaceful, unsustained, unified protest—could make the Native Department and the Europeans of the region. Preventing such unified resistance through social atomization and the promotion of individualism had been one of the original purposes of the civilization policy. But this episode also showed that European officials could rely on neither customary African leaders nor educated young men as automatic allies for the native administration. The protest had been phrased in terms of customary demands: the return of Lobengula's heir, the limitation of the royal salute to the Kumalo family, and the emphasis on the royal responsibility to provide land for obedient subjects. But at least some of its leaders had been the most educated and acculturated Africans of the region, including "town boys" and Mfengu immigrants, who had demanded preferential treatment on the grounds of superior education and civilization.[55]

The incident highlighted the sociopolitical and economic crisis within the African community, as the elders claimed inability to control the young or, indeed, to prevent them from starving. The chief native commissioner, commenting on that incident and the other events of 1909, emphasized that the system of chiefs and customary control must be used, and enforced, or it would be lost. There was a "tendency of the natives to break away from tribal control" despite the fact that

> according to all recognised rules governing the natives, the chiefs are the medium between the Government and their people. They are the mouthpieces of the people, and all questions relating to their welfare are voiced by them, through the proper channel.[56]

The earlier, essentially negative and disruptive, policies of civilization and labor recruitment, which emphasized individuation, training in European culture, and capitalistic materialism, vanished in the face of such a threat to social order. Taylor did not believe that the civilizing process could be fully halted, but he did advocate an increasingly active policy of control that would enable native commissioners to act to supervise and control the changing society. And as long as traditional authority and the leadership of the chiefs survived, he advocated using them. The increasing inability of those authorities to control the aspects of society that mattered to the developing European-dominated economy and society forced Taylor to recognize that the contemporary, haphazard system of government and social design was unstable and untenable, useful only in the short term as the region engaged in a massive project of social architecture to design a more manageable balance of power. For the future, Taylor emphasized that the administration had a duty to guide the education that was, increasingly, shaping Africans.[57] Officially, the administration sought to manage change through an authoritarian Native Policy governed by a supervising native commissioner in alliance with customary authorities working to promote social control, and through an education policy that cultivated discipline.

Settler Fears

Settlers, afraid from the beginning of the century that a policy of civilization might erode distinctions between the European community and a growing class of educated Africans, were even quicker than the administration to realize the dangers of competition inherent in the translation of the ideas of civilization into the legislation, funding, and institution building of policy. And in the context of the early twentieth century, settlers steadily increased their influence within, and power over, the complex politics and economics of the region.[58] That ascendancy, relative to the Company and the imperial government, increasingly provided them with the power they needed to design a racially hierarchical society, in opposition to the cultural hierarchy implied in developmental and teleological notions of civilization. By 1904, in their compulsive interest in the Russo-Japanese War, settlers who followed the cable news as Asian Japanese thoroughly defeated European Russians saw what they feared might be the fate of their own community. Japan's rise, the *Bulawayo Chronicle* argued, provided a cautionary tale:

> . . . there has occurred very recently in Japan what, in a former age, would have been explained away as a miracle. Within a generation we have seen a race that was regarded as a medieval society of no importance undergo such a change as has placed it amongst the great nations of the world. . . . In view of such a phenomenon, who shall say that anything is impossible in history?

The article went on to emphasize the causes of this miracle and to link the threat of "native progress" more closely to southern Africa: Japan's rise, it argued, was caused by

> the grafting of a western education upon an intense national spirit. . . . Amongst the teeming native population of South Africa there is growing up just such a desire for a greater share in the knowledge which is seen to be the chief strength of the whitemen . . . the natives are now realising that it is not what a man believes but what he knows and can do which makes him a power and brings him the good things of this present existence.

That Western education, the article asserted, laid the groundwork for "a racial problem which shall put the similar one of the Southern States of North America completely in the shade."[59]

Fearing African progress, settlers shifted from a post-Risings support for African economic change to an increasing nervousness about the social consequences of that change. That nervousness was labeled the Native Question, and talked about, written about, and argued over incessantly. The label, *Native Question,* referred to the questions colonial development raised concerning what the role of Africans was to be in the changed and changing society. Settlers worried by the possibilities of change were not naive enough to believe that they could stop the economic, social, and political transformation of the region. Grudgingly, they admitted that change, transformative change, was inevitable as a result of the economic progress they had immigrated to the region to find. But settlers hoped to remain in control of the change and the society produced by that change through aggressive control over education.

The European settlers feared for the education of their children and the sustainability of a European domination based at least partially on control of educational capital and cultural knowledge.[60] In a territory where advanced education was unobtainable, the training of the next generation of businessmen, or gentlemen farmers, required expensive foreign study. And for the majority of young men, who would never attend university and left school by age fourteen, dominance was possible only if the jobs they could acquire, ranging from farming to carpentry to shopkeeping, were not equally obtainable by Africans. On this frontier of Southern Africa, educating the next generation for leadership and domination was not easy.[61] The European population was diffuse, scattered haphazardly over prohibitive distances. The most isolated families were likely to have the fewest resources available to devote to their children's education. The profitability of agriculture slid according to the difficulties of moving produce to markets, and mining tended to be scattered, with few European families at each small, marginal, and sometimes temporary mine. From 1900 to 1906, with the region's economy on the skids, European families found it increasingly difficult to pay for their children's education.[62] And part of the population was Dutch-speaking, not literate in English, and, in some cases, marginally literate in any language. These parents might place little value on education or be unable to teach their children more than the alphabet. The administration's educational resources were limited by its desire to show a profit and by the marginal profitability of the European enterprises that theoretically formed its tax base. Worse yet, with a scattered European population amid a vast African majority, and with weather that frequently tempted children to escape the classroom, educators contended that the African environment was inimical to the formation of healthy English characters through the rigors of proper British schooling.[63]

Concerned and patriotic British Southern Rhodesians viewed the situation with alarm and worried over the possibility of degeneration.[64] The fears evoked by this image of a degenerating European population and a progressive class of Africans shaped the development of educational policy in the region.[65] The conquest and rule of the region, settlers asserted, had been made possible at least partially because Europeans formed "a highly cultured community [that] possesses for our small population an extraordinary standard of education."[66] If European children were not being educated to maintain this standard, they would, under African pressure, be likely to lose their ability to rule.

Africans, after all, were rapidly demonstrating to a suspicious and increasingly fearful European population that they sought education and learned quickly. Already in 1904, the *Bulawayo Chronicle* was asserting, with fear, that Africans were "strong and virile . . . imitative, quick to learn, naturally vain and fond of power."[67] Discussion surrounded not whether Africans were able to learn, but whether it was advisable that they be taught and, if so, what the curriculum should consist of. The ease with which Africans learned was, indeed, a source of settler anxieties.

The fear of degeneration meant that Europeans, particularly upper-class Europeans, worried about the quality and universality of European education, and sought to channel resources into education as a crucial determinant of the region's future. W. H. Brown was one of the earliest speakers for the expansion of resources for European education when he argued that if the Dutch of Melsetter district were allowed to grow up illiterate they would become a serious regional problem, and he declared to the Mashonaland Farmers' Association in 1902 that

> it is one of the first duties of the Government that every white child should have the means provided for its education, and this should be compulsory, and in English . . . [It is] nothing short of criminal to spend money and waste good talent on the education of blacks so long as one white child in Rhodesia is left without a means of education.[68]

Brown was, however, soon joined by others as European education became one of the most popular demands of the settlers who spoke at Farmers' Association events or at public meetings.[69]

In 1906 concern over European education reached crisis proportions among settlers who read the Education Department's report and realized that government funding for schools had actually decreased from the previous year, despite increases in the number of students.[70] Over the course of the next year, the settler community sought to gather statistics to show the need for an expansion of educational resources for Europeans, and in May 1907, Col. Raleigh Grey confronted the administration with a resolution "that the present system of [European] education in Rhodesia is inadequate, and that immediate steps be taken to improve and enlarge the system in accordance with the growing needs of the country."[71] The statistics of education in the region worried him as they showed, he argued, that less than half the region's European children of school age were in school. Expansion would be expensive, he recognized, but "to teach the young of Rhodesia a knowledge and appreciation of their adopted country and also the sense of their responsibilities as future citizens of the British Empire was an object upon which neither time, trouble nor expense should be spared."[72] Grey spoke for a substantial constituency, and his resolution was intended to provoke the administration and promote discussion. It did both. The 1907 session of the Legislative Council passed a new Education Ordinance that provided the basis for an expansion in governmental support for education. Education funding—nearly all of which went to European education—which had declined from £6,481 for the budget year ending 31 March 1904 to hover around £5,500 for the next two years, went up to £7,943 for 1907 and advanced to £11,173 for 1908.[73]

The administration sought to manage European concerns for education through this expansion and through an Education Committee, which began its deliberations in January of 1908, under orders to weigh the possible against the necessary and to produce solid proposals regarding compulsory or free education for the European children of Rhodesia.[74] When it published its report in 1908, the committee emphasized the importance of primary education, asserting that "the first object to be aimed at is to bring within the reach of every European child the opportunity of acquiring a thorough grounding in the standards usually accepted as constituting the education which boys and girls up to the age of 14 ought to possess."[75] And the committee accepted that "the responsibility for providing these facilities is, in our opinion, a national one; it should be accepted as such by the Government, and the cost borne by the public exchequer."[76] Primary education, the committee argued, needed immediate government attention. Higher education should not be ignored, but could wait.

Yet despite this attention, Europeans continued to worry. The administration of Southern Rhodesia lacked the financial or organizational resources necessary to take the initiative in the expansion of education. Despite widespread support from legislators and the director of education as well as the Education Committee, primary education was not made free or compulsory in 1908, or, indeed, until 1930.[77] For settlers, the fact that a diminishing minority of European children continued to escape formal education remained a threat to the sustainability of European dominance in the economy, society, and polity of the region. Even relatively trivial snags in funding for European education sent up howls of protest from settler representatives in the Legislative Council. When the dormitories at Gwelo school were so full that boys and girls were within sixty to seventy feet of each other, an indignant legislator protested to the government that money was needed to build, and "the one department which they had no right to restrict was the Education Department," regardless of the severity of the government's financial crisis.[78] The representatives of the European community were willing to argue that the government should use both its coercive power and its financial resources to ensure that all European children received a respectable education. "It seems only right," argued an editorial, "not only in the interests of the children themselves, but in the interests of the whole country, that the many white children now running 'wild' and illiterate should be brought under regular school discipline and instruction."[79] Schooling was too important to continued European dominance for the settler community to feel comfortable about leaving it to individual choice. Poor whites might make the wrong choices. One prominent settler argued that

> we get a lot of people in Africa who are not fitted by desire, intelligence, or training to represent, even for a moment, a dominant race. . . . it ought to be possible to prevent by legislation the upbringing of white children in a state of ignorance or degradation. . . . Let us . . . insist upon the children of the unambitious or ignorant of our own colour being improved by the state.[80]

In the face of rising competition from Africans, "No matter," declared the *Bulawayo Chronicle* in 1911, "more vitally concerns the well-being and orderly development of a young country than . . . the instruction of its children."[81] The consistent failure of the administration to find the resources necessary to implement these pleas for universal, compulsory, and free education only increased European leaders' sense that their community was endangered by the prospect of educational decline.[82]

African education, however, appeared to settlers to be experiencing positively metastatic growth, growth that was beyond control by Europeans—be they missionaries, settlers, or officials—and dangerous to the stability of African society. Some Africans were demanding education and, through whatever means necessary, procuring it. Settlers were worried not merely by the existence of this education, but by the fact that it was under the control of Africans or, at best, missionaries, rather than the settler community or regional officials, over whom the settlers possessed increasing influence. Observers noted that at least a few Africans sought education, and some argued that Africans transformed their workplaces from sites of indoctrination in labor discipline to study halls in which they frequently abandoned paid labor to study to puzzle out books either by themselves or with the help of itinerant teachers.[83] Critics may have exaggerated the prevalence of education in labor compounds or servants' huts, but they did point to the threat that even a small class of educated Africans could pose to Europeans.

Africans who sought education, and educated others, in systems independent of European control threatened the conceptual delineation between the educated, civilized European and the ignorant, savage African by offering a model of educated African leadership. The pride and joy of an Anglican missionary was an African who, after studying at St. Augustine's mission in Penhalonga, went to work as a "police boy" at Ayrshire mine. He had "put up a hut for school and church and gives his spare time to teaching and preaching; and, being a police boy, he has the additional prestige of carrying a sjambok."[84] In this combination of education, religion, labor, and authority, he embodied the settlers' nightmares.

The independent and self-motivated "mission boys," who possessed skills and knowledge relevant to maneuvering within the European-directed economy and society, were feared by those Europeans who saw them as having the energy and education that sections of the European population lacked. As they were "more independent and inclined to approach the level of the white man," their education, initiative, and ambition "almost amounts to impertinence, which is absolutely intolerable."[85] Settlers rationalized their dislike by arguing that these men were not necessarily orthodox Christians in the sense of being subject to an established church. Religious education, they emphasized, was being spread by African teachers, and "the present system of allowing Native teachers to expound the Bible to a lot of raw Mashonas is ridiculous, not to say dangerous."[86] It led, critics asserted, not to converts, but to dishonest opportunists.[87]

Literate Africans possessed some concrete advantages in the expanding labor markets of Southern Rhodesia. In 1904 one farmer was already complaining that literate Africans had "the idea that they are too good for ordinary manual labour."[88] Instead, they formed a labor elite that included such trained workers as the "police boy" of the Ayrshire mine, the "office boys" of Salisbury or Bulawayo, or the construction workers that missionary industrial training produced. And that elite was not a mere figment of settlers' imaginations. Jonas Hlatywayo, a student of Mt. Silinda, reported that of the men who had been at school with him, all were employed or looking for work. He and another man had held relatively lucrative jobs as prison guards, two friends were working for the railway in Salisbury, and others (that he planned to join) held jobs in Selukwe.[89] Settlers could be disconcerted or infuriated when a former mission pupil came "to ask—in English—for work, dressed as often or not better than him from whom he seeks it . . . and wearing a hat which, of course, he is careful not to remove."[90] And literate African workers could, to at least a limited extent, write their own passes, which could allow them to move about the country illicitly seeking the most favorable labor conditions, or to expunge from their passes or testimonials the written record of disagreements with employers.[91] Literate Africans were also more likely than Africans unfamiliar with the way Europeans ran things to be aware that they had rights even within the minimally regulated labor law of Southern Rhodesia, and to appeal to the law when beaten or denied their pay. Since many European employers believed that their farms, mines, or businesses could not function without arbitrary authority over their employees, and since literate Africans could object to abuse not only of themselves but also of fellow workers, knowledge had the potential to disrupt the normal abusive course of labor relations.[92]

These "mission boys" threatened more than the deference required by the economic order of settler society. They also threatened the political ascendancy of the settler community. The threat was hardly immediate as, in 1905, there were only fifty-one registered African voters in all of Southern Rhodesia.[93] But the franchise law was based on that of the Cape Colony, without any race-based legal barrier to political participation. Furthermore, imperial authorities such as high commissioners Lord Milner and Lord Selborne emphasized that "if a black man raises himself to the level of the white, he should be accorded the same privileges."[94] Property and education qualifications for the franchise were low in Southern Rhodesia, designed to permit even marginally literate poor whites to vote, and observers worried that the fifty-one African voters would soon become a multitude because "with the spread of native education and the increased wages paid to unskilled labourers, it will be seen at once how slight the qualification really is."[95] At a time when settlers were only beginning to win political power away from the Company and the imperial government's oversight, they dreaded wresting power from London to Salisbury only to lose it within a few years to Africans. Politicians opposed attempts to limit the voting rolls through rises in property or educational qualification. Raising the voting qualifications would merely strike European voters from the rolls, and "why should the white man be penalised? This was a country in which the qualifications of the white man should be as low as possible"—or even approach universal suffrage for white Rhodesians.[96] Confronting the issue head on, and invoking the language of justice, a settler declared, to applause, that under the current political regime "the native has a right equal to myself. He has a right to vote and take any political status he likes, he has a right to return to Parliament and so forth. I say that is wrong."[97]

Settler fears of "mission boy" or "educated native" power in the economy and politics of settler society were not necessarily rational. Certainly the number of Africans falling into those categories before 1910 was minuscule.[98] Progressive Africans who acquired an acquaintance with the culture and economy of the European community might blur the delineation between settlers and Africans, but when the most elite and highly educated Africans ended their education with Standard IV, a level appropriate for a European twelve-year-old, distinct differences remained. Educated Africans had little direct effect on the hierarchical, racially ordered structure of settler society.

Settler society, though, could function effectively only when supported by a peaceable and subordinate African economy and society. By 1909 settlers were aware of the dangers offered to the customary African leadership by educated Africans, who were the embodiment of the new sources of authority and independence. And, the settlers argued, as the customary leadership was undermined, the African social order was threatened by anarchy.

In the immediate aftermath of the Risings, around the turn of the century, Europeans in Southern Rhodesia welcomed the ideas and ideology of civilization as strategies for subordinating the African economy and society to European needs. But by 1909 or 1910 settlers and, increasingly, the officials of the Native Department and the administration of Southern Rhodesia were confronting the problems inherent in the translation of ideas of civilization from philosophy to policy. As education, tax, and labor policies produced a group of "civilized" Africans—men and women broken loose from subordination to customary authority, familiar with the ground rules of European culture, and highly conversant with the opportunities and costs of participation in the European-directed capitalist economy of the region—the policies' costs became clear. Settlers and officials, and eventually missionaries and some Africans, called for a change in direction.

Mission Discipline

Missionaries were slower to abandon the ideals of civilization than either the officials or settlers. Missionaries were not, however, slow to begin to recognize the problems inherent in the translation of ideology to policy, or in their attempts to address the fears raised by officials and settlers. In response to those fears, missionaries moved from unilinear models of change, which sought to defuse competition by uniting Africans and Europeans as civilized people, toward a multilinear model. Within a multilinear model of social change, missionaries argued that they could promote African progress most effectively by promoting the construction of disciplined communities of African Christians who would be taught to accept duties and responsibilities rather than to enjoy the rights and opportunities of a humanistic and individualistic European civilization.

In 1906, during the Anglican Synod, missionaries were once again forced to face settler fears and skepticism when the week's editorial on the missionaries declared, the fact is that, as a rule, the educated native is not liked, is not trusted, and is not held in esteem as a servant. He has already established some slight reputation for forgery, and has frequently been known to tamper with his own and less educated brothers' passes. . . . His usual manner is one of careless disrespect. . . . the contrast between what is known as the "raw" native and the educated variety is commonly very much in favour of the former.[99]

The missionary response to such accusations—accusations aimed at the missionaries as the principal educators of the region—was to hold a public meeting on the subject that sought to delineate what was good education and what was bad.

This delineation between good and bad education was crucial because, by that 1906 synod, the missions had lost at least some of their faith in transformative conversions. Years of disappointments, of (at best) slow progress, had made them receptive to local settlers' negative characterizations of Africans. Negative characterizations of Africans had always been part of the stock of mission literature; the more dreadful the original state, the more glorious any change at all appeared, and early missionaries had taken full advantage of negative characterizations as a rhetorical device.[100]

The mission agenda revolved around the conversion, civilization, and, ultimately, transfiguration of Africans from a simple existence to a complete Christian life. What missionaries got was rapid social change of a sort they often found difficult to classify, led by both Europeans and Africans who proved far from perfect models of Christian sainthood. During the first decade of the twentieth century, occasional European missionaries became involved in various sorts of misconduct—including assault on students, illegal cattle dealing, and interracial adultery—that they could not want their charges to emulate. And even missionaries who did not become notorious among their colleagues for their misdeeds lived the lives of European settlers, relying on control over the lands of the mission station and employing Africans as construction workers, day labor, or domestic servants. With their materialism and their leisure, their ability to provide behavioral models was limited.

For expansion, missions relied on African teacher-evangelists. African teachers cost the missions less than European teachers and were more likely to speak local African languages fluently and to be accessible to the local population. These factors were undoubtedly important. But the evangelists were also important as role models for Christian converts. By living their lives, they were supposed to provide other Africans with a glimpse of the future that could be theirs if they converted to Christianity and followed the way of civilization. They also provided missionaries with living exemplars of the limits of perfectibility or change. Some missions, such as the American Board or the Anglican Society for the Propagation of the Gospel (SPG) imported evangelists from South Africa, recruiting from among Zulu or other South Africans who had experienced decades of mission activity. But, like European missionaries, African evangelists were far from perfect. And missionaries, who struggled to recruit evangelists, educate them, supervise them, and ensure that their lives reflected the appropriate standards of Christian moral and physical discipline, saw perhaps more clearly than anyone else in the region the limits of the transformative process. Too many evangelists, and other professed Christians, "fell."

Missionaries were careful to interpret those falls as individual, isolated events, rather than as indictments of the ideology of transformation. As a picture of the future, teacher-evangelists often functioned admirably, leading exemplary lives, accepting low pay, and enthusiastically teaching what they had learned. But there was always a potential for disaster that no missionary could afford to ignore. Missionaries had difficulty recruiting teachers, complaining from before the turn of the century that teachers were difficult to hire, both because of the minimal wages offered and because individuals with the requisite minimum of education were scarce.[101] And then there were the falls when those teachers rejected the missions' moral strictures.[102] Teachers or evangelists could be implicated by lack of activity as much as by specific misdeeds if their schools or congregations began to appear slack, lacking in discipline or vitality. Transforming Africans into obedient exemplars of mission morality, discipline, and enthusiasm was, at best, a difficult endeavor.

Missionaries realized that the teachers and teacher-evangelists were in a difficult position, with little more education than those they were supposed to teach, minimal salaries, and an ambiguously oppositional position within local society as they taught Christian concepts of marriage, rejected communities' attempts to protect themselves from witchcraft, or provided in their schools and churches an alternative source of community for the young people of the area. Disillusioned concerning the possibility of employing perfect teachers, missionaries became bluntly realistic. Teachers who repented after their falls were accepted back into the fold. When Ndonga, a head teacher for the LMS, was charged with and found guilty of molesting female pupils, his mission superiors were perfectly willing to accept him back, though he was told, "for the sake of example," to wait three months and reapply.[103] And the LMS was not the only missionary society to accept a policy of repentance and reinstatement after failings by its teachers. The Anglicans expressed pride in one of their teachers when "after one sad fall" he was working with both initiative and effect.[104] And the American Board accepted and negotiated with the teachers' organizations that rejected subservience by demanding better pay and fewer responsibilities.

Missionaries did more than just develop mechanisms to redeem the fallen, though. To the limits of their resources, they sought to develop systems of disciplined training that would engrain in the would-be teacher both faith and obedience. And they developed systems of supervision and control by central missionaries, usually European, over the evangelists in remote areas, systems designed to ensure that the discipline instilled by training did not yield to the inertia or temptations of the unsupervised setting. In the early twentieth century, missionaries moved from the hope that faith would transform the Africans into proper Christians to a belief that transformation could come only through the inculcation of a discipline that affected both mind and body, engraining time discipline and obedience into the mind, and work discipline and materialism into the body.

Missionaries chose their central schools as the sites of that training in discipline. The earliest mission schools had not sought to provide any sort of specific teachers' training, instead working for the more minimal goal of acquiring converts in the only way possible, by catching them young and training them up right. But with the early-twentieth-century expansion in African demands for education, it was clear to all the missions that a system of European-directed missions training boarders would never be able to expand sufficiently to meet Africans' demands, and the rivalry between various mission groups meant that none viewed without resentment and frustration the prospect of other mission organizations expanding and occupying territory they had hoped to evangelize. Teacher training was therefore high on the mission agenda before the government made even tentative provisions to fund it, and missionaries increasingly saw central institutions as the training grounds for a new African leadership cadre.

Discipline was the most important rallying cry of these schools in their search for a pattern of socially acceptable "good" education. Three schools received early official recognition: Chishawasha, St. Augustine's, and Mt. Silinda. All worked hard, using staffs of white missionaries that were, for the region, remarkably extensive, to achieve this discipline. Emphasis, though, varied from school to school. The Fathers of Chishawasha emphasized that Chishawasha was a farm, and potentially a profit-making enterprise, and pursued a disciplinary strategy similar in many ways to that of other employers in the region.[105] Children were recruited to Chishawasha through the expedient of compulsory education. Parents had to pledge to send their children to school as the price of remaining on mission lands.[106] Once held by the mission, they did not merely study, they worked. The Jesuits in Southern Rhodesia had a low opinion of book learning, asserting that while "we are by no means averse to teaching the Kaffirs to read and write," such teaching was complicated by

> the fact that even a very slight amount of learning is sufficient to turn their heads and spoil the characters of a good number. . . . caution should be exercised in cultivating their mental faculties. . . . The training which we are convinced they are ready to receive and profit by is that of the hands rather than that of the mind.[107]

Already in 1899 one observer of the bustling activity of the station reported, "At present they trust chiefly in incessant work. They say that if the children are not at work they are in mischief, so they are taught to read, to sing, to carpenter, and to garden."[108] By 1902 Father Richartz was able to write to the Inspector of Schools that the junior school had eighty boys, who were taught for four to five hours each day, learning oral English, Christian catechism, arithmetic, reading, writing, singing, band, and drill, and then put to industrial work in the gardens, the houses, or the craft workshops for an additional five hours each day. Older boys, more prone to difficulty with free time, were circumscribed even more tightly, being tutored in the same subjects, but with seven to eight hours each day of industrial work.[109] This strategy worked admirably to promote the image of Chishawasha to the settler community; Father Sykes noted proudly that while "a dead-set is being made in this country against so-called Christianised natives . . . *we* are exempted by practically all."[110] At Chishawasha, the students' hours were occupied, and they were removed from the "leisure" or laziness Europeans saw as characteristic of their home lives.

Planning work or study for all, or at least most, of the pupil's time was not a tactic limited to Chishawasha. St. Augustine's also required hours of work. Early supporters emphasized that "the most powerful work here is to get orphans, and to be allowed to bring them up in the way of Christian truth and *industry*."[111] And the school wanted to cultivate the reputation for work not merely among Europeans, but also among Africans, as a way of allowing potential students to accept before arrival that St. Augustine's was a place of labor as well as a school.[112] The leaders of the St. Augustine's mission sought to run a disciplined school according to a strict monastically inspired timetable that prescribed prayer, work, and study from matins at 6:30 A.M. to the 6:30 P.M. evensong.[113] Manual labor was important enough to the missionaries for them to insist emphatically on it even in the face of a student strike in 1901 and steady pressure for a greater ratio of literary education to the work of gardens or the thinly disguised unskilled labor of "industrial education."[114]

Anglican missionaries argued that labor was not merely, as at Chishawasha, a tactic for teaching obedience or preventing idle hands from finding mischief. It was a strategy for moral transformation, working on the body, through the timetable of prescribed hours and the physical training of agricultural or craft work, and on the mind, through the emphasis on discipline that pervaded both work and rote learning and the bracketing of work and education by prayer and reflection. St. Augustine's supplemented Chishawasha's strategy of exhausting the body to prevent youths from finding trouble with a school capable of exhausting the mind and leaving room for "habits of discipline, industry and respect" to form.[115]

Mt. Silinda, initially a racially integrated school, was less obsessed with either pupils' labor or strict discipline than the other schools receiving government funding before 1907. American Board missionaries actively complained of governmental policy. They objected vehemently to attempts to increase the taxes on Africans while decreasing to fourteen the age at which taxation began; complained in 1906 that though the schools at Chikore and Matangas had met the government's requirements, the government was refusing them grants; and noted that for some students, the mission provided a refuge from European mistreatment. Some unfortunate students, missionaries observed, arrived long distances from "where they were so badly treated and in such peril of imprisonment and from the lash that they made their escape to this place, which was to them a haven of rest where they could study without molestation."[116]

The American Board mission substantially rejected government policies that put industrial education in the place of literary education. But that did not mean it neglected to teach discipline or that it ignored industrial education. Its central school, Mt. Silinda, provided the most academically disciplined education available to Africans in early Southern Rhodesia. By 1899, Mt. Silinda was a graded school, with Africans separated into various classes according to their knowledge and classes that organized the student's school day into a series of twenty-minute recitations for different teachers on different subjects, punctuated by room changes.[117] And Mt. Silinda emphasized efficient training, stating as a goal that after less than a year's study, the student should learn and retain the ability to read the Bible in the vernacular.[118]

Discipline through labor was not ignored at Mt. Silinda; it was treated as something too serious to be dismissed by merely assigning schoolboys to make bricks, a frequent ploy elsewhere. Ironically, this academic stronghold probably had a higher proportion of industrial missionaries than any other mission station.[119] Mt. Silinda's industrial mission paid its workers, and expected serious labor from them. It was not fully integrated with the school, but it was perceived as a potential source of income where pupils could work, for wages, to earn the money to put themselves through school.[120] Instead of Chishawasha-style attempts to discipline students through intensive work, or St. Augustine's efforts to inculcate discipline through work and timetables, Mt. Silinda sought to discipline students through study and to teach them profitable work by putting them on the job, alongside day laborers, as paid workers. Students were supposed to work at their education, and work for it, as the mission insisted on higher academic standards than the rudimentary levels of most other schools, but refused to support special help for ambitious scholars lest "special privileges" be "injurious to the best development of character."[121] This policy encouraged students like Jonas Hlatywayo—who studied, then worked at a series of relatively lucrative jobs, and finally returned to teach for the mission—and, on an even more ambitious scale, such educational stars as Pambani—who returned to Southern Rhodesia in 1913 with a teaching certificate from Lovedale.[122] More than any other mission, Mt. Silinda turned out students who were not merely taught to work to exhaustion or to follow timetables, but who learned the self-discipline of study and the potential rewards of disciplined labor in the workplace.

Missionaries, constantly at watch over African teachers and evangelists, servants and students, were aware of the difficulties social change created for officials concerned with Native Policy and settlers worried about both the labor supply and the maintenance of European supremacy. They did not directly refute official fears of disorder or settler fears that Africans would cease to defer to Europeans if they became educated and espoused a religion that emphasized that all Christians were brothers and sisters together as the children of God. Missionaries responded to fears of social disintegration by emphasizing that education must be disciplined, training students in work and obedience to Christianity even as it offered them a way out of customary strictures. Missionaries, seeing the loss of control that rapid change brought with it, did not respond by attempting to hit the brakes. Attempting to halt change, they argued, would only lead to a loss of control as society skidded out of European control.[123] Instead, they advocated grabbing the initiative and accelerating into the future as the only way to pass through the difficulties on the way to their goal of a reordered Christian society. As schools provided a way for some children to escape their parents' discipline, the schools must discipline the children to a new, Christian, morality. Since undereducated teachers knew little more than their students, they must be taught. And when Africans demanded more money or better working conditions, missionaries sought to train them in skills that would make them productive workers well worth the extra wages.

Missionaries in the midst of rapid change sought the resources to achieve balanced and controlled change, not to halt that change. Rejecting unilinear notions of progress, in which social change led inevitably to a humanistic, individualistic, European-style civilization, they developed a concept of an alternative path forward, through a disciplined community of Christians steeped in obedience and duty rather than rights and freedoms. Within that cognitive framework, change continued to challenge Europeans, but missionaries could respond to the crises caused by the breakdown of customary authority, the increasing independence of women, and the commercialization of alcohol and sex, without sacrificing concepts of progress. Through discipline and Christianity, missionaries promoted a new African social order and a new basis for both the productive and reproductive economies. Missionaries could control and justify their support for social change through an emphasis on their cultivation of divergence.

Disorderly Transformations

The first decade of the twentieth century ended in a clamor for the management of change that brought the appointment in 1910 by the Legislative Council of a new Native Affairs Committee of Enquiry. This Southern Rhodesian committee, which contained the administration's attorney general, representatives of both mining and farming sectors of the settler community, and a native commissioner, was designed to look at the social, economic, and political implications of Africans' presence in a region that Europeans were increasingly occupying and exploiting. Unlike the earlier SANAC, this committee lacked any blithe assurance that contemporary difficulties were a mere stage on the road toward a new progressive civilization. Instead, the committee emphasized problems, arguing that

> the natives have degenerated in some respects, and that contact with civilization has had a retrograde effect. . . . This may be attributed largely to the weakening of tribal control which has resulted from a civilized system of government, and to the discouragement, which is inevitable, of time-honoured ceremonies which . . . have . . . played an important part in compelling respect for tribal, parental and marital authority. . . . it is questionable whether it is wise to suppress them suddenly. . . .[124]

The committee painted a bleak picture of a disintegrating society which lacked the strength to absorb the more positive features of the civilization with which it was in contact, and which therefore suffered from anomie, amorality, and a lack of discipline.

In drawing this picture, the committee argued that mere ideologies of civilization could no longer provide for the progress of either the African or European communities. Instead, the committee called for a reinculcation of social discipline through strengthened native commissioners, reempowerment of customary authorities, and the reimposition of family discipline through a reassertion of marital and parental control, or their new administrative replacements. The committee suggested that the Native Department intervene to strengthen customary authorities where they had lost power, modifying patterns of succession to assure strong heirs, and granting chiefs the power of acting as sole interlocutors between their communities and the European-directed state.[125] When husbands and the customary leadership could no longer control women, senior men were to be helped through the criminalization of adultery.[126] And if parents lost control of their adolescent children, officials were to ensure children's obedience by binding them into apprenticeship to an approved employer or industrial institution.[127]

The committee's report in 1911 represented the end of civilization as the dominant ideology of social transformation within Southern Rhodesia. Civilization, the committee argued, putting together previous criticisms, had proved incapable of providing for constructive and orderly change. It had wrecked customary African society, but no new, civilized African society was emerging from that wreckage. In observing that progress was not automatic, and that degeneration was possible, the committee's report provided a foundation for future policies of social architecture that presumed that the new society could not be an organically grown civilization, but must be planned and constructed, with architects and builders capable of considering not merely the destruction of previous social edifices, but the careful and coherent design and construction of future ones, from a foundation in an African society strong enough to support a superstructure of European design, to the bricks and mortar of mobilized economic resources and disciplined social relations. The committee's indictment of laissez faire attitudes toward social change cleared the way for the administration to develop a native policy emphasizing the Company state's reenforcement of discipline, for the settlers to advocate the active cultivation of racial difference, and for missionaries to strengthen and extend their efforts toward educating Africans in managed change toward a designed future.

NOTES

1. "To-day, the laws for the administration of natives were the laws which were applicable to the white race. There was no code of law for the native alone, and that was, he thought, a great mistake under which they laboured." Grey, *Legislative Council Debates* December 1907:18. Concretely, Grey proposed an expansion of Native Commissioners' powers, to encompass magistrates' judicial authority, and allow them to administer corporal punishment. He wanted native commissioners empowered to act as active and forceful labor recruiters, preaching "the Gospel of work" (p. 19). Grey's suggestions were seconded by Forbes, and Napier spoke in support of the resolution (pp. 17, 22-23).

2. Grey, *Legislative Council Debates* (1909): 75-81, 108.

3. Ian Phimister, *An Economic and Social History of Zimbabwe, 1890-1948* (London: Longman, 1988), 45-64; esp. 61. Between 1904 and 1911, Phimister notes, the number of European farms increased more than two and a half times, cultivated acreage expanded by a factor of four, and the quantity of maize harvested by a factor of more than eight. Tobacco, too, first became noticeable during those early years, though not in the quantities of the later boom.

4. Phimister, *Economic and Social History,* p. 61.

5. The very concept of a Native Question was and is highly political. See Adam Ashforth's argument that its construction was part of a political discourse to legitimate domination in South Africa. *The Politics of Official Discourse in Twentieth-Century South Africa* (Oxford: Clarendon Press, 1990), 1-21.

6. See the discussion of the Rising in Shula Marks, *Reluctant Rebellion: The 1906-8 Disturbances in Natal* (London: Oxford University Press, 1970), esp. 52-84, 307-37. Native Department officials compared Southern Rhodesia more frequently with Natal than with any other colony or territory, despite quite different laws and regulations. Many of the native commissioners were recruited from Natal, and some had even been born there and grown up speaking Zulu in families where their fathers were native commissioners (e.g., S. N. Jackson and H. M. Jackson). Mission societies also made comparisons, and drew many of their early evangelists and teachers from Natal (especially the Anglicans and the American Board), and a few European missionaries had been born there and grown up on mission reserves (e.g., G. Wilder of the American Board).

7. Clarke to High Commissioner Milner, 31 December 1902, CO 417/371/332-33.

8. J. H. Williams, deposition, 3 December 1902, CO 417/371; Clarke to HC Milner, 31 December 1902, CO 417/371/332-33.

9. W. W. Taberer to Administrator, 10 September 1902, CO 417/371.

10. Administrator Milton to HC, 24 December 1902, CO 417/371.

11. de Laessoe to Chief Secretary, 27 December 1906, NAZ A3/18/13.

12. H. J. Taylor, Report on Enquiry into NC Belingwe H. H. A. de Laessoe, 5 February 1907, NAZ A3/18/14. This was, he argued, the very kraal where the 1896 rising had first broken out, and it had never been adequately punished.

13. (Twenty signatures) European residents of Filabusi to CNC Bulawayo, 14 January 1907; and Attorney General, "Alleged administrative abuses by de Laessoe—Belingwe," NAZ A3/18/14. The attorney general adovcated a reprimand and a partial reduction in salary.

14. H. J. Taylor, Report on Enquiry into NC Belingwe H. H. A. de Laessoe, 5 February 1907; Attorney General, "Alleged Administrative Abuses," NAZ A3/18/14.

15. Minutes, Executive Council of Southern Rhodesia, 20 February 1902, CO 603/1; Report of the CNC Matabeleland, for the year ending 31 March 1901, CO 603/3; Report of the CNC, Mashonaland, for the year ending 31 March 1904, CO 603/5.

16. Wilder to ABC, 26 October 1905, ABC 15.4 vol. 28, item 252, commented bitterly on the difficulty of getting inspectors to visit schools: "it seems to be the policy of the government not even to visit any more schools, even though they may have filled all the conditions for obtaining a grant. The Chikore and Matanga schools have long been entitled to grants; but no amount of coaxing brings the inspector down to examine these schools." The Education Department's lack of interest was not merely a figment of the missionary imagination: annual reports of the inspectors of schools or the director of education (available from at least 1901 on; CO 603) include pages of information on schools for Europeans, but mere paragraphs on schools for Africans.

17. See, for example, the written evidence submitted by the future CNC of Southern Rhodesia, H. M. Jackson, then NC Fort Usher, *SANAC Report* 5:340-43; or NC Umtali and Inyanga, T. B. Hulley, *SANAC Report* 5:337-39.

18. The first government school for Africans, Domboshawa, did not open until after the First World War. It was joined by a second industrial institution at Tjolotjo, but that was, during the period under discussion, the entire extent of the government's school-building activity.

19. Report of the Director of Education (Duthie), for the year ending 31 March 1907, CO 603/7. Mt. Silinda and St. Augustine's received £60 each, Chishawasha received £50. This represented a level of funding unchanged from the previous year, and only a small fraction of the department's total education budget, which spent £5,371 on schools for European children. Note that the grants are insufficient to pay the salary and benefits of even one white teacher per school.

20. R. J. Challiss, "The Foundation of the Racially Segregated Educational System in Southern Rhodesia, 1890–1923, with Special Reference to the Education of Africans" (Ph.D. University of Zimbabwe, 1982), 28, argues that industrial education formed a powerful bar to the educational activities of underfunded missionary organizations.

21. The London Missionary Society, with its weblike configuration of central stations with numerous outstations operated by marginally literate catechist-teachers, had a particularly acute problem with this requirement, but the difficulty was widespread. Some non-British missions, such as the Dutch Reformed Church missionaries from South Africa or Catholics from France and Germany, had problems because even the missionaries did not speak English fluently.

22. A Seventh Day Adventist school in Gwelo (twenty-five boys and fifteen girls) received no grant, and the various schools of the London Missionary Society at Hope Fountain, Inyati, and Centenary were all too small or too erratic to qualify.

23. Wilder to ABC, 26 October 1905, ABC 15.4, vol. 28, item 252; Report of the Director of Education (Duthie) for the year ending 31 March 1907, CO 603/7. In Melsetter, both Chikore and Mt. Silinda were growing. Chikore in 1906–7 had an average daily attendance of eighty-seven, with over a hundred on the roll. Wilder, Chikore School Report, 17 June 1908, ABC 15.4, vol. 23, item 107. It received no funding. Mt. Silinda was grossly overcrowded by 1908, with classes forced out of doors from lack of classroom space, and an official enrollment of 172, many of them boarders who slept on the floors of missionaries' or teachers' kitchens, or crammed together in cattle sheds. Report of the Mt. Silinda School, June, 1908, ABC 15.4, vol. 23, item 155; Fuller to ABC 26 March 1908, ABC 15.4, vol. 25, item 185.

24. See Challiss, "Racially Segregated Educational System," 70–71, for a discussion of the ephemeral nature of some of the education of the region, and consequent limitations on the data for African-operated independent schools.

25. See, for example, Edwards' (NC Mrewa) complaint to the Southern African Native Affairs Commission (SANAC) 5:323–27, or H. M. Jackson's condemnation of singing, hymns, and the 'sol-fa' system, *SANAC Report* 4:186.

26. J. W. Posselt (NC Charter) *SANAC Report* 5:351–53. Posselt went on to become a notable segregationist, but he was one of the first to pose the education question seriously within the Southern Rhodesian context.

27. Direct evidence of these challenges, as opposed to generalized statements by Europeans, is scarce without the advantages of oral history research. The history of the young African men educated at the American Board missions is, however, suggestive. Not only did some of these young

men go to school, they even left the region, traveling to the Rand, to Natal, to Kimberly and even to Lovedale (possibly the top educational institution in South Africa for nonwhites) and to Hampton and Columbia in the United States, in pursuit of education. This had an effect not merely on their personal lives, but on the community as a whole: these young men returned to become the teachers of outschools for the American Board, and even to enter the selection process for the next chief of the region. The repercussions were, however, delayed by the length of time it took a student to work to pay his way through school. See, for examples, Fuller to ABC, 4 January 1927, ABC 15.4, vol. 35, item 48; Chikore Station Report, June 1927, ABC 15.4, vol. 35, item 150—note that the American Board pupil did not become chief, though the older man who did succeed proved to be quite willing to work with the mission. At least one early pupil of Chishawasha, did become a chief, although not until 1948. He had been away from his locality, teaching for the mission, from around 1913. (Chief Chivero, autobiographical narrative, JAH, box 328).

28. Probably all mission societies sheltered at least a few runaways. The American Board Mission was particularly notable in its attempts to found a home for runaways, and the Anglican St. Monica's, the girls' wing of St. Augustine's Penhalonga, initially appeared to consist primarily of runaways.

29. C. T. Stuart, quoted in the Report of the CNC Matabeleland (Taylor), 1907, CO 603/7.

30. The difficulties included: need for closer surveillance for law enforcement, implying both more staff and more expense; an increased resentment by Africans towards Europeans, complicating labor recruitment and labor discipline; the possibility of economic damage, particularly agricultural disruption, leading to famine and regional depression; and, ultimately, the possibility that Africans would once again rise in revolt, as they did in Natal and in Nyasaland even later, causing economic disruption for European enterprises as well as African, and endangering both European property and Europeans' lives. All these problems are discussed more specifically below.

31. Report of the CNC Matabeleland, 1907, CO 603/7. Syphilis was widely used by authorities within the British empire to point to breakdowns in customary systems of sexual control, and to indicate the development of prostitution. See J. Walkowitz on England, K. Ballhatchet on India, or E. van Heyningen, "The Social Evil in the Cape Colony, 1868–1902," *Journal of Southern African Studies* 10:2 (April 1984): 170-97, and C. van Onselen, *Chibaro* and *Studies in the Social and Economic History of the Witwatersrand* (New York: Longman, 1982) on Southern Africa.

32. Senior African men were the principal group worrying about young

men's tax evasion. But even CNC Taberer complained about the "almost nomadic existence" of some of his charges. Report of the CNC Mashonaland . . . , 1907, CO 603/8. Regarding women, the Southern Rhodesia Native Affairs Committee of Enquiry [NACE] Report, (Salisbury: Government Printer, 1911), 2, 6–7, stated the issue most clearly, asserting that "the immorality of women, both married and single, in the vicinity of mines and other industrial centres, is a growing danger to the future welfare, both moral and physical, of the native races." The danger was based partly in the perception of urban women as "loose" women, partly in concern over sexually transmitted diseases, and partly in the committee's recognition of the importance of women's agricultural labor to Africans' ability to produce maize in quantities large enough for both subsistence and sale. Domestically grown cheap maize was vital to employers' profit margins.

33. Report of CNC Matabeleland, for the year ended 31 December 1907, CO 603/9.

34. See J. J. Taylor, "The Emergence and Development of the Native Department in Southern Rhodesia, 1894–1914" (Ph.D. dissertation, University of London, 1979), 155–61. He emphasizes that the Native Department's effort to gain magistrate's authority sought to forestall any appeals by Africans to the Law Department. In combination with the department's reforms of the messengers into an alternative police force, this was an attempt to achieve control over all channels of communication between Africans and the administration.

35. The BSAC report for year ending 31 March 1911, 41, declared that the NC, strengthened, "is now the person who supplies the blank left through the taking away of the Chief's power, consequent on the removal of the tribal system." The Native Department was administratively different from the rest of the BSAC administration in that its officials, down to the lowliest assistant native commissioner, were subject to imperial approval, and the department was officially supposed to be a protective, paternalistic conservation agency, providing Africans with protection. During the early years, however, it functioned to circumvent imperial influence rather than to provide a direct link between Africans and their distant imperial protectors. See J. J. Taylor, "Emergence and Development of the Native Department," 2, 74.

36. Taylor, Report of CNC Matabeleland for the year ended 31 December 1907, CO 603/9. This is the second of the annual reports for 1907. The reporting year changed in 1907 from an administrative year ending 31 March to a calendar year.

37. *NACE Report* (1910), 5.

38. *NACE Report,* 5–6.

39. This policy also had clear implications for the reimposition of

elders' power over women. Schmidt describes these initiatives as a collaboration by government officials with male elders to assert expanded powers over women. Elizabeth Schmidt, *Peasants, Traders and Wives: Shona Women in the History of Zimbabwe, 1870–1939* (Portsmouth, NH Heinemanns 1992), 6–9, 98–110, 121.

40. Taylor, Report of CNC Matabeleland, 1908, CO 603/9.

41. Taylor, Report of the CNC Matabeleland, 1908, CO 603/9.

42. Taylor, Report of the CNC Matabeleland, 1908, CO 603/9.

43. The changes in education policy in Southern Rhodesia followed and resonated with contemporary changes in educational policy within South Africa, which Southern Rhodesians frequently contemplated joining, and constantly drew on for models of either desirable or undesirable policies. For a study of South African educational policy during this period, see Frank Molteno, "The Historical Foundations of the Schooling of Black South Africans," in Peter Kallaway, ed., *Apartheid and Education: The Education of Black South Africans* (Johannesburg: Ravan Press, 1984, 1988), 45–107. Molteno emphasizes that in the late nineteenth and early twentieth centuries, while Africans "voted for an academic form of education in the only way open to them, with their feet," the state sought to ensure that much of the students' time was occupied in labor, and that the literary schooling was merely elementary.

Another source of ideas and influences for Southern Rhodesian educational policy, though, was the movement for the expansion of education into the working classes of Great Britain. An emphasis on manual labor as vital to education for the working classes also emerged in Britain, through movements such as the nineteenth-century movement for "half-time education," which argued that the factory child learned best when academic education was supplemented with hours of manual labor, or the twentieth-century emphasis on vocational education. See Harold Silver, *Education as History* (London: Methuen, 1983), 35–59, 151–72.

44. As late as 1927 moves to develop an efficient system of inspection were greeted by missionaries as something of an innovation, an innovation that would make more work for them. For a candid indication of the superficiality of early oversight, see Father Bick's concern about the new Department of Native Education Inspectorate: "The new Native School Inspectors are bound to be more exacting in their examinations. It was easy enough to throw sand in the eyes of inspectors who did not know a word of the language." Bick to Fr. Superior, 28 August 1927, JAH, box 126/4.

45. And mission initiatives touched off by the offer of government support for normal training often faltered. Williams's effort to build a training school at Hope Fountain (LMS) had collapsed by 1910, the Dutch Reformed Mission at Morgenster was notorious for the poor education of its

teacher-evangelists, and as late as 1922, Fr. Bert complained that the new Jesuit training school at Driefontein was doomed, as it was impossible to pull enough students up to the Standard III level required for government-funded normal training. 9 October 1922, JAH box 124/1. The only notable exception to this miserable state of education was the American Board's enterprise in Melsetter, where they were graduating certificated teachers educated to Standard VI by the mid-1920s, and at the Standard VII level by 1928. The slowness of the teacher improvement initiative is most graphically demonstrated, though, by the fact that, after years of government and mission initiatives, the 1931 Department of Native Education report noted that 40 percent of the teachers held qualifications below Standard III, and that, under government pressure to raise standards, the number of kraal schools had actually begun to decline.

46. Duthie, Report of the Director of Education, 1908, CO 603/9.

47. James Anderson, *The Education of Blacks in the South, 1860–1935* (Chapel Hill: University of North Carolina Press, 1988), 33–78. Keigwin, earlier a native commissioner, became the most explicit Southern Rhodesian exponent of this philosophy by 1918. South African educators also drew heavily on this Hampton-Tuskegee model. Keigwin and Taylor, though, anticipated Loram's enthusiasm. See, for example, R. Hunt Davis, Jr., "Charles T. Loram and the American Model for African Education in South Africa," in Kallaway, ed., *Apartheid and Education,* 108–26. Even missionaries accepted some aspects of this ideology: the American Board sponsored a student to Hampton (Kamba Simango) and employed him on his return. And at least one of the heads of the Mt. Silinda school had spent seven years teaching at Hampton (Julia Winter).

48. Note that Mt. Silinda, the first American Board school in Southern Rhodesia, was integrated, and initially headed by a black American woman. Jones to ABC, 26 October 1896, ABC 15.4, vol. 20, item 84. Even after Jones was pushed out to make way for a white school head, the school remained integrated, declaring a 1897 student body of 4 Americans, 1 Dutch, 3 Zulu, 2 Ndebele, and 71 Ndau. H. J. Gilson, Report of Mt. Silinda School, 28 May 1897, ABC 15.4, vol. 19. Missionary societies tended to develop schools for single ethnic groups, but often paid less attention to excluding white or "coloured" children than the administration might wish. Furthermore, though African children were concentrated in the lower classes, it was possible for a missionary society, such as the American Board, to offer a unified, nonracial curriculum. During 1898, at Mt. Silinda, Standard II was fully integrated, with 7 European pupils and 6 Africans, and within the entire school, even as the African students learned English, the European students studied Zulu (the school's working language). Report of Mt. Silinda School 4 July 1898, ABC 15.4, vol. 19, item 13. And as late as 1909 Williams of the LMS was proposing to teach stu-

dents motivation through the study of the evolution of the "British Race" and of the rise and decline of nations. Williams, "Scheme for the Establishment of a Proposed Native Institute," September, 1909, CWM 71/4.

49. Rote learning and automatic obedience were a form of intellectual discipline insofar as they represent a form of teaching that trains students to turn off their critical minds, and suppress the automatic caveats that occur to any creative student faced with large amounts of information. While the time discipline and the bodily discipline were primarily active, or positive, in that they trained pupils to *do,* this intellectual discipline was substantially inactivating, or negative; it trained pupils to *not* think.

50. The entire Order D of this Education Ordinance is relevant here, and may be referred to later. The following is quoted or paraphrased from *Legislative Council Debates* (May 1907), 114–15:

Order 'D' Schools for Natives

—"Native schools of the first class are those where there is a boarding establishment under the supervision of a European, and which can satisfy the Director that (a) industrial work is systematically taught at least two hours a day during the school year; (b) a sufficient number of pupils are taught to speak and understand the English language; (c) pupils are taught habits of discipline and cleanliness; (d) that the school hours, inclusive of the hours devoted to industrial work, shall be at least four hours a day for 180 days during the year.

"An annual grant of £1 will be given for every boarder who has attended 120 full school days during the year and made satisfactory progress."

—"Second-class native schools are those which are under the supervision of a European teacher and provide for day scholars, and satisfy the Director that, (a) a sufficient number of pupils are taught to speak and understand the English language; (b) the school is open 180 days during the year for two hours a day; (c) pupils are taught habits of discipline and cleanliness.

"An annual grant of £10 will be given in second-class schools for every 20 pupils who attend 120 full school days a year and make satisfactory progress. A further annual grant of 10s. per head will be given to those who are trained industrially for two hours a day for 120 days during the year in addition to the two ordinary school hours."

—"Third-class native schools are those under native teachers where the school is open 180 days of two hours each during the year, and where pupils are taught habits of discipline and cleanliness. An annual grant of £5 will be given for every 20 pupils who attend 120 full school days during the year and make satisfactory progress."

—Schools with both boarders and day scholars can apply for both first- and second-class grants.

—"An annual grant of £1 will be given for every female native who is trained 120 days of two hours a day in domestic work and makes satisfactory progress. The domestic work must include sewing, cooking, washing, ironing and general housework."

—Grants of half the cost of equipment are available for female domestic training.

—"Industrial work for natives may include farming, brickmaking, roadmaking, building, carpentry, iron work or domestic work."

—"The maximum grant to any native school shall be £125 per annum."

51. "Native Indaba: An Unfortunate Episode," *Bulawayo Chronicle,* 19 November 1909. Though the specific demands for restoration of Lobengula's heir were solely Ndebele, other sociopolitical issues were echoed by leaders in Mashonaland. Corresponding to Ndebele worries about their ability to control wives, CNC Taberer noted that "the natives view with alarm the increase of adultery, and constantly ask that it be made a criminal offense. I am of the opinion that the question of making adultery a crime should be considered with the utmost seriousness and earnestness." Report of the CNC Mashonaland for 1910, CO 603/11.

52. "Native Indaba," *Bulawayo Chronicle* 19 November 1909.

53. "Native Indaba," *Bulawayo Chronicle* 19 November 1909.

54. "Native Indaba" and "Friday's Indaba," *Bulawayo Chronicle* 19 November 1909.

55. When officials looked across the border into Natal, they could see a similarly ambiguous situation. Many Europeans and Africans believed that the 1906 "disturbance" in Natal was the work of "the younger generation, the wild youngbloods, who had no memory of war against the Europeans and who, in addition, had experienced the demoralizing influence of the towns." Yet those disturbances, Marks notes, were "basically tribal in origin and organization, and many features of Zulu militarism were invoked through "traditional war doctors" and chiefs' leadership. See Marks, *Reluctant Rebellion,* 308–13.

56. H. J. Taylor, Report of the CNC, Matabeleland, 1909, CO 603/9.

57. Taylor, reports of the CNC, Matabeleland, 1909, 1910, CO 603/9, CO 603/11.

58. See J. A. C. Mutambirwa, *The Rise of Settler Power in Southern Rhodesia (Zimbabwe), 1898–1923* (Cranbury, N.J.: Associated University Presses, 1980), esp. 65–69; 167–87.

59. "Natives and Education," *Bulawayo Chronicle,* 24 September 1904. The effect of the Japanese victory in the Russo-Japanese war seems to have had an effect on public opinion similar to that of the dismantling of the Berlin Wall during 1989. It was such a surprising event that it forced all observers to question old certainties.

60. One article put it this way: Africans' "compelled submission to white rule results at present mainly from the fact that he is uneducated." "The Native Problem," *Bulawayo Chronicle,* 17 September 1904.

61. See Philip Mason, *The Birth of a Dilemma* (London: Oxford University Press, 1958), 282-83, for a short discussion of the relationship between paternalism and education. New arrivals to the region, Mason notes, needed more educational help than they would have received in England or South Africa, as they were more scattered, and distance increased costs.

62. R. J. Challiss, "The European Educational System in Southern Rhodesia, 1890 to 1930" (*Zambezia* supplement, 1982), 4.

63. "The South African Schoolboy: His Disabilities," *Bulawayo Chronicle,* 26 August 1905.

64. Dane Kennedy, *Islands of White* (Durham, N.C.: Duke University Press, 1987), 173.

65. British educational concerns did provide grist for discussions of education in Southern Rhodesia, but the British system, which did not make full-time education to age fourteen the rule in England and Wales until 1918, was thought to be insufficiently ambitious, as it contended only with class distinctions, and not with the problems of racial dominance crucial to Southern Rhodesian and South African educational policy. For a discussion of the extension of British education, see J. S. Hurt, *Elementary Schooling and the Working Classes, 1860–1918* (London: Routledge and Kegan Paul, 1979), esp. 188-213 and Pamela Horn, *Education in Rural England, 1800 1914* (London: Gill and Macmillan, 1978).

66. "Report on Education," *Bulawayo Chronicle,* 11 June 1904.

67. "The Native Problem," *Bulawayo Chronicle,* 17 September 1904.

68. W. H. Brown to Mashonaland Farmers' Association, *Rhodesia Herald,* 10 May 1902.

69. For example, see "Town Council," *Bulawayo Chronicle,* 25 August 1906, which was a part of the public demand ultimately leading up to the 1908 Report of the Education Committee (CO 603/9), which focussed exclusively on white education.

70. "The Education Report," *Bulawayo Chronicle,* 9 June 1906 declared that "in view of the importance of the subject, we consider it [the *Annual Report of the Director of Education,* for the year ending 31 March 1906] to be but a shabby document."

71. Grey, *Legislative Council Debates,* May 1907, 47-49.

72. Grey asserted that 795 European children of school age attended school, but 804 did not. Grey, *Legislative Council Debates,* May 1907, 47-49.

73. Reports of the Director of Education, for 1904-8. CO 603/5, CO 603/7, CO 603/8. Note that from 1907 on, reports covered the calendar year rather than the cycle from 1 April to 31 March previously used.

74. *Rhodesia Herald,* 24 January 1908.

75. H. M. Hole, chair, "Report of the Committee of Inquiry into Education" (Salisbury: Government Printer, 1908), CO 603/9.

76. Ibid.

77. Editorial, "Compulsory Education," *Bulawayo Chronicle,* 26 May 1911.

78. Heyman, *Legislative Council Debates,* 1913, 162-63.

79. Editorial, "Compulsory Education," *Bulawayo Chronicle,* 26 May 1911.

80. Mowbray, "The Poor White," *Bulawayo Chronicle,* 2 August 1912.

81. Editorial, "Compulsory Education," *Bulawayo Chronicle,* 15 September 1911.

82. Note that the provision of European education was considered vital not merely for the cultivation of the next generation, but also for the recruitment of European settlers. Educational inadequacy therefore threatened both domestic and imported civilization.

83. For example, H. M. Jackson, *SANAC Report* 5:340-43; or, more disapprovingly, S. N. G. Jackson, *SANAC Report* 5:344-46: "they neglect their work and rush off on the slightest pretext to some teacher or friend for educational instruction. When supposed to be performing their duties they may frequently be found in their huts studying some book or scrawling on some scrap of paper."

84. The school was clearly the ex-student's enterprise—not merely a mission outstation. E. J. Parker, *Mashonaland Quarterly* 56 (May 1906): 9-11.

85. F. Rochfort Byron, *SANAC Report* 5:309-13.

86. W. Edwards, *SANAC Report* 5:323-7.

87. For example, L. C. Meredith, *SANAC Report* 5:349-50.

88. P. D. Crewe, *SANAC Report* 5:317-18.

89. Jonas Hlatywayo to Gilson 21 March 1901, ABC 15.4, vol. 25, item 221. Hlatywayo kept in touch with his friends by mail, and was able to pass on news about all of them, and about job opportunities for others at the school. The jail job paid £4 a month, plus food, uniform and lodging, but he was leaving it because he objected to the police's tendency to shoot prisoners. He explained his decision saying, "God said thou shalt not kill," a moral statement which probably infuriated his employers.

90. "Educating the Native," *Bulawayo Chronicle,* 21 July 1906.

91. The simplest tactic was simply to lose a pass that bore an unfortunately negative testemonial. But there were other possibilities. The educated African, some noted, "has already established some slight reputation for forgery, and has frequently been known to tamper with his own and less educated brothers' passes." "Educating the Native," *Bulawayo Chronicle,* 21 July 1906. The police court reports of the *Bulawayo Chronicle* carry frequent reports of Africans caught forging passes. (For example: Mabunga, charged 15 January 1909; Dachiganidza, charged 13 September 1912; Tjutju, charged 15 January 1914; and an unnamed offender, charged 5 February 1914.) Mabunga's statement, that he would not have done it if he had thought he would get caught, implied that such forgery was not uncommon. And Dachiganidza was charged with having forged signatures of his employers at least twice, to facilitate his desertion. Tjutju's case was reported most poignantly: "Tjutju pleaded guilty, but added with a show of emotion that he regretted not having stayed long enough at the mission station where he learned to write. Had he learned to write better, he said, the present attempt would not have been a failure, and he would not have had to return to the service of a hard master." In the last case, the offender had forged not merely a signature, but testimonials for his application for a job as an "office boy." Changes in the pass laws, Col. Heyman reminded the Legislative Council in 1914, had to "take into consideration that there were a large number of educated natives . . . and they could, with the document in the possession of the ordinary native, gain a livelihood by forging that document." The police, he noted, could only catch some. *Legislative Council Debates* (1914), 174.

92. Evidence on this is sketchy, but it does exist. "Fingos," for example, members of a Mfengu immigrant community that valued education highly, intervened in objection to forced labor in 1905, and were reviled in the *Bulawayo Chronicle* as a bad example, and "a school from which the other natives will learn disrespect." "The Fingo Location," *Bulawayo Chronicle,* 23 September 1905. And when William Napier expressed a preference for the uneducated worker over the educated worker, as more amenable, and disapprovingly noted that two or three African teachers unaffiliated with a missionary institution were teaching on his land, he apparently worried about the dangers of African initiative. "You know what a clever Native can do with the uneducated . . . ." he remarked to his examiners, and emphasized that he, personally, would prefer to keep the African as an uneducated, unskilled worker. *SANAC Report* 4:165–68.

93. "Native Franchise," *Bulawayo Chronicle,* 18 February 1905. Of these fifty-one, an unspecified number were probably Mfengu ("Fingo") immigrants from South Africa, Mosotho workers, or even, possibly, Indian merchants. "Alien natives" were far more likely to acquire access to the political system than local Shona or Ndebele.

94. Lord Milner, quoted in "The Question of Colour," *Bulawayo Chronicle,* 30 May 1903. Note that this statement was perceived as a call for controls on the actions of missionaries, not as a radical declaration of potential equality. Lord Selborne emphasized that whatever the current state of affairs, it would be irresponsible for the government to deny the franchise for all time, and "arrest the development of the native, a human being, at a certain point and say, in effect 'thus far shall you advance, but no further'. . . ." Lord Selborne, "The Native Question," *Bulawayo Chronicle,* 5 March 1909.

95. "Native Franchise," *Bulawayo Chronicle,* 18 February 1905.

96. Grey, *Legislative Council Debates,* 1912, 45.

97. Hans Sauer, speech on the Native Question, *Bulawayo Chronicle,* 13 June 1905. Similar sentiments were declared by Charles Coughlan, "Rhodesia and the Union," *Bulawayo Chronicle,* 5 February 1909: "The decision to give the franchise [to Africans] in Rhodesia was the most absurd blunder that was ever perpetrated."

98. In 1910, *after* a massive expansion in African education between 1907 and 1910, the Department of Education reported grant-earning attendances at 973 pupils in first-class schools, 2,874 pupils in second-class schools, and 5,693 pupils in third-class schools. Report of Acting Director of Education for 1910, CO 603/11.

99. "Educating the Native," *Bulawayo Chronicle,* 21 July 1906.

100. An impressive example of this genre is G. W. H. Knight-Bruce, *Journals of the Mashonaland Mission, 1888 to 1892* (London: USPG, 1892), 9: "No one who has not had dealings with the really heathen native can credit what a degradation of humanity they are. To live somewhat intimately among them is the best refutation of the belief that heathen natives are better than Christian, and is the strongest argument for the necessity of raising them." The genre did not, however, die out. In 1909 a Jesuit editorial defended education by arguing that "the raw native" lacked the virtues ascribed to him: "He has no idea of morality. . . . Steeped in all that is vile and low, . . . he gives . . . full vent to his passions. . . ." Editorial, *Zambesi Mission Record* 3 (1909): 524–25.

101. For example, the 1898 annual reports of Hope Fountain and Figtree emphasize the scarcity of teachers and the inadequacy of mission pay as an inducement. Helm, Carnegie, Wilkerson CWM 3/1.

102. For example, within the LMS alone, Qazeyena was fired for trying to abandon his wife (Helm to LMS 16 August 1907, CWM 68/4), and the teacher of Dagameta outstation, a bright and promising teacher, "got entangled in his home affairs and committed a grave offense in our eyes"— leading to dismissal (Bowen Rees, Annual Report, CWM 3/2). Another serious case was reported by Cullen Reed in 1905, when he found a head teacher guilty of molesting female students, and realized that the reluc-

tance of people to attend that school may have arisen from people who knew "of this from other girls who had been so treated." Cullen Reed to LMS, 12 January 1905, CWM 66/1.

103. Cullen Reed to LMS, 12 January 1905, CWM 66/1; Reed to LMS, 4 August 1905, CWM 66/3.

104. E. J. Parker, *Mashonaland Quarterly* 56 (May 1906): 9–11.

105. Chishawasha's financial statements are not entirely clear, but, at least after its reorganization in 1909, the farm was clearly making some sort of profit. For example, see Propaganda Fideii Statistics, 1913–1914, JAH, box 49/2. Furthermore, Chishawasha may have used that profit to help underwrite other Jesuit missions which were chronically in deficit. See, for example, Propaganda Fideii estimates for 1915–16, JAH box 49/3, which appears to show a profit of £472, out of revenues totalling £3,530 (13%). And when the farm or the government subsidies failed to cover costs, there was the lime quarry.

106. Richartz to Inspector of Schools, 12 June 1902, Richartz Letter Book, JAH, box 356. This became a popular strategy for mission recruitment after the Private Native Locations became legally formalized. Chishawasha, though, was one of the first stations to exercise this tactic.

107. Editorial, *Zambesi Mission Record* (ZMR) 2 (1902):84–5. These sentiments were constantly reaffirmed over the next few years. See Editorial, ZMR 2 (1903): 204. By 1911, though, the Jesuit leaders were beginning to note that it was impossible merely to teach Africans to be "respectful, honest and industrious . . . without teaching a good deal more." Christianity, and at least an elementary education, was at that point acknowledged as crucial, though the editor concluded more conservatively, pointing out that "Surely in this matter of native education it ought to be born in mind that the blacks are, and must for generations to come remain, the inferior race. It is our duty to raise them from the state of barbarism and heathenism; but they should also be taught to submit cheerfully." Editorial, ZMR 4 (1911): 163–64.

108. H. C. Thomson, *Zambesi Mission Record* (ZMR) 1 (1899): 82–83.

109. Richartz to Inspector of Schools, 12 June 1902, Richartz Letter Book, JAH, box 356.

110. Sykes to Provincial, 28 November 1902, JAH, box 12.

111. Rev. W. J. Roxburgh, *Mashonaland Quarterly* 31 (February 1900): 5–6.

112. "It is most important . . . to get a reputation among the natives as a place where boys have to work hard. Thus will the humbugs be kept away . . ." Brotherhood Diary, *Mashonaland Quarterly* 32 (May 1900): 19–21.

113. Wimbush, *Mashonaland Quarterly* 45 (August 1903): 9–10, describes a timetable with Matins at 6:30 A.M., gardening from seven until

nine, school from 9:00 A.M. through 1:00 P.M., industrial work from 2:00 until 6:00 P.M., evensong at 6:30 P.M., and "everything methodical and no time for idling." Students also worked on a rotation system to do the cooking and serving of meals. See Brotherhood Diary, *Mashonaland Quarterly* 38 (August 1901): 15–20. Even the potential leisure of a holiday for saints' days was considered problematic, and abandoned quickly, at least temporarily, as "many holidays being bad for the boys." Brotherhood Diary, *Mashonaland Quarterly* 38 (November 1901): 11–18. Bishop Gaul was emphatic in his support for a monastic-style life and for Holy Orders. He recruited Anglican Orders to staff both St. Augustine's and St. Monica's.

114. For one of the first examples, see the Brotherhood Diary, *Mashonaland Quarterly* (August 1901): 15–20.

115. Wimbush, *Mashonaland Quarterly* 45 (August 1903): 9–10; Wimbush's comments were echoed by Gaul's emphasis on "habits of industry" and the "gospel of labour," *Mashonaland Quarterly* 46 (November 1903): 3–9, and elsewhere, including Upcher, *Mashonaland Quarterly* (August 1907): 8–10 and Leary, *Mashonaland Quarterly* 64 (May 1908): 7–8.

116. Minutes, ECAM, July 1903, ABC 15.4, vol. 21, item 30; Annual Report of the American Board of Commissioners for Foreign Missions, 1906, 40; Annual Report of the ABC . . . , 1907, 30–31. Some of these protests about abuse, though, may have been aimed at the Portuguese rather than the government of Southern Rhodesia.

117. This status as a graded school with many rooms distinguished it from the schools of many British mission societies, which seem to have been modeled on the large, single-roomed monitorial school of nineteenth-century Britain. See P. Silver and H. Silver, *The Education of the Poor* (London: Routledge and Kegan Paul, 1974).

118. Report of Mt. Silinda School, 1899, ABC 15.4, vol. 19, item 18. Since Mt. Silinda school was at this time conducted in Zulu and English, students learned two new languages, and reading in the vernacular (in this case Zulu) meant deciphering a text in an unfamiliar language. This level of efficient literacy training was not common in mission-run schools. Without qualified teachers, outschools could train students for years without providing the knowledge necessary to read with facility, or to enter Standard I.

119. Dr. Thompson was notable for his building, and for his original promotion of the industrial program. More formally trained industrial missionaries—Orner, Fuller, Dart, and Alvord—came out as specifically designated industrial missionaries. Julia Winter had industrial ambitions and training after teaching seven years at Hampton, Clio Wilder had been formally trained in Domestic Science, and other individuals were hired locally to work with the industrial plant and industrial training, including some of the Zulu teachers, Mr. Hirst, and a South African woman hired to teach spinning and weaving.

120. Minutes, 8–10 January 1906, ABC 15.4, vol. 21, item 57; ABC Annual Report, 1907, 31; C. C. Fuller, "Industrial Work in the American Board Mission . . . Rhodesian Branch," 1910, ABC 15.4, vol. 32, item 47. Fuller emphasized that "the industrial work gives the boys in school a chance to support themselves while securing an education . . . ," noted that pupils were expected to work at least five hours a day, and calculated that trained pupils received four to sixteen times the wages of unskilled laborers when they left the mission to seek work on the open labor market.

121. Minutes, 12 July 1907, ABC 15.4, vol. 21, item 77.

122. Gilson to ABC, 15 March 1913, ABC 15.4, vol. 33, item 152; Gilson, Annual Report, Rhodesia Branch, 31 May 1913, ABC 15.4, vol. 32, item 69. Pambani spent five or six years in school at Silinda, worked at Kimberly for three years, and then studied for six years at Lovedale, finishing with a third-class teacher's certificate from Cape Colony.

123. Ethiopianism—a Christianity led by Africans without European input or control—was the bogey with which missionaries threatened nervous Europeans. Ethiopianism, which had political as well as religious and social implications, stood for a process of change beyond any European control. The *Bulawayo Chronicle* (17 April 1904) worried that "from the Zambesi to Table Mountain the country is overrun with missions and teachers, both white and coloured . . ." Without the white teachers, the African would have a monopoly on the formation of the future educated classes. John White, of the Wesleyan Methodists, told the SANAC that the Ethiopian churches provided a haven for malcontents: "if we have to exercise discipline over any of our members for misconduct, they generally go to the Ethiopians and are received there with open arms." *SANAC Report* 4:90. Rev. H. P. Hale informed a public meeting that "the natives generally displayed an intense desire to be educated. It was no use fighting against it, and it would be a short-sighted policy not to give him what he asked," for if they did not, Ethiopianism was the sure result, and an educational system that, struggling against opposition, "would engender racial hatred" rather than peaceful coexistence. "Native Education," *Bulawayo Chronicle,* 21 July 1906.

124. *NACE Report,* 2.

125. *NACE Report,* 5–6: "The Committee have no hesitation in recommending that the authority of the chiefs and headmen be fully recognised as a necessary element in administration, and that all chiefs should be subsidised, in order to fix definitely their status and responsibilities."

126. The proposed Native Adultery Punishment Ordinance was strongly backed by African male leaders, who disapproved of women who left husbands in favor of making a living in urban areas through some combination of beer brewing, prostitution, and cooking, or who ran off with "alien natives" from whom no bridewealth had been received. See, for example,

the Legislative Council Debates on the subject in 1912, or Report of the CNC Mashonaland (Taberer) for 1911, CO 603/11. The committee also recommended restrictions on "the irregular sexual relations which it is alleged frequently exist between white men and black women. The question is an extremely important one. Apart from the moral aspects of the matter . . . the prestige and influence of Europeans are seriously affected by such incidents." *NACE Report,* 8, 6–7.

127. *NACE Report,* 7. The commission's suggestion was that between the ages of fourteen and eighteen, a child could be bound if it was not being effectively disciplined, even without the parents' consent.

CHAPTER FIVE

"A Different Sort of Civilisation"

THE IDEALS OF NATIVE EDUCATION POLICIES, 1913–1934

From 1910 through the late 1920s, Africans who sought access to the benefits of the European-dominated economy and society pushed for a rapid development of educational opportunities and knowledge as an alternative to the acceptance of permanent subordination.[1] The missionaries also sought the development of education, seeing it as an aspect of evangelization and conversion. More reluctantly, a few European leaders of Southern Rhodesia acknowledged that civilization, and the education necessary to spread it, was important because they could admit of no way of life superior to European civilization. "Unless," H. M. G. Jackson wrote, "our belief in our civilisation is beginning to totter, our only policy must be the enforcement of what we conceive to be its principles."[2]

But while a few European leaders worried about the implications of refusing education and civilization to Africans, many within the European community worried about the implications for the future of European domination of an increasingly educated and skilled African population both capable of and interested in competing with Europeans economically, politically, and intellectually. Competition became a nightmare for settlers as they became increasingly unsure that they would win in struggles for agricultural markets, entry level jobs, automatic deference, and educational superiority. This tension between civilization as an inherently proselytizing ideology, and the settlers as a community that hoped to protect itself through characterizing itself as a civilized island amid a sea of savages, led settlers to a passionate interest in social engineering as a way of resolving fundamental social conflicts and contradictions. As their control of the Southern Rhodesian state expanded, settlers increasingly sought to use that state to design a future in which Southern Rhodesian society was differentiated between a civilized European community and an "advanced" African community with a different, inherently African, form of civilization.

From 1907, when the Company granted settlers a majority on the Legislative Council and began to disentangle its administrative and business functions, through the establishment of responsible government in 1923, Southern Rhodesia's government grew from a dictatorship by the Company into a limited parliamentary system. The settler community, though, took years to achieve the limited self-rule of responsible government. In addition to the delays brought by the the First World War, two problems stalled the process: land ownership and Africans' rights. From the Native Reserves Commission of 1915, through an appeal to the Privy Council against the commission's division of lands led by the Aborigine Protection Society in conjunction with some Africans and missionaries, to the final settlements written into law in the much-debated Land Apportionment Act of 1930, the question of land made the reality of conflict between African and European interests unmistakably concrete. At the center of the land issue were two questions: Who—Africans, Company, crown, or settlers—owned the land, and Who should own the land? The question of aborigine rights was related, but even more complex. What rights did Africans have? What rights should they have: Was it the African community's right to be left alone, or the right of individual Africans to participate in the economic and political development of the region, prospering through maize and cattle production, or skilled labor, competing with Europeans for limited markets and good jobs, and acquiring the material and educational capital that would allow them to vote on the common voters' rolls?

During those years, the leaders of the administration and the settler community emphasized to both their internal settler constituency and their external Colonial Office overseers that the settler society of Southern Rhodesia was potentially workable if these questions were answered carefully. European and African interests need not necessarily collide. Native Policy, though, became an increasingly contentious political issue. Native Policy was so vital to the survival of the government that early premiers invariably held the portfolio of minister of native affairs. The topic arose frequently in campaigns for the Legislative Assembly, and Native Policy was rambunctiously debated in public meetings even though it was considered too central to the survival of the settler community to be legitimate as a partisan political issue.[3] Legislators and members of the government sought a politics of reconciliation that would balance imperial arguments for a rudimentary level of fairness against the demands from their settler constituencies.

It was in this atmosphere of attempts to justify a settler state to London that the administration of Southern Rhodesia oversaw the implementation of two inherently contradictory policies designed to provide a model image, if not the substance, for a solution to conflicts over land and rights. The Native Reserves, paltry but away from centers of European activity, or indeed any form of economic development, were formalized in the aftermath of the Native Reserves Commission (1915). On these reserves, the Native Department promised a paternalistic rule that would buffer backward Africans from the effects of change. Within the reserves, the rights of the African community would prevail over the rights of dangerously ambitious individuals. "The reserves will eventually be for the accommodation of the backward," asserted one prominent Native Department official.[4] Even as the Native Reserves were established, though, a faction within the Native Department, the administration at large, and the settler-dominated Legislative Council, organized around a policy of Native Development designed to provide African individuals with the education, skills, and opportunities they needed to promote both economic development and social change.[5]

The two contradictory initiatives were rhetorically reconciled and made to serve the settler-dominated state within the ideology of a separate "native," or community, development. The idea of native development postulated that Africans could make progress culturally, socially, and economically, without following in Europeans' footsteps toward European culture, European social practices, and competitiveness in the European-dominated economy. It offered social planners a new, planned, multilinear teleology of progress to replace long-held notions of organic, unilinear social change. Moving Africans into reserves away from the temptations of European-dominated cities was supposed to preserve the communal core from "de-nationalisation" and disintegration.[6] Development projects that focused on the mass of Africans, rather than the ambitions of individual young men, were to allow the African community to move cohesively toward increased productivity and prosperity, rather than being torn apart by rivalry, competition, and inequity. Furthermore, within the political constraints of the period—settler fears of economic competition from Africans and British demands that the Africans be provided with the resources necessary to survive—a distinct policy for African development on reserves was the only feasible solution. Braked by the burden of the larger African community, and forced to work with the limited resources of the reserves, progressive Africans would be less likely to threaten the ascendancy of the Europeans. And some development within the reserves was crucial to their economic viability. Reserves, small in size, far from markets, with poor soil and limited water, could not be expected to support the growing population of Africans unless agricultural productivity per acre increased sharply. The commission that originally delineated them argued that "it cannot be assumed that every unborn native is to enjoy an indefeasible right to live on the soil under tribal conditions and by the primitive and wasteful methods of cultivation practiced by his forefathers." But the commission went on to assert that development would speed up in future, allowing Africans to manage with less land.[7]

During the transition from Company rule to Responsible Government, the administration, settlers, missionaries and Africans were aware that *something* needed to be done to resolve an increasingly unstable Native Question. Few of those arguing for *something* had any clear or practical vision of what it should be. Within the administration, support for some change in policy grew from a realization that the situation of larger and larger numbers of Africans crowded onto the economic backwaters of the reserves was inherently unstable. "[I]mproved methods in the cultivation of the soil and a greater degree of industry on the part of the native become year by year a more pressing necessity," argued a Department of Education official faced with limited reserves and an increasing population. And his argument was supported by serious segregationists such as C. Carbutt, later the chief native commisioner, who argued that agricultural techniques and knowledge on the reserves must improve, or overpopulation, dependence, and poverty would make true segregation impossible.[8] Officials feared "the disintegrating effect of civilisation on tribalism," but realized that the problem was only made worse when disaffected youths were given no opportunities for advancement within either the customary system or the new European-dominated workplaces. Without reform, the more political aspects of Ethiopianism appealed to these young people, exerting "a dangerous influence on the good relations between the Europeans and natives."[9] Furthermore, the Native Department faced the fact that the living conditions in areas set aside for Africans were unappealing, and sometimes actually "inimical to domestic and family welfare." The chief native commissioner argued that Africans in such an environment saw education as a way out and wanted education for material reasons. If their material wants could be answered, some of the dangerous political implications of increased mission activity might be circumvented. The Native Department sought a policy of Native Development that would transform the reserves into centers of economic activity without threatening social peace within the African community, or between Africans and Europeans.[10]

The settler-dominated Legislative Council was also convinced that *something* really ought to be done. Members of the Legislative Council, though, focused more on the political than the economic ramifications of Native Development. Speaking for a British audience evaluating the region's ripeness for Responsible Government, the members were careful to deny racial conflict, advocate African advancement, and claim that "no freedom [is] denied to the native at present in Rhodesia."[11] Drawing direct parallels between settlers and Africans, members emphasized that just as they demanded education for European children, they must advocate education for Africans; that they could not deny the right of Africans to develop; that the settler community had a duty to Africans to civilize Africans into good subjects rather than merely forcing them to be beasts of burden; and that it was time for some of the money collected in Africans' taxes to be used for their benefit, to show them that the settlers were not "antagonistic to them."[12] Members went on to explore the public relations value of the plan in convincing Africans that taxes were for their own good, rather than merely serving to mark them as subservient to the settler government.[13]

The Legislative Council approved the native development plan of 1920 after a closing speech in which F. L. Hadfield, a mission-affiliated settler, emphasized that "would it pay" should not be the relevant question in deciding native policy. Explicitly differentiating native policies in Southern Rhodesia from practices in South Africa, Hadfield emphasized that it was impossible to block education merely because, at some future time, it might lead to competition with the European population. The only option was to design an education that would divert competition by addressing the real concerns of Africans, making interracial competition unnecessary.[14]

Reassuring their local constituents, the members emphasized that a properly guided native development plan was a politically useful program for Africans' benefit because, unlike other possible initiatives, it did not promote conflict between Africans' and settlers' interests. Its industrial training might spur Africans to greater efforts, expanding the tax base.[15] The development scheme might help pacify Africans caught by the unrest of the First World War and the influenza epidemic, inflation, and the land squeeze.[16] And, if the plan proved a success, it might make Africans work more efficiently when employed by Europeans.[17] But ultimately, the plan could not be expected to allow Africans, who could rarely get more than a smattering of education, to compete with Europeans.[18]

Missionaries, the principal educators of Southern Rhodesia, were as convinced as the Native Department or the Legislative Council that the government needed to do *something* about African education and development. For years, the missionaries had struggled, with limited resources and personnel, to expand their educational programs. The African demand for education had continued to increase.[19] And by 1920, some of the missions' efforts were finally beginning to produce the stable central schools and functioning school systems that were the prerequisite for further educational and economic development. The LMS had a successful girls' boarding school at Hope Fountain by 1918 and was attempting to begin a boys' school. The Wesleyan Methodists' Waddilove Institution impressed the government inspectors despite its acute staffing problems. The American Methodists had a strong educational program at Old Umtali. And at Mt. Silinda and Chikore, the American Board ran what was probably the most effective educational system in the country. Even the more educationally backward missions were expanding and improving their educational efforts from the end of the war into the 1920s. The Catholics, concerned that they would soon be shut out of the mission field, began to attempt to catch up with the Protestants through educational initiatives at Kutama and Driefontein, and even the Dutch Reformed Church began to consult with the American Board about possible collaboration in South Melsetter.

This growth, though, had been difficult, and missions, squeezed by demands from Africans for expansion and demands by their societies that they cut costs, were becoming increasingly vocal in asking that the government begin to provide them with more than mere token funding for their educational efforts. The Southern Rhodesia Missionary Conference, the missions' interdenominational organization, asked in 1915 that the government provide more money for mission education.[20] In 1920 it once again asked for money, pointing out that if educational training was to expand, the government needed to increase its financial aid both to central schools, which trained teachers, evangelists, and artisans, and to the entire web of third-class schools, which the missions oversaw.[21] Despite this missionary hunger for educational grants, the Southern Rhodesia Missionary Conference initially welcomed the government's native development proposals, seeing them as complementing the mission effort rather than competing with it. The missionaries hoped that this development initiative meant that the government was finally taking the problem of African education seriously. Like the Native Department and the Legislative Council, they sought to see in the proposals what they wanted to see—a change of heart by an administration that had previously been conspicuously stingy with educational funds. Welcoming this philosophical change, the conference recorded its "sincere desire to cooperate with the administration in making a success of this important new undertaking."[22]

In 1920, balancing the political, economic, and cultural interests of the Europeans in Southern Rhodesia, the administration of Southern Rhodesia, supported by the Legislative Council and the Southern Rhodesia Missionary Conference, designated H. S. Keigwin, a former native commissioner, as the first director of native development, responsible for formulating and enacting the policy of community-based industrial development. The administration, the Legislative Council, and the missionaries had, on a trial basis, accepted Keigwin's development plan, generally called the Keigwin scheme, which was intended to give substance to the widely used rhetoric of social harmony. The Keigwin scheme had three parts. First, there was the school, the first government-initiated or government-operated school for Africans in Southern Rhodesia. Ideally, the school would deemphasize literary education, emphasize industry, and train men who would work for their own communities, as builders or commercial farmers, or at crafts ranging from blacksmithing to basketry. Second, the school would not merely teach industry; it would be a research center, seeking to search out indigenous African industrial techniques and skills that, improved, were capable of benefitting the community. The third element of the scheme was a trust fund to market the anticipated products of these refined home industries, which ranged from tanned skins to improved beer pots. In theory, the scheme would transform the African reserves from the depressed backwaters they were rapidly becoming into bustling centers of activity by yeoman farmers and craftworkers who, buying from and selling to each other, would transform everyone into rich and dutiful citizens. The Keigwin scheme was a rhetorically elegant attempt by the government of Southern Rhodesia to provide a reasonable and just solution to the Native Question. It was enacted to nearly universal, though unenthusiastic, approval.[23]

The Keigwin scheme represented an attempt to reconcile liberal notions of individual progress, the value of civilization, and the missionary agenda of communal transformation, with conservative Native Department concerns over the stability of African societies, and settlers' communal fears of competition between progressive Africans and degenerate Europeans. Before the First World War, when Keigwin had submitted his initial suggestions on native education, he had argued for what he acknowledged would be an expensive system of education: state schools in Native Reserves staffed by European teachers and providing education "from an early age" to puberty, at which time the former student could be apprenticed elsewhere. Literary education, he argued, should come first, while the child's mind was maleable, and should include education in English. Industrial education should begin around puberty and last through adolescence. This educational system, he argued, should be compulsory, and its graduates should be compelled to accept work contracts for six months per year when they left school. Such a system, he argued, would instil discipline, banish ignorance, and encourage Africans to become both needed workers for the European-directed economy, and peasant producers of such lucrative commodities as cotton.[24] This early proposal was nearly utopian in its optimism that money could be invested in Africans, that all sectors of the African community would welcome such a demanding proposal, and that it could be implemented to the benefit of all.

By the end of the war, though, Keigwin had become far more clearsighted and realistic about the politics of such a proposal. His plans in 1919 and 1920 were much more limited, and were explicitly designed not to help the African community achieve its full potential, but to control the disintegration of African communities and the growth of competition between educated Africans and underskilled Europeans. Like the missionaries before him, Keigwin realized that change could not be stopped. Africans demanded education and were willing to work hard for improvements in their material conditions. But instead of the convergent changes of individuals seeking education and civilization in mission schools, he proposed that the government promote divergent patterns of change for the Africans and Europeans of the region, so that each could develop, but conflict or competition could be averted. Keigwin promised a controlled system of education. Africans, he argued, must maintain contact with their homes and with the land. Even as they become more productive workers, they should understand that duties came along with possibilities, and remain under the influence of chiefs and headmen.[25] Keigwin argued that the literary education of mission schools was

> foreign both in language and matter. . . . There is very little in it at all which deals with every day subjects, with industrial occupations and vocational aims. In short, it seems to be too much imposed from without rather than springing from within. It almost panders to the native's undoubted imitative powers, instead of developing in him the creative faculty.[26]

Unlike mission schools which emphasized a literary education that he regarded as "too European, both in motive and form," a government school would be a "school of work" and emphasize industrial training.[27] By changing the structure of education, Keigwin believed he could transform it from a process that produced Africans who threatened culturally based delineations between the European and African communities, into a process of socializing Africans to improve their own communities, using this "creative faculty" to pursue a specifically African progress rather than employing the "undoubted imitative powers" of the educated Africans who threatened the exclusiveness and privilege of the European community. Though Keigwin sought to civilize Africans, he worked for a different civilization than that promoted by missionary training. In place of individuation, identification with European culture, and entrance into a market economy, Keigwin hoped to see a reformed community that would identify with specifically African home values, and participate in the larger capitalist economy only in niches that did not conflict with Europeans. Keigwin planned to contact the masses in their homes, "and endeavor to lift them little by little, and as much as possible all together," in a way that would actually decrease "racial friction" in part by decreasing racial interdependence and racial contact.[28]

Keigwin recognized that some, perhaps even most, of his students intended to leave the reserves and seek paid work, but he did not initially regard that as a danger to his central task of cultivating a core of progressive individuals within the reserves. Instead, he emphasized that his educational structure would

> assist the native to greater knowledge, a knowledge which will both help him in his home life, and increase his value when he offers his labour. . . . The progressive native finds his needs involve an increasing expenditure, and he knows, or readily understands when told, that it is only by efficiency and by increased application that he can hope to earn higher pay.[29]

An improved home life on the reserves, Keigwin expected, would keep progressive Africans under control even when they did temporarily leave their homes to seek the higher wages of the European-dominated mines, towns or farms. An education which emphasized homes and the African community was, therefore, crucial in efforts to keep cultural distance between Africans and Europeans by keeping Africans' homes, culture, and identifications away from the European regions by ensuring that Africans had a reason to return to the reserves.

Maintaining cultural differences was one important feature of the Keigwin scheme, but equally important was the maintenance of physical distance. Operating in the aftermath of the Native Reserves Commission (1915), which mapped out separate regions for European farms and provided the administrative basis for the relocation of Africans onto inadequate African reserves, the Keigwin scheme not only accepted the allocation of the land, but sought, through development policies, to make it viable. Keigwin defended the reserves policy vehemently, arguing that while "conservative and unprogressive" Africans opposed relocation, their reasons were unworthy: a reluctance to engage in the mental and physical effort of moving and an objection to losing the income obtained by living near European areas from illicit sales of beer, prostitution, fraud, and theft.[30] By locating his project on a reserve, spending little time on literary education, and centering instruction around ways to improve the material standards of homes on the reserves, Keigwin sought to keep progressive young men at home as catalysts for economic change within the African community, stemming the destabilizing movement of young men away from the home jurisdiction of the African community onto the fringes of the European community.

That agenda contrasted sharply with the social effects of mission education. Mission schools had never seriously attempted to maintain physical separation between Africans and Europeans. Organized around a core of European missionaries and a farm, they were modeled on the basic institution of the settlers' economy—the farm—and as such could serve as training grounds for Africans considering employment on European-run farms or in European-dominated industries. Stations near towns actually thrived as bedroom communities for respectable families headed by men who worked for Europeans.[31] Missions were often sought out by Africans precisely because they provided literacy and the knowledge of English that would enable the progressive African to find relatively tolerable employment within the European community.[32] The missions also trained African women to emulate the cleaning, cooking, sewing, and childcare that took up the time of European housewives. Missionaries promoted both paid employment for women as domestic laborers, and unpaid work as wives within restructured African families and homes modeled on European ideals.[33] And even peripheral schools run by African teacher evangelists promoted cross-cultural contact through the training they offered in Christianity and basic literacy and numeracy. These cultural links with Europeans tended to be reinforced through visits and correspondence, as the peripheral schools were denser on accessible lands owned by the missions or by European farmers than on the hinterland of the reserves.[34]

The Keigwin scheme quickly ran into practical difficulties that exposed the fundamental conflict of interests between the various factions of the Southern Rhodesian polity and society. Keigwin and his supporters developed and attempted to implement a policy of native development as a solution to European concerns regarding the Native Question. They did so, however, without confronting the realities of African social or educational ambitions. And Africans protested and worked to reformulate the curriculum of the government schools as they realized that the education the schools were intended to provide offered few opportunities for individual advancement. The Keigwin scheme was not, even in theory, a plan for a separate but equal school system. Instead, it sought to develop the non-European path in ways separate and appropriate to European images of non-Europeans. Initially, Keigwin had difficulty recruiting either staff or students for this educational program. When the first government school, Domboshawa, opened in January of 1921, it was headed by a disgruntled missionary and had only one teacher, a graduate of St. Augustine's, Penhalonga, one of the mission schools Keigwin had viewed as misguided. Domboshawa immediately suffered student strikes. Furthermore, several would-be students had to be sent away as they were too small to manage the work required.[35]

When students did come to Domboshawa, or to Tjolotjo, its Matabeleland counterpart, their reasons for doing so conflicted sharply with the goal of a humble school of work that Keigwin had so loudly espoused. At Domboshawa in Mashonaland—a region where government and commercial work for clerks or literate employees was expanding rapidly—African students sought literary education, preferably in English, as a qualification that would permit them to find better and more lucrative jobs with European employers. At Tjolotjo in Matabeleland—a region where artisanal work for the railway, the mines, or at construction in the European-dominated sector provided major opportunities—Africans sought to acquire the training necessary to gain employment as skilled artisans. The government schools opened with great fanfare, and recruited some of the most ambitious of the students then studying in mission schools or teaching in mission outstations. These students were not shy about expressing their problems with the school's philosophy and practice. Toward the end of 1921, twenty-nine of Domboshawa's students went on strike, asking that their curriculum be expanded to include reading in English. After they marched the nineteen miles into Salisbury, Keigwin intervened, and the issue was settled when Keigwin agreed to expand the hours of literary education. After the curriculum revision, Domboshawa students spent more than four and a half hours a day on nonindustrial schoolwork. Mt. Silinda, the most academic of the mission schools, compressed its scholastic work into a mere three and a half hours each schoolday.[36] Students struck again over the Domboshawa curriculum during 1922, when approximately half the students walked out, protesting that they wanted more time for scholastic work and less for industrial training, and this strike was settled more quickly than the earlier one, with another capitulation by Keigwin.[37] By the mid-1920s, the students had impressed the principal with their need for literary education so thoroughly that he opposed attempts to increase the school's teaching of agriculture, asserting that the students would leave if forced to study farming.[38]

Tjolotjo's beginnings were even rockier. The students used their social connections to spread news of their protests, and then struck directly. One native commissioner reported that his head messenger visited Tjolotjo and reported that the pupils and their parents were quite dissatisfied, not merely unhappy about the lack of literary education, but frustrated because the principal refused to teach European-style, skilled work.[39] And Manzatunywa, a protégé of the Hope Fountain mission, gave such a dire report of the school's state that Neville Jones, normally one of Keigwin's strongest missionary supporters, fired off a note of protest to the Native Department.[40] The pupils presented a list of their complaints to the local native commissioner, noting that they were not being taught either literary material or industrial work, but were, instead, being used as unskilled labor. Furthermore, the principal had announced his intention of keeping them from competing with European labor by confining their training to the construction of round rather than square buildings and by avoiding training in the skilled tasks of building and carpentry.[41] Keigwin arrived quickly in an attempt to deal with the situation but recognized that this was an even more serious crisis than the controversies over literary education at Domboshawa, as it had entered the gossip circuit. The principal, he noted, had been tactless and had nearly wrecked the school.[42]

J. J. Alexander, the Tjolotjo principal, had undoubtedly been tactless. But the problem was not merely one of rhetoric. Substance was also involved. Alexander got into trouble because he attempted "to impress upon the pupils the primary importance of their learning to build better houses for themselves, and not to think too much of rivalling white men in trades."[43] The pupils did not attend government schools, though, to learn to build improved round houses for themselves. When questioned by inspectors, students admitted that they had come to the government school as part of a plan "to obtain work either on farms or in town, in European employ."[44] That training ran directly into European settler opposition. In a Bulawayo meeting, a European artisan informed Alexander to his face that if he was teaching skills to Africans, he deserved to be shot.[45] Such a stark breakdown of consensus was difficult to work around.

Both Domboshawa and Tjolotjo continued as schools, but by the end of 1923 the Keigwin scheme was in serious trouble. Tjolotjo was the site of continuing trouble as African teachers and a series of acting principals fought over status, respect, and control.[46] Dombo-shawa retained its popularity among students, but did so by preparing students to find remunerative work for Europeans—as builders, teachers, interpretors, or clerks—rather than by training peasant farmers to live on the reserves.[47] And the plan's European constituencies were disgruntled. Plans for more "schools of work" were shelved.[48] The idea of a special plan targeted at education for industrial development vanished into the underfunded morass of the government's general efforts to develop a policy on African education. And the original ambitious proposals for a research institution and a marketing trust collapsed in the face of Africans' response to the proposals as inadequate, government worries over the potential expense, and legislative opposition to policies that settlers increasingly viewed as vaguely dangerous. No simple plan could correct the social, economic, and political tensions that continued to make the Native Question explosive.

Native Affairs Department Revisions

In Southern Rhodesia, the Native Department was responsible for "keeping the natives loyal and orderly" through "control of the internal economy of native society," and by "obtaining and preserving their confidence in the Government."[49] Unlike the order-preserving work of the British South Africa Police (BSAP), who dealt with crime, went armed, and represented the military wing of the administration, the Native Department was supposed to maintain order by anticipating problems and designing ways around them through reshaping African society. During a period when the reports of the BSAP indicate few problems of order, the Native Department kept busy by borrowing trouble from the future.[50]

When the Native Department accepted the Keigwin scheme, it accepted a type of education that was specifically antiliterary, an education designed to address the material conditions of African life without exacerbating an increasingly apparent social crisis. The African community and customary sources of authority were disintegrating in the face of the economic and cultural changes brought on by contact with the European-dominated capitalist economy and with "civilization"—which ranged from the mission school to the experiences of ambitious young men who traveled to Lovedale for advanced educations.[51] At the lowest level of the educational pyramid, the department alleged that the influence of widespread third-class schools "has not been beneficial," but had produced moral and disciplinary problems.[52] At intermediate levels of education, more than just moral problems arose. The department saw economic distortions and the possibility of discontent as education "tends to make the native unwilling to work in a capacity in which there is scope for him, yet eager to engage in work for which there is no demand." Would-be clerical workers were multiplying.[53] As for more advanced and thorough education, it was a direct challenge to the assumptions and organization of Southern Rhodesia. After hearing of Southern Rhodesian students going to South Africa to complete their educations, the Native Department approved of the increased level of literary education at Domboshawa as an appropriate defensive measure, as "we ought to make it unnecessary for [the native scholar] to leave the Territory and become subject to unknown and perhaps unsuitable influences" in pursuit of an education.[54]

Opposing the expansion of education was difficult for the Native Department. Even as the chief native commissioner worried about the destabilizing effects of education and "civilisation" on the coherence and stability of African communities, he wrote that "progress is necessary for the native. . . . He cannot be kept back, and it is our responsibility to guide him: we must train him through the missions and schools."[55] The authority young native commissioners of indifferent educational backgrounds held over experienced elders was justified by the expertise of the NCs in the knowledge and skills of civilization, which the department valued above knowledge of and experience with the African past. Ideally, the chief native commissioner argued, the Native Department would be a shoehorn, "drawing the shoe of civilisation onto the shapeless foot of barbarism; exercising pressure to that end, but minimising pain and economising force."[56]

Yet not all the NCs shared Keigwin's or the other development advocates' belief that African life was so backward that only an intensive effort could rescue it from degradation. One chided him, pointing out the fallacies inherent in

> postulating the occupation 'in idleness and in squalid contentment' of 'huge grants of land' by the bulk of the natives. It is a

> reasonable complaint, you say, that the natives are being en-
> couraged to live in idleness and degradation. These conclu-
> sions are extravagant and cannot be admitted, and . . . should
> not have been advanced by one who has seen, as you have
> seen . . . the struggles of these quarter of a million people in
> wresting from a not too bountiful nature the means of subsis-
> tence . . . cattle owners . . . railways, [etc.]. Rhodesia is not
> and never has been a land of lotus-eaters. 'Root! hog! or die'
> applies.[57]

Keigwin, a former native commissioner, had dwelt in his arguments
for the development program on African backwardness. The administration, he argued, must intervene to promote appropriate
progress. Indirect rule through collaboration with established African elites, which would institutionalize customary law and expand
'traditional' authority, was not initially a popular solution among
the officials of Southern Rhodesia, who tended to argue that it
would represent "the surrender of basic civilised principles."[58] Returning power to the chiefs, one argued, was "pure wind":

> What power have the chiefs lost? The power of the despot, a
> power fostered and kept up by witchcraft and superstition, the
> power of 'might is right,' the old days of 'let him take who has
> the power and let him keep who can.' Yes, he has lost all that,
> but what other power did he possess that he has lost? None.
> . . . We have taken nothing from the chiefs that we could give
> them back.[59]

But as the Keigwin plan showed its inability to answer the questions raised by social disintegration, increased economic competition between Africans and Europeans and among Africans for access
to land, or the fundamental issue of order in an increasingly differentiated African community, some within the Native Department
began to wax nostalgic over the "tribal system," and to see as potential dangers any education, civilization, and other development
initiatives that emphasized individuals above the mass of the African
population.

While rarely willing to argue that African life before the European conquest was ideal, a strong movement within the Native Department of the 1920s began to look backward to the period before
the social and economic dislocations of colonialism as a time characterized by an appropriate form of governmentally imposed social
order and a rational economic system. The *Native Affairs Depart-*

ment Annual (NADA), established in 1923, provided a forum for proponents of different systems to work out their ideas and attempt to persuade those within the region who shared their interest in the issues of African life. Early articles included some diatribes against what was perceived as the backwardness of the customary social system and economy by advocates of aggressive development policies, such as Keigwin, N. H. Wilson, P. H. Moyo, and H. M. G. Jackson.[60] But despite these, *NADA* increasingly carried the views of those who challenged the development advocates. The "most advanced all around" African women she had met, argued Agnes Sloan, were not those in contact with Europeans, but those way off in Dande, Mt. Darwin district, where they were safe from European influence. Sloan argued that there, amid a relatively undisturbed culture, women were happy, living with

> a sense of what is becoming and proper in their relations with their elders, their relatives, their husbands, their husbands' other wives, their children; and in their relations with the world about them and with the opposite sex. . . . From the time when, as a little girl, she plays [house] . . . the black woman knows all there is to know of life and death, of sickness and health, of marrying and bearing children. . . . The communal life she leads has many advantages. She lives on good terms with many neighbors, and with other women in particular. . . .[61]

Sloan's advocacy of women's customary life flew in the face both of mission characterizations of that life as a degrading struggle of forced marriage, polygyny, and overwork, and of development advocates' arguments that uneducated African women were the regressive force precluding African workers from making economic, moral, or intellectual progress.[62]

But Sloan was not alone in arguing for a careful, anthropological reevaluation of customary culture. Even H. M. G. Jackson, who advocated development programs, became, during the 1920s, increasingly cautious about characterizations of customary law as inferior to European models. In 1925, he had argued that

> to enlarge the powers of a tribunal of old men . . . who believe in the righteousness of destroying twins at birth and the drowning of witches, in the efficacy of ordeal trials and bone throwing, to whom the pledging in marriage of infants and

young girls is a humane and reasonable transaction, would be . . . incompatible with . . . civilisation.[63]

But by 1927, he was advocating a more respectful attitude toward "Native Customary Law," and describing nonjudgmentally what he viewed as a coherent system for coping with torts, contracts, and social control.[64]

Native Department opinion, by the late 1920s, had moved away from an earlier advocacy of development programs to promote guided change, and many of the department's strongest proponents of interventionist policies had retired.[65] Increasingly, officials emphasized the need for an anthropological reevaluation of the uses of custom, and for the control, rather than the promotion, of change. This attitude increased tensions between the Native Department and the new Department of Native Education (later the Department of Native Development).[66] When M. W. Waters, the domestic education inspector for the Department of Native Development, wrote a melodramatic condemnation of the moral and physical conditions of customary life, she was admonished by the Native Department editor, who argued that African huts were the most appropriate, and even hygienic, solution to the environmental conditions of Southern Rhodesia.[67] And by 1932, the Native Department was at least willing to contemplate preserving "all that is good and precious in Bantu institutions" through measures that included licensing diviners. "It seems to me that it would be better to have these people as friends rather than as enemies," a writer observed. "Cannot we meet them half-way?"[68]

By the end of the 1920s the Native Department consistently disapproved of attempts to force Africans to abandon practices viewed as backward. Attempts to reform African marriage regulations had become total fiascos, according to not merely Native Department officials, but nearly all observers of the confusion that interference had caused.[69] Instead, discussion centered around the need to strengthen, retain, or even resurrect the increasingly decrepit structures of African society. "I am emphatically opposed," declared one native commissioner in 1927,

> to the view that the tribal system itself, as a whole, is antagonistic to civilisation. . . . Native tribal life itself has been the genius of the people as its most moral, social and legal force. . . . we, as trustees of the natives, should exercise the very

> greatest caution not to destroy any feature of such system which may assist in the general uplift of the natives. . . .[70]

In the 1920s, native commissioners disagreed over the question of whether segregation was a possible or profitable solution to the Native Question. But they did, increasingly, reach consensus on the argument that earlier concepts of African progress, based on the idea that once African societies were broken down, a new, European-style society would spring up, were both incorrect and scary. For the Native Department, its mission of spreading civilization ceased to be one of pushing for the spread of European culture. Native commissioners instead brainstormed on how to reinforce the paternalistic, "tribal" authorities they viewed as quintessentially African. Uniforms, some suggested, would impress other Africans and lend the chiefs authority.[71] A new succession law, others argued, would ensure that the posts of authority were filled by more forceful men.[72] Women, others noted, must be managed more effectively, enlisted in support of the government rather than in opposition to it.[73]

The Native Department's new emphasis on social conservation did not, in the 1920s, represent a total repudiation of the idea of civilization or an unreserved acceptance of African culture.[74] Instead, the department's policy was stretched, during the 1920s, between the fundamental commitment to order, potentially best secured through reactionary means, and the justification of the department's authority through its civilizing mission. Under CNC Taylor and his successor, H. M. G. Jackson, the department gave limited approval to Native Development initiatives, viewing them as the best available means to reconcile these potentially contradictory interests. After H. M. G. Jackson retired in 1930, though, he was succeeded by the more conservative C. L. Carbutt, who held strictly segregationist views and pushed the department to abandon or modify its limited native development programs lest they threaten the authorities and order that made Africans governable. In place of education-based social engineering, the department increasingly promoted segregation by blatantly deploying state power. Carbutt himself advocated sending the educated, troublesome Africans of the region off to Uganda or Tanganyika.[75] And he headed a department that, unable to manage mass deportations, sought to maintain control by cultivating the barriers between European and African society, limiting physical contact through a pass system for Africans and a license system for European traders in African Reserves, and blocking transfer of ideas by establishing native purchase areas as a buffer zone between Europeans and the reserves and by ordering European native commissioners within the reserves to shore up the "traditional" authorities.

The Growth of Mission Alternatives

Many missionaries in Southern Rhodesia were opposing the government schools by the time the Southern Rhodesian Missionary Conference met in 1922. Realizing that the missions and the government schools had become competitors for scarce government grants rather than complementary institutions working to transform Africans' lives, they argued that Domboshawa and Tjolotjo were part of a deeply flawed policy, representing a wholly inadequate method for dealing with African aspirations and the idea of development. The conference passed a resolution opposing the government's schools on a vote of twenty-eight to two.[76] The government schools were so expensive that it was impractical to expect them to reach the mass of Africans. The mission schools, through the development of teacher-training institutions and the gradual extension of outstations, were a far more effective, and underfunded, means of providing a real system of mass education. E. H. Etheridge, a Church of England missionary, pointed out that in 1921 the two government schools received £7,500 from the government, while the 856 mission schools approved by the government received a total of less than £16,000. Yet, after pressure from students, the government schools taught the same literary and industrial subjects as first class mission schools, and differed only insofar as they did not evangelize within the student body and lacked the webs of evangelical outstations which surrounded most mission institutions, employing graduates and extending the influence of the central school into the wider African community.[77]

The lack of evangelization was indicative, though, of a fundamental conflict between most missionaries and the Native Department regarding the future of Southern Rhodesia. Keigwin defended his schools as attempts to teach the Africans to make the most of the resources available to them—not to seize new resources.[78] Essentially, he was attempting to teach economic activity and political passivity simultaneously. Missionaries, teaching skills and preaching a potentially transformative religion, sought to provide individuals with the skills they needed to transcend their resource base. Though nervous about the possibility of Africans becoming political actors in their own right, missionaries accepted the necessity of social change.[79] They recognized—and increasingly disapproved of—Keigwin and the Native Department's inherently contradictory visions of the future. In his presidential address at the 1924 meeting of the SRMC, Samuel Gurney of the American Methodists declared that educators "would not be guiltless before God if they ministered merely to the spiritual and neglected the intellectual," and went on to mock the fears that Keigwin's emphasis on the development of the reserves was designed to sidestep, noting that it sounded "a little absurd that a white man, with centuries of culture behind him, was going to be worsted in this competition by the man who was just emerging from heathenism."[80] Gurney's speech followed that of the governor of Southern Rhodesia, who had argued that Africans should not be taught to become imitations of white men, and that some, though not total, segregation was essential.[81]

By the 1920s missionary school systems throughout the region were expanding rapidly, and their quality gradually began to improve as some trained teachers began to replace the earlier semiliterate teacher-evangelists. The American Board was probably the most educationally effective mission in the country, aggressively seeking to show what could be done in African education if reasonable resources were devoted to it. In 1921 the mission redesigned its teacher training into a three-year certificate course during which the student teachers would be expected to pass Standards IV through VI and accomplish two and a half hours each day of practice teaching the lower standards and substandards.[82] And by registering all births on the mission station, and enrolling children through compulsory education policies, the missionaries ensured that these teachers would have students to work with. The missionaries tried to ensure that all children on the mission station started school young, with time enough to complete an elementary education before the boys reached the taxpaying age of fourteen or the girls were old enough to marry.[83] And even the lower classes were taught with increasing competence, allowing students to pass a Substandard A or B or Standard I in a year each, or at most two years each, rather than getting bogged down in elementary courses past the point of boredom.[84] By 1926 Mt. Silinda was once again raising the academic standards of its teacher training program, requiring a pass in Standard IV for entry, and a pass in Standard VII for certification.[85] That expansion did not transform education in the entire territory. In 1928, despite an acute cry throughout the region for any teachers qualified above Standard IV, there were only forty pupils in the graduating classes of all the teacher training centers of Southern Rhodesia. But of those forty, seventeen graduated from Mt. Silinda.[86]

Other mission societies were slower, through lack of resources or differences in priorities, to move toward an effectively educated African population in their districts. But by the 1920s, most sought to establish or improve central schools in response to Africans' increasing sophistication in seeking useful education, education which taught more than prayers, Bible stories, and a nodding acquaintance with the European world.[87] And all were expanding their webs of the rudimentary local schools referred to as third-class, kraal, or community schools.

Gradually, many of the missions whose educational programs had previously faded into and out of existence—depending on mission staffing levels and the local young people's willingness to tolerate poor food, hard work, and the deference of studying at the missions—began to stabilize. After suffering from a nearly total absence of staff at the beginning of 1919, the Wesleyan Nengubo institution, renamed Waddilove, finally emerged during the early 1920s with a competent teacher-training course and prizewinning domestic program.[88] St. Augustine's, the flagship Anglican school, gradually began to reemerge, after a lull, as an improving school and a rudimentary teacher-training institution. Increasingly, it emphasized the training of children who, born to Christian families, started schooling early, and therefore had time for a number of years of education before marriage or the need to leave school to earn money for taxes began to intervene.[89]

In Matabeleland, the London Missionary Society's transformation was dramatic. In 1909 it had shut down its central school, temporarily abandoning any prospect of educational development. But in 1916 Hope Fountain reopened as a girls' school under Rachel Masinga, a qualified Zulu teacher. By the end of her first year, she was attracting boarding students to the mission school from throughout the region and adding additional staff. In 1918 her superior, Neville Jones, pronounced the girls' school a success and began to argue for a boys' department, pointing out that the mission's policy of sending select students off to Tiger Kloof (a South African school for Setswana speakers) was both expensive and, given the extremely low standard of the select students, incapable of providing the mission with teachers qualified beyond Standard III.[90] Inyati school was opened in 1921, under a teacher who had passed Standard IV at Tiger Kloof, to provide upper-elementary training for men, as even conservative missionaries could not avoid seeing that "our chief need throughout the district is a more intelligent and better equipped staff of evangelists and teachers."[91] In 1922, Neville Jones, the most educationally ardent of the LMS missionaries, had to admit that the mission still lacked the necessary pool of educated students to sustain a teacher-training program.[92] LMS efforts toward expanding and improving educational opportunities in Matabeleland suffered from two major roadblocks: a shortage of staff and a lack of money. Perhaps the more important of these was the staffing problem—the fact that at some basic level one needed teachers in order to train teachers. Initially, the missionaries of the LMS confined themselves to merely supervising African teachers. This technique for circumventing the shortage of European staff members exacerbated the funding problems of the schools, as the government provided grants on the basis of European staff members and training in English. By the end of the decade Hope Fountain and Inyati had grown, and the missionaries and government agreed that staffing levels were clearly inadequate. Jones pleaded with the home committee to find him a professional teacher and administrator, rather than another missionary, to run the institute. Hope Fountain, he pointed out, was no longer a small mission boarding school, but a complicated educational enterprise including not just the schools, but also additional departments for the Jeanes program (for domestic demonstrators) and women's work.[93] And at Inyati, W. G. Brown complained that with 145 boarders, "the Institution is really too successful for the amount of staff we have."[94] By the mid 1920s Hope Fountain and Inyati were among the most successful missionary educational institutions in the country. Hope Fountain provided academic and industrial tracks for girls who wished to be educated up past Standard VI. In 1926 it graduated four students from Standard VI, five from Standard V, nine from Standard IV, and much larger numbers from the lower standards.[95] Inyati was comparable, with similar numbers of graduates from the higher standards in 1926.[96]

The Catholics also began to realize the importance of education during the 1920s, though by then Chishawasha was in decline, and the mission was short on students with the educational background necessary to qualify for entrance into a teacher-training program.[97] During the 1910s the Jesuit mission had emphasized industrial missions and the development of communities, rather than following the Protestant model, in which the primary purpose of the central station was to train teachers and evangelists to run the outstations. This meant that it was ill-prepared to meet government demands for higher standards of literary education, or even the demands from Africans for qualified teachers. The most prominent Catholic mission of this period was Kutama, under Fr. Loubiere. Loubiere had little interest in literary training.[98] Instead, he tried "to instil into the Natives under my charge love of work in general, and in particular the love of useful manual trades," such as carpentry and masonry.[99] Loubiere believed that Africans could be transformed by industrial training, acquiring "habits of industry, order, moral and material cleanliness, and such measure of skill as he is capable of."[100] Despite his industrial emphasis, Loubiere was skeptical of Keigwin's schools, arguing that industrial training could catalyze individual and communal transformation only when it was combined with intensive religious instruction.[101] Kutama, however, changed rapidly. The African catechists themselves pushed for a more systematic training.[102] By the mid-1920s, it was becoming a teacher-training school, providing education in the upper standards.[103]

Opening up teacher-training programs was difficult, though, when the general level of education was so low that recruiting qualified students was impossible. When Driefontein was established as a center for teacher training during 1922, Fr. Bert, the missionary in charge, realized that he could not turn out certified teachers in three years. None of his students passed Standard III when the government examiner administered the tests after their first year of study, and, even more discouragingly, the government examiner informed him that it might well take them another two years to get to that point.[104] After Bert and the Diocese temporarily gave up on teacher training, Driefontein was reorganized in an attempt to provide a boarding school with high enough educational standards to eventually produce teachers. It made progress, but the actual educational standards remained below those of most of the centers of Protestant missions: by 1926 it was beginning to be popular with African students, and government inspectors were impressed by its disciplined atmosphere, though even in 1927, it could boast only nine girls attending Standard II and seventeen in

Standard I, along with six boys in Standards I and II combined. No students had passed Standard II.[105]

Nearly every mission society in the region, large or small, Protestant or Catholic, shared a basic educational strategy of combining religious and literary training with both unskilled physical work and intermittent efforts toward systematic training in the skills of agriculture, construction, and domestic work. The missionaries found, however, that the government was willing to provide neither the money nor the supportive policies that might have permitted the missions to develop a nationwide system of mission education. Missionaries could see quite clearly that their schools fell short of providing ideal literary or industrial educations to their students. But they argued that the blame rested squarely on the government's stinginess.[106] In choosing to fund the government schools rather than put the same, or more, money into the missionary educational system, the administration and the Legislative Council chose to fund programs they could control rather than programs that were cost-effective.[107]

Mission educational systems were designed to be catalytic programs that used a small core of Europeans to train elite African teachers, who would then go out and train the African masses. Missionaries did occasionally worry over their inability to supervise or control the proliferating outstations, but their worries centered around specific cases where misconduct by a teacher or evangelist had come to light. Missionaries found constant supervision of outschools neither necessary nor practical.[108] Instead, mission notions of improvement centered around professionalization. Trained, certified teachers who could be relied upon to work professionally in rural schools away from European oversight were vital to the expansion of missions onto reserves. These teachers were so important to expansion that many missions regretfully agreed to dip into their scarce resources to increase teachers' pay to reflect this growing level of skill and professionalism. The American Board was probably the most up-front about its efforts, and its difficulties, in making teachers' pay commensurate with teachers' training, experience, and responsibility. The mission committee negotiated wages with a committee of teachers and evangelists,[109] took into account whether the teacher was expected to assume extra responsibilities, such as sewing classes,[110] and by 1925 negotiated with its teachers for a formal wage contract.[111] Other missions were less successful in coming up with the money to fund a cadre of professional teachers, but it was difficult to miss the consequences of failure: as an LMS missionary noted, the mission's outreach relied on "inspired zealous teachers and evangelists," who were in short supply and, as his station had lost two specifically over pay during the previous year, would continue to be in short supply until the mission did pay them adequately.[112]

More than just the concept of the independent professional teacher threatened the relationship between a government intent on European oversight and control and a missionary emphasis on catalysis and self-fueled change. Many mission organizations were, by the 1920s, beginning to push for a change in the relationship of the European missionary to the scattered outstations. To be successful, African Christian communities needed to begin to take up for themselves the responsibilities of fundraising, operating the outstation church and school, and minding the behavior of the community's Christians. If a Christian community were fully successful, European oversight would become obsolete. The LMS was particularly emphatic about the need for African churches to take responsibility for themselves and for their children's education.[113] By 1917 it was already employing two Ndebele men, Shisho Moyo and Mtompe Kumalo, to itinerate, undertaking some of the work of supervising and maintaining the African community churches and schools.[114] Missionaries discovered that successful outreach demanded changes in the relationship between the European missionaries and the African charges as Africans became more educated and more capable of taking on intermediary roles. In Southern Rhodesia, influenced by the dominant settler society, not all mission societies promoted the concept of African supervision of schools, and of an African church. The American Methodists' parent organization expressed frustration at opposition to the promotion of Africans to supervisory roles.[115] But as missionaries grew more flexible, accepting as a necessary part of the catalytic process of conversion the organizations of increasingly professional teacher-evangelists who participated as partners in the design of mission policy,[116] the government became more worried about maintaining European control.

The conflict between a growing mission ideal of African leadership and the administration and settlers' desire for control broke out most clearly in debates over the Jeanes teachers. Under the direction of Harold Jowitt, the director of native development, both the Department of Native Development and the missions received a grant from the Carnegie Endowment to train some of the missions' best teachers in the supervision of other teachers, and in rural development work. Ideally, the Jeanes teacher program would have allowed Africans, after training, to take on responsibility for the supervision and coordination of development work on the reserves. Male Jeanes teachers were trained at Domboshawa as school inspectors and development agents; female Jeanes teachers studied at Hope Fountain, learning basic first aid, midwifery, preventive medicine, dispensing, and sanitation. The program was an elegant attempt to stretch limited government funding for development by paying African salaries, rather than recruiting and paying smaller numbers of far more expensive Europeans. In other regions, such as Nyasaland and Northern Rhodesia, the administration had found the program unproblematic. Female Jeanes teachers, working out of their homes on an extremely limited scale, caused few conflicts between missions, officials, and settlers.

Male Jeanes teachers, though, became the primary symbol for Native Department officials of the uncontrollability of educated African men. Furthermore, as they worked on reserves—areas where change was supposed to be slow and under the control of the Native Department—they triggered protests, bureaucratic squabbling, and ultimately the closure of their training program by officials worried over the possibility of new, African or missionary, loci of power. By 1933 the first Jeanes teachers had completed their training and had returned to the missions who had originally sponsored them. The missions were then supposed to tell them where to settle, give them responsibility for certain schools and villages, and supervise their work. Early missionary supervisors' reports were enthusiastic. "[T]his venture is one of the most significant single steps in the progress of Native education in Rhodesia," argued one impressed observer, and other observers, while noting some friction, concurred in their praise of and hopes for the new program.[117]

Native commissioners, however, were, from the beginning, dubious and worried about the implications of African teachers assuming the authority of development coordinators. First, they tended to complain that reports of Jeanes teacher accomplishments were exaggerated, possibly even untruthful. Then, if the Jeanes teacher did not defer entirely to the NC, the NCs launched campaigns of intimidation. The SoN Victoria, E. G. Howman, accused the two Jeanes teachers in his territory of using force, or at least threats, against the local people, and threatened to "inform village heads and others that the Jeanes teachers (JTs) are not allowed to give orders or ride rough shod over the community," though he noted that "the consequence of doing so would be that the efforts of the teachers would be nullified as one can hardly imagine any decent Native putting up with the impertinances inflicted upon them by the Teachers under the catch word of 'community work' if . . . aware that the teachers were not carrying out the wishes of the government."[118] Howman may have been one of the most vocal opponents of the program within the Native Department, but he was not alone. From the time the first JTs went into the field in 1933 to 1935, several JTs were accused of using force to make schoolchildren work on road building or in gardens and families to move their farms and allocate separate lands for grazing and arable; they were also accused of disobeying the direct orders of an NC.[119]

Though some NCs did complain about specific actions by Jeanes teachers, missionaries defended their protégés, even against charges of the direct disobedience of NC orders.[120] The conflict over the Jeanes teachers was not a battle over specific actions of road building, construction of outhouses, or the planting of school gardens. It was a fight over who would control those innovations, and how that control would be exercised. For the NCs, development projects could only be controlled if Europeans maintained the initiative, and supervised their servants closely. For the missions, the essence of guided change was to train Africans who would then be capable of both promoting and guiding the future of their own people. Control, for the missions, was in the indoctrination of the student, rather than the micromanagement of the project.

Settler Nuances

When settlers discussed African education or development programs, they discussed themselves and the effects that education or development would have on settlers as employers of Africans and as parents concerned over their white children's ability to rule Africans. During the 1920s and early 1930s settlers debated education and worried about the ability of the European community to educate its own children: the topic of free and compulsory education for European children remained on the agenda of every Legislative Council or Legislative Assembly session from at least 1907 until 1930, when the education of European children was finally made compulsory.

Settlers sought to develop an educational system for European children that would teach civilization and communal solidarity.[121] When, in 1920, surveys showed that many European children in rural areas were not being educated, some alleged that illiteracy rates of 30 percent among European children in some rural areas meant that settlers "had no claim to call themselves a civilised country."[122] Many also opposed "invidious distinctions" between those whose families could afford to pay for education and those whose families could not. Social inequalities within the white community must, they argued, be wiped out at the level of the primary school if European democracy was to survive and a new, national Rhodesian identity to form.[123] Despite this emphasis on educating Rhodesians to overcome class, ethnicity, and distance, settlers sought to ensure that the curriculum of their schools would promote children's domestic relationships of faith and family. Bible reading, they declared, could impress moral values.[124] Settlers argued for domestic education classes for girls, and industrial and agricultural education for boys, both to instil moral values and to suit European children to the available niches in the Southern Rhodesian economy.[125] White children in Southern Rhodesia were sent to boarding schools for much of their youth, and settlers acknowledged the contradictions inherent in inculcating identification with family and community by removing them from home. Some argued that though the boarding system provided the solid foundations of a literary education, "if that progress was made at the expense of a general appreciation of home life and duties, then it was a loss rather than a gain."[126]

Settlers also worried about African education. They viewed it as one of the hazards of a racially mixed society—it could not be avoided, given imperial oversight and African initiatives, but the settlers' leaders worked hard to stunt it, or at least to twist it into paths away from competition or equality with Europeans and toward a system of training that would instil deference and difference rather than independence and ability. Settlers, used education as an implement capable of shaping their society through increasingly professional pedagogical techniques which cultivated communal or "home" values within both the European and African communities.[127] Settlers objected vehemently to the attitudes of individualism which the missions allegedly taught. Many employers argued that they would not knowingly employ a "mission boy." And a settler-dominated Committee of Enquiry urged that "missionaries should examine the position closely and consider whether humility . . . should not be more fully inculcated . . . in an essentially unequal environment to preach equality is far removed from being in the best interests of the Natives"[128] The government schools, Domboshawa and Tjolotjo, were the first attempt by the settler-dominated government to bring African education under a tight professional control capable of limiting it to the teaching of low levels of skill for home use, deference, and discipline.

In this context of education as a necessary evil, some settlers may have backed the government schools for Africans precisely because they were inadequate and inefficient. In the debates over funding of European education, settlers discussed both how the limited funds could most efficiently be allocated to provide the maximum amount of European education, and the question of standards—what the minimum level was below which no European child should be allowed to fall.[129] These issues were not invoked in discussions of African education.[130] Pleas to increase the funds devoted to African education requested money less to educate Africans than to "show that the country was developed from the native point of view, and the natives were being brought up under discipline and under control."[131] And H. U. Moffat, a sceptic regarding the actual usefulness of the Keigwin plan, emphasized that though it was an experiment that showed no signs of success after two years, "it was a visible sign of their earnest desire to do the best they could for the native."[132] When Jock McChlery repeated the SRMC's criticisms of the inefficiency of the Keigwin scheme to the council, his calls for "something more like justice" in educational funding were dismissed by his colleagues as irrelevant.[133] All acknowledged that, whatever its ideals, the Keigwin scheme in practice left the vast majority of Africans almost entirely unaffected.[134] But the settler community wanted neither solid literary instruction nor skilled industrial work for the African population. The administrator expressed this hesitance toward solid instruction when he echoed common sentiments that "the African has learned so much in the previous few years that they should be left alone for ten years to digest it."[135] Instead of providing a newly advanced system of education for the country, the government schools spent relatively large quantities of money to provide a retarded system. The academic quality of the government schools was too low to produce qualified teachers, but settlers advocated these schools even at a time when some missions were finally beginning to put resources into teacher training.[136] Even the industrial training was watered down lest African artisans compete with Europeans.[137] The Keigwin scheme was for show, not for results.

The government schools taught few students. And many of the students were ambitious and sought education as a means of entering the European economy rather than as a source of basic skills for improving life on the reserves.[138] The government schools failed to contain African educational efforts or the expansion of mission schools. Faced with what they perceived as a dangerously out-of-control education movement capable of spreading ideas of equality and the knowledge necessary for Africans to compete with Europeans in the skilled trades and low-level clerical jobs that provided entry posts for inadequately educated colonial children, the settler community developed two new initiatives: an emphasis on the training of African women in morals and the skills of domesticity; and legislation to cripple mission attempts to expand teacher training and block the growth of professional networks of teachers supervised by educated African supervisors.

African women did not compete with European men for skilled work during the early twentieth century, and settlers did not fear that they would.[139] In funding domestic education for women, the European community could safely spend money for the educational benefit of Africans without fear that it would promote an educated African elite capable of displacing European workers. African women in Southern Rhodesia did not usually seek any form of wage work. Instead, they farmed at home. In the early twentieth century, as the government promoted plows for the sake of more extensive farming, women's agricultural labor—sowing, hoeing, weeding, harvesting—increased dramatically.[140] And though women did not retain control of much of what they produced, their work created the agricultural surplus that provided a basis for the European-dominated expansion of cash crops, mining, and industry. But women's importance was more than merely economic: as both wives and the mothers and principal teachers of African children, the discipline they imposed and the domestic environments they provided were, according to worried settlers, crucial to the development of communal cohesion and values within the African community, and to the economic and social viability of a separate African sphere. Some settlers began to argue as early as 1923 that the training and transformation of African women was vital to any hope of success for efforts to train men in work discipline while maintaining their cultural identification with the Africans of the reserves rather than with the mixed society of the towns. No community could be transformed when only half its population was addressed.[141] The government tacitly promoted girls' education by enforcing the poll tax on boys from the age of fourteen while leaving girls exempt.[142] Settlers, though, suggested that the government ask missions to take over the work of girls' education as an active concern, emphasizing the teaching of domestic virtues and the "moral or spiritual tenets . . . the things that really count and that shape the future of the race."[143]

Both the government schools and the push for the domestic education of African girls were relatively simple to portray as paternal, humanitarian initiatives, efforts which directed the development of African society into a separate track from that of European society, but which sought to ensure that that track was well provided for. Settler efforts in the wake of the Committee of Enquiry (1925) to put limits on the most volatile class of African education, the rapidly spreading kraal schools and their relatively independent teachers, were justified using similar language, a language that emphasized the settlers' need to protect African society from demagogues and disruption, and to provide quality education. But settlers were also both aware of and willing to discuss what they perceived as the dangers of uncontrolled education. African education, settlers feared, was a phenomenon that was "bound to grow, and ultimately to become very strong. . . . There are things that grow without cultivation, and often the plants that so grow are the most difficult to eradicate. . . ."[144] In 1927 the Legislative Assembly debated what to do about this weedlike form of education. "It is not satisfactory," Tawse Jollie argued, "that the State should subsidise schools in which an unsatisfactory form of education is being carried on."[145] The diluted, out-of-control teaching of missions stretched beyond their resources was not better than no education, she continued. It was dangerous. All people teaching or preaching among Africans, she argued, should be required to hold government licenses. Government inspectors should harden their hearts and shut schools that did not meet government standards.[146] Tawse Jollie was backed up even by strong advocates of African education such as Hadfield. Consolidation, not extension, he agreed, was what the educational system needed, though "there will have to be extension and material extension later, otherwise there will be an outcry on every hand that the needs of native education are not being met. The natives will raise it themselves." The government will learn, he continued, "how insistent that demand is and how extremely difficult it has been and still will be for the missionaries or for the Government to refuse the demand that the natives are constantly making for education. . . . The demand is there, and practically every native wants it. . . ."[147]

In 1927 the Legislative Council discussed legislation designed to control Africans and African educational initiatives in several ways. First, it removed African education from the jurisdiction of the Department of Education and placed it under a newly created Department of Native Education, where Africans could be managed not by educationalists, but by specialists who "know the way of life of the native, his way of thinking, his tradition, his customs, and everything that has to do with the kraal."[148] And the government hoped that this new educational system would be more carefully managed than the previous haphazard oversight of the mission schools by the Department of Education. "Native education," the government believed, should be conducted by a person who

> knows the end which he wishes to achieve by educating the
> native, which must necessarily be a different end from the object in educating the white child. . . . If the native here is educated to-day to fulfil exactly the same social function as the
> white child, we are going to be in difficulties at once.[149]

But the new, settler-inspired policy was not limited to this administrative transfer of responsibility for African education from the department interested in the educational progress of individuals to the hands of specialists in African "kraal life" and customs, who were intent on social engineering.

In rearranging the administrative structure to emphasize control, the settler-dominated government dropped any remaining emphasis on the education of individual Africans and instituted a new priority for "character" training, on which the grants of all schools were to become dependent. The government argued,

> Character is much more important than literary training for
> the native, not only to himself in raising him in the scale of civilisation, but also, more important, in his contact with white
> people in this country. . . . if we can do anything to bring in a
> public opinion . . . that looks on untruthfulness as something

> not right and has some conception of fair play and realises that
> discipline is a good thing, we are well on the way. . . .[150]

Character training, promised the government, would emphasize respect for authority, punctuality, cleanliness, orderliness, self-control, and service to the community—all of which, it alleged, some mission schools had neglected. By threatening to halve school grants, the government sought both to increase the level of European supervision of the African educational system and to bring the mission schools ideologically into line with the settler view of education.[151] And if that crippled African education, so be it. "Sufficient emphasis has been placed," the government argued, to assembly approval, "on the literary side of native education."[152]

When legislators supported African education or development, they did so with statements that Africans were "one of the laziest races on the earth,"[153] who thought communally,[154] were weak morally,[155] and lacked the necessary discipline to get up and do what needed to be done.[156] If settlers had believed those characterizations, they might have been more willing to promote effective educational policies. Instead, they supported policies targeted toward specific goals or specific sectors of the economy, and worried about the effects on the European-dominated economy of energetic,[157] individualist,[158] Christian or Christian-influenced,[159] productive Africans.[160] Settlers both sought and feared changes in what they perceived as the nature of Africans. As farmers, supervisors, traders, or housewives, all classes of Europeans in Southern Rhodesia employed African workers, and many saw proletarianized, trained, and disciplined workers as desirable after their experiences with chronic problems in recruiting enough labor, boredom from teaching tasks repeatedly, and frustration at feeling unable to transfer oversight responsibility to their employees.[161] If the government schools taught wants, rudimentary skills, and discipline, employers might benefit. But those very traits that made Africans more useful to their employers eroded the differences between African and European workers, fundamentally altering the shape of the labor market. Educated Africans, unwilling to continue as cheap unskilled labor, would be socially disruptive either by competing directly with the lower classes of Europeans or by demanding a class of work and scale of pay that took account of their skills. Such demands would promote class tensions within the African community and cause problems for employers unwilling to pay higher wages.[162]

Keigwin's reassurance that his educational system would lead Africans to remain on the reserves to use their new skills left unconvinced those settlers who knew that Africans were willing to migrate in search of better wages.[163] The specter of competition worried all who feared the loss of the European community's absolute domination, even if they personally need not fear competition.[164]

The Commission on Native Education of 1925, appointed by the Legislative Assembly, acknowledged the central problem of educational policy in Southern Rhodesia when it stated that African education could not be wholly divorced from European culture and European skills. The commission noted

> that the existence of a different sort of civilisation to our own, unrelated to and uninfluenced by the changing phases of modern European thought and literature can hardly be imagined as practicable. To put it bluntly, we cannot teach what we do not ourselves know, and there is no other available source of inspiration and instruction than ourselves.[165]

The commission provided no answers to the problems that had led to its formation: the Native Department's desire to cultivate the reserves as conservatories of increasingly endangered "traditional" culture and authority, settlers' fears of economic competition from educated Africans, and missionaries' and Africans' demand for increases in the minuscule resources devoted to education. Established within an atmosphere of increasing worry over the nature and content of African education and an increasingly vocal segregationist movement among settlers, the commission proved something of a disappointment to those who hoped for a way out of the tension through native development policies that, by promoting some "different" sort of civilization or progress, could help the African community to "realize the best of which it is capable and to advance along the path of civilisation, though not necessarily the same path as that trodden by the white people."[166]

While settlers clearly wished African and European education were entirely different issues, they acknowledged that they were in many ways linked. Africans' demand for education, and the gradual improvements in the education available for Africans, were directly linked to legislators' demands for free and compulsory education for Europeans. For example, Tawse Jollie moved for free and compulsory education for European children up to Standard VII in 1925, the year after the American Board announced plans to add Standard

VII to its school, Mt. Silinda. Her motion was seconded by Eickhoff, a member who put the question even more clearly, noting that "the native is receiving education up to a higher and higher standard" and that "it is rather surprising the number of advanced natives there are who are beginning to press for compulsory education for native children, and that is a factor which should influence us very much" in deciding whether or not to make education compulsory for European children.[167] The Legislative Assembly also acknowledged parallels between Europeans and Africans in its promotion of industrial education and the importance of home life. Matopos, the industrial school for Europeans, like Domboshawa and Tjolotjo, industrial schools for Africans, was designed to fit children to their environment through practical training.[168] And even as the Keigwin plan emphasized the importance of cultivating African home life as a resource for social development and social peace, Europeans critically debated the curriculum and practice of boarding schools, arguing that European children must be given more training in homecraft and in the values of home life.[169] Even the drive toward putting education into the hands of the professionals was roughly the same: even as African education was transferred after 1927 out of the Department of Education into the Department of Native Education, vocational education for Europeans at the Matopos school was moved in 1930 to the jurisdiction of the Department of Agriculture.[170] Settlers realized that totally divergent educational curricula for the European and African students were not feasible either theoretically or practically.[171] If African and European education had been viewed as totally different problems, there would have been no need for such intense struggle over the level of funding for European education and the nature of African education.[172]

Real education, settlers argued, could be dangerous. Supporting first the Keigwin scheme, out of a desire to be seen doing something, settlers became frustrated when it failed to be the sovereign band-aid of its advance publicity. Optimists merely declared that the potential results of educational initiatives such as Keigwin's were unknown.[173] Others assessed the problem more bluntly. The Keigwin plan did not prevent Africans from seizing the educational initiative, the administrator declared. And as Africans pushed, education was expanding, and was going to continue to expand, probably leading to a future of direct competition between Africans and Europeans.[174] Ultimately, most settlers believed education could not solve the Native Question; it could only add to it.[175] But the question of the shape and velocity of that expansion was important, and in order to have some control over education as the principal tool for social control, the Legislative Assembly unenthusiastically renewed the funding of government schools each year, promoted communal identification and nonliterary education through domestic education programs for girls, and eventually sought to defuse education for competition through an emphasis on education for communal divergence, which used administrative reorganization, new conditions of funding, and intensified oversight of the schools' ideological base to enforce governmental control on the expanding mission schools system.

Developing Domination

From the early 1920s, the administration of Southern Rhodesia pursued the ideal of a native development policy capable of providing answers to the Native Question. As the land of the country was formally divided between Africans and Europeans, confining African rights to overcrowded and infertile reserves, and as European settlers solidified their control over the state, limiting Africans' ability to elude or appeal the state, the ideals of native development offered a common ground on which officials, settlers, missionaries, young African men, and African elders could compromise. But compromise between such fundamentally opposed groups was possible only because the ideals of native development were themselves contradictory. To officials, native development meant improving the economic productivity of the reserves, making them economically and socially viable, and protecting the European society from the dangers of ambitious African competitors. To settlers, native development meant either a policy that made it feasible to restrict Africans to smaller and less productive portions of the land, leaving more for the European farmers, or policies designed to make Africans into a more effective body of laborers by inculcating skills and discipline and by providing reasons for them to work. Missionaries saw in native development policies the promise of more governmental resources for the economic, social, and spiritual transformation of Africans. Young African men saw the possibilities of personal advancement through improved commercial farming techniques at home or more skilled labor in the European sector. And African elders recognized the policy as one designed to strengthen the reserves, the sole areas where their power and influence was supported rather than fought by the state.

Few of those hopes and agendas fit together comfortably, or indeed workably. The history of Southern Rhodesian native development programs is a history of the gap between rhetoric and substance, as attempts to argue for mutual interest broke down in the region's all-too-real conflicts of interest. The educational component produced conflict as the administration's stinginess with funding and staffing ran into Africans' demand for more effective education, and as settlers sought to defend their community's monopoly on forms of work that required cultural and intellectual capital. Productivity increases in agriculture exacerbated conflict both between Africans and settlers who were competing with equivalent products within a limited market, and within the African community as the more "progressive" farmers fought with subsistence farmers and pastoral specialists for limited land resources. Artisanal skills bred conflict between African artisans who sought new, more lucrative work using their skills and European settlers who, feeling threatened by this prospect of competition, argued for a color bar. And ultimately no rhetoric could paper over the African community's frustration with the division of resources between the strained African reserves and the protected European sector.

The elaborated Native Education programs and Native Development policies of the 1920s represented an attempt to use the power of the state and a rhetoric of conciliation to achieve a future which lacked social, economic, or political competition across racial lines. But in an economy where European dependence on local African workers was only increasing, a society characterized by an increasingly independent and vocal class of educated Africans, and a polity where, despite a theoretical division of responsibility between the Native Department and the rest of the administration, all inhabitants of the region were fundamentally governed by the same tiny minority, progress toward even modified concepts of civilization could not be sorted into progress by an African community and progress by a distinct European community. And stagnation during the economic crises of the late 1920s only produced more competition, dependence, and the reinforcement of domination. Fundamentally, settlers and the Native Department recognized that the prosperity and livelihoods of Africans and Europeans were closely related. Acknowledged a legislator in the 1929 debate on the Native Development Ordinance,

> We are not going to raise ourselves up by depressing the other
> people whose homes are in this country. You can do that if you
> are a race that is temporarily here; but, if you are going to
> make your home here, then your children are going to feel
> whatever efforts you make to depress the other people that are
> here. I think it is almost axiomatic to say that people are raised
> by their, so to speak, polishing up of one another, not by one
> race depressing another, because the mediocre of the domi-
> nant race will always sink, and you cannot help it. . . . If you
> have a depressed race living amongst you, well, then the less
> fortunate, and the less talented in your own race are bound to
> sink down toward them. . . .[176]

And even the segregationist forces within the Native Department emphasized the economic importance of Africans—as workers, as consumers, and as taxpayers—to the European-dominated civilization of the region. "The advancement of the Native," Carbutt therefore acknowledged, "becomes, from an economic point of view, not a matter . . . of negrophilist sentiment, but a sound business proposition on which the prosperity of Africa largely depends."[177] Native development was a compromise ideology, but its compromises produced little peace. The acknowledgement of interdependence by the European community or administration was a mere prelude to statements of the need for more aggressive efforts for separation. Even as settlers acknowledged that they could not in conscience or as a workable policy dominate Africans, they demanded separation. And even as Carbutt acknowledged the economic importance of Africans and the importance of their progress to the survival of the European community, he wrote that they endangered it. Fearing African political and economic competition, the settler-dominated state must intervene, Carbutt wrote, and settlers affirmed. "The white man," repeated the Europeans of Southern Rhodesia in what became a near refrain to any substantive political argument, "will never submit to . . . domination by the black man."[178]

During the 1920s, some elite Africans who had grown up in a settler-dominated Southern Rhodesia sought to proceed, as individuals acquainted with European culture and the skills and economic logic of the European-dominated economy, into the web of civilization the settlers had woven round their own community. But, fearing this competition, the European community rebelled, arguing that civilization should not provide entrance into the ruling community. Dependent on African labor, African consumption, and African acceptance, the European community continued to advocate a form of civilization for Africans. But, despite its own acknowledgment of the contradictions inherent in segregation, it hoped and pushed Africans toward a dependent, communally defined African civilization, a "different sort of civilisation to our own."[179]

NOTES

1. For example, governor's observations, "Conference of Superintendents of Natives and Native Commissioners of the Colony of Southern Rhodesia, December 1927" (Salisbury: Government Printer, 1928), 2.

2. H. M. G. Jackson (of the Native Department; Jackson became CNC in 1928), "Indirect Rule in Southern Rhodesia," *NADA* (1925): 57–58.

3. L. H. Gann, *A History of Southern Rhodesia* (New York: Humanities Press, 1965), 208–51, 263. And for examples of the importance of the issue in electoral politics and public meetings, see, for example, the furor over the Sinoia resolutions, reported in "Mr. Eaton Replies to Sinoia Resolutions," *Rhodesia Herald,* 7 January 1927.

4. Carbutt (SoN Victoria), "Conference of Superintendents of Natives and Native Commissioners . . . December 1927" (Salisbury: Government Printer, 1928), 14. See also Benjamin Davis and Wolfgang Doepcke, "Survival and Accumulation in Gutu: Class Formation and the Rise of the State in Colonial Zimbabwe, 1900–1939," *Journal of Southern African Studies* 14 (October 1987): 64–98.

5. For one version of the bureaucratic infighting between the Southern Rhodesian Missionary Conference, the Native Department, the Native Christian Conference, the Native Education Advisory Board, and the Department of Native Education/Native Development, see D. J. Murray, *The Governmental System in Southern Rhodesia* (Oxford: Clarendon Press, 1970), 271–343. For a partisan description of what this meant to the agricultural demonstration program, see E. Alvord, "The Development of Native Agriculture and Land Tenure in Southern Rhodesia" (undated carbon, received 1959, U.S. Department of Agriculture Library, 35.3AL8) 13–20, 26–36, 44.

6. Rev. J. Reyneke (Dutch Reformed), "Christianity and Denationalisation," *Proceedings of the Southern Rhodesia Missionary Conference* (1920), 15–16.

7. See *Papers Relating to the Southern Rhodesia Native Reserves Commission* (London: HMSO, 1915). With development, Africans could manage with less land. The resident commissioner echoed this theme to the

Legislative Council in 1923, when he explained that the Keigwin scheme for development was intended "to teach the native how to make better use of the reserves and how to help himself" since, though there would still be a bit of time, the reserves would eventually fill up. Development policy was insurance against the time when the African "might find himself in a very difficult position" economically and socially. Resident Commissioner, *Legislative Council Debates* (1923), 582–89. African leaders who were aware of this argument frequently tried to block agricultural development projects. See, for example, the argument by "Chief Nema," paramount on the Selukwe Reserve, that attempts to increase productivity per acre were only a scheme of the administration's to test the land. If the land became productive, Nema continued, the administration would take it for the European settlers. Alvord, "The Development of Native Agriculture," 19.

8. S. de Lenfestey, Memo, "Imperial Education Conference," 1923, IMC/CBMS, box 1221; Carbutt, "Conference of Superintendents of Natives and Native Commissioners, December 1927" (Salisbury: Government Printer, 1928), 15.

9. *Report of the Chief Native Commissioner for 1919* (Salisbury: Government Press, 1920), 1, 16–17; Davis and Doepcke, "Survival and Accumulation in Gutu," 75–84.

10. The home industries plank of the plan was therefore crucial, as it suggested a way for older, nonmigrants to gain monetary incomes, and thereby maintain their influence over young migrating men. See, for example, Bulawayo to Keigwin, 8 March 1920, NAZ N3/9/1–2, who suggested confining the plan to the revival, stimulation, and improvement of home kraal industries.

11. L. Cripps, *Report of Debate on Motion as to Responsible Government, in the Legislative Council of Southern Rhodesia,* 12–17 May 1920 (Salisbury: Government Printer, 1920), 28–31.

12. *Legislative Council Debates* (1920), Gilchrist, 495–98; Stewart, 535; Coughlan, 528–31; Hadfield, 525–27.

13. Leggate, *Legislative Council Debates* (1920), 523–24.

14. Francis Leslie Hadfield, *Legislative Council Debates* (1920), 545. Hadfield was comparing Southern Rhodesian native policy to the color bar policies of the Transvaal rather than the segregationist ideas informing Natal's policy or the more liberal approach of the Cape. For a contemporary account of the basis of South African native policy, see E. H. Brookes, *The History of Native Policy in South Africa,* 2d ed. (Pretoria: van Schaik, 1922, 1927).

15. Leggate, *Legislative Council Debates* (1920), 523–24.

16. Hadfield, *Legislative Council Debates* (1920), 525–27.

17. Coughlan, *Legislative Council Debates* (1920), 528–31.

18. Stewart, *Legislative Council Debates* (1920), 542. Stewart noted

that few Africans in the region received more than a Standard III education, and inferred from this that Africans were wholly unable to advance to the level of Europeans.

19. See, for example, Neville Jones (LMS) to Oldham, 28 December 1922, IMC/CBMS, box 1221.

20. *Proceedings of the Southern Rhodesian Missionary Conference* (June 1915).

21. *Proceedings of the Southern Rhodesian Missionary Conference* (June 1920), 5.

22. *Proceedings of the Southern Rhodesian Missionary Conference* (June 1920), 6, 9–10.

23. Keigwin even managed to mobilize part of the African community for his scheme. After initially arguing that the opposition of elders should not be allowed to stop the advancement of the African people (Keigwin to CNC, 6 January 1921, NAZ N3/9/1–2), he decided to extend the public relations effort to persuade elders that the schools' efforts were worthwhile. See the description of 120 chiefs' and leaders' visit to Domboshawa (NC Goromonzi to Superintendent of Natives, Salisbury, 28 June 1923, NAZ N3/9/1–2).

24. Keigwin, "Native Education: A Suggestion (1914?)," NAZ A3/18/21.

25. Keigwin, "Native Development" speech (1919?), IMC/ CBMS, box 1221.

26. Keigwin, "Report of the Director of Native Development, 1920," in the *Report of the Chief Native Commissioner of Southern Rhodesia . . . for 1920* (Salisbury: Government Printer, 1921), 22.

27. H. S. Keigwin, "Report of the Director of Native Development for 1920," 20–23.

28. Ideally, the scheme would have decreased European employers' demands for workers by increasing the efficiency of the workers they could hire, and, by developing the reserves, would have decreased the dependence of Africans on European employers for opportunities to get paid for skilled work. H. S. Keigwin, "An Educational Experiment," *South African Journal of Science* 18 (December 1921): 172–82.

29. Keigwin, "Report of the Director of Native Development for 1920," 23. This belief that outside employment and a vital home life were consistent with each other persisted among Europeans who needed labor, but sought some form of social segregation. See, for example, Frank King's discussion of enlisting the chiefs and paternal authorities to recruit labor on the reserves and export it to the European farms and mines. *Rhodesia Herald,* 28 January 1927. By 1927, though, most Native Department officials and retired officials were beginning to realize development and neo-traditionalism were inherently contradictory. See, for example, Alfred Drew, "Native Labour Controversy," *Rhodesia Herald,* 11 February 1927.

30. H. S. Keigwin to Colonial Office, forwarded to the Aborigines Pro-

tection Society, 18 December 1919, in "Correspondence with the Anti-slavery and Aborigines Protection Society Relating to the Native Reserves in Southern Rhodesia" (London: HMSO, 1920), 37-39.

31. Tsuneo Yoshikune, "Black Migrants in a White City: A Social History of African Harare, 1890-1925" (Ph.D. thesis, University of Zimbabwe, 1989), 81-82, 138-39.

32. A remarkably high proportion of urban Africans were Christians: Yoshikune suggests that as early as 1911, when only one-sixteenth of the Africans of Southern Rhodesia had encountered even rudimentary contact with Christianity, 28 percent of the Africans working in Salisbury claimed to be full fledged Christians. Yoshikune, "Black Migrants in a White City," 81. Jobs open to Africans varied dramatically within Southern Rhodesia during the 1920s, and Africans worked hard to find the best jobs they could, balancing wages, rations, accommodations, amount of work, and severity of discipline. Rural farmers on the verge of bankruptcy were not, for example, ideal employers, and during the 1920s sent up cries of labor shortage, despite the fact that few other sections of the economy were willing to back their arguments of labor shortage. See the letters to the editor on the subject of labor shortage, arising from a meeting of radical farmers at Sinoia, *Rhodesia Herald,* January-March 1927, for numerous examples.

33. Runaways were incorporated into mission households as servants and not necessarily given any choice in this training. Some women trained by the missions, though, were betrothed to teachers or evangelists and went to the mission station specifically to learn the skills of Christian housekeeping. See, for example, the discussions of St. Monica's Penhalonga (Anglican) or early descriptions of Mt. Silinda (American Board), Mother Annie, *Mashonaland Quarterly* 49 (August 1904): 18-20; King, Mount Silinda Station Report for 1909 and 1910, ABC 15.4, vol. 32, item 58. For a general discussion, see Elizabeth Schmidt, *Peasants, Traders, and Wives,* 129-69.

34. Many mission stations were zoned as European areas, and the Africans who farmed in the villages surrounding them were covered by the provisions of the Private Locations Ordinance (1908). That ordinance, designed for the use of European farmers, and for the control of "kaffir farming" (in which absentee or inactive Europeans allowed Africans to farm all the land using customary measures, rather than reorganizing around European commercial logic), allowed missionaries the powers of landlords—such as levying taxes for school fees, making school attendance mandatory, or expelling troublesome families from the region. But the ordinance put limits on the numbers of Africans legally permitted to live on the private location. (See, for sample discussions, "Agreement under Section 5 of the Private Locations Ordinance" 1912, Jesuit Archives, Harare, box 126/5, which notes that Hope Fountain, an LMS station, has a

similar agreement. The problems of the ordinance are discussed by Fuller to ABC, 1 December 1916, ABC 15.4, vol. 33, item 131 and Fuller, Chikore Station Report, June 1917, ABC 15.4, vol. 32, item 130.) The paucity of mission stations in reserves was a major item of concern for some of the mission societies in the wake of the population movement which followed the Native Reserves Commission's allocation of land. The LMS, in particular, had difficulty following its people onto the reserves, and the American Board missionaries felt limited by the mission's centralization and the difficulty it had finding land where it could establish outstations. For examples, see Helm, Annual Report of Hope Fountain, 1912, CWM 4/4; Wilkerson, Annual Report of Centenary, 1911–12, CWM 4/4; Dart to ABC, 23 November 1912, ABC 15.4, vol. 33, item 29; Dr. Lawrence, Conference with Zulu Helpers of Rhodesia Branch, 17 December 1912, ABC 15.4, vol. 32, item 17.

35. Broderick, the first head of Domboshawa, was a Church of England missionary frustrated at being transferred out of Manyikaland into Matabeleland. He may also have needed the extra money of a government salary. GEP Broderick, "A History of the Diocese of Southern Rhodesia . . . , 1874–1952" (unpublished manuscript, 1950), USPG X563; Broderick to SPG (1919?) and Bp to SPG (1919?), USPG/CLR 142. Keigwin had reported that in the mission schools he visited, he saw "very little evidence of industrial work being systematically taught. Even at the larger institutions, where there are qualified men on the staff, there is little of what could be termed organised instruction. Work is done for a set period . . . but almost always without a thought to that detailed explanation which amounts for instruction." Keigwin to Administration, "Industrial Training for Natives," 28 December 1920, NAZ N3/9/1–2. One wonders how the product of such inadequate training could be viewed as a suitable solo teacher for the more ambitious government school. For an early report on doings at Domboshawa, see Keigwin to CNC Salisbury, 5 January 1921, NAZ N3/9/1–2.

36. Keigwin, Report of the Director of Native Development, *Annual Report of the Chief Native Commissioner of Southern Rhodesia. . . . , 1921* (Salisbury: Government Printer, 1922), 15. B. W. Lloyd, "Early History of Domboshawa School Period, 1920–39," *NADA* 39 (1962): 4–13, esp. 6; J. Condy, Mt. Silinda Inspection, 16 October 1923, NAZ N9/5/8.

37. CNC Taylor to Administrator, 15 September 1922, NAZ N3/9/1–2; B. W. Lloyd, "Early History of Domboshawa School Period 1920–39," *NADA* 39 (1962): 4–13.

38. Alvord, "Development of Native Agriculture," 16–17.

39. Lanning, NC Plumtree, to Keigwin, 1 September 1922, NAZ N3/9/1–2.

40. Neville Jones to Keigwin, 1 September 1922, NAZ N3/9/1–2.

41. Sixty-four students appeared in Johnstone's office to present their

grievances. Johnstone, ANC, to NC Nyamandhlovu, 29 August 1922, NAZ N3/9/1-2.

42. Keigwin immediately set off on a damage control effort, visiting the homes of the students who had left the school in disgust and attempting to convince students to return, and trying to "correct the unfavourable impression that might have got about." Keigwin to CNC, 14 October 1922, NAZ N3/9/1-2.

43. Reported by Keigwin, Keigwin to CNC, 14 October 1922, NAZ N3/9/1-2.

44. Lenfestey and Brady, Report of Visit of Inspection: Domboshawa School, 3 December 1923, IMC/CBMS, box 1221.

45. Johnstone to NC Nyamandhlovu, 29 August 1922, NAZ 3/9/1-2.

46. See, for example, the dismissal of F. R. Mills as acting principal after he assaulted one of the three African teachers with whom he had had repeated confrontations. Various correspondence, October–November 1923, NAZ S138/69, vol. 2.

47. See, for example, the tally of where students have ended up, Domboshawa Principal's Report for 1924, NAZ S138/69, vol. 2.

48. One responsibility of the Commission on Native Education (1925) was to look into the government schools. The commissioners and their witnesses disagreed over Tjolotjo, and some argued that it should close. *Report of the Commission on Native Education* (Salisbury: Government Printer, 1925). In any case, the government halted early plans to expand the government school system into a net of advanced schools throughout the region. Contrast Keigwin in "Report of the Chief Native Commissioner for 1920," 8, with the reluctance of the commission even to permit the continued operation of Tjolotjo, and the skeptical reaction of the SRMC and Legislative Council to the expense of the schools, below. The "school of work" idea was briefly resurrected in the early 1930s in the Umchingwe School experiment, but the absolute and rapid failure of this experiment further damaged the concept. See Carol Summers, "Demanding Education: African educational agendas in Southern Rhodesia, 1900-1934" (unpublished paper, 1993).

49. Taylor (CNC), Conference of Superintendents of Natives and Native Commissioners (meeting held December 1927), 1.

50. The British South Africa Police admittedly did little work on the reserves, but nevertheless, their concern with order among Africans is quite low. Their commissioner appeared to believe that problems among Africans were "largely due to excessive beer drinking, and the attendant results," and that crimes between Africans and Europeans were "few in number" and all too often "due to temptation and provocation on the part of the European." Edwards, "Commissioner's Report on the British South Africa Police for the year 1921" (Salisbury: Government Printer, 1922), 8. The BSAP tended to be rather blasé about even the most emotional of in-

terracial crimes—the rape, attempted rape, or indecent assault of white women or children by black men—suggesting that the crimes were brought about by the failure of Europeans "to adopt the most rudimentary precautions, such as the secure fastenings of doors and windows, and use of blinds in all sleeping rooms occupied by female members of the family. . . . It was felt by all concerned in the investigation of these cases that in many instances had reasonable precautions been taken cases would not have occurred." G. Stops, "Report of the Commissioner, British South Africa Police, for the Year 1926," 7. The native commissioners did not receive legal permission for law enforcement activities until the Native Affairs Act, 1927, which went into effect in 1928. Bill: "To make certain provisions for the control of natives and the conduct of native affairs," *Government Gazette* (1927), vol. 5 (AB 15, 1927).

51. Report of the Chief Native Commissioner for 1920, 7; Report of the Chief Native Commissioner for 1919, 1, 16.

52. Report of the CNC for 1921, 4.

53. Ibid., 4.

54. Ibid., 15, 19.

55. Herbert J. Taylor, preface, *NADA* (1923), 1.

56. Taylor, Conference of Superintendents of Natives and Native Commissioners, (December 1927) 1.

57. Bulawayo (H. M. G. Jackson?) to Keigwin, 8 March 1920, NAZ N3/9/1–2.

58. H. M. G. Jackson, "Indirect Rule in Southern Rhodesia," *NADA* (1925), 57–58.

59. W. Edwards (NC Mrewa) to CNC, 22 February 1927, NAZ S170/164; quoted by Leggate (Colonial Secretary, MLA), "Native Labour Shortage in Lomagundi," *Rhodesia Herald,* 23 March 1927.

60. H. S. Keigwin, "Native Development," *NADA* (1923), 10–17; N. H. Wilson, "The Development of Native Reserves," *NADA* (1923), 86–94; Keigwin, "Segregation," *NADA* (1924), 52–57; P. H. Moyo (teacher, Tjolotjo school), "Native Life on the Reserves," *NADA* (1925), 47; H. M. G. Jackson, "Indirect Rule in Southern Rhodesia," *NADA* (1925), 57–58.

61. Agnes Sloan, "The Black Woman," *NADA* (1923), 60–69.

62. See, for example, E. T. P., "Native Labour," *NADA* (1925), 122–23, who argued that "Much of our labour is wasted by this return of a few months to the kraal life, where conditions are such that lessons of industry are soon forgotten and filth, indolence, beer and superstition regain a hold." Or, even more emphatically, the Native Education Commission's (1925) fear that the slow development of the mass of Africans was caused by the reluctance of Africans to allow women to be educated: "The efforts to elevate touched only half the race, with the result that the untouched half tended to keep the other down." Report of the Commission on Native Education (1925), 93–94.

63. H. M. G. Jackson, "Indirect Rule in Southern Rhodesia," *NADA* (1925), 57-58.

64. H. M. G. Jackson, "Notes on Matabele Customary Law," *NADA* 5 (1927): 7-14; and Jackson, "Some Reflections on the Relation of Law to Social Anthropology," *NADA* 5 (1927): 26-29.

65. Retirees included Chief Native Commissioner Taylor, Alfred Drew and others who had been more willing to intervene in African home life than the more cautious successors. See, for example, retired NC Alfred Holland's denunciations of alcohol, "Native Policy," *Rhodesia Herald,* 8 January 1927, and compare his vehemence with the care of the younger generation.

66. The Department of Native Education was established under H. Jowitt in 1928. In 1929 it changed its name to the Department of Native Development, but Jowitt remained in charge. It continued under Jowitt until 1934, when Jowitt, concerned about the direction Native Policy in Southern Rhodesia was headed, left to take work in Uganda. Before he left, he wrote that he wanted to leave because he had become tired of fighting "week after week and month after month" the "consistent hostility and opposition from the Native Affairs Department, consistent opposition from the Government." H. Jowitt to Oldham, 20 April 1934, IMC/CBMS, box 1221.

67. M. W. Waters, "The Tragedy of the Home" [and editor's note], *NADA* 6 (1928): 79. In 1931 H. T. Tracey, *NADA* 9 (1931): 111-12 further objected to the idea that African arts and crafts were mere inferior forms that deserved to disappear, arguing that there should be an exhibition of them "to combat thereby the evils of social disintegration and denationalization."

68. "Mushoma" [European with pseudonym], "The Native Approach to Religion," *NADA* 10 (1932): 27-32.

69. See, for examples, F. W. Posselt, Conference of Superintendents of Natives and Native Commissioners, held December 1927 (Salisbury: Government Printer, 1927), 6, who worried about losing what was good, and Coughlin and McChlery, *Legislative Council Debates* (1917), 185-87, who referred to the marriage legislation as the "Native Women's Further Enslavement Ordinance." For a more complete discussion, see Diana Jeater, *Marriage, Perversion and Power: The Construction of Moral Discourse in Southern Rhodesia, 1890-1930* (Oxford: Oxford University Press, 1992).

70. Posselt, "Conference of Superintendents of Natives and Native Commissioners" (meeting held December 1927), 9-10.

71. Ibid., 10.

72. Bullock, Lanning, "Conference of Superintendents of Natives and Native Commissioners" (meeting held December 1927), 11.

73. Lanning, Howman, Posselt, "Conference of Superintendents of Natives and Native Commissioners" (meeting December 1927), 19, 27.

74. Murray, *Governmental System,* 271–343.

75. Ibid., 288–93.

76. Of the two votes against, at least one was cast by a missionary of the Dutch Reformed Church (Rev. Reyneke). Etheridge, *Proceedings of the Southern Rhodesian Missionary Conference* (PSRMC) (July 1922), 13–20.

77. Etheridge, PSRMC (July 1922), 13–20. Even the staff of the government schools was recruited from the mission community, earning the antagonism of missionaries who felt that the government had no business luring away mission staff with relatively high government salaries when replacements were so difficult to come by. The first head of Domboshawa, Broderick, was recruited from the Church of England mission, leaving his bishop to remark, "He cannot serve two masters! and is under the entire control of H. S. Keigwin. . . . Our clergy resent Broderick's school . . . and I think quite rightly, too." The Bishop pointed out that he, himself, had no more control over Domboshawa than over some school in Australia. Bishop to SPG (1919?), USPG/CLR 142. Alvord, an agricultural specialist, was recruited in 1925 against the American Board's protests (Alvord to ABC, 16 July 1926, ABC 15.4, vol. 36, item 236). And when W. G. Brown of the LMS was recruited to head Tjolotjo after Alexander's resignation, the local missionaries were irritated (Jones to LMS, 20 July 1923, CWM 85/3) and succeeded in blocking his release from the society.

78. Keigwin, PSRMC (July 1922), 13–20.

79. In 1915 the Southern Rhodesian Missionary Conference had narrowly (8 to 7) rejected a proposal for a "Native Christian Workers" Conference (PSRMC, June 1915). Such a forum was considered premature. But despite lags and misgivings, the major mission societies recognized the necessity of developing not merely an African church, but a society in which improved, educated, and transformed Africans could take part as full citizens.

80. *PSRMC* (June 1924), 15–16.

81. *PSRMC* (June 1924), 12–14.

82. Annual Report of the Education Department, 30 June 1920, ABC 15.4, vol. 35, item 122.

83. Annual Report of the Education Department, 30 June 1921, ABC 15.4, vol. 35, item 125.

84. Mather to ABC, 30 March 1918, ABC 15.4, vol. 34, item 4, placed a heavy emphasis on the need to acquire skilled primary teachers. And when improvement came, it was probably partly brought by training in teaching techniques, and partly because these lower elementary pupils were finally being taught by teachers who had more than a lower elementary education. Chikore, a large American Board station, had a staff in 1921 that included 2 Europeans, 2 certificated teachers from Natal, and 2 Standard VI graduates, 2 Standard V graduates, and 4 Standard III graduates from Mt. Silinda. J. Condy, Inspector's Report, Chikore, 16 September

1921, ABC 15.4, vol. 35, item 127. It took longer to provide certified teachers for the outschools, but by 1927 nearly all outstations had 2 teachers, both of whom were graduates (Standard VI), and the board was experimenting with paying women teachers on the same salary schedule as men. Report of Silinda Outstations for June 1927, ABC 14.4, vol. 35, item 258. Chikore's outstations were slower to recruit fully qualified teachers, but even so, by 1928, there were 35 men and 14 women teaching in Chikore outstation schools, of whom one had passed Standard VII, 17 graduated Standard VI, 3 completed standard V, 18 standard IV, 5 standard III, and 5 standard II. Many of the less-educated would have taught in two-teacher schools. Chikore had 23 outschools. Annual Report of Chikore Outstation Schools, June 1928, ABC 15.4, vol. 35, item 156.

85. Report of Mt. Silinda School for the year, June 1926, ABC 15.4, vol. 35, item 235.

86. "The Future of the Educational Work of Mt. Silinda Station," 1929, ABC 15.4, vol. 35, item 247.

87. See the discussion of improving standards in the Dutch Reformed schools during the late 1920s and 1930s, in Carol Summers, "Educational Controversies: African Activism and Educational Strategies in Colonial Zimbabwe, 1914–1934" (seminar paper, 1992).

88. In 1915 six students passed Standard IV at Waddilove (Stanlake, Waddilove Training Institution Report for 1915, WMMS 826/5), an entirely respectable number for the time, but John White pointed out that the institution was barely scraping by, and that for twelve years the work had been carried on in inadequate buildings and with inadequate staff (White to MMS, 31 August 1915, WMMS 826/5). At the beginning of 1919 Nengubo was missing two European staff members (the schoolmaster had left after his wife sought a divorce, the industrial specialist had left to take up farming, and the woman teacher's health was failing) and had just dismissed two African staffers for immorality. It began the year with Loveless temporarily transferred in as the schoolmaster, and the girls' school closed. Loveless to MMS, 22 January 1919; Loveless to MMS, 13 May 1919; WMMS 827/8. Nevertheless, by 1923 it had increased in size, and twenty-seven students passed Standard IV, four from Standard V, two completed Standard VI for certification as teachers, and in addition to academics, the mission became notable for the girls' program in domestic training. J. Condy, Gov. Inspector's Report, Waddilove Training Institute, 1923 and Needlework and Handwork Exhibit, 1923, WMMS 827/13. Waddilove lost another schoolmaster in 1923, but by then the institution had begun to build momentum, and things did not grind to a halt. White to MMS, 24 November 1923, WMMS 828/1.

89. In 1920 the Anglicans were bemoaning the state of their educational program in comparison with that of the American Methodists and the American Board, but they were trying to correct some of the most se-

rious problems. SRQ 114 (November 1920): 8-9; Rev. H. Barnes (St. Aug's), SRQ 101 (August 1917): 5-7; Baker, SRQ 103 (February 1918): 4-6. And the policy of accepting younger students was not limited to St. Augustine's. Subsidiary institutions also began to place more emphasis on educating children. Upcher, SRQ 104 (May 1918): 6 (St. Faith's, Rusape, accepting younger children). There was, though, a split between those at St. Augustine's who wanted increased investment in the central institutions (above), and those who glorified the idea of a Christian community centered around a kraal school with little more than a rudimentary education—for example, E. W. Lloyd (at Rusape), SRQ 117 (August 1921): 10-12.

90. Jones to LMS, 18 April 1918, CWM 81/2.

91. It opened with eighteen boarders, Whiteside to LMS, 28 March 1921, CWM 84/1.

92. Jones to LMS, 2 August 1922, CWM 84/5. By 1923, though, Inyati managed to convince a government inspector that at least one of its students was up to Standard IV. This represented notable progress over a short period. R. MacIntosh, Government Inspection report on Inyati, 1923, CWM 85/1.

93. Jones to LMS, 12 December 1929, CWM 91/Jones.

94. Brown admitted in 1929 that he had been turning away would-be students. Brown to LMS, 5 August 1929 and Brown to LMS, 16 February 1930, CWM 90/ W. G. Brown.

95. The school had a total of ninety-five boarders in 1926. Jones, Hope Fountain Girls' School Annual Report for 1926, CWM 6/4. The girls' school was, indeed, so successful that some of the government inspectors expressed reservations, afraid it was "proceeding too far beyond the simple needs of native life." Cowling, Inspector's Report on Hope Fountain, 1927, CWM 7/1.

96. W. G. Brown, Inyati Boys' School Annual Report for 1926, CWM 6/4. While Hope Fountain continued to improve and diversify, Inyati ran into problems during the late 1920s, related to both staffing problems and increasing dissatisfaction with Brown's management style. Its difficulties culminated in the 1932 student strike, after which Brown left. See Brown, Annual Report for Inyati 1929, CWM 7/1; Brown, Principal's Report on Inyati for 1932, CWM 8/1, or Carol Summers, "Educational Controversies."

97. Fr. Biehler to Johanny, 23 January 1923, JAH 126/3.

98. Loubiere's school at Kutama claimed to offer two hours a day of elementary literary education. Loubiere, comments on industrial training in response to questionnaire (1920?) NAZ N3/9/1-2. Most missions who were serious about education offered substantially more than this governmentally imposed minimum for third-class schools.

99. J. E. Loubiere, "Native Industrial Training in Rhodesia," *Zambesi Mission Record* 6 (April 1921): 399-408.

100. Loubiere, "Native Industrial Training," 399–408.

101. Fr. Loubiere to Fr. Superior, 10 May 1921, JAH, box 134/2.

102. Lorenzo [catechist] to Fr. Loubiere [Kutama] (report of discussion with Joseph, another catechist), 30 December 1921, JAH, box 134/2. Lorenzo and Joseph may have originally come from South Africa.

103. Callan to Director of Education (Foggin), 30 November 1925, JAH, box 134/3. Callan proposed that students be recruited from among those who had passed Standard II for a four-year certification program, and that the entry standard should soon be raised to Standard III, in accordance with the government's requirements for three-year teacher certification programs.

104. C. Bert [Driefontein] to Rev. Father, 9 October 1922; Bert to Johanny, 9 March 1923, JAH, box 124/1.

105. Bert, Notes on the Condition of the School (January 1925?) and Gardner to Fr. Superior 5 December 1924, JAH, box 124/1; Gardner to Fr. Superior, 7 January 1925 and Gardner to Fr. Superior 18 February 1925, JAH, box 124/2. Lenfestey, Education Department Native School Inspection Report [Driefontein] (copy), 9 April 1926, JAH, box 124/2. Foggin to Collingridge, 25 April 1927, JAH, box 124/3.

106. See, for example, Archdeacon Etheridge (Church of England), and John White (Wesleyan Methodist), *PSRMC* (July 1922), 13–20; and John White's reaction to the Phelps-Stokes criticisms of mission education, *PSRMC* (June 1924), 22. *Report of the Commission on Native Education in Southern Rhodesia* (1925), 86.

107. For examples of this logic, see Leggate, *Legislative Council Debates* (1–25 May 1922), 380–82; Ethel Tawse Jollie (MLC Umtali), *The Real Rhodesia* (London: Hutchinson and Co, 1924), 270–74.

108. See, for example, Whiteside, Tjimali/Dombodema Report for 1933, CWM AR 8/2, who explained that it was impossible to ensure that a European missionary visited each remote school on the reserves four times each year. Whiteside expected to lose government grants for several of his outstations.

109. For example, Conference with Zulu Helpers, 28 July 1920, ABC 15.4, vol. 35, item 5.

110. For example, "Minutes, Rhodesia Branch," 3 June 1918, ABC 15.4, vol. 32, item 37.

111. For example, "Rules Governing Assistant Teachers," August 1925, ABC 15.4, vol. 35, item 253.

112. W. W. Anderson, Dombodema Annual Report for 1920, CWM 6/1; Whiteside, Dombodema/Tjimali Annual Report for 1927, CWM 7/1. Not all the missions paid their teachers in cash, though. The Catholics, who were notorious for announcing that their teachers worked for devotion alone, suffered a high attrition rate, but the teachers who stayed managed to enrich themselves at the mission's expense through the use of land,

expense money for housing and food, unpaid labor by schoolboys, and the authority they garnered as the local representative of The Mission. See, for example, the history of Lorenzo, a catechist who, cozily ensconced at Mkaya, inquired when the mission sought to transfer him, "who would put up his houses" at the new station. Fr. Bick was quite incensed that Lorenzo required more than one house. Fr. Seed reported that Lorenzo refused to move unless paid reasonable compensation for his huts and fields. Originally, Lorenzo officially worked for no pay beyond his keep. This arrangement ended up costing the mission quite a bit more than a salary would have, but when the mission sought to change him from keep to salary, Lorenzo objected, asking, "What about the pay for my wife?" J. H. Seed to Fr. Superior, 30 November 1927; J. H. Seed to Fr. Superior, 1 January 1928, JAH, box 126/4.

113. The Tati school committee was expected to come up with the money for two-thirds of the teachers' salaries the first year, and the full salaries in subsequent years. It was paying for the privilege of having qualified teachers rather than whomever the mission happened to have available. Whiteside, Dombodema Annual Report for 1925, CWM 6/3.

114. "Minutes of the Hope Fountain District Teacher's Committee," 10 December 1917, CWM 81/1. The meeting as a whole is interesting. Though clearly scripted to some degree by Neville Jones, who acted as the committee's chair, all other members were Africans, and the committee was the context for policy decisions on morality, discipline, and finances.

115. Donohue (Methodist Episcopal, USA) to Oldham, 15 August 1929, IMC/CBMS, box 1221.

116. In addition to the LMS, the ABC has left written records of such an organization, and such committees were common, though not universal. In 1915 there was enough interest in a nation-wide, interdenominational "Native Christian Workers' Conference" to parallel the Southern Rhodesia Missionary Conference that seven of the fifteen missionary delegates voted for its formation. Some of the votes against may have been cast by missionaries from societies that had organizations, but worried about large organizations of Africans, or about other societies making attempts to lure their teachers away.

117. J. Marsh, Report on the work of Jeanes teachers, Chikore Kraal schools January–June 1933; Orner, Report on the work of Jeanes teacher Mac Sitole, 2d half 1933, 31 December 1933; Ibbotsen, Report on the work of A. Zhakata (JT Selukwe), July–December 1933, and others, NAZ S1542/J1, vol. 3.

118. SoN Victoria (Howman) to CNC, 23 February 1934, NAZ S1542/J1, vol. 3.

119. James Stewart, Report on J. Ndebele, 1934; G. Stark (acting DND) Minutes, 27 March 1935; Superintendent's Half-Yearly Report on the Jeanes teacher at Chibi, Josias Cipato, July 1935; Report on Jeanes teacher work

at All Saints Mission Wrenningham for half year ending June 1934, NAZ S1542/J1/vol. 1; Bullock (Assistant CNC) "Control of Native Demonstrators in Native Reserves," undated; DND to CNC, 18 April 1934; SoN Victoria to CNC, 29 March 1934, NAZ S1542/J1, vol. 2; CNC to Minister of Native Affairs, 9 March 1934, NAZ S1542/J1, vol. 3.

120. Louw [Dutch Reformed] to CNC, 11 April 1934, NAZ S1542/J1, vol. 2, defended Lysias, a JT who was secretary of the Southern Rhodesian Natives' Association, involved in organizing opposition to an agricultural demonstrator's plan for centralizing grazing and arable land, and accused of the direct defiance of an NC's orders. The Salvation Army objected vehemently when an NC attempted to question a JT's actions. Territorial Commander, Salvation Army to CNC, 15 March 1934; CNC to Maj. Stoyle, 13 March 1934; CNC to Minister of Native Affairs, 9 March 1934; and NC Mazoe to CNC 6 March 1934, NAZ S1542/J1, vol. 3.

121. R. J. Challiss, "The European Educational System in Southern Rhodesia, 1890 to 1930" (*Zambesia* supplement, 1982) argues that this attempt to promote European solidarity through the school system was unique to Southern Rhodesia, transcending issues of Dutch versus English that tied up South African European education, and reacting to a far stronger threat than Kenyan settlers ever experienced.

122. Gilchrist, *Legislative Council Debates* (1920), 495-98.

123. Tawse Jollie, McChlery, *Legislative Council Debates* (1920), 480-84, 491-94; Gilchrist, *Legislative Council Debates* (1922), 332-36.

124. Tawse Jollie, *Legislative Council Debates* (1921), 675-76.

125. See, for example, Leggate, Mennell, Tawse Jollie, *Legislative Assembly Debates* (1925), 675-80; 881; 662-69.

126. Hadfield, *Legislative Council Debates* (1922), 346-47. See also the comments by Tawse Jollie and Boggie, *Legislative Council Debates* (1921), 675-77.

127. Challiss, "European Educational System," 1-4.

128. *Report of the Commission on Native Education in Southern Rhodesia* (1925), 86-87.

129. By 1915 settlers were asking questions in the Legislative Council over the shortage of certified teachers in the government's European schools, as they were concerned over the quality of teaching. In 1915, 114 of the 146 teachers in government schools for Europeans were certified. *Legislative Council Debates* (1915), 255, 266. Gilchrist emphasized that given the immense need for European education in the country, and the difficulties of distance and diffusion which must be overcome, a cost-effective program was vital. As it was, too great a part of the budget had been spent on buildings. *Legislative Council Debates* (1923), 559-61. And in 1924 Tawse Jollie moved to reduce the salary of the director of education, arguing that the Education Department was failing in its mission to give every European child in the country the best possible educa-

tion. Instead, when the school system expanded, it expanded in the form of farm schools with inferior education. *Legislative Council Debates* (1924), 687-88. By 1920 some settlers were arguing not only that education was vital to European children, but that free primary school would not be enough. Secondary school was important, and should be government funded. Moffat, *Legislative Council Debates* (1920), 484-91. Moffat's argument was restated repeatedly, most emphatically by Tawse Jollie: "I think we all agree that we cannot afford to have white children growing up in this country at a low level of education, or at a lower level than some of the natives. . . ." *Legislative Council Debates* (1925), 662-69.

130. Educational cost-effectiveness, however measured, was not a requirement or a value until 1927, when, for the first time, the grant for mission schools was divided into a portion assessing "literary efficiency" and a portion indicating training in character. Colonial Secretary (Leggate), *Legislative Assembly Debates* (1927), 37-43. The Native Education Act, of which this initiative was a part, was not, however, designed to improve the efficiency of education. It worked to limit education. New funds were not made available. Judgments on efficiency were mere excuses to close schools or reduce funding. Ultimately, this led to the reduction in the numbers of schools, and of the number of Africans receiving schooling, which took place in the early 1930s. For examples of the effects of the changed rules, see H. Jowitt, "Report of the Director of Native Development for the year 1929" (Salisbury: Government Printer, 1930), 55: "Many schools have been closed rather than replace poor teachers with more poor teachers"; G. Stark, "Report of the Acting DND for the year 1934" (Salisbury: Government Printer, 1935), 1.

131. Douglas-Jones, *Legislative Council Debates* (1922), 368-69.

132. Moffat, *Legislative Council Debates* (1922), 375-79.

133. McChlery, *Legislative Council Debates* (1922), 369-72. Douglas-Jones accused the SRMC of being envious, and Tawse Jollie argued that McChlery was merely confusing matters (373-76).

134. Gilchrist, *Legislative Council Debates* (1923), 595.

135. Administrator, *Legislative Council Debates* (1923), 600.

136. Boggie, *Legislative Council Debates* (1923), 575.

137. Tawse Jollie, *Legislative Council Debates* (1922), 374-76. She points out that the scheme was not to turn out highly skilled workers, but to provide Africans with craft skills they could use in their own homes. Her impressions were confirmed by the prospectus of the government schools, which asserted that the aim of government schools was "to turn out men who shall be able, both by their conduct and their knowledge, to set a higher standard of life to those around them. . . . It is not contemplated that a complete preparation for trades shall be given." Keigwin, "Report of the Director of Native Development for 1922," 23.

138. *Report of the Commission on Native Education in Southern Rhodesia* (1925), 97.

139. Ironically, African women's success as agricultural producers meant that they were actually competing more successfully with European men than African men were, as they could grow high-quality maize in large quantities more cheaply than the European-run farms could. Elizabeth S. Schmidt, "Ideology, Economics, and the Role of Shona Women in Southern Rhodesia, 1850–1939" (Ph.D. dissertation, History, University of Wisconsin, Madison, 1987), 184. European settlers, though, do not seem to have conceptualized this agricultural production as competition by women. Instead, it was regarded as competition by Africans, since African men controlled the marketing. It is interesting, however, to speculate whether settlers' interest in domestic training for women may have been associated with a desire to handicap settlers' African agricultural competitors.

140. Schmidt, "Role of Shona Women," 156, 173, 197, 204, 206, 347.

141. Tawse Jollie, Gilchrist *Legislative Council Debates* (1923), 580–82, 593–94. These mentions of the importance of girls' education were mere foreshadowings, though, of the emphasis put on it by the *Report of the Commission on Native Education in Southern Rhodesia* (1925), 93–96, which deplored what it regarded as the conservative mass of African women, who tolerated polygyny, brideprice, the pledging of female children, and widow inheritance. The commission asserted that the slowness of civilizing advances to penetrate the female population explained the "slow development of the mass of indigenous Natives. The efforts to elevate touched only half the race, with the result that the untouched half tended to keep the other down."

142. R. J. Challiss, "The Foundation of the Racially Segregated Educational System in Southern Rhodesia, 1890–1923, with special Reference to the Education of Africans," (Ph.D. dissertation in History, University of Zimbabwe, 1982), 92.

143. *Report of the Commission on Native Education* (1925), 67.

144. Eickhoff, *Legislative Council Debates* (1925), 670–72.

145. Tawse Jollie, *Legislative Council Debates* (1927), 86–88.

146. Tawse Jollie was particularly worried by the ratio of European supervisors to African students; in Southern Rhodesia 128 missionaries were engaged in educational work. That educational work taught over 90,000 Africans. *Legislative Council Debates* (1927), 86–92.

147. Hadfield, *Legislative Council Debates* (1927), 126–29.

148. Leggate (Colonial Secretary), *Legislative Council Debates* (1927), 37–40.

149. Leggate, *Legislative Assembly Debates* (1927), 37–40.

150. Leggate, *Legislative Council Debates* (1927), 37–40.

151. Leggate, *Legislative Council Debates* (1927), 41-43.

152. Leggate, *Legislative Council Debates* (1927), 43. Tawse Jollie approved this sentiment, noting that "a great number of people in this country are asking themselves the question: what is education, especially what is education as applied to the native peoples?" The new emphasis on character, she noted, simplified matters, though she still worried about "what you are going to do after the education. . . . We should make no pretence of educating them in exactly the same way as we do Europeans" (pp. 82-86). Sir Ernest Montagu applauded the government emphasis on inspection and character (pp. 133-34), and other legislators grudgingly acknowledged that despite their suspicions of education, the new legislation seemed something of an improvement: see Mennell, Thomson, Moffat, Gilfillan, and Inskipp, pp. 136-51.

153. Gilchrist, *Legislative Council* (1923), 593-94.

154. Leggate, *Legislative Council Debates* (1922), 380-82; Leggate argued that Africans thought all workers should be paid the same regardless of their training, and he labeled this communistic thinking.

155. Examples are far too numerous. A good one is Hadfield, *Legislative Council Debates* (1922), 384-89.

156. See, for examples, Gilchrist, *Legislative Council Debates* (1921), 688, who argued for training in the personal qualities necessary for punctual, disciplined police work; or Leggate, *Legislative Assembly Debates* (1927), 37-40, 43, who wanted to see Africans taught discipline and character because without such training "little there is in kraal life to produce what we know as character. We do not have any strong public opinion here which ostracises a person who has no self-control and is fond of self-indulgence. . . ."

157. Africans throughout the country were making a "tremendous effort" to get the rudiments of an education, pointed out Major Boggie, *Legislative Council Debates* (1922), 366-38.

158. For example, Gilchrist bemoaned the individualism of educated Africans. *Legislative Council Debates* (1923), 593-94.

159. For a rabid example, see Boggie, *Legislative Council Debates* (1922), 366-68: separatist Christian religious groups, he feared, were impressing on Africans that they were in every way equal to Europeans. These groups, he thought, were teaching socialism, and even "Bolshevism."

160. Africans, McChlery pointed out to his colleagues, were adopting modern methods of agriculture, such as the plow and selective cattle breeding, and Europeans must realize that "the natives in this country are the real workers of the country, they are the real wealth producers of the country. . . ." *Legislative Council Debates* (1920), 532-37.

161. The secretary of the Department of Agriculture consistently pushed farmers to find or train more skilled labor, pointing out that "a cheap and plentiful supply of inefficient labour is never likely to be either satisfactory

or economical, and the want of knowledge, energy and intelligence makes labour of that class too costly for the average farmer." "Report of the Secretary, Department of Agriculture, for 1926" (Salisbury: Government Printer, 1927), 7. His opinion was supported by some settlers, such as Tawse Jollie, a housewife and legislator experienced in living in rural areas. Tawse Jollie attested to the differences between hiring servants in Britain and in Southern Rhodesia, pointing out the near impossibility of recruiting female servants, workers' lack of skill, and the employer's inability to surrender any of her supervisory functions lest the food be inedible or the children maltreated by incompetent or undisciplined servants. Tawse Jollie, *Real Rhodesia,* 200-203. Nor were these practical reasons the only justification for supporting development programs. There was also the moral issue that the legislators discussed at length during the initial approval of the Keigwin scheme. Sincerity probably varied, but many, including Tawse Jollie, asserted that it would be demeaning to Europeans' sense of themselves as civilized not to seek to teach Africans what they themselves knew. See also Tawse Jollie, *Real Rhodesia,* 262. The gap between Tawse Jollie's public and private statements, though, may have been substantial. See Alvord's discussion of his feud with her (the unnamed Lady Member of the Legislative Assembly) in "Development of Native Agriculture," 14-16.

162. Boggie, *Legislative Council* (1922), 366-68, predicted that education would lead to incongruities between the sorts of jobs available and the qualifications of the workers—"something radically wrong" and potentially dangerous.

163. For examples, Stewart, *Legislative Council Debates* (1922), 394; *Commission on Native Education* (Salisbury: Government Printer, 1925), 97.

164. Even Hadfield, an advocate of education for Africans, acknowledged that European children were growing up in the region and quitting school, "mentally saturated," after only a primary education. These young people needed jobs. In 1924 he asserted that jobs were present in the economy. But it was difficult to be confident of the future. Hadfield, *Legislative Assembly Debates* (1924), 705; Tawse Jollie, Eickhoff, Leggate, Mennell, *Legislative Assembly Debates* (1925), 662-69, 670-72, 675-80, 892.

165. *Report of the Commission on Native Education in Southern Rhodesia* (1925), 116.

166. Tawse Jollie, *Real Rhodesia,* 293.

167. Tawse Jollie, Eickhoff, *Legislative Assembly Debates* (1925), 662-69, 670-72 and Annual Report of Mt. Silinda School, 1 June 1924, ABC 15.4, vol. 35, item 231. Challiss, "European Educational System," 27, argues that numbers were also important, and that the increased enrollments of Africans in mission schools after 1900 was the principal factor pushing the development of European education well into the 1930s.

168. Resident Commissioner, *Legislative Council Debates* (1923), 582-89.

169. For examples, H. S. Keigwin, "An Educational Experiment," *South African Journal of Science* 18 (December 1921): 172-82; and, for concerns about the boarding system for European children, Tawse Jollie and Boggie, *Legislative Council Debates* (1921), 675-76, 677. Tawse Jollie feared the loss of "the moral influence of the home." Also, compare the conclusions of the Commission on Native Education (1925) and the arguments of the Education Commission (1929), which confined its work to Europeans. The Native Education Commission worried over the moral state of African communities and sought industrial and home education capable of correcting perceived problems (pp. 10-13, 67, 70, 94-96, etc.). The Education Commission acknowledged that education could only do a limited amount, as "the real educator is always the community itself in the end" (p. 10). It then went on to argue that "practical" and "intellectual" training could not be distinguished (p. 30). And it advocated home training for girls alongside of industrial training in disciplines such as agriculture for boys (pp. 61, 76). Finally it acknowledged that education must be regarded above all else as a "character-forming process" (p. 111). In all, these educational policy outlines were remarkably similar. And both Commissions saw education as a tool in the construction of the future.

170. "Report of the Director of Education for 1927," 14; "Report of the Director of Education for 1930."

171. *Report of the Commission on Native Education* (1925), 116.

172. Challiss, "Racially Segregated Educational System," ii–iv, argues that settlers and administrators in Southern Rhodesia tended to view African and European education as two totally different problems, a perspective he sees as having reached its ascendancy through the legacy of "Phelps-Stokesism." It is true that the resources available to educate African and European children differed widely, and while Europeans were to be educated to rule, Africans were to be educated to be productive servants. But the lines clearly blur over when policymakers discuss poor whites and the African elite.

173. Leggate, *Legislative Council Debates* (1922), 380-82.

174. Administrator, *Legislative Council Debates* (1922), 389-93.

175. L. Cripps (not to be confused with A. S. Cripps of the Church of England), *Legislative Council Debates* (1922), 383.

176. Bertin, *Legislative Assembly Debates* (1929), 127-28.

177. C. L. Carbutt (CNC), "Address delivered to the Rotary Club, Salisbury, March 1932," *NADA* 10 (1932): 57-59.

178. C. L. Carbutt (CNC), "The Racial Problem in Southern Rhodesia," *NADA* 12 (1934): 6-12; and, for a settler example, Tawse Jollie, *Legis-*

lative Assembly Debates (1927), 84. "We do intend that the Europeans shall occupy a certain position in the country. Let us frankly say that within these limits, we shall give the native child an education. . . . [But] We do not intend to hand over this country to the native population or to admit them to the same social or political position as we occupy ourselves. . . . we should make no pretence of educating them in exactly the same way as we do Europeans."

179. Quotation, and the acknowledgement of the contradictory nature of the concept of a different civilization, drawn from the *Report of the Commission on Native Education* (1925), 116.

CHAPTER SIX

Imposing Differences

FROM SOCIALIZATION TO SEGREGATION, 1927–34

At the end of 1929, his first full year as chief native commissioner of Southern Rhodesia, H. M. G. Jackson looked back over his thirty-five years in the region and acknowledged that change was no longer something that Southern Rhodesia could look forward to in the distant, or even the immediate future. Change had already happened. During any one year, the African population might appear to experience little social change, but between the Africans of thirty-five years ago and those of 1929, lay a "gulf" of social, economic, and political transformation.[1]

By the end of the 1920s, settlers, government officials, missionaries, and Africans could see a new Southern Rhodesia. In less than forty years, the economy had moved from its precolonial roots in subsistence agricultural labor and the accumulation of surplus stored up in cattle, gold, and cloth, to a diversified colonial economy, where access to markets was all-important, and monetization had spread from the region's urban and mining centers to the agricultural hinterland. Forty years of intercultural contacts—ranging from trading relationships to tax collection to wage labor—also complicated the social relations of the region, leaving African authorities battered, Europeans competing with each other, and authority contingent on placement and access rather than on absolute power. And during those forty years, as the economy and society became increasingly complex, knowledge about those complexities and the changing politics of the region spread to an avid public anxious to survive and profit from transformation.

The possibilities of this changed economy and society scared many settlers. The country was no longer inhabited by two separate communities, marked off from each other by history, culture, and appearance. From a simple racial hierarchy, in which those of European descent had dominated those of African descent, the European community was dissolving into factions with jobs and without jobs, urban and rural, immigrant and Rhodesian-born, English-speaking and Dutch-speaking, rich and poor. The African community, always heterogeneous, had become increasingly divided. Literacy, skills, English-language ability, access to money, access to land, and divisions between the urban and the rural populations became nearly as important as earlier distinctions of seniority, age, or gender. Both competition and interdependence between the European and African communities sharpened as the rise of a generation, both black and white, that had grown up in a colonial Southern Rhodesia blurred differences based on socialization and knowledge. Years of education and legislation promoting communal cohesion had not been markedly successful. The future that had arrived was characterized by intracommunal social differentiation, and intercommunal convergence and competition.

Africans and Europeans struggled over the management of the new society. Education and labor policies designed to spread individualism, cultural knowledge, and monetization increasingly appeared to have worked far more quickly than their initial sponsors had anticipated. Even as some Africans embraced change and sought prosperity within the European-dominated sector, others clamored for the reinforcement of earlier structures of power within African communities, parents over children, men over women, and elders over young progressives. And a vocal faction of the Europeans of Southern Rhodesia increasingly attempted not merely to half assimilationist civilizing policies, to develop social policies to promote discipline instead of change, or to create a coherent blueprint for a future of divergence of European and African societies, economies, and polities, but to use state power to shape the present, to block a present threat.

The logic of segregation was rooted in the straightforward idea that the community rather than the individual was the appropriate unit for social analysis and policy, and a conviction that communities had different attributes and different histories, which made their separation and independence important. Within Southern

Rhodesia, though, this simple logic produced many different segregationist proposals.

At a very basic level, most Southern Rhodesians, including many Africans, proposed "social segregation." That could mean illegalizing sex or marriages between Africans and Europeans.[2] More broadly, though, it meant ensuring, formally through laws or informally through social sanctions, that Africans and Europeans did not meet as equals over the dinner table, in the club room, or in any other situation where they might be expected to talk with each other.

Economic forms of segregation were debated even more vigorously than social segregation. In an agricultural setting, economic segregation could mean territorial segregation, designating areas as African or European. This territorial segregation could be envisioned in various ways. Many Europeans merely wanted to ensure separate core areas where the interests of one racial group would predominate, but which would be permeable to migration for labor or trade. A minority, though, advocated total separation, either by exporting the Africans beyond the colony's borders or by creating sharp racial boundaries within the colony over which not even workers would be able to pass.[3] Proposals for territorial segregation could also be based in very different concepts of how much land Africans needed, with perspectives ranging from the employers' view, that Africans should not be granted enough land to support an increasing population, to the missionary argument that territorial segregation should leave African communities viable, with enough land to live and prosper.[4]

Some Europeans who supported economic segregation, but could not quite visualize carving the colony up into racially distinct units, opposed territorial segregation. These segregationists advocated other forms of economic segregation. The state could allocate agricultural markets, some suggested, according to the race of the farmer. Or it could designate specific jobs or sectors of the civil service or the industrial economy for Africans or Europeans. Such a policy could take the form of horizontal segregation—reserving good jobs for Europeans regardless of applicants' qualifications. A more common proposal, though, was vertical, sectoral industrial segregation, in which certain trades, such as engineering, might be set aside for Europeans, and others, such as shoemaking, for Africans.

Both Europeans and Africans also floated concepts of cultural segregation. Cultural segregation was rooted in the idea that there was a distinct African culture which was inherently different from that of the Europeans, and which should be kept separate from European culture lest Europeans degenerate and Africans become confused. Like social and economic segregation, advocates of cultural segregation could suggest various intensities. Many settlers, government officials, missionaries, and even some Africans, merely voiced a conservationist support for African arts and crafts,[5] or advocated supporting "traditional" authorities on reserves.[6] Other settlers, though, condemned missionaries, and called for their elimination from the African cultural atmosphere as intolerable contaminants.[7]

Finally, akin to both social and cultural segregation, segregationists contemplated political segregation. Most Europeans emphatically resisted the idea of African participation on common voter rolls, let alone African admission to the Legislative Assembly. Under imperial oversight, though, Africans' status as potential citizens was difficult to remove. Instead, through attempts to restrict African political rights to the reserves, political segregationists sought, simultaneously, to safeguard the European polity by blocking African participation, and to force educated and "traditional" African leaders to come to terms with each other, blunting the African community's potential for unified complaint about colonial policy by putting African progressives and elders in direct competition with each other.

Advocates of segregation also disagreed over how segregation fit into the grand scheme of Southern Rhodesia's history and future. Many of the most vehement segregationists saw segregation, of whatever form, as a permanent solution—indeed the only possible permanent solution—to the Native Question. Others, particularly missionaries, saw it as a temporary solution, appropriate to a specific point in time. Eventually, these temporally limited segregationists argued, Africans would cease to be too fragile to expose to the dangers of European civilization, the European economy would become less vulnerable to African competition, and progress would make segregation irrelevant.

These quite different understandings of what segregation meant allowed the logic and language of segregation to remain remarkably flexible, expressing the interests of different groups within Southern Rhodesia's colonial society. And, during the depression, settlers, government officials, missionaries, and Africans used segregationist language to argue for and against a wide variety of specific political initiatives. During the period from the labor crisis and Native Affairs Act of 1927 to the election of the explicitly segregationist Huggins government in 1933, debates over how to segregate the economy, society, administration, and politics of Southern Rhodesia edged out debates over whether segregation was sensible, appropriate, possible, or desirable.

And segregation was not merely an ideology to shape the society of the future. Segregation's advocates sought to use the state's coercive power to shape the present, to enforce a logic of communal solidarity that previous policies had promoted through education and socialization. Increasingly, debates over social policy became segregationist debates over dividing shares—whether of land, markets, political power, or knowledge—between racial communities. A need to create and enforce these distinctions by race formed the background for political discussions of the Land Apportionment Act of 1930, the Maize Control legislation of 1931 and 1934, the Native Councils Act of 1930, and the explicit censorship legislation published as the Prevention of Unrest Bills in various versions from 1928 through 1932. And the argument that the historically defined racial community rather than the educable individual was the relevant unit of social analysis and social policy provided the basis for a series of reforms altering the structure of the administration's bureaucracy to reflect segregationist norms in the most basic divisions of law, education, and agriculture. The Native Affairs Act provided for separate legal mechanisms and courts to try African cases and hear Africans' appeals. The Native Development Act separated African education off from the Education Department as a whole. And the same legislation provided the basis for dividing agricultural extension work into separate, race-based offices, with Africans in the Native Affairs Department or the Native Development Department, and Europeans in the Agriculture Department.

Southern Rhodesia was not officially a segregated state during the late 1920s and early 1930s. But many factions within the polity and society were increasingly arguing for segregation as an ideal. And by the end of 1930 Southern Rhodesia was moving so quickly toward instituting some policy of segregation that Governor Cecil Rodwell declared the country to be moving effectively to avoid "those difficulties which are vexing men's minds both to the north and south of us."[8] In his two years in office as the representative of the crown in Southern Rhodesia, Rodwell asserted that he had observed "the soundness and justness of the attitude and the outlook, not only of the Government, but of the whole European community, towards the native population.[9] Instead of a solution to the Native Question through a policy of "equal rights for all civilised men South of the Zambesi," which would have promoted social change and ultimately threatened Europeans' political and economic control, Southern Rhodesia moved toward segregation.

Changes

All groups within Southern Rhodesia shared a perception of transformation based, to a limited degree, on empirical realities of change. Farmers and farming organizations, both African and European, could point to technical, social, and commercial changes in Southern Rhodesian agriculture. Observers in both mining compounds and towns noted the growth of a class of Africans who were accustomed to working for wages, semiskilled or skilled, and increasingly distant from their presumptive rural origins.[10] And within the Legislative Assembly and the Native Department, politicians and officials alike increasingly expressed their fears of the effective demands that educated, skilled Africans were making on the state. The numbers of Africans involved in new types of agriculture, or the new urban culture, were small. But while empirical, quantitative changes in African economic, social, and political organization were minuscule in relation to the continuities provided by the colony's large food-producing African population, the changes that did occur had a qualitative impact out of all proportion to any quantitative measures of innovation. African and European perceptions of reality changed in response not to aggregate statistics, but to exceptional, vocal, or threatening individuals or small groups. "It is not the bulk of the natives that counts; it is the few who think and can organise," argued a critic of earlier government policies.[11] Both the demands for state intervention in the economic and social development of the colony, and the interventions that occurred, were responses to the threats individuals posed to the defensive communal logics of some Africans, and many settlers, officials, and missionaries.

In Southern Rhodesia's largely agrarian society, extensive changes in agriculture marked a fundamental transformation of the relationships both among Africans and between Africans and Europeans. Africans had sold grain and cattle to Europeans since at least the earliest European incursions of the 1880s. But by the 1920s, the sales were routine, and substantial. And in addition to large numbers of families who sold limited amounts of surplus grain for taxes or extras, a new class of small African commercial farmers began, during the 1920s, to gain the attention of Europeans.[12]

The numbers involved in this movement toward African commercial agriculture were not large. In 1921, only eight Africans bought land outside reserves, paying for freehold tenure through commercial farming and accumulated cattle. And even by 1925, Africans, including South African immigrants, had purchased a total of only fourteen farms, covering 46,966 acres.[13] But this movement toward land ownership and market-oriented production gradually grew from microscopic to small. And it had a symbolic significance out of all proportion to its quantitative impact. An African like Frank Sixubu—who, as an individual farmer, bought a 618-acre farm only seven miles from Salisbury, employed eight full-time laborers and fourteen squatter families, and earned extra income from cattle, donkeys, and wood—challenged comfortable demarcations between African and European production.[14] Land ownership, a process requiring time, energy, and connections, as well as money, was an important sign of capitalist agriculture in the region. With ownership, and security of tenure, came an intellectual and economic acknowledgement that all in life, from the land, to the labor that farmed it and the commodities that grew on it, was potentially a part of the cash economy.

While purchases of land were the most dramatic indication of the changing rural economy, some Africans who lacked official ownership also participated vigorously in the market economy. Africans could learn extensive farming techniques by working on European farms,[15] or experimenting with indigenous farming technologies. Some African farmers used plows and other equipment to harvest hundreds of bags of surplus grain through extensive agriculture.[16] By 1926, 27,584 plows were in use in the colony.[17] And between 1931 and 1934, under the new Land Apportionment Act, the government sold 160 substantial farms, with an average size of 360 acres, to Africans.[18]

The government also began to train Native Demonstrators in intensive, scientific agriculture. Each demonstrator was supposed to supervise new intensive farming techniques on a number of one-acre demonstration plots. Native Demonstrators were supposed to support subsistence activities, but their training provided them with knowledge of new farming technologies, a status as representatives of the state that they could use to recruit nonfamily labor, and the knowledge and connections they needed to market their surpluses. Though their salaries were paid by the government and the yields of demonstration plots belonged to the plots' owners rather than the demonstrators, demonstrators had to be restricted on how much land they, or their wives, were allowed to farm for themselves. And cooperators did not put the extra effort into demonstration plots merely for subsistence purposes. They grew maize to sell, resisting government attempts to push alternative, subsistence, crops such as *rukweza* (millet) that had little market value. The head of the training program admitted that demonstrators' innovations made little sense unless used as a means through which to become commercial farmers.[19]

Market-oriented agriculture, extensive or intensive, involved changes in the technology, social organization, and economic relations of production, and of African society as a whole. Technologically, both extensive and intensive agriculture relied on plows and quality cattle and seed supplies. Socially, plows and manuring increased each male farmer's demand for women's labor. Plows conserved male labor, and enabled each male farmer to extend planting, but did nothing to decrease women's labor of weeding and harvesting. And intensive manuring actually directly increased women's work by increasing the weed burden and forcing women to more vigilant supervision of growing crops. Commercially, the differential access of men and women to land, to the resources of production, and to markets, tended to undermine women's control over the proceeds of agricultural production. These changes in the balance between men's and women's labor, in a system that was slow to alter the sexual division of labor, affected both the social and economic implications of marriage, and may even have pushed increasing numbers of overworked girls and women into fleeing the rural areas for the towns and mining compounds.[20]

And just as the new agriculture bent and reformed the structures of African families, the new combination of resources and market opportunities affected other social relationships. By 1927 parents came into conflict with teachers over teachers' demands for mandatory unpaid labor from both students and their families in school plots and teachers' plots.[21] By 1929 Africans were organizing farmers' organizations—such as the Progressive Native Farmers' Associations of the Chindamora and Zimunya reserves, and Shiota, Wedza, and Umtali districts—and investing collectively in transport to market.[22] And throughout the 1920s, prosperous farmers attempted to participate in colonial politics through such organizations as Ndebele royalist movements, the Rhodesia Bantu Voters' Association, and the various Native Welfare Associations.[23]

The growth of this small group of market-oriented farmers set the stage for a backlash from both other Africans, and from Europeans. Not all market-oriented farmers owned land. Many farmed on the communally owned reserves. Large-scale farming for the market on limited reserve lands was both contrary to the point of the reserves and potentially dangerous to their effectiveness as regions of sustainable agriculture, or extractable labor. By 1929 the overstocking and extensive plowing of the reserves by market-oriented farmers anxious to make the most of their opportunities was beginning to produce visible ecological deterioration through the loss of fallow periods, poor crop rotation, and increasing erosion.[24] As the quality of reserve land deteriorated, African competition for increasingly limited quantities of land intensified as individual market-oriented farmers needed increased quantities of land, and Africans were pushed off "unalienated" or "European" land, increasing the population of the reserves.[25]

African farmers faced substantial and increasing obstacles to market participation at the end of the 1920s. There were not many conspicuously prosperous African commercial farmers. Even missions and schools, which had worked to develop a successful African peasantry capable of producing a marketable surplus to finance the clothes, schooling, and church contributions of the Christian African, had little success. In the early 1920s the agricultural work at Mt. Silinda, directed by E. D. Alvord, a professional American agronomist, was not effective by even rudimentary standards; the school, complete with an agriculture program, failed to feed itself, let alone grow crops to demonstrate commercial success.[26] And Alvord's judgment of agriculture on the reserves was even more critical. Africans' lives, he alleged, were centered around a "low type" of agriculture, characterized by techniques that degraded the land and promoted famine. "Because of their poor farming methods," he argued, "the lives of the great mass of our Rhodesian Natives are filled with poverty. They have worn-out lands, poverty-stricken cattle, poorly constructed huts, and undernourished, naked children."[27] Although a few visible Africans were leading a transformation in African agriculture, Africans "just emerging from heathenism" could not, missionaries argued, provide serious competition for Europeans "with centuries of culture."[28]

The state, first through the Native Department and then from within the new Native Development Department, attempted to shape a new, progressive African agriculture that would feed Africans and not threaten European farmers. Pursuing that goal, officials moved the government school at Domboshawa from an emphasis on industrial training, to focus on agriculture, used it to train Africans in agriculture, and then hired former students as agricultural demonstrators to work on the reserves showing other Africans the benefits of agricultural innovation. From 1927 to 1933 the number of demonstrators on the reserves grew from eleven to thirty-five, and the acreage they farmed from just over 93 acres to over 532 acres. During that same period, the yield per acre of the demonstrator's plots, while more erratic than the yields of the average African farm, was consistently at least twice that of the national average, and more often five or six times the average productivity of African-farmed land.[29]

Both mission- and government-sponsored agricultural initiatives advocating an African peasantry and intensive rather than extensive farming were, however, insignificant in comparison with the larger changes occurring within the colony as Africans competed with each other and restructured the systems of agricultural production which were at the root of rural Africans' lives. The very size of the gap between the productivity per acre of demonstration fields and those of the average producer indicated that demonstrators' techniques were hardly transforming the productivity of African agriculture as a whole. And without diffusion of the technology to the general African farming population, those 533 acres under scientific cultivation in reserves did not allow the African community to become rich, or to dominate the grain market. The demonstration program failed.[30] The other source of agricultural innovation, mission school farms, was no more revolutionary. Collectively, missions had farmed on far more land than 500-odd acres without significantly altering the economic status of the local African farmers.[31] Both mission and government initiatives were minuscule; the population of Africans on the reserves alone was, during this period, estimated at up to 660,000, and total land cultivated by Africans was estimated at up to one and a half million acres.[32] African grain production did not rise markedly in the 1920s or 1930s, and during the late 1920s and early 1930s African maize sales never amounted to more than 15 percent of European sales.[33] Thus, while not insignificant to the food security of the African population, changes in African farming practices showed no signs of providing prosperity for large numbers of Africans, or of suddenly threatening European farmers' preeminence in the grain market.

While agriculture dominated the economy of the colony, the most marked social changes were occurring in the urban or mining areas of the region. By 1928, when the weight of the Depression turned African unemployment into a serious problem, a full generation had been going to mines and towns to seek work, and patterns of labor migration and permanent, or at least long-term, urban immigration had transformed the nature of African labor. Large numbers of African men left the rural areas to find paid work. In some areas, such as the Makoni District where in 1926 the NC reported that 60 percent of able-bodied African men were away at work during the previous six months, wage labor had become the rule rather than the exception.[34]

Increasingly, these workers were knowledgeable job hunters. By the end of the 1920s, the day of wholly unskilled, "raw," African labor was over, if, indeed, it had ever existed. Under the economic, social, and political pressure of the settler economy, wage labor had become vital to the survival and prosperity of large sections of the African community, despite the government's continuing tendency to view that labor as migratory and volatile. Money, frequently gained through wage labor, was not merely useful to pay taxes; it was vital for survival and reproduction. Africans did not merely sell grain, they also bought it. They did not merely store wealth in cattle, they sold cattle as meat in order to buy grain or consumer goods, and paid cash for dipping fees levied on their growing herds. And bridewealth was increasingly quantified not merely in cattle, but also in money, with hefty monetary components of between £6 and £34.[35]

In both the urban locations and mining compounds, some workers—such as government messengers, clerks, "police boys," or relatively skilled workers—were not temporary migrants. They were almost wholly dependent on wages, or the proceeds of their skilled craftwork.[36] In the 1890s, when Africans had received relatively high wages, they had been paid more because African labor was a scarce commodity, rather than, necessarily, because the individual worker possessed a skill. By the end of the 1920s, though, the labor market had become more differentiated, from the low pay of agricultural workers or short-term contract workers, to the relative affluence of settled urban skilled or literate employees such as carpenters, servants, or clerks. Africans who showed up at mines to look for work had specific jobs in mind.[37] And Africans, even settled workers, could change jobs frequently in attempts to move up to better working conditions, better pay, or higher status. This was so well known by the government, which paid its African workers enough that their jobs were increasingly coveted by lower-class Europeans, that it bluntly rejected pleas from employers who wanted to coerce workers, pointing out that "a contented native is the best advertiser you can get," but that "if he feels that he is being paid below what he can get elsewhere, he will go there."[38]

Even before the Depression was in full swing, mines were no longer having trouble acquiring workers. From 1921 on, the proportion of mine labor recruited by the Rhodesian Native Labour Bureau's (RNLB) coercive tactics dropped markedly, amounting to less than 10 percent of the labor employed on Rhodesian mines.[39] That decline was not merely due to the increase in the numbers of indigenous African workers in Southern Rhodesia. Even workers from Northern Rhodesia, Nyasaland, and Portuguese East Africa increasingly entered the region of their own volition. And though farmers in Mashonaland complained vehemently about their labor problems during the tobacco boom, mines, particularly in Matabeleland or on the route to the Rand, had few problems acquiring enough workers.[40] Mine work paid better than farm work, and conditions could be better than on farms. Workers made decisions about where to work on the basis of knowledge, not chance, and spread information regarding working conditions through both word of mouth and extensive letter writing.[41]

The Depression had a catastrophic effect on the conditions and pay of African workers. By 1928 African labor was no longer scarce. African workers found themselves putting up with abuses they might once have changed jobs to avoid.[42] And as mines shut down or businesses reduced their workforce, employers were increasingly able to selectively employ only the most skilled or diligent.[43] But much though some urban or industrial Europeans might wish it,[44] settled urban Africans were not likely to pick up and leave the towns for the rural areas and reserves. Many of the Africans of the towns, wrote representatives of both the Salisbury Native Welfare Association and the Matabele Home Society, were born and raised in towns and industrial centers, without knowledge of reserve life.[45] European concerns about African landownership and competition in market gardening had kept pressure on the land available for Africans near urban areas. By 1930 government estimates of the population suggested that 5,540 Africans lived on less than 65 acres in the Bulawayo location, and while the Salisbury location was much less densely populated, with 2,976 living on 290 acres, it, too, had become an urban area with an urban population and urban problems, rather than a location of part-time farmers.[46] And mobility, which had historically provided the African answer to difficult conditions, was no longer practical; rural areas were already full of unemployed Africans in search of work, and the land shortage and low commodities prices made a return to agriculture a difficult and unpromising option.

Unemployed Africans were not the only source of social tension in the towns or on the roads of Southern Rhodesia: large numbers of indigent European settlers were even more disconcerting to the region's racial order. The European community formed some voluntary relief organizations, such as the Society for the Amelioration of Unemployment of Bulawayo.[47] And the government also worried. Southern Rhodesia did not have the "poor white problem" of South Africa, but it did appear to be moving in that direction. Gladys Maasdorp, campaigning for the Legislative Assembly on a government ticket, demanded immediate action to halt the descent of Europeans to the levels of Africans.[48] And after his 1933 election as prime minister, G. M. Huggins emphasized the dangers posed to European prestige by a poor white class. People who could not keep a job, he argued, must be given a bit of land and put in a labor colony, under close supervision. Their children, he argued, should be taken away and installed in boarding school to keep them from becoming as shiftless as their parents.[49] By the mid 1930s, government relief programs had installed unemployed Europeans in work programs on roads and afforestation projects, and other Europeans in the region were becoming increasingly resentful of those who did not keep up racial standards.[50]

Perceptions

Whatever the extent or limits of actual changes, Africans, missionaries, officials, and settlers had quite different perceptions and understandings of both the social changes of the 1920s, and the impact of the Depression.

In rural areas, the settler perception of aggressive African commercial agriculture produced conflict between Africans and Europeans. During the late 1920s and early 1930s, some European farmers voiced concern about the directions in which African agriculture was moving. In 1927, in the midst of European farmers' tobacco boom,[51] Rhodesia's farmers complained that Africans were not volunteering to work for Europeans in the large numbers needed to grow that labor-intensive crop.[52] Furthermore, they worried that the missionary and native development policies, by strengthening African education and productive capabilities, were only going to make matters worse, making workers more difficult to recruit, and African producers into serious competitors for agricultural markets. In 1927 the most outspoken complaints came from tobacco farmers, who demanded government policies capable of procuring more African laborers for European farms.[53] European farmers argued that increased levels of state control over conditions on the reserves were crucial to attempts to expand the labor force. An intensified Native Department presence and Native Department control could, they hoped, block such disturbing trends as economic reliance on beer brewing and bridewealth, which redistributed wages earned by a few migrant workers more widely to the women and older men of the reserves, and the increasing influence of missionaries, who advocated the development of an African peasantry rather than a migrant labor force.[54]

The labor shortage tobacco farmers complained of was short-lived. By the 1930s, a surplus of labor existed in Southern Rhodesia and, though Africans tried to choose where to work by leaving farmers who paid little or acted brutally toward them, the problem for European farmers at the end of the decade was no longer one of labor shortage, but of unemployed Africans wandering about looking for work.[55] But as the labor problem resolved itself, European farmers acquired other concerns.

By 1928 European farmers were already complaining that the government's cures for labor shortages—taxation and native development policies—were worse than the initial problem. Despite Native Development Department statistics indicating that Africans' grain production remained fairly steady from 1915 through 1939, and that average yields per acre might actually be declining, differentiation was occurring within the African community, and European farmers feared a revolution in African agriculture.[56] As the tobacco boom collapsed and attempts to find alternative crops failed, European farmers returned to a reliance on maize and cattle, both of which were also produced for market by African farmers. European farmers under these conditions found themselves competing with African agriculture not merely for labor, but also for markets. European farms lacked a substantial edge over African farms in technology, or even productivity. European farmers had improved their methods since the conquest, but not by much. Though some managed yields of nine bags an acre, most managed no more than five, and farmers frequently neglected fertilizer, rotation, or any attention whatsoever to the sustainability of their farming practices. By the 1930s many European fields were all but ruined.[57] To the north, in Nyasaland, these farmers could observe how African peasants had outcompeted a fledgling settler population.[58] And observers of African agriculture could point to increases in both the technical and the commercial skill of some African farmers. Technically, plows increased the possible scale of African farms, manuring made it possible to use increasingly scarce fields repeatedly rather than expending time for fallow or effort in clearing new fields, and improvements in seed quality and in cattle breeding made Africans' products comparable to those emerging from European farms.[59] Commercially, Africans in some areas worked together to improve the marketing of their produce, as on the Chindamora reserve (around Domboshawa school), where some farmers founded a Native Farmers' Association, with seven wagons to transport members' grain for large-scale marketing.[60] The Rhodesian Agricultural Union (RAU) feared that these changes, emerging from both African entrepreneurial activity and the government's native development policy, could provide the African farming sector with the resources it needed to drive an increasingly precarious European farming sector out of business. Two thousand European farmers would be forced off the land, and their places taken by Africans, warned the RAU in 1928.[61] By 1930 the president of the RAU was condemning Africans for scientific agriculture, and calling for controls on local markets.[62] And demands for controls became increasingly forceful as Africans diversified their production, and competed in all branches of agriculture. Agricultural markets within Southern Rhodesia, European farmers asserted, were

> the Europeans' own creation, and they [Europeans] should
> have the right to use them for their own purposes. The native

> owing to his lower standard of living, his rent-free land, his
> free child labour, can always sell products such as maize, milk,
> potatoes, eggs, wheat, fire-cured and later on flue-cured to-
> bacco, beans, pigs, etc. at a price far below that which a Euro-
> pean can possibly sell at and yet live and rear a family as he
> should be able to do.[63]

In these assessments of technological and commercial extensions
and improvements in African agriculture, these worried farmers
were almost certainly overstating changes in African agriculture.
The Farmers' Associations even had some difficulty convincing their
own members that European farmers were about to be outcompeted, as many felt it beneath their dignity to feel threatened by Africans.[64] European farmers suffered in the market not merely because
their maize and cattle competed with maize and cattle from African
producers, but because the markets for both were so seriously depressed that their marginal agriculture was inherently unprofitable.
Complaints regarding competition merely provided a convenient
way to argue for state intervention in the commodities market, limiting Africans' access through the Maize Control Act, and to use tax
income, including taxes on Africans, to prop up a sagging rural
economy.

While the claims of agricultural transformation were clearly overstated by nervous farmers seeking state intervention in the present
rather than social planning for the future, changes in the African
population of the mining and urban sectors of the economy clearly
had occurred by the end of the 1920s. In this context of economic
depression and decreasing mobility for Africans and Europeans
alike, three types of people were particularly dangerous to the stability and hierarchies of Rhodesian urban society: unemployed or
unsupervised Africans, elite skilled or educated Africans, and frustrated, lower-class Europeans.

Africans without steady work, or living from marginal, possibly
illicit, labor such as theft, beer brewing, or prostitution, made Europeans nervous because such marginal people lacked decorum. Europeans even considered the leisure time of employed Africans as
potentially dangerous. According to many Europeans, when Africans
were not employed as supervised labor, they did not belong in the
towns. When a plainclothes European police trooper in Bulawayo
slammed an African through a plate glass window, injuring him seriously, he defended his actions by arguing that the African should
have been brought to court for loitering on the sidewalk, and that

violent action was appropriate to the "insolence" and "nuisance" the African's presence had caused him.[65] And even worse than insolence in settlers' eyes was the potential embarrassment or danger these "loitering" African men could offer to European women by sitting on the sidewalk with their legs outstretched so that women had to walk over them, as the men laughed and commented.[66]

And unsupervised Africans in urban areas were considered dangerous not merely to the relations between Europeans and Africans, but also to the orderliness of the African community. Locations were settlements of Africans who lacked a common history or common authority figures. Inhabitants were not merely from Southern Rhodesia, but from throughout the southern African region. Many of the people, particularly the women in the locations, had left the rural areas to avoid customary authorities of one sort or another, such as husbands or fathers.[67] These people were therefore seen by Europeans and many Africans alike as "detribalised" and beyond customary control.[68] And by the late 1920s, life in the locations was dangerous as unemployed mine and tobacco workers flocked to the locations, scrambled for work, and, sometimes, resorted to gambling, prostitution, assault, and robbery.[69] This perception of danger became a reality in Bulawayo at the end of 1929 not merely for the individual victims of assault or robbery, but for the social order itself, when large-scale fighting broke out, centered on the Bulawayo municipal location and the Rhodesia Railways compound, with hundreds of Africans involved in the fighting. The authorities called up the local European Citizens' Defence Force, brought in police reinforcements from Salisbury, and, over a period of several days, stopped the fighting, leaving two dead, forty to fifty seriously injured, and almost 350 arrested—most of whom were sentenced to pay a £5 fine or serve one month in jail. Nor were these major riots the only violence to hit the Bulawayo location. "Faction fights" became common during the Depression, to the point that some Europeans saw them as both unavoidable, and institutionalized. "In fact, I think the natives rather enjoy these incidents," asserted one legislator who had previously served on the Bulawayo council responsible for the Bulawayo location.[70]

Control over urban African men was a problem. But urban women seemed, to many observers, an even greater threat to orderly urban life. With the Depression, increasing numbers of women moved into the locations or the periphery of towns to make what kind of living they could.[71] Women "of doubtful character," argued

Walter Chipwaya, should be prevented from entering and renting huts in locations, lest they damage the reputation of all location women, and the peace and quiet that the workers and their families needed.[72] And women, in addition to any prostitution they may have been carrying on, brewed beer, which was frequently blamed as the root of most African disorderly conduct.[73] Beer brewing in urban locations should be banned, argued one prominent expert, for both its devastating effects on order, and its promotion of de-generation.[74]

Leisure, prostitution, alcohol abuse, and fights were not entirely new to the locations of the late 1920s and early 1930s, but the De-pression intensified both the actual danger to the respectable Afri-can population living in the locations, and Europeans' sense of themselves as a community endangered by low-life Africans. With the Depression, asserted the head of the BSAP in 1932, came

> increased numbers of native loafers in and around townships . . . a large number of natives who have become "urbanised" and have no desire to work continuously, but who drift from one employer to another between periods of loafing. It is this type of native which constitutes the potential evil-doer.[75]

The police, he admitted, could not control the locations closely enough to prevent these dangers. "It is not easy," he pointed out, "to differentiate between the genuine visitor or unemployed native and the loafer element."[76] And even the genuinely unemployed African could be dangerous in the desperate environment of the Depression.

Both organizations of urban Africans, such as the Rhodesian Na-tive Welfare Associations, and such conservative settler notables as Ethel Tawse-Jollie worried over rootlessness and economic pres-sure in African urban areas. Africans raised those issues diffusely through the Bulawayo unrest, advocacy of "Native Welfare" pro-grams such as permanent villages, demands for education, and-condemnations of prostitution.[77] Tawse-Jollie was more articulate. Concerned by the specter of Bulawayo-style riots in those African areas that were becoming larger and more populous, and encir-cling the relatively small European towns, she argued that urban Africans had pulled up their roots and had forced themselves too quickly "along the path which the northern Europeans hacked out, step by step, in long years of training and discipline." Without a change in policy, she warned that Africans might "blow away from reality altogether," implicitly endangering anything in their path.[78]

But if order and public safety were endangered by unemployed, underemployed, or unsupervised Africans, pressed and scrambling to survive the Depression, European settlers found the upper end of the urban locations' society even more threatening. Tawse-Jollie, in marking out the dangers social change posed to urban life, pointed to "the detribalised, landless and yet educated and progressive native . . . inevitably the leader of the younger generation" as "the most dangerous class of all."[79] Government clerks, messengers and police boys, private servants or clerks, and independent artisans, were the relatively elite groups within the urban locations, and with the spread of African literacy, and increasing numbers of skilled Africans workers, these men were coming into direct competition with the most vulnerable level of European society: the young Rhodesian-born, European school-leaver with minimal skills, minimal discipline, and hefty expectations.

Just as European farmers had, under economic pressure, complained vehemently of competition from progressive Africans, so European artisans and would-be clerks or government employees, and even some of the more prosperous members of the European community, were asserting by the late 1920s that unless competition was constrained, Europeans would not be able to maintain their elite position in the region. One observer, who had earlier commented on African competition in agriculture, announced in 1932 that "this country is overrun with native carpenters, brickmakers, tinkers, motor mechanics, etc. etc. Our Mashona native has shown himself to be extraordinarily capable of learning these trades."[80] Quite skilled African carpenters, he continued, would work for as little as £2 a month. These were carpenters with the skill to make chairs and chests of drawers. African builders, too— not merely laborers, but contractors who supervised construction and additional workers—were available for rates far below those demanded by Europeans. European brainpower alone, the observer commented ruefully, was not enough to overcome the advantages Africans had in competition with Europeans.[81] Europeans, meanwhile, chose unemployment and government-sponsored work camps, where they were given at least £6 15s and food each month, rather than accept "absurdly low wages."[82]

Under financial pressure, European employers also became increasingly likely to put work up for bid, and to take the lowest bid, even if that meant that the contractor would be African. Making this point, Max Danziger asked "how many hon. members of the legislative assembly have not at some time employed natives to do skilled work, such as building a barn or room?" answering his own query by noting that "I do not think . . . that any of us could stand here and say that we have not done so."[83] Even the settler-run government of Salisbury considered employing African builders, and other municipalities and individuals did so.[84] But skilled European workers did not accept the propriety of direct competition. Some suggested the government impose a "colour bar," a system of job reservation by race. Others, responding to the government's statements that such legislation would be disallowed by imperial oversight, advocated a minimum wage high enough for Europeans to live on, with the argument that if the employer had to pay so much anyway, he would go ahead and hire the European rather than the African applicant. Making explicit the linkages between economic, social, and political position, a representative for the Rhodesia Amalgamated Building Trades Union wrote, sarcastically,

> We merely ask Councillor Reid Rowland [Mayor of Salisbury] to be logical. If he believes in natives doing the skilled building which has hitherto been the prerogative of the white man, will he object to going a step further and saying that they shall be permitted to enter any and every branch of skilled and professional industry, even to the extent of controlling the destinies of the town, from a seat on the Council? . . . where does he intend to draw the line?[85]

Skilled work, artisans argued, should be reserved for "those who have served arduous apprenticeships and are now maintaining white civilisation in Rhodesia."[86] Allowing competition between educated Africans and Europeans, these Europeans argued, was based in the "fantastically weird theory" that "a mere veneer of education and civilisation of the native gives him equality with the European."[87] Cultural—racial—values, and careful consideration of the politics of civilization should, these settlers argued, enter into employment decisions.

Africans had learned their trades at mission schools, at the government schools, or on the job, and Europeans debated back and forth the question of who was responsible for these elite Africans. One small contractor argued that graduates of government industrial institutions and the missions were responsible for the debilitating competition.[88] But others pointed directly to on-the-job education as the primary path for the transfer of skills. European artisans, employing cheap African laborers, would stand back and direct, teaching as they worked, and ultimately making their employees into competitors. Face facts, one settler argued: "the native is here, he will stay, he will multiply, and he will learn trades unless expressly prevented."[89]

Under Depression conditions, it was possible for very small numbers of skilled Africans to challenge Europeans' craft dominance. A survey of Salisbury location in 1930 pointed out 13 tailors, 3 bricklayers, 3 carpenters, and a small assortment of plumbers, clothes cleaners, and other semiskilled or skilled artisans, out of a total location population of 2,976.[90] In all of Southern Rhodesia, the Native Department counted 1,586 African "tradesmen" in 1932, including 423 builders, 179 carpenters, 74 painters, 238 shoemakers, and a wide variety of others.[91] These numbers were not large. But they rose each year in which the Native Department reported statistics.[92] And as the numbers of unemployed Europeans increased and European youths found it impossible to find jobs, the European community squirmed to avoid a "poor white" problem, and protect racial status, led by politicians who could never forget that, unlike all but a few Africans, Europeans voted, and the politicians' power rested not merely on support within the European community, but on the continued exclusion of Africans from politics. As premier, H. U. Moffat estimated in 1933 that out of a total voting roll of 24,000 there were 58 African voters, and that between 100 and 500 more Africans were probably qualified, but unregistered. Moffat urged a cautious response, but other members reacted more emphatically, particularly H. H. Davies, an opposition member who suggested that there might soon be 100,000 African voters on the roll, eliminating the control by the European community that had been achieved through Responsible Government.[93]

Europeans who were less affluent, less educated, less skilled, more violent, or somehow less civilized than the ideal held up for a minority culture in a settler colony had always posed a problem for European and imperial policymakers. Rhodesia was built on dreams of riches, but those riches had never really materialized. Gold fizzled. Cattle died of diseases. Agriculture was vulnerable to fluctuating commodities prices and high transport costs. And in this context, with the increasingly severe economic pressures of the Depression, many Europeans complained publicly that the community was no longer able to keep up standards.

Direct competition in the labor market, vocal Europeans argued, was inherently unfair. "The white," one asserted, "is labouring out of his element under conditions he was not born under, which makes the position very favorable to the black."[94] And settlers argued that the inability of Europeans to live on the same wages paid to Africans, to do the same work as Africans, or to work effectively enough to be worthy of higher wages, was damaging the ability of Europeans to perpetuate the culture they had inherited. "It is not possible for us to contemplate that the white race could be maintained in this country on the economic standard of the native," argued one Labour legislator intent on advocating segregation.[95] As workers and employers increasingly relied on Africans rather than on themselves and their community, and accepted African standards rather than those they had inherited from Europe, settlers feared the end of their culture, civilization, and power. Ease was insidious: "Civilisation, history proves, is the result of centuries of mental, moral and physical discipline, and in all countries which claim civilisation, discipline has been enforced, often, indeed, by repressive measures."[96]

Degeneration, or the loss of civilized status, was most worrisome for the European community when it contemplated its own young men. To maintain Europeans' status, young men, whether native born or immigrants, needed to be able to acquire good jobs. But the "small but not uncompetitive force" of African graduates of mission schools provided "the germ of unfair competition," and neither coercion nor sentiment were likely to halt that competition.[97] Furthermore, as Africans competed eagerly for clerkships, apprenticeships, skilled jobs, or government work, European elders increasingly feared that European youths were losing their will to compete. By 1931 there were more than a hundred Europeans living in Salisbury who had registered themselves as unemployed, most of whom had few skills for anything beyond clerical or construction work.[98] And the problem of unemployment was most severe for those on the threshold between school and their first jobs.[99] Some prominent settlers feared that such unemployment was not merely because of the economic downturn, or African competition, but because the average youth was "worse than useless . . . lazy, indolent, more or less impudent . . . [and] not worth employing."[100]

In 1929 a commission on education, inquiring into European education in Southern Rhodesia, published its report. It focused on the needs of an educational system designed to maintain its European inheritance, create a new Rhodesian culture, and "develop in the youth of the country the moral stamina to overcome the strong and subtle influences which in a mixed society like that of Rhodesia, are constantly at work to sap the energies and weaken the moral tenacity of the privileged Europeans."[101] Something, it acknowledged, must be done to control the pervasive influence of "the ubiquitous native" on European youths' diligence, attitudes toward family and sex, and concepts of moral obligation. Education must impart a "tradition of hard work, of self-reliance and initiative, and of honest satisfaction in honest work, however lowly it may be." Otherwise, it would be impossible to produce "manly men and womanly women, efficiently trained to follow some worthy career and serving in it with good will to their fellows."[102] The report called for educational reforms that would integrate literary training (with its preparation for crucial South African Matriculation exams) with more practical forms of education designed to push each pupil "toward an intelligent understanding of his world and the attainment of power to bend his world to his purpose."[103]

The Depression was not merely an economic crisis for the European community of Southern Rhodesia. It was a crisis of socialization and social engineering, as the young people who had been trained within the colony proved inadequate to the challenges that confronted them, and as competition and conflicts, which education was supposed to resolve, grew rather than receded.

Early attempts to resolve the crisis revolved around reconstructing the education of young men. Education was supposed to inculcate the will to work in each student and to provide the majority of European students with practical training: preparation for the work they should be finding as school-leavers, and indoctrination to make them content with it. In 1927 the most powerful aspect of this was the government's emphasis on keeping children in a rural setting, rather than allowing them to be attracted to the boarding schools of the urban areas, and training them in more effective agricultural techniques. During the 1920s school attendance among European children had increased through the expansion of boarding schools, and in 1930 school attendance finally became mandatory for all children of European ancestry under the age of sixteen.[104] Parents wanted the stronger education a boarding school could provide, but both the parents, and observers of the social effects of boarding schools that took children from rural to urban surroundings, eliminated the daily chores of a farm child, and exposed that child to the bright lights of the city, worried. Allowing children to grow up with a taste for the city could be dangerous, pointed out one legislator well aware of the colony's reliance on agriculture.[105] Tawse-Jollie, another member of the Legislative Assembly, was one of the principal advocates of secondary education in smaller towns. She advocated siting good schools in small, rural, towns, to become "centres of thought and intellectual endeavour."[106] This was not a movement back to the low-quality "farm schools" that were the European equivalent of the African "kraal schools." Instead, even those who had government-sponsored farm schools on their land advocated changes.[107] The upper-class Europeans of Southern Rhodesia complained that their educational system was producing neither educated scholars nor skilled artisans, but poor imitations of both.[108] Worse yet, the president of the Chambers of Commerce condemned the training as inappropriate. Graduates, he complained, lacked ordinary common sense and the ability to take simple instructions and execute them, unsupervised.[109] Thomas Thompson, a legislator and successful mine manager, was even more vitriolic:

> My opinion is that it is a waste of education to educate a child beyond the sixth standard [U.S. eighth grade] when such a child has not the capacity likely to fill a post where the educational standard is higher. . . . In a new country we do not want those super-educated men, men who are turned out machine-like from the different colleges all doing the same thing and repeating the same things like a parrot, from a text book. We do want a man . . . who . . . can forge ahead in a new country.[110]

Appropriate education, even for the European children of the divided society, became an increasingly appealing concept to a financially strapped elite.

During 1927 the reorganized Matopos school was the most concrete initiative toward providing lower-class youths with agricultural training and a work ethic. W. M. Leggate, the colonial secretary, argued that in Southern Rhodesia, with its "sharp distinction" between "the town, with a high standard of living, high wages coming in regularly" and the country, characterized by uncertain, low incomes, education must be designed to teach people to cope with the social divide.[111] He pointed to the Matopos school as providing an agricultural training that offered a way out of an unnecessary emphasis on secondary education and exams.[112] The Matopos principal stated that the philosophy of the school was "to develop the boy on all sides, and to make a man of him," and he emphasized that it provided good housing, "every comfort," "manly sports," and an agricultural training that took boys in at age fourteen, kept them in school for two years, and then enlisted them for two years of work for the Agriculture Department.[113] The Matopos school, though, had as many difficulties as Tjolotjo did, and for many of the same reasons. Like Tjolotjo, it was to instill discipline, demand hard work, and require contentment with subordinate status. European parents rejected Matopos in droves. The school had space for sixty students when it opened, but only twelve arrived.[114] Parents of potential students saw it as a labor colony for juveniles. "Had I wanted [my son] to do manual labour I could have put him on my own farm," complained one disgruntled parent.[115] Even the students who attended did not continue in the agrarian track the school laid out, but left the school for commerce and the towns.[116] The school remained so unpopular, even in the midst of the Depression, that by 1932 the Matabeleland Agricultural Union was asking for an enquiry.[117] And by 1934 the Commissioner of Labour warned the European community that agriculture alone was not an answer. The "peasant type" of European youth was just as difficult, and potentially dangerous to European dominance, as the "difficult" unskilled urban worker.[118]

Even less wholesale attempts to rewrite the curriculum and training of European students were met with resistance from parents who, though possibly supporting the idea that someone had to do the not particularly prestigious work of the working-class, Europeans, rejected the idea that their own children should be tracked for those positions. These parents saw the matric exam as a way up for their children, and were extremely reluctant to consent to any system of education that abandoned it.[119] They objected to introducing African languages into an "already crowded curriculum."[120] New curricula, decreasing the prominence of Latin, and providing the possibility of an alternative track for professional education, were pushed by some professional educators and prominent Europeans, and fought by ambitious parents. Bluntly, a dubious editorial asked "are parents content that their children should be lower down the labour scale than they are themselves?"[121] Appropriate education was a problematic policy even for Europeans worried about the survival of their own racial community.

A 1930 editorial in the *Rhodesia Herald* stated the problem of European young men quite pointedly. The typical Rhodesian youth, it pointed out, was accused of being

> unambitious, unable to seize opportunities, dull, without polish, lacking in initiative, inefficient, undisciplined, unstable, purposeless, superficial, and further from the fulfillment of Rhodes' ideals than the youth of any other part of the British empire. Finally, he is smug and has no wish to improve.[122]

This was a damning indictment. But the editorial went on to explain that these shortcomings were caused not by inherent weakness in European children, but by their maturation as members of a European minority surrounded by Africans. European youths were lazy, argued the editor, because they left as much work as possible to Africans. African labor, after all, was cheap, and willing. Europeans were unable to seize opportunities, he continued, as Rhodesia was a poor country, with few opportunities to seize. And they were unpolished because "centres of civilization" were far away. Segregation, the editor continued, or leaving Africa entirely, might be the only solution to these problems. The young men were not bad, the editorial concluded, but they were average. And "with our black population we need an aristocracy"—average simply would not do.[123]

Policies

From the foundation of Southern Rhodesia, many factions of an increasingly fractured society had sought, through concepts of civilization, a disciplined Native Education, or a differentiated system of native development, to design a future of either unity or peaceful divergence, without racial conflict. But under economic pressure, the ideals of a conflict-free future were no longer enough to reconcile the leaders of colonial society, whether missionaries, government officials, elected representatives, or elite Africans, to the demands of three increasingly dangerous classes of that society: unsupervised Africans, "progressive" Africans, and marginal Europeans. The costs of incorporating everyone in the colony into a social whole became more than settlers, the administration, the missions, or even the Africans, were willing to pay. As children grew to adulthood within a hierarchical society, they made demands that violated ideologies of reconciliation. The people of the new generation, white or black, could not be assimilated immediately to a common colonial civilization. They fought for survival.

And it was within this atmosphere of acute social and economic danger that ideas of segregation grew from the margins of the region's politics to dominate discussions by settlers and their representatives, government officials, missionaries, and Africans concerned about the region's future politics, society, and economy. Fear pushed each of these groups toward accepting segregation. Whenever, and on whatever issues, settlers were fully convinced of their own political, economic, or moral superiority, they saw segregation as expensive, inconvenient, and unnecessary. Missionaries strong in their knowledge of the appeal of Christianity and Christian and material ideals of civilization did not back segregation; but competing with a European secular materialism for the souls, lives, and resources of Africans, missionaries quibbled only about the terms on which segregation should take place. Africans confident of their ability to take advantage of Europeans to further their individual well-being, or that of their communities, had argued for access to European towns, markets, and mines. Africans worried by the increasing dependence of the African economy on Europeans, by the disintegration of African society, or by the increased dominance of the settler state, backed segregation as a way of managing these increasingly apparent threats.

For the Europeans of Southern Rhodesia, particularly the non-elite Europeans and their spokespersons, segregation was not a new idea. Over the years, it had been advocated by various individuals and a few groups, notably the Labour Party both during election campaigns and within the Legislative Assembly. Early advocates had propounded segregation as the only true way to make and keep Southern Rhodesia as a "white man's country." But with the Depression, the settler rhetoric of segregation grew both more vehement and more widely accepted.

During 1927 settlers discussed segregation in the context of a labor shortage as European farmers anxious to expand their tobacco production realized precisely how dependent they were on African labor. In earlier years, farmers had, under such conditions, called for the forcible recruitment of African labor. But in 1927 various commentators looked for alternative ways out of their dependence. Some still argued for a type of forcible recruitment, either directly through the Native Department, or mediated by "chiefs" and "headmen" employed by the administration.[124] Some modified that position slightly to advocate improving health conditions as a way of increasing the available pool of workers.[125]

But the *Rhodesia Herald* chastised those who continued to debate labor policy using an assumption of dependence on African labor. "Interference with the liberty of the black subject," it argued, could not be justified merely "on the grounds that the white settler wants labour and wants it at moderate prices."[126] Responding to this challenge, some Europeans called for mechanization, others for increased reliance on European family labor.[127] Frank Johnson, a radical segregationist, proposed "A Whiter Rhodesia," in which whatever *could* be done by Europeans, would be done by them, and not by their African employees.[128] Segregation was a way out of dependence on African labor, and a move toward a self-reliant European population, he and his supporters argued. For radical segregationists, such as Johnson, Africans were a danger to Europeans as long as they were a factor in the colony, whether they worked and competed, or refused to work and undermined an economy that was dependent on them.

Johnson won his 1927 by-election in a working-class district of Salisbury quite removed from the labor-hungry employers of the tobacco-growing regions, on a platform advocating strict segregation. But he lost that seat during the 1928 general election.[129] A segregationist's argument that "the white population must revolutionise its methods of living and recognise that it did not consist of super-men fitted only for supervision and overseeing"[130] presented a direct challenge to workers' status. Strict segregation and self-reliance would be dangerous to the prestige of many Europeans who, in the face of economic problems, relied on race to provide them with access to the state, and social and economic privileges. These Europeans reacted in anger when told by the government that they should work harder, and give up their privileged position of directing African labor.[131] Even unemployed Europeans argued that they should not be forced to manual labor, and that the government should provide them with dignified work as overseers.[132]

At the top of colonial society, elite Europeans also disliked ideas of strict segregation, viewing it as unnecessary interference in the running of their businesses, farms, or mines. They reacted with scorn toward working-class Europeans, or farmers when, arguing unfair competition, the nonelite asked for help from the government on the grounds of European solidarity: ". . . in meeting native competition . . . the white man . . . must be the force that leads and governs. He must not rely all the time on the Government helping him."[133] And even Prime Minister Huggins, while advocating segregation, realized that racial phenotype was not the only qualification for participation in the life of Southern Rhodesia. He differentiated between those who were "really white inside," and others who, he alleged, were chameleons, capable of adapting to their surroundings, and undermining the prospect of Southern Rhodesia "remaining white even unto the tenth generation."[134] Unemployment relief, argued the government, must differentiate between "men who really wanted work" and "men who did not want work, who were, in effect, unemployable."[135] These elite Europeans argued that the European workers and farmers were seeking unfair competition through their control over the government, after having failed to compete through discipline or hard work.[136] And for those who lacked the discipline, skills, education, or capital associated with a European heritage, they felt little sympathy.

Though Frank Johnson's radical segregationist initiatives did not become law in 1927 or immediately afterward, ideas of segregation were becoming important to both the elected government and the bureaucratic structures of the administration as they introduced a new system of values and policy that responded to an increasingly tense political and economic situation. The new perceptions and values emerged most sharply during the Legislative Assembly's debates over Native Education and Development, Land Apportionment, and Huggins's motions for segregation.

During 1929, legislators nervous about the relative positions of Africans and Europeans in Southern Rhodesia, debated a much postponed Native Development bill, which its primary sponsor, Leggate, the colonial secretary, described as using a change in administrative structure—the establishment of the Native Development Department—to implement a shift in the principles guiding African education. After years of rhetoric, this new department was to enforce an education which "will . . . be treated in its broadest aspect, so that it comes very near to the native's everyday life, and will have an effect on his every day life though he never leaves his kraal."[137] The education Leggate was suggesting to his peers was a conditioning education, to improve the lives of Africans in their place, the reserves, and not to assimilate them into European culture or European opportunities. Despite these careful caveats, though, the debate permitted many legislators to both state their opinion of education, and their assessments of Africans' progress and knowledge. Some condemned poorly supervised kraal schools, which they contended broke discipline rather than imposing it.[138] These legislators wanted to see African education controlled, however they defined control. Thompson advocated emphasizing the mass rather than the individual.[139] R. E. Downes emphasized the need to control the information available to intelligent Africans by restricting their access to materials intended for Europeans.[140] And Captain Guest, reminding others again of rapid changes, emphasized that "it is of the utmost importance that native development should be properly directed, and the white people are the people to direct it."[141] Others, though, joined in contending that even education under control was potentially dangerous to European dominance. Competition was an ever-present fear for legislators such as Mac-Gillivray, Davies, and Eickhoff. "No one," one legislator asserted, "can place limits to the development of the native."[142] And Davies made the implications of competition for his constituency clear in examining the various proposals for the channeling of Native Development initiatives:

> One suggestion has been made that the form of instruction should be in agriculture. Well, I wonder how comfortable the dairy farmers, for instance of Salisbury and Bulawayo, will feel if a dairying instruction school is started in one of the native townships . . . the logical application of the principle to natives must result in consequences flowing to the whole white population. The economic pressure that could be applied by the native when properly trained would be so great that it would not be possible for the present standard of white civilisation to be maintained in this country.—I wonder how far the question has to be examined before it becomes self-evident . . . to-day, with the output of native bricklayers trained in the native schools of this country, we could practically eliminate from our economic life every white brick layer . . .[143]

Davies, and his Labour Party and Reform Party colleagues, continued to emphasize competition as inherent in a multiracial context, and to use fears of competition to stir up support for segregation.

Denouncing competition as a dreaded prospect, these legislators made, both in the native development debate and subsequent debates over Land Apportionment and segregation, remarkable statements about Africans' progress and potential to participate in a common nonracial society. "To suggest . . . that it would take these natives 2,000 years to reach the stage of civilisation that we have reached is . . . foolish," one legislator pointed out, labeling economic competition as not speculation regarding the future, but a fact of life in the present.[144] Legislators relied on their own experiences of change to provide them with assessments of African potential. And despite their emergence from a culture proclaiming European superiority, these observers, perhaps for rhetorical flourish, portrayed African equality as a real possibility. "The capacity of the native . . . is not a matter of 1,000 years; it is not even a matter of one generation—it is only a matter of a few years," asserted a legislator for whom this was not a sign of hope, but of danger. One African, "with less than one generation of education, was cleverer than most people at picking up bacilli under the microscope . . . We see mail trains and goods trains run by black engine drivers in much less than one generation . . . We see [change] all round us," he continued.[145] A few legislators resisted these apocalyptic assessments, and considered segregation unnecessary.[146]

But for many European politicians, African potential and progress created a danger that had no solution short of segregation—a segregation that, if it could not be justified as humane or in the best interests of the African, should be implemented forcibly by the state, in defense of the European population. "This world is not governed by ideals" such as liberal notions of individual rights, argued C. S. Jobling, MLA.

> We have to deal with things as they are, and not as they ought to be or as we would like them to be. And, however deplorable it may sound, I state without any hesitation that under existing conditions we cannot be governed entirely by ethical considerations . . . the relations between races are not so governed . . . however regrettable it may be, we still live in the jungle, and . . . to clip our claws . . . is to invite certain extinction.[147]

For Jobling and others, their comfortable assumptions of European superiority had been undermined by the impact of the Depression, and the experience of living within a changing Southern Rhodesia. And if scientific racism, pure economics, or intellectual and cultural knowledge were not sufficient to maintain European dominance, they were willing to abandon those ideals, in favor of using state power to preserve their ultimate value, European culture and the European community. The language of segregation was a language of communal values, capable of allowing elite legislators to speak with stressed European farmers and townspeople. And with the victory of Huggins's segregationist Reform Party in the October 1933 elections, segregation became institutionalized as the most successful language of values accessible to politicians.

The Legislative Assembly's debates did not occur in a vacuum. The rhetoric and communal values of segregation were translated into policy through a reconstruction of the region's administration. In 1927 the government revised the administration's Order D, which had, with few alterations, governed the administration's contribution to African education since 1907. It also separated the administration and inspection system for African education from the jurisdiction of the nonracial Education Department.[148] The Legislative Assembly's discussion of the changes revolved around how different Africans were from Europeans, and how vital it was to the colony's peace and prosperity that the difference be handled professionally, by experts on Africans rather than experts in education, with an emphasis on maintaining "character" and "respect for authority" rather than book learning.[149] Another major segregationist initiative went into effect when the Native Education Act (1928) was postponed and transformed into the Native Development Act of 1929. By creating the Native Development Department, and endowing it with authority over "all work necessary and incidental to the control of native development"—which its director defined as "the education of natives and any other work primarily designed to further the agricultural, industrial, physical or social advancement of natives"—the administration neatly shifted authority for Africans from departments such as Agriculture or Health over into a separate division.[150]

While both the revision of education regulations and the establishment of the independent Native Development Department could be seen as part of a continuing pattern of government attempts to control socialization through Native Education and social engineering, even more explicitly segregationist legislation and regulations went into effect in the next few years. The government published a new Native Affairs Act in 1927, designed to segregate administrative authority by increasing the power of both Native Department officials and "customary" leaders such as department-appointed "chiefs," and to channel all other functions of government related to Africans, such as the judiciary, through a system distinct from that which handled Europeans.[151] And just as the Native Affairs Act provided for separate administrations for Africans and Europeans, the Native Councils Act (1929) provided the beginnings of political segregation, as it provided a system of African representative government that was subservient to the increasingly powerful bureaucratic administration of the Native Department, and distinct from the European politics of the colony.[152] Preparing for the 1933 general elections, Huggins sought to take the political segregation one step further, advocating some method of political representation that would eliminate even urban, educated Africans from the common parliamentary elector's roll.[153] While Moffat, as premier, mocked him for being scared by fifty-eight African voters on a voters' roll of 24,000, Moffat did promise to consider the problem, and Huggins's supporters emphasized that those fifty-eight were just the beginning, unless action was taken immediately.[154]

And, even as the government attempted to divide the nation's administration and politics by race, it attempted a formal division of the land itself in the Land Apportionment Act, which was passed in 1929, sent back without the royal assent, and passed again in 1930. The act was segregationist legislation, rather than merely a new attempt to expropriate African land. It was a rational, not a dogmatic, piece of legislation. It provided for the formal division of the land of the colony into Native, European, and Undetermined, Forest, and Unassigned areas. Based on a close classification of all of the land of the region, it enacted the principle that "no native shall . . . hold or occupy land in the European Area" and "no person other than an indigenous native may hold or occupy land in the Native Area." But it did provide for exceptions: European mining rights remained in effect in Native Areas, the government reserved the right to allow people of the "wrong" racial group to remain until it was convenient to move them, missionaries located in European Areas were allowed to continue to operate their farms by leasing land to Africans, Europeans could continue to establish Private Locations on which their workers could live, and land near European urban settlements could be set aside for Village Settlements or municipal locations. This was legislation that divided the land, and affected the mobility of African, but permitted European miners and employers a nearly free hand in prospecting, or in recruiting, settling, and employing African workers.[155]

This spate of segregationist rhetoric, legislation, and administrative changes produced neither a peacefully segregated African community, nor a comfortably protected European working class. With the reinforcement of the Native Department, allied with an elderly African leadership, and the establishment of the Native Development Department, which worked with younger, often Christian, educated and "progressive" Africans, African communities shattered into argumentative collections of individuals—elders and progressives—searching for allies and opportunities. Clashes occurred at all levels, from the highest reaches of African administration, characterized by conflict between the Chief Native Commissioner and the director of Native Development, through the division of Native Councils between "the old induna type" and the young progressives, to local-level resentments over land, resources, schooling, and morality.[156]

These education and administrative initiatives, while announced with a considerable amount of emphasis by a government that wanted to be perceived as solving the country's Native Question, provided no more increased cohesion to the European population than to the Africans. Segregationist legislation limited Africans' rights, making it more difficult than ever for Africans to take the initiative in schools, courts, politics, or economic activity. But it did not seriously attempt to end the interdependence between Africans and Europeans in the colonial society, polity, and economy. Africans' education might be moved out of the European Education Department, but debates continued to rage in the European community over what the content and extent of African education should be in order to provide an African population most suited to meeting European demands for workers. And settlers also worried about how to alter the education of their own children to provide them with the necessary knowledge of Africans, and the skills they needed to prosper in a multiracial society. The Native Councils might theoretically provide for the separation of African and European politics, but during elections European politics revolved around Africans, as the question of how far segregation was to go provided the major political divisions within the European community. And the Land Apportionment Act, while central to government attempts to provide for separate African and European economies, did not exclude Africans from European areas. Instead, it may have promoted increased levels of African urban immigration, and provided for increasing contention within the European community over how best to use African workers within a multiracial colonial economy.

Each of the major segregationist initiatives ran into major practical problems in implementation. The Native Development Department found itself unable to hire the necessary inspectors, and by 1934 its director, Harold Jowitt, quit, exasperated both by his fights with the Native Department, and by the depressing prospect of presiding over a contracting system of African education as schools under economic pressure closed down, one after another. Administratively and politically, the Native Department found that neither its attempts to resurrect "traditional" authority on the reserves nor the establishment of Native Councils was effective in calming and coercing an increasingly urban or migrant African population. Indeed, rather than contact between the "traditional" and the urban providing a calming influence, in the 1930s political activism in the form of organizations such as the Industrial and Commercial Workers' Union (ICU) extended from urban areas into the rural hinterlands, bringing political consciousness, and potential conflict, with them. And while the idea of the Land Apportionment Act appealed to the Native Department, settlers and missionaries, its realities proved aggravating. A segregationist Chief Native Commissioner admitted in 1933 that "there seems to be some doubt as to whether it will be possible to accommodate the whole of the . . . native population in the Reserves and native areas as they exist today."[157] Even though unwilling to do without African labor, settlers in Bulawayo reacted with horror to the government's attempts to force them to come up with Native Villages near the European municipality.[158] And missionaries objected to the terms of the division, pointing out that Africans had not been allocated enough land to enter the market as prosperous peasant producers.[159]

The segregationist legislation of the 1920s and 1930 did not immediately translate into a segregated Southern Rhodesia. In the late 1920s, despite facets of the idea of state-imposed segregation that appealed to different constituencies, strict segregation was usually viewed by thoughtful Rhodesians as "one of those remedies which looks splendid on paper, and sounds inviting if you do not stop to think about it, but . . . is Utopian . . . impractical."[160] And during the 1933 general elections, even as political parties campaigned for one form of segregation or another, editorials in the colony's principal newspaper, the *Rhodesia Herald,* suggested that while segregation might have a notable appeal to unemployed Europeans, as it would eliminate African competition for scarce work, its supporters should consider "whether in practice it would provide fair play to the European," and "where it would ultimately lead." If implemented, its separation of Africans and Europeans could promote African competition in both agriculture and secondary industries and alienate Europeans from a substantial domestic consumer market. During the election campaign of 1933,[161] the editors labeled segregation "economic suicide."

Yet despite the practical problems all segregationist legislation experienced, segregation appealed to people who worried about jobs, markets, and competition rather than capitalistic economic rationality or comparative advantage. The rhetoric of segregation tied culture and history tightly to what might otherwise have been seen as purely economic or bureaucratic questions. Worried people used it as a way to reintroduce questions of values into debates over Southern Rhodesia's present and future. When general elections were held in 1933, segregation of one sort or another was advocated by all participants, and the election was won by the Reform Party, which had campaigned for a "two pyramids" policy of separate development attributed to N. H. Wilson, a former native commissioner. Wilson's proposals promised state-sponsored segregation substantially stricter in its conceptualization of what should remain separate than the Rhodesia Party's advocacy of Land Apportionment and the Native Councils Act as ideal segregationist initiatives.[162]

Missionaries, long-term stalwarts of the ideals of a common Christian civilization, were slower than nervous settlers to use the language of segregation to define their policies and express their goals and hopes. But by the end of the 1920s and the early 1930s, missionaries embraced a modified form of the segregationists' language. Missionaries had initially responded to the dangers of aggressively ambitious Africans through a training that emphasized discipline, deference, and membership in a Christian community. But, like the settlers and the government, missionaries in the 1920s faced all the changes and challenges brought on by monetization, labor migration, and urbanization. And with that perception of danger, prominent missionaries embraced the notion of separating Africans from the sin and secularism of colonial culture, and promoting a separate form of development.

Missionaries attempted to use segregationist language and segregationist policies obliquely—not to block Africans' access to education and economic opportunities, but to oppose immorality and conflict. During the 1920s, in response to African pressure, missions were expanding their educational systems and working to train more qualified teachers. Evangelically, the mission societies were increasingly attempting to develop African churches, with African congregations, church committees, catechists, ministers, and even interdenominational councils. Some missions, notably the Anglicans of St. Faith's, the Jesuits at Driefontein, and the LMS at Inyati, emphasized adapting European knowledge to an African context, and building a specifically African Christianity. Socially, missions backed the Native Welfare movements in urban areas, which emphasized the need for respectable African villages, and supported Christian villages in rural areas, becoming uneasy when they had to contend with Africans scattered inaccessibly about the private locations of European farmers. Segregation was not the aim of these policies. Missionaries emphatically declared Christianity—a common Christianity—to be the ultimate goal of all their activities. In a context of economic depression, tension between Africans and Europeans, and state concerns over order, however, segregation provided a path to that end.

Even as they acquiesced to or supported segregationist initiatives or segregationist language, missionaries relied on the metaphor with which they had begun the century, of Africans as children in need of protection. Missionaries opposed segregation when they saw it as unfair, or designed to deprive Africans of their rights, demanding "opportunities for progress,"[163] objecting to the reinforcement of reactionary leaders over educated Christians,[164] and moving from generalized support of the Land Apportionment Act to vehement opposition when their demands for more land for African farmers were ignored.[165]

Using the metaphor of Africans as children in need of protection during a dangerous adolescence, though, missionaries accepted the logic and language of segregation as the best short-term strategy available for reconciling Africans and Europeans. "I suppose we are all segregationists of one sort or another," asserted Frank Noble to his synod in 1934, as he agreed with settlers and the government that, "it is no doubt a desirable and advantageous thing to put children away in the nursery provided for them. They are then out of the way, they can . . . play their own games without disturbing their parents."[166] But, expressing the mission's reinterpretation of the implications and uses of separation, he emphasized that the nursery of segregation was a temporary expedient, not a permanent solution.

> In every nursery worthy of the name we provide for supervision, education, training. And if we want our children to be-

come men and women, and not feeble-minded parasites, we
are careful to see that in due time the nursery conditions must
cease and they are given every chance of attaining full manhood and womanhood. If it is thought that we can keep the
largest section of our community in segregated conditions,
which are a hundred or two hundred years behind the other
section, in a sort of permanent nursery, we shall attempt a socially impossible and ridiculous task. Any segregation that involves or implies . . . the permanent subjection of any section,
or the imposition of anything like perpetual childhood, will
just mean that we have missed our way and forgotten God.[167]

And while the Wesleyans, under White and Noble, were the
most radical of the missionaries, most others concurred that segregation was not a permanent solution, and that Africans could not
be held to a perpetual childhood. Samuel Gurney, of the American
Methodists, argued that "God's people ought to teach every part of
those to whom they ministered" and emphasized that "they would
not be guiltless before God" if they constrained education and industrial training to prevent competition.[168] The conservative Jesuit
mission condemned Protestants, but echoed the belief that segregation was only a temporary solution. "Because a race is uncivilized," it asserted in an editorial,

it does not follow that it is uncivilizable . . . When . . . the
natives have been fairly drawn into the swing of civilization, it
will be seen that they are eager enough and capable enough to
attain a level of culture which will cause doubts to arise in the
minds of many who insist in regarding them as an inferior race.
The inferiority may exist. It may go on for a long time . . . but
it is a dangerous thing . . . to use suppressive means to make
it more of a reality than it naturally is.[169]

Bishop Paget, the head of the Church of England in Southern Rhodesia, also emphasized that the church had a responsibility for the
souls of all, European and African alike, and asserted that while the
relationship between the races might be that of father to child, it
should not become oppressive or overly restrictive. "There must
be equality of opportunity provided," he argued, "which enables all
to rise to the great destinies God has in mind for them."[170]

Missionaries accepted segregation to protect a childlike people.
But they worked within the language and policy structures of separation to undermine segregation's stability and make it short-lived.

Missionaries were the principal educators of the region, and "knowledge," one missionary pointed out, "is dynamite, and if with it be not imprinted the reverences and responsibilities of men towards God and towards men, knowledge itself is a very dangerous gift."[171] Missionaries accepted knowledge as valuable enough to justify danger, worked closely with the government to make that danger manageable in the present, and prepared their congregations for a future challenge to a segregated society.

Despite the government's push toward segregation, the Southern Rhodesian Missionary Conference, long the voice of missionaries advocating African opportunities, increasingly sought to work with rather than against the government. Missionaries supported Jowitt's Native Development Department in educational changes, village settlements, and the development education initiatives such as the Jeanes teacher program and the agricultural demonstrators.[172] And even the missionaries who were ambivalent about the new alliance found themselves so closely tied to the government's policies that they had to ask, "Are we missionaries or are we Government servants?"[173] The answer was all too clear: missionaries had not only accepted the government line, but accepted its implications for "the colour question," "white prestige," "slave psychology," and segregation.[174] Missionaries taught a government-prescribed curriculum, expanded only in the directions the government was willing to fund, accepted a position of dependence, and waited, at their interdenominational conferences, to be given the latest government position by such establishment luminaries as Keigwin, Jowitt, various native commissioners, the governor, or the prime minister.[175] Missions worked with government officials, vied with each other for prominence in government reports, and accepted the segregationist elements of the NDD's educational goals in their efforts to remain in the front of the educational movement.[176] Like the government, they increasingly saw their position as educating and improving communities, not reaching out to evangelize or civilize individuals.

Missionaries were ambivalent about the Native Affairs Act (1927) and the Native Councils Act (1930), segregationist initiatives to restructure the administration and political position of Africans. Some missionaries shared the government's interest in reinforcing "traditional" authority.[177] But many urged caution. "Not a few people, once they understand its far reaching implications, will be astonished at the precipitancy with which the 'Native Affairs Act' has been introduced and is being rushed through the Legislative Assembly," warned John White, worried about its implications, particularly its bestowal of "near absolute" power on the native commissioners and its designation of "chiefs" as constables with power to punish.[178] Frank Noble, his colleague within the Wesleyan mission, stated the social tensions between the elders and the new educated class even more bluntly, arguing that "you cannot get natives who have passed Standard VI or VII to submit to the authority of what may be an ignorant and degraded chief."[179]

The Native Councils Act, by opening a way for educated Africans to express themselves politically, provided a measure of relief to missionaries worried about government attempts to reinforce tradition at the expense of Christianity. Structurally, by providing for a segregated system with administrative oversight by Europeans, it paralleled closely the missions' own innovations in African administrative participation. During the 1920s, organizations for educated or Christianized Africans had multiplied and increased in stature within the missionary organizations. Some missionary societies had formal organizations of catechists or teachers.[180] Others had church councils whereby African mission churches managed their own affairs, or denominational conferences with African representatives from many stations.[181] By the mid-twenties, the SRMC had sprouted an interdenominational Native Christian Conference, which, attended by prominent educated Africans from various missions throughout the colony, provided an opportunity for Africans to become acquainted, and to raise the issues that mattered to them, within a context of supervision and control by European missionaries.[182] Missionaries understood, particularly during the financial crunch of the Depression, how important it was to cultivate an African leadership. Even two of the most conservative societies, the Jesuits and the Dutch Reformed church, put increasing emphasis on training Africans at more than just a rudimentary level. The Jesuits upgraded their educational system, hoping to train young men "who can express and fight for the Catholic point of view."[183] And the Dutch Reformed church both cooperated with the NDD to upgrade Morgenster, its central school, and negotiated with the American Board, hoping to take over Mt. Silinda, the most advanced school for Africans in the region.

For these missionaries, segregation was the best immediate solution to the social tensions of a rapidly changing colony. Like settlers and government officials, they condemned disorder and immorality, and saw segregation as a partial response. But it was a segregation that incorporated many of the missionaries' earlier ideas about civilization. Missions, though frustrated by lack of funds, were faced with African demands for expansion and upgrading of the educational system.[184] Missionaries were pressuring the government for enough African purchasable land to enable the most "progressive" African farmers to enter the colonial commodities market.[185] Missionaries provided Africans with the opportunity to participate in church business and mission politics, albeit overseen by the European missionaries and the SRMC. Though complaining constantly about Africans who they saw as troublemakers, undisciplined individuals, or "Bolshis,"[186] missionaries' view of progress continued to label these difficulties as growing pains, and expected Africans, eventually and with the help of God, to outgrow the nursery and join a common Christian civilisation.[187] Missionaries cautiously viewed segregation as a temporarily expedient way to handle a difficult and dangerous social adolescence, but a policy dangerously close to godless repression, and therefore one to be watched closely.

African perspectives were even more complex. "Traditional," rural, African leaders were aware that the social and economic changes of the early twentieth century had taken power away from them, and some wanted that power back, advocating segregationist controls over youths and women as a path to that goal. These men used the segregated Native Councils to request that the Native Commissioners force their sons to remit more money from the cities, and their daughters and wives to return home.[188] With power to control youths and women, whether through enforcement of the Native Juveniles Employment Act or the Native Adultery Punishment Ordinance, they would be in a position to ensure order and deference, and to use their authority to bolster attempts to buy land and sell agricultural products in the market.[189] Educated Africans both rural and urban, wanted new opportunities, but worried about the dangers of chaos underlined by the Bulawayo riots. Seeking order, both "traditional" and educated African leaders argued for hierarchy, order, and cohesion in the African community, especially through control of women and unskilled, unaffiliated African men.[190]

Africans judged new government-sponsored segregationist policies, most notably the Land Apportionment Act and changes in the educational and development systems, in the same ways they had judged earlier legislative attempts to control African women and youths. They asked how these policies affected order and opportunities for themselves, and their people. Segregationist initiatives were potentially capable of altering the entire menu of choices and opportunities facing Africans. Africans who gave evidence to the commission that drew the boundary lines for the Land Apportionment Act wanted more land, and wanted to be able to buy land. Segregation, for them, was relevant only insofar as it affected more central concerns. They did not explicitly volunteer to support it, but of 1,753 African witnesses, only seven actually opposed the principle of segregation. Africans viewed segregation in a fashion remarkably similar to European settlers. They were ambivalent, but desperate. At least some of these African witnesses saw segregation as a bad choice among worse choices.[191] The African community as a whole reached no consensus about the Land Apportionment issue.

Education and development initiatives were equally problematic for Africans, who suspected them of hiding European attempts to enable settlers to seize more land from Africans. The NDD designed those programs, such as the agricultural demonstrators, the public health Jeanes teachers, or the reorganized schools, to improve the standard of living on the reserves. But history had made African observers suspicious. The new programs offered opportunities for trained individuals to acquire status and wealth in rural African communities at the expense of other Africans who lacked access to such education, equipment, or capital. As third-class (kraal) schools increasingly shut down, the higher standards of surviving schools continually redefined what it meant to be an educated African. Some missions restricted access to the remaining third-class schools, attempting to eliminate "the elderly loafer type" of school attender.[192] Students who lacked Christian affiliations or the support of an affluent or educated family also had increasing difficulties in getting their feet onto the educational ladder.[193] This meant a nearly total inversion of precolonial distribution patterns for educational capital. Instead of the elder being the source of knowledge, and the young son of an older man being the most likely to have access to that knowledge, the elders were increasingly the least likely to have access to knowledge of colonial culture, and their children were at a competitive disadvantage to the children of younger evangelists, teachers, European-employed workers, or government-educated progressive farmers.

In that context, segregation provided some Africans with a way to address their increasingly acute intracommunal problems. By reifying the community over the individual, it suggested the continued responsibility of the straying township dweller or educated agricultural demonstrator to maintain connections with a larger African community. Segregation both promoted and smoothed over conflict. It prevented educated Africans from seceding from the larger African community to struggle with Europeans for limited resources, and forced them to compete within the African community for racially delineated opportunities. But even as it put "traditional" and "progressive" leaders into contention, the logic of segregation pushed for intracommunal solidarity in the face of outside threats.

The Native Department's notion of segregation, instituted in the Native Affairs Act (1927) promoted the idea of a separate African way, providing a last gasp of authority and legitimacy to "traditional" African leaders even as it undermined that authority by making it contingent on appointment and oversight by the European-run Native Department. The restructuring of Native Development programs at Domboshawa and Tjolotjo to emphasize agriculture rather than industry both worked to bring the educated back onto the land under the purview of the leadership, and to cultivate these rural progressives as a present economic and political challenge to "traditional" authority.[194]

Segregation condemned individual "detribalized" Africans. But as it did so, it offered educated or skilled Africans a language of leadership for communal progress that, borrowing from the missions, could be used to enhance their position rather than threaten it. Rather than being Africans who were marginal to a common colonial culture, this mission-influenced strand of segregationist ideas made these young men and women into potential leaders of a transformed African community. Africans, argued Bradfield Mnyanda, should reject European-style education in favor of a curriculum specifically based in the needs of the community. "Social efficiency" and trades, Mnyanda argued, should come first.[195] Segregation provided new opportunities even for progressive or educated Africans once they had shifted their goals from competition with Europeans to competition with the "backward" Africans for the political and economic leadership of African communities. And, as the colonial society and economy reeled from the effects of the Depression, these progressive Africans used all the tactics learned from the missionaries—Native Welfare Associations, strikes, and Native Villages—to establish and solidify their position as leaders of the new African communities, and the vital link between the two imperfectly segregated worlds.

Implications

Segregation was a compromise strategy. No one's first choice, it was nevertheless something that almost all within the colony could live with or work within. That flexibility and appeal was possible because while the basic idea of segregation—separation—was simple, its policy applications were almost infinitely flexible. The ideas of segregation provided policymakers with the racial community as a fundamental unit of social analysis. And they provided a language of possibilities with which to discuss the future of that unit. But, like ideas of civilization in which the individual became the unit of analysis, ideas of segregation could be deployed in service of the interests of many quite antithetical factions. In practice, segregation meant very different things to the various factions of an increasingly divided population.

Segregation was not unique to Southern Rhodesia. South Africa and the American South also, during this period, both developed and reinforced their own versions of segregationist rhetoric. But the forms segregation took were tied closely to the immediate history of each area. Reflecting a substantially more industrialized and differentiated society than Southern Rhodesia, South African segregation may have been substantially more complex than the Rhodesian form. While Southern Rhodesia's efforts at segregation responded directly to the Depression, and grew from attempts to comprehend and simplify a rapidly diversifying society, South Africa's segregation instead appears to have been designed to balance the contradictions of rapid industrial development, and, abandoning Southern Rhodesia's intense interest in boundaries, control differences through a focus on nuclei of community identity.[196] The segregation of the southern states of the United States was even more fundamentally different from that of Southern Rhodesia, as it took place in areas where whites were more than just a minuscule minority, where whites and blacks could look back on a substantially longer historical relationship, and where the dynamics of industrial and commercial agricultural development differed substantially from the marginal profitability of Southern Rhodesia. Some settlers in Southern Rhodesia found their own situation so different from that of the American South that they argued, inaccurately, that the American South had no racial problem, having exported the former slaves to Liberia.[197]

Individuals within Southern Rhodesia chose their notions of segregation carefully, combining items from the menu of choices offered by concepts of social, economic, political, and cultural segregation, usually worrying far more over expediency than ideological consistency. The language of segregation, with its multiple meanings, its unclear relationship to time, and its advocacy of state intervention, proved even more all-encompassing and flexible than earlier languages of civilization or discipline. Frank Johnson, with his advocacy of a "whiter Rhodesia," and Chief Native Commissioner C. L. Carbutt, with his proposals for the export of Africans to some separate political entity, possibly north of the Zambezi, represented only two paths within a segregationist debate that ranged as far as the Rev. Frank Noble's denunciation of "any segregation that involves or implies the establishment of two wholly different levels of civilisation in one country, or the permanent subjection of any section, or the imposition of anything like perpetual childhood."[198] Noble's acceptance of segregation as a temporary expedient was itself a far cry from Governor Cecil Rodwell's belief that the economic and political segregation of the Land Apportionment Act would provide a long-term solution to problems of inequality and competition.[199]

Growing from Southern Rhodesia's history as a colony shaped by attempts to promote discipline, and channel social change through socialization and social engineering, segregation's ideas and policies embodied a theory of social change. Segregation advocates, though, did not merely seek to control change in the future. They demanded state intervention in the present. Civilization, during the colony's early years, had sufficed as a language to describe social, economic, and political changes occurring in a cosmopolitan Southern Rhodesia of imperial and mission activity. But segregation was distant indeed from the laissez faire, organic approach to the colony's present and future suggested by the ideas of civilization at the beginning of the century. Segregation was an ideology and strategy of desperation, a bad choice among worse choices for many of its advocates, and a radical attempt to simplify society in the face of dangerous and alarming differentiation and economic collapse. Segregation expressed multiple interests, but a new immediacy. Not merely a way of delineating the future, segregation provided a way of imposing values and culture onto discussions of social policy designed to affect not merely the distant future, but also the dangerous present. The language of segregation was used within the specific internal Southern Rhodesian context, during struggles for comprehension of the colony's economic and social woes and prognosis, and for control of the colony's government and administration. While civilization had provided a language for divergent interests to express their imperial opportunities, segregation invoked economic, social, and cultural dangers through a language of fear, or even, as Premier Moffat pointed out in 1933, a language of unreasoning terror.[200]

By the end of the 1920s, social policy in Southern Rhodesia was ceasing to be a matter of planning educational programs to socialize the inhabitants of the territory for the society of the future. Instead, social policy was becoming a matter of the deployment of state power in attempts to delineate the people of the colony into racial communities, and to push those communities into specific economic, social, and political configurations within the present. Educational activities continued, but just as the notion of an assimilative civilization had become increasingly untenable in the colony's early years, the economic pressures of the Depression marginalized even the notion that contemporary social problems could be sorted out through socialization for a future of separate civilizations. Under economic pressure, Europeans and Africans alike sought to survive in the present. And as economic collapse pointed up the failures of social engineering, Europeans, increasingly sure of their control over the mechanisms and ideology of the state, began to argue for, and to use, state power to impose social designs directly to an extent not seen since the beginning of the twentieth century. Segregation emerged in the early thirties not as a mere blueprint for social planning, but as a disputed language describing possible uses of social and state power. Debates surrounded segregation, but by the accession to power of the Huggins government of 1933, those debates revolved around which form of segregation was most appropriate, rather than the question of whether segregation was desirable, necessary, or inevitable.

Notes

1. H. M. G. Jackson, *Report of the Chief Native Commissioner for the year 1929* (Salisbury: Government Printer, 1930), 1.

2. Educated Africans tended to oppose sex between white men and black women, arguing that their community needed legal protection against interracial sexual liaisons or assaults. For a discussion of the complex issues involved, see John Pape, "Black and White: The 'Perils of Sex' in Colonial Zimbabwe," *Journal of Southern African Studies* 16.4 (December 1990): 699–720. Many missionaries agreed with settler opinion that intermarriage was a problem. Rejection of interracial marriages provided a way of denying fanaticism, while at the same time rejecting stronger segregationist measures. See, for example, Bishop Paget, "Opening of Diocesan Synod at Salisbury," *Rhodesia Herald,* 5 September 1933. Marriage, as a legitimate form of contact, was seen as more dangerous to the segregationist agenda than mere sex. See, for example, the "Reform Party Policy," *Rhodesia Herald,* 14 July 1933, which, as part of the election platform, indicated that miscegenation must be stopped, but not criminalized.

3. These strong opinions were not merely held by powerless lunatics. They were propounded by such notables as Danziger, a member of the Legislative Assembly, and C. L. Carbutt, a native commissioner who succeeded H. M. G. Jackson as chief native commissioner. Danziger, *Legislative Assembly Debates* (1929), 765. C. L. Carbutt, "The Racial Problem in Southern Rhodesia," *NADA* 12 (1934): 6–11.

4. A. S. Cripps to Editor, *Rhodesia Herald,* 6 May 1927; A. S. Cripps, *Africa for the Africans.*

5. H. T. Tracey to Editor, *NADA* 9 (1931): 111–12.

6. Walter Chipwaya to Editor, *Rhodesia Herald,* 4 February 1927. Also repeated statements by prominent members of the Native Department, notably C. L. Carbutt and F. Posselt.

7. F. C. Peek to Editor, "The Decay of Discipline," *Rhodesia Herald,* 7 January 1927.

8. Governor Cecil Rodwell, "The Colony's Agricultural Outlook," *Rhodesia Herald,* 24 September 1930.

9. Rodwell, "The Colony's Agricultural Outlook," *Rhodesia Herald,* 24 September 1930.

10. See Danziger, *Legislative Assembly Debates* (1929), 757–59; Thompson, *Legislative Assembly Debates* (1929), 1175–76.

11. Danziger, *Legislative Assembly Debates* (1929), 763–64. Danziger was worried about the possibility of an African Robespierre at the head of a Rhodesian Revolution.

12. CNC Taylor, Annual Report for 1920, 2.

13. Taylor, CNC Annual Report for 1921, 2. Robin Palmer, *Land and Racial Domination in Rhodesia* (Berkeley: University of California Press,

1977), 279-81, provides a detailed list of purchases. Half of the fourteen purchases were made by South African immigrants, including mission teachers and prosperous cattle owners. And at least five were collective purchases, either by subjects anxious to protect an "ancestral home" (Makoni) or, more commonly, by small groups of retiring wage earners (one case) or teachers who wanted to farm (all of the first seven sales Palmer lists). Some were subsequently farmed through the use of either paid labor or of squatters. And purchases continued to be made through the 1920s in such small numbers that many Europeans were unaware that Africans were even allowed to buy land, until the Land Apportionment Act restricted that theoretical free market and confined African land purchases to specifically designated Native Purchase Areas. The African landowners who testified before the Morris Carter Commission of 1925 had generally paid for their land with cattle, using European intermediaries. NAZ ZAH 1/1/1-4.

14. Palmer, *Land and Racial Domination,* 280-81. Sixubu was exceptional, but visible. A Zulu missionary who arrived in Southern Rhodesia with the Anglican mission during 1891, Sixubu bought his farm for £400 in 1911, with the proceeds from cattle sales. After Land Apportionment, Sixubu's land became part of a European area. Larger purchases were made by prosperous cattle owners in Matabeleland, but many of them became tenuous as cattle prices fell. See, for example, Madhloli Kumalo's purchase of 6,417 acres in Nyamandhlovu District in 1921; Kohle Sekani's 1,000 acres in Bulalima-Mangwe in 1920; and George Nyangazonke's 7,258 acres in Matobo in 1920.

15. Alfred Drew to Editor, *Rhodesia Herald,* 24 April 1931, downplayed the importance of specific institutions such as Domboshawa, arguing that the most successful African producers picked up their knowledge on European farms. Despite this common suggestion, innovative European farming technologies were not always adopted by men who had worked for Europeans (see Moffat, *Legislative Assembly Debates* [1928], 811-14). This may have been because most European farmers in the region simply did not use the intensive methods advocated by Domboshawa or the agricultural demonstrators. See the allegations of European inefficiency reported in Palmer, *Land and Racial Domination,* 211. Paul Mosley, *The Settler Economies* (Cambridge: Cambridge University Press, 1983), 170-93, argues against the general assumption that European farms were undercapitalized and used labor wastefully by asserting that they chose the most economically rational path available given lack of knowledge of their environment, and the relative factor input prices of capital and labor. Merely asserting the economic rationality of extensive land use patterns, though, does not eliminate the possibility that Africans could not learn intensive agriculture from Europeans because Europeans did not practice it. What the European farmers did use, though—the plow and extensive

farming—was rapidly adopted by Africans, when they could gain access to the equipment and markets.

16. Eric A. Nobbs (Ph.D.), "The Native as Maize-Grower," *Rhodesia Herald,* 27 July 1928. Nobbs alleged that 150 bags, 300 bags, or even 600 bags were produced by some individual African growers. A bag is equal to approximately 200 pounds of grain. Given rough estimates of yields ranging from two to a maximum of around ten bags per acre, these yields indicate large farms with between 15 and 200 acres under cultivation. Furthermore, these farmers were seeking to expand. L. H. Gann, *History of Southern Rhodesia,* 274, notes applications to buy land from Mupe Sipopa, of Bulalima-Mangwe, who sought 1,000 acres and Oliver Somkence, of Bubi, who sought 100 acres.

17. Taylor, CNC Report for 1926, 6.

18. Carbutt (Chief Native Commissioner), "Organisation and Activities of Native Department," *Rhodesia Herald,* 2 February 1934. Note that this compares to an average size of over 3,000 acres for the fourteen farms sold to Africans or groups of Africans before Land Apportionment. Palmer, *Land and Racial Domination in Rhodesia,* 279–81.

19. Alvord and Carbutt quoted in Steele, "Foundations of Native Policy," 381. Steele points to Alvord's private statements—that European fears of competition should not be allowed to block African commercial farming—and contrasts them with Alvord's public disclaimer of competition.

20. Elizabeth S. Schmidt, "Ideology, Economics, and the Role of Shona Women in Southern Rhodesia, 1850–1939" (Ph.D. dissertation, History, University of Wisconsin, Madison, 1987), 156, 173, 177; Diana Jeater, "Marriage, Perversion and Power: The Construction of Moral Discourse in Southern Rhodesia, 1890–1930" (Ph.D. dissertation, Oxford University, 1990).

21. Taylor, CNC Report for 1927, 5.

22. HMG Jackson, CNC Report for 1929, 5.

23. Rex v. Rhodes Lobengula, Rex v. Baby Usher, High Court of Southern Rhodesia, 17–30 March 1932; Palmer, *Land and Racial Domination,* 280; Terence Ranger, *The African Voice in Southern Rhodesia* (London: Heinemann, 1970), 98–109.

24. Alvord, Agriculturalist's Report, *Native Development Department Annual Report for 1929,* 85. Alvord argued that the reserves were sufficient if used for subsistence production, but were degraded by market-oriented extensive farming.

25. Phimister, *Economic and Social History,* 143. Phimister points to two cases: that of Solomon Ndawa, who farmed 500 acres in the Wedza reserve through encroachments on land held by others, and that of Ndawana Sinyanga, who plowed nineteen acres and ran thirty head of cattle on the Chindamora reserve, who tried to take the land he felt he needed,

and when his neighbors objected, complained, "I am surrounded. They ploughed there all around me but they have not cultivated their fields. They did this out of spite to prevent me from enlarging my land."

26. J. Condy, Inspector's Report, Mt. Silinda, September 1921, ABC 15.4, vol. 35, item 126. Alvord to ABC, 20 February 1922, ABC 15.4, vol. 36, item 218. The students worked full time outside of school hours, and school hours had included instruction in the technology of agriculture, not merely explanations of how to hoe. Alvord, Annual Report of Agricultural Dept, Silinda, 31 May 1921, ABC 15.4, vol. 35, item 177. But the school was farming only forty acres of land to feed 200 working students, despite the mission's larger, undeveloped, holdings. And despite the generally good quality of that land, its harvests were poor. Alvord to ABC, 20 February 1922, ABC 15.4, vol. 36, item 218.

27. Alvord left the mission and accepted a job with the administration. Alvord to ABC, 16 July 1926, ABC 15.4, vol. 36, item 236. For his observations on reserve conditions, see E. D. Alvord, "Agricultural Life of Rhodesian Natives," *Native Affairs Department Annual, NADA* 7 (1929): 9–11.

28. Samuel Gurney (American Methodists), Presidential Address, *Proceedings of the Southern Rhodesia Missionary Conference* (1924), 15–16.

29. For statistical tables, see Steele, "Foundations of Native Policy," 554. The statistics are drawn from the annual reports of the Native Department and the Native Development Department. Several explanations for this discrepancy exist beyond just the assumption that demonstrators had additional knowledge of farming technology. They may also have had better land, more access to labor, and better seeds than the other Africans of the region. It is also entirely possible that the figures on the national average yield for African farmed land was kept low by an underestimate of the grain actually produced. The data is merely suggestive of a growing gap between the agricultural demonstrators and the majority of African farmers.

30. Alvord, its director, admitted this in 1944. Steele, "Foundations of Native Policy," 374.

31. See, for example, W. G. Brown, at Inyati Institute in Matebeleland, who reported in 1930 that the school had 150 acres under cultivation with 123 to 145 boys in the boarding school working on the land. He had expected a harvest of 600 to 700 bags of grain, a yield somewhat below the average achieved by the demonstration plots, but above the national average. When, with poor rains, the school harvested only 200 bags, he was faced with a yield well below the national average. Yet government inspectors commended his work and tried to hire him to run Tjolotjo. Brown to LMS, 24 June 1929, 5 August 1929, and 16 February 1930, CWM 90/W. G. Brown.

32. Steele, "Foundations of Native Policy," 549, 555. Acreage estimates included not merely reserve land, but also plots farmed by Africans in

undesignated or European areas. Statistics drawn from annual reports of Native Department. All population estimates are almost certainly underestimates.

33. Steele, "Foundations of Native Policy," 555–57, statistics drawn from the annual reports of the CNC, the Department of Agriculture, and the Maize Control Board.

34. NC Makoni, CNC Report for 1926, 7. The NC also pointed out that this represented the absolute maximum of labor extraction which was possible, as "the women cannot possibly do all the necessary work at the kraals, especially such men's work as building huts and cutting down bush for new lands. Continual absence of the greater part of the able-bodied males tends to cause famine, immorality and disease."

35. The actual range of bridewealth was probably much larger. These statistics are from civil cases before the Native Appeals Court from 1928 through 1934, regarding payments which had been transferred any time from the twenties to the early 1930s. See Nyamadzawo v. Mandaza (7 January 1930), which mentions bridewealth in 1925 of £21 and 8 head cattle; Masawi v. Mzanenamu (1 November 1932), bridewealth in 1929 of £34 and 4 head cattle; Gatsi v. Dokasi (8 December 1932), a 1919 marriage by Christian rites with bridewealth of £20 and 11 head cattle; and Zimunu v. Chakawarika (26 February 1934), regarding a 1928 marriage agreement with £6 and 7 head cattle. Not all marriages involved such high bridewealth payments, but senior men frequently resisted attempts to limit bridewealth by asserting that "Our daughters are our banks." Pfende, minutes of the Marandellas native board, 26 February 1932, NAZ S1542/N2 M.

36. James Ferguson, "Mobile Workers, Modernist Narratives: A Critique of the Historiography of Transition on the Zambian Copperbelt," *Journal of Southern African Studies* 16.3 (September, 1990): 385–412, makes this point for Northern Rhodesia, arguing that workers became an urban, stabilized work force well before those workers began to hold jobs for long periods. Instead, a worker might move from job to job, seeking mobility by changing positions, rather than by moving up in a single job. Ferguson also points out that, in Northern Rhodesia, most men did *not* leave their wives behind in the villages. Many of Ferguson's points are equally relevant for Southern Rhodesia. See, for examples, H. Taylor, CNC Report for the year 1920, 2, which pointed out that a "large proportion" of township Africans had their wives with them, or the running discussions of township conditions and "Native Welfare" published in the *Rhodesia Herald* during the first few months of 1930, or for a more complete treatment, Tsuneo Yoshikune, "Black Migrants in a White City: A History of African Harare, 1890–1925" (Ph.D. dissertation, University of Zimbabwe, 1990).

37. See Thompson's comments in the *Legislative Assembly Debates* (1929), 1175–76. Familiar with the labor practices of the Wankie Colliery, Thompson argued that African workers had changed. Twenty or thirty years earlier, they had been "very inefficient," kept at work only through vigilant European overseers. But in 1929, "he comes along and asks for specific jobs and he is learning in many directions at a rate which is really astounding."

38. Premier (Coughlan), "RAU Congress and Native Labour," *Rhodesia Herald,* 5 April 1927. Government jobs paid quite well by African standards, with the average wage for Africans calculated at £4 per month in 1933. O'Keeffe (Minister of Internal Affairs), "Mining Men and White Youths," *Rhodesia Herald,* 13 October 1933.

39. Charles van Onselen, *Chibaro: African Mine Labour in Southern Rhodesia* (London: Pluto Press, 1976), 114. RNLB (Rhodesian Native Labour Bureau) workers were unable to choose their employers, and may therefore have been used in mines that had bad reputations among workers for management brutality, excessive work, or poor or unsafe working conditions. By the 1920s, though, RNLB labor was more expensive for mineowners than "free labor." It was not employed during the late 1920s to keep wages down. By 1927 the only employers who had to rely on RNLB labor were either new to the area, or old hands with nasty reputations. Reliance on RNLB labor, considered "poor quality and very expensive," was seen as a major factor discouraging new settlement. "Veritas" (New Settlers' Survey) to Editor, "Native Labour," *Rhodesia Herald,* 15 January 1927.

40. J. W. Downie (MLA), meeting of the Mazoe-Glendale Farmers' Association, "Government and Native Labour Supply," *Rhodesia Herald,* 1 April 1927.

41. "A Letter from Matabeleland," *Rhodesia Herald,* 20 July 1928. See also the expressed willingness to travel as far as the Rand for work with better pay in "The Labour Shortage: From the Native Point of View," *Rhodesia Herald,* 23 March 1927 (excerpts from a letter from an African at Chikore mission station: ABC, South Melsetter).

42. See, for example, Tahomo and Inyeboe's remarks regarding beatings they received from the compound manager of the Gaika gold mine. Tahomo, a "police boy" who received 6 cuts with a sjambok, admitted that he hadn't objected to the beating as he wanted to keep his job. And Inyeboe accepted the beating he received, despite its severity, because the compound manager was the best "master" he was likely to get. "Alleged Extortion by Compound Manager," *Rhodesia Herald,* 4 July 1930.

43. Editorial, "Native Labour," *Rhodesia Herald,* 19 September 1930; C. L. Carbutt, "Report of the Chief Native Commissioner for 1931," 8.

44. Thompson, of the Wankie Colliery, was one of many who distin-

guished between African and European unemployed on the grounds that Africans could merely return to the land, but Europeans could not. See Thompson, "Budget Debate," *Rhodesia Herald,* 22 April 1932.

45. M. J. Rusike (Salisbury Native Welfare Association) to Editor, *Rhodesia Herald,* 20 May 1932. Not only did these urban, "detribalized" Africans lack the knowledge to prosper in the reserves, Rusike continued, they would never be content with mere subsistence. They needed money, more money than would be available on overcrowded reserves, with which to buy the new consumer goods they felt vital to life. Guka Kumalo (Matabele Home Society), cited in L. H. Gann, *A History of Southern Rhodesia: Early Days to 1934* (New York: Humanities Press, 1965), 282.

46. "Municipalities and Native Locations," *Rhodesia Herald,* 3 June 1930. Actually, these population statistics were probably serious underestimates, as many Africans may have lived illicitly in the locations, avoiding the surveyors. Davies, *Legislative Assembly Debates* (1931), 552, feared that the Bulawayo location was becoming a hotbed not merely of loafing, but also of prostitution.

47. "Unemployment in the Colony," *Rhodesia Herald,* 30 November 1933. The society could stage a public meeting in which 200 to 250 people showed up. It was chaired by Mrs. J. McKeurtan, OBE.

48. Gladys Maasdorp, "Rhodesia Party Candidates and Government's Record," *Rhodesia Herald,* 23 August 1933. Maasdorp lost, and the new government was formed by the Reform Party under Huggins.

49. "The Prime Minister on the Government's Policy," *Rhodesia Herald,* 2 December 1933.

50. Commissioner of Labour (CE Wells), "Examination of Unemployment Position in the Colony," *Rhodesia Herald,* 26 March 1934. Wells counted 1,581 unemployed Europeans in the colony, pointed out that "not a few men were out of work because they refused to accept less than the standard rate of wages," argued that the government must recognize that "there was very little scope in Southern Rhodesia for the [European] semi-skilled artisan, and still less for the unskilled man," and found that most men working in the relief camps had "not the slightest desire" to leave, as the pay in the camps was substantially higher than they could earn elsewhere. (Base pay was £6 15s., plus food, per month.)

51. For a quick discussion of the tobacco boom, see Ian Phimister, *An Economic and Social History of Zimbabwe, 1890–1948* (London: Longman, 1988), 135–39.

52. See, for example, H. Barnes Pope to Editor, "Native Policy," *Rhodesia Herald,* 1 December 1927; F. C. Peek to Editor, "The Decay of Discipline," *Rhodesia Herald,* 7 January 1927; Arnold Pearson, "Native Labour," *Rhodesia Herald,* 14 January 1927; J. H. Milward, "Disciplinary Measures Essential," *Rhodesia Herald,* 22 January 1927; and CE to Editor, *Rhodesia Herald,* 28 January 1927.

53. "Farmers' Council Formed," *Rhodesia Herald,* 1 April 1927. A meeting of the Mazoe-Glendale Farmers' Association was also highly concerned about the labor situation, and speakers at its meeting attributed the shortage variously to the wastefulness of employers, who allegedly held 25 to 30 percent more laborers than they needed, and to conditions on the reserves, where Africans allegedly could make enough money from beer and "immorality" to escape economic pressure to work (Austen); to high mortality among Africans which decreased the pool of available labor (Appleyard); to the success of Africans' cattle enterprises (White); or to the conditions of or returns from labor on farms (J. W. Downie [MLA]). "Government and Native Labour Supply," *Rhodesia Herald,* 1 April 1927.

54. For a discussion of bridewealth as a way of redistributing money from young wage-earning men to older men, see Elizabeth Schmidt, "Negotiated Spaces and Contested Terrain: Men, Women and the Law in Colonial Zimbabwe, 1890–1939," *Journal of Southern African Studies* 16.4 (December, 1990): 623. Col. Frank Johnson, an outspoken segregationist, argued that in a relatively uncontrolled reserve, rural councils in charge of their own trust funds might use that money to fund "sloth, vice and idleness." He advocated increased taxation of those on reserves as a way of forcing them into employment. "RAU Congress and Native Labour," *Rhodesia Herald,* 5 April 1927. Even the possibility of forcing women into the work force appealed to some labor-hungry farmers, who pointd out that African women were the biggest potential suppliers of labour in the country, if they could be pushed into working. J. A. Halliday, Dobbin, "RAU Congress Continues," *Rhodesia Herald,* 6 April 1927. The Secretary of the RAU condemned the missions as dangerous to the authority of the NCs, arguing that NCs "must be absolute and not impugned by any one." In this, he was backed by Beamish, Begbie, Rawson, and Frank Johnson, who emphasized that the state, and the state alone, should be in charge. "RAU Congress and Native Labour," *Rhodesia Herald,* 5 April 1927. For a close analysis of the potential importance of beer brewing, see E. Coulson and T. Scudder, *For Prayer and Profit* (Stanford: Stanford University Press, 1988), 72–95, a case study on the social economy of alcohol in Zambia, and van Onselen, Chibaro, 166–74, for a discussion of alcohol and the mines.

55. For example, Editorial, "Native Labour," *Rhodesia Herald,* 19 September 1930. Ian Phimister argues that by the late 1920s, "Southern Rhodesia was well on the way to becoming a labour surplus economy." *Economic and Social History,* 142. This is not, however, to say that farmers' anxieties about their labor supplies ceased. Farmers suggested that the government supply food and government roadwork to foreign Africans looking for work, lest the labor supply dry up. Mashonaland Farmers' Association Resolution, "RAU Congress and Native Labour Supply," *Rhodesia Herald,* 16 October 1933. And they resisted, with support from the

prime minister, South African recruitment for Rand mineworkers in their territory. "Recruitment of Native Labour in Southern Rhodesia," *Rhodesia Herald,* 22 December 1933. The labor problems of the most vocal farmers probably originated in the fact that working tobacco was one of the most unremunerative jobs an African could take in Southern Rhodesia.

56. Statistics can be drawn from the annual reports of the CNC, or see tables in Steele, "Foundations of Native Policy," 555–57.

57. Gann, *History of Southern Rhodesia,* 284.

58. Most complainants did not bother to make this comparison explicitly, but Nyasaland has since gone down in the historiographical literature as a case study of the demise of settler agriculture in the face of competition from African farmers unwilling to sell labor, but willing to grow a cash crop. On cotton, see Elias C. Mandala, *Work and Control in a Peasant Economy* (Madison: University of Wisconsin Press, 1990), 108–34; and on tobacco, Landeg White, *Magomero: Portrait of an African Village* (Cambridge: Cambridge University Press, 1987), 146–99.

59. E. Plewman de Kock, "The Advance of the Native," *Rhodesia Herald,* 2 March 1928. Plewman de Kock had been absent from Southern Rhodesia for ten years, and found striking differences when he returned, though, to lend punch to his call for segregation immediately, he may have been exaggerating the difference between 1917—when "the Mashona was an uncouth raw savage; all he was capable of doing was the simplest form of agriculture, he had little idea of work, being still imbued with the hereditary notion that the male should only hunt and do light jobs whilst the female made the gardens, reaped and prepared her lord's food and beer"—and the "wonderful aptitude" of 1928. However, see the previous note: for quality, productivity, or sustainability, European agriculture was itself evidently nothing to write home about.

60. Eric A. Nobbs, "The Native as Maize-Grower," *Rhodesia Herald,* 27 July 1928. Nobbs saw the scale of maize growing increasing, as some individuals (presumably with family or client labor) begin to produce 150, 300, and even 600 bags of maize within a single season. He sees the technology of farming as improved, but not as wholly transformed as Plewman de Kock (above) reported. Ian Phimister asserts that from 1924 through 1929, there was a "modest recovery" on the reserves, marked by growth in the numbers of carts, wagons, motor vehicles, and cattle owned by Africans. The individual farmers producing over 150 bags of maize a year, though, were not the norm. The period was also marked by increasing differentiation and even, according to Phimister, proletarianization—not just growing gaps between subsistence and surplus producers. Phimister, *Economic and Social History,* 141.

61. Editorial, "The Farmer and Competition," *Rhodesia Herald,* 5 October 1928. The editor was, however, sceptical of such claims.

62. Basil Christian, "Facts about Farming That Have to be Faced," *Rhodesia Herald,* 24 September 1930.

63. "Rusape Memorandum to Inquiry Committee on Agriculture," *Rhodesia Herald,* 22 December 1933.

64. For example, Barry, president of the Farmer's Association, Umtali, who spoke for his meeting in asserting that they should not be afraid of African competition as European farmers should be able to maintain superiority. Despite the extreme positions taken by Col. Valentine, who warned that Africans were becoming serious competitors to Europeans, the consensus of the meeting was that, at least in the Umtali region, "the supposed native menace is not taken seriously." "Native is Farming Competitor," *Rhodesia Herald,* 9 November 1928. See also "Hartley Farmer" to Editor, *Rhodesia Herald,* 19 October 1928.

65. "Policeman and a Native," *Rhodesia Herald,* 31 October 1928. The magistrate thought the argument overly self-serving, noted that the push must have been hard, and ruled for a fine of £5.

66. A. Edwards to Editor, *Rhodesia Herald,* 28 November 1928. The police, according to Edwards, were far too lenient about this damage to European prestige.

67. Or, if they were not in the towns to avoid their relatives, they might be there as prostitutes to support the failing rural economy. See Davies, *Legislative Assembly Debates* (1931), 552. Davies's allegations fit with Luise White's argument in *Comforts of Home* (Chicago: University of Chicago Press, 1990) that in Kenya urban women were far from independent of social ties and authorities. Many women became urban prostitutes in support of an indigenous agriculture battered by drought and expropriation.

68. For example, see H. J. Simons, "European Civilisation and African Crime," *African Observer* 2 (1934): 20-27, esp. 26. See also Elizabeth Schmidt, "Negotiated Spaces and Contested Terrain: Men, Women and the Law in Colonial Zimbabwe, 1890-1939," *Journal of Southern African Studies* 16.4 (December 1990): 623-48.

69. Phimister, *Economic and Social History,* 152-53.

70. The main Bulawayo riots broke out on 27 December 1929. Phimister, *Economic and Social History,* 154-55; Cowden, *Legislative Assembly Debates* (1931), 554.

71. Carbutt, "Report of the CNC for 1932," 10.

72. Walter Chipwaya to Editor, *Rhodesia Herald,* 16 May 1929.

73. For example, A. H. M. Edwards, "Report on the British South Africa Police for the Year 1921," 8; G. Stops, "Report on the BSAP for the Year 1926," 8. Even nonofficial observers argued this. See, for example, C. Southey, "RAU Conference Continues," *Rhodesia Herald,* 6 April 1927.

74. Alfred Drew (former NC, frequent letter writer) to Editor, *Rhodesia Herald*, 25 January 1930.

75. J. S. Morris, *BSAP Report* for 1932, 13.

76. Ibid.

77. Terence Ranger, *The African Voice in Southern Rhodesia* (London: Heinemann, 1970), 88–109, 138–40, discusses African political organizations such as the Rhodesian Bantu Voters' Association, the Rhodesian Native Welfare Association, and the ICU. Ranger emphasizes attempts to link urban and rural Africans, and asserts that, with fewer than 16,000 Africans in the colony who could be considered "urbanized," a specifically urban political agenda was slow to form. But the few sources available on urban Africans do indicate a serious concern with urban order. Walter Chipwaya's comments on prostitution and order, and their discussion by the Native Welfare Association, are one example of this (mentioned by Ranger, and see Chipwaya to Editor, *Rhodesia Herald*, 16 May 1929). Phimister, *Economic and Social History*, 150–56, discusses a breakdown in order, and how that pushed people to find new links however possible, even through organizations based in ethnicity.

78. Ethel Tawse-Jollie, "The Urban Native," *Rhodesia Herald*, 31 January 1930.

79. Ibid.

80. E. Plewman de Kock, "Unemployment and the Native Artisan," *Rhodesia Herald*, 29 April 1932.

81. Ibid.; Plewman de Kock to Editor, *Rhodesia Herald*, 19 October 1928.

82. "Examination of Unemployment Position in the Colony," *Rhodesia Herald*, 26 March 1934. Elite Europeans were disgruntled by Europeans who chose the camps over lower wages. Far from competing, Thompson asserted, "I could give the house many instances where the European has thrown away his position almost willfully." *Legislative Assembly Debates* (130), 1624.

83. Danziger, *Legislative Assembly Debates* (1929), 758–59.

84. Reid Rowland, the mayor of Salisbury, defended his position before an irate Salisbury Ratepayers' Association, arguing that "whatever one's opinion as regards a white or black Rhodesia . . . the native is essential for labour reasons in the towns" and that those workers would have to have some place near the European city where they could live. In African locations, "it was only right and proper that the natives should be allowed to build the houses." "Native Village Settlements near Towns," *Rhodesia Herald*, 18 May 1934. Rowland's arguments were blocked by vehement European protests for Salisbury. But in Bulawayo, and elsewhere in the region, Europeans employed African builders. Danziger, *Legislative Assembly Debates* (1929), 758–59.

85. H. C. Goodall to Editor, "Builders and Native Labour," *Rhodesia Herald,* 5 February 1929.

86. H. C. Goodall to Editor, "Builders and Native Labour," *Rhodesia Herald,* 5 February 1929.

87. W. B. Collyer to Editor, *Rhodesia Herald,* 16 April 1929.

88. "Small Contractor" to Editor, *Rhodesia Herald,* 13 May 1932. During the war, he continued, when young men and able-bodied older men had left to fight, their places had been taken by these skilled and semi-skilled Africans.

89. John de L. Nimmo to Editor, *Rhodesia Herald,* 6 May 1932.

90. "Native Welfare Society," *Rhodesia Herald,* 14 June 1930; "Municipalities and Native Locations," *Rhodesia Herald,* 3 June 1930.

91. "Increase in Number of Native Tradesmen," *Rhodesia Herald,* 9 May 1932. These were the numbers from the CNC's Report for 1931.

92. See *CNC Report for 1933,* 1934, etc.

93. Moffat, Davies, *Legislative Assembly Debates,* 520, 528–30.

94. F. C. Peek to Editor, "The Decay of Discipline," *Rhodesia Herald,* 7 January 1927.

95. Davies, *Legislative Assembly Debates* (1930), 1619.

96. J. W. Milward, "Disciplinary Measures Essential," *Rhodesia Herald,* 22 January 1927.

97. "Skilled Labour," *Rhodesia Herald,* 6 June 1927. By the end of 1926 there were 7,125 European pupils in school in Southern Rhodesia.

98. Estimates of Salisbury's European unemployment were, in 1931, around 140. Editorial, "Unemployment," *Rhodesia Herald,* 29 December 1931. When, in 1933, the government first attempted to acquire systematic statistics on unemployment in the region, over 100 in Salisbury registered as unemployed, most of whom had held clerical positions, and a handful of whom, painters and carpenters, were involved in the building trades. "Salisbury's List of Unemployed," *Rhodesia Herald,* 14 December 1933.

99. "The Government and the Problem of Juvenile Unemployment," *Rhodesia Herald,* 26 January 1932. This, at any rate, was the public perception, although Gladys Maasdorp debates the factual basis of this alarm, reexamining the statistics for 1932, and arguing that of the 369 juveniles leaving school who needed jobs, more than two hundred had been placed within a couple of months. Maasdorp, "Good and Efficient Government," *Rhodesia Herald,* 19 August 1933.

100. Capt. W. H. Kimpton to Juvenile Affairs Board, "Responsibility for our Youth," *Rhodesia Herald,* 3 March 1932.

101. *Report of the Education Commission for Southern Rhodesia* (Cape Town: Cape Times, 1929), 12–14.

102. *Report of the Education Commission for Southern Rhodesia* (1929), 14–18.

103. *Report of the Education Commission for Southern Rhodesia* (1929), 30. The commission's arguments for educational reform were quite similar to the director of Native Development, Harold Jowitt's, ideas about reform of African education. This emphasis on practical education was opposed both by such health and education politicians as Gladys Maasdorp, who noted that of 33 boys in 1932 who had been unable to find work, 25 were graduates of Bulawayo's technical school (Maasdorp, "Good and Efficient Government," *Rhodesia Herald,* 19 August 1933), and by professionals such as L. M. Foggin, the Southern Rhodesian director of education, who argued that much of what was termed practical or commercial education was no more practical, and possibly less so, than Latin. *Education Department Annual Report for 1927* (Salisbury: Government Printer, 1928), 6–7.

104. Bill: "The Compulsory Education Act, 1930," *Government Gazette* 8 (1930).

105. Walsh, Debates of the Legislative Assembly (1928), 843.

106. Tawse-Jollie, "How Can We Stop the Drift to the Towns?" *Rhodesia Herald,* 17 August 1927.

107. See, for example, a meeting at Chipinga, where sixty-four (European) residents showed up, four of whom had farm schools on their land, and unanimously voted for a better central school in Chipinga. "Farm Schools Not Adequate," *Rhodesia Herald,* 15 April 1927.

108. Editorial, "Our Education," *Rhodesia Herald,* 2 July 1927.

109. President of Congress of Associations of Chambers of Commerce, "A Business Critic of Southern African Schools," *Rhodesia Herald,* 18 April 1928.

110. Thompson (of Wankie Colliery), Debates of the Legislative Assembly (1928), 849.

111. Leggate, Debates of the Legislative Assembly (1928), 886–89.

112. Leggate, "RAU Congress," *Rhodesia Herald,* 7 April 1927.

113. Voss, "RAU Congress," *Rhodesia Herald,* 7 April 1927.

114. Editorial, "The Matopos School," *Rhodesia Herald,* 7 April 1927.

115. Discussion of the Theo Hastings case, 1927, NAZ S824/844; "Report of the Director of Education for 1926" (Salisbury: Government Printer, 1927), 11.

116. Editorial, "Agricultural Education," *Rhodesia Herald,* 1 April 1929.

117. "Matopos School of Agriculture," *Rhodesia Herald,* 13 May 1932.

118. CE Wells (Commissioner of Labour), "Examination of Unemployment Position in the Colony," *Rhodesia Herald,* 26 March 1934.

119. Editorial, "Education in Rhodesia," *Rhodesia Herald,* 19 October 1933. Parents also cited the abandonment of preparatory courses for Ma-

tric as a reason to pull their children out of the Matopos school. A. Raymer [accountant] to Inspector of Schools, Bulawayo, 12 June 1926; E. F. Henderson to Inspector of Schools, 14 June 1926; K. Stewart to Inspector of Schools, 14 June 1926; H. G. Constable to Inspector of Schools, 15 June 1926; Olive Barron to Inspector of Schools, 28 June 1926, NAZ S824/844.

120. "Native Languages in Schools," *Rhodesia Herald,* 6 May 1930.

121. Editorial, "Competition and the Pyramid Policy," *Rhodesia Herald,* 15 August 1933.

122. "Critics of the Rhodesian Youth," *Rhodesia Herald,* 16 April 1930.

123. Ibid.

124. For example, CE to Editor, *Rhodesia Herald,* 28 January 1927, who asserted of the average young African, "I do not think that he will voluntarily become more industrious unless compulsion is used in some form or other. . . ."; or Frank King to Editor, *Rhodesia Herald,* 4 January 1927 and Walter Chipwaya to Editor, *Rhodesia Herald,* 4 February 1927, both of whom advocated paying chiefs to supply labor.

125. For example, R. I. Collings (Rhodesia Party candidate for Salisbury South), *Rhodesia Herald,* 24 February 1927.

126. Editorial, "A Thorny Subject," *Rhodesia Herald,* 31 January 1927.

127. For example, A. E. W. Stead to Editor, *Rhodesia Herald,* 22 January 1927; R. C. Munch, "Black and White: Segregation and a Solution," *Rhodesia Herald,* 22 January 1927; and comments on public discussions, by "Old Hand" (trader and prospector) to Editor, *Rhodesia Herald,* 28 January 1927.

128. "Col. Johnson Opens His Campaign," *Rhodesia Herald,* 8 February 1927.

129. Gann, *History of Southern Rhodesia,* 263–64.

130. Connelly, "Segregation of the Native," *Rhodesia Herald,* 27 October 1933.

131. For example, "Old Hand" to Editor, *Rhodesia Herald,* 28 January 1927; W. S. T. to Editor, "Native Labour," *Rhodesia Herald,* 31 January 1927; or, most emphatically, Danziger, Legislative Assembly Debates (1929), 760–64.

132. For example, "Mining Men and White Youths," *Rhodesia Herald,* 13 October 1933; R. C. B. to Editor, "White Status," *Rhodesia Herald,* 1 December 1928.

133. Thompson, *Legislative Assembly Debates* (1929), 1178.

134. G. M. Huggins, "A Vital African Problem," *African Observer* 2 (February 1934): 18–25, esp. 20.

135. O'Keeffe (Minister of Internal Affairs), "Mining Men and White Youths," *Rhodesia Herald,* 13 October 1933. These sentiments were echoed by the prime minister, Huggins, who went on to declare that European people who could never keep a job "would have to be put in a la-

bour colony," with a bit of land, while their children were removed to boarding schools and training as upright citizens. "The Prime Minister on the Government's Policy," *Rhodesia Herald,* 2 December 1933.

136. Farmers, the *Rhodesia Herald* alleged, were trying to compete through legislation even as they failed to compete by any other means. Editorial, "The Farmer and Competition," *Rhodesia Herald,* 5 October 1928. Farmers, they argued, must bestir themselves: "amongst the farming community there are many who grouse about the 'rotten nigger,' and yet are too tired themselves to institute any form of discipline or regular system in the management of their natives." Cecil J. Shirley to Editor, *Rhodesia Herald,* 27 September 1929.

137. Leggate, *Legislative Assembly Debates* (1929), 115-20.

138. Green and Bertin, *Legislative Assembly Debates* (1929), 121-23; 127-28.

139. Thompson, *Legislative Assembly Debates* (1929), 123.

140. Downes, *Legislative Assembly Debates* (1929), 123-25.

141. Guest, *Legislative Assembly Debates* (1929), 121-22.

142. Jobling, *Legislative Assembly Debates* (1929), 1184-85. This pronouncement was greeted with shouts of "Hear! Hear!" by his audience.

143. Davies, *Legislative Assembly Debates* (1929), 133.

144. Eickhoff, *Legislative Assembly Debates* (1929), 122-23.

145. O'Keeffe, *Legislative Assembly Debates* (1933), 1003.

146. For example, Easton, *Legislative Assembly Debates* (1929), 1179, who declared that in twenty years in Southern Rhodesia "there is not one single native I have ever had in my employ—and I have had thousands—to whom I could confidently assign a piece of work of any importance and leave him to make a satisfactory job of it."

147. Jobling, *Legislative Assembly Debates* (1933), 512-16.

148. "Order D: Schools for Natives," *Government Gazette* 5 (3 June 1927): 210-13. In theory, the new rules, with their more stringent evaluation of the quality of education, went into effect 1 January 1927. In actuality, it took time to constitute the new Department of Native Education, and hire the requisite inspectors who, as specialists in Africans rather than in education, were supposed to know African languages. The head of the new department, Harold Jowitt, was appointed in December 1927, and the inspectors of native schools were officially installed at the beginning of 1928. *Government Gazette* 5.51 (23 December 1927); *Government Gazette* 6.3 (20 January 1928): 19. Jowitt was hired from Natal, a protégé of C. T. Loram, and an expert in African education and administration. Steele, "Foundations of Native Policy," 313.

149. Leggate (Colonial Secretary), *Legislative Assembly Debates* (1927), 41-43, stated the government position. Other commentators expressed doubts about the activities of missionaries, and support for increased government intervention in the mission-staffed expansion of African education

(esp. Tawse-Jollie, 84–88; and Gilfillan, 147–48). And others advocated the legislation not out of concern for supervision or standards, but because "the mind of the black man is very different from that of the white" (Mennel, 136)—and therefore should be trained within a separate administrative structure.

150. Bill: "To establish a Department of Native Development," *Government Gazette* 7 (1929): AB 23, 1929; Jowitt, *Report of the Director of Native Development for the Year 1929,* 5; Steele, "Foundations of Native Policy," 314, 316.

151. "Bill: To make certain provisions for the control of natives and the conduct of native affairs," *Government Gazette* 5 (1927): AB 15, 1927. In the definition of the bill, "Chief" meant "a native appointed by the Governor-in-Council to exercise control over a tribe . . ." Legally, the position had nothing to do with custom. A segregated Court of Appeals for Native Civil Cases began hearing appeals in 1928, removing civil cases among Africans from the docket of the High Court, except in very exceptional circumstances, such as Dayimano v. Kgaribaitse, one of the only cases during the 1930s when a Native Court of Appeals decision was appealed to the High Court.

152. Bill: "To provide for the constitution of Native Councils and to define their powers and duties," *Government Gazette* 7 (1929): AB 18, 1929. Councils were to be chaired by the local native commissioner, with six taxpaying members, two who would be direct government appointees, and four who were to be nominated by taxpayers and approved by the governor (in fact, the Native Department). In any case, the native commissioner chairing the meeting would "in respect of any resolution which has been passed, decide upon the action to be taken, and shall if necessary apply to the Chief Native Commissioner for authority to carry out the proposal or take such other steps as may be required." (line 35) Authority was clearly defined as running downward, from the governor in council to the minister of native affairs (the European-elected prime minister), to the chief native commissioner, the local native commissioner, and only then to what was a fundamentally advisory council. Council resolutions within such an administrative structure were more akin to petitions than to acts, particularly given the NC's ability as chair to control the agenda (line 25) and outcome of the council's meetings.

153. Huggins, *Legislative Assembly Debates* (1933), 510–12. Huggins's motion was seconded by Jobling (512–16). Davies supported it (520).

154. Moffat, *Legislative Assembly Debates* (1933), 528–30; Davies, *Legislative Assembly Debates* (1933), 520. Moffat mocked, but accepted the sense of the motion. Davies argued for action immediately, since "if one considers the native schools of Rhodesia and what they are doing and may do, one can hardly resist the conclusion that sooner or later we shall have on the voters' rolls a native electorate of 100,000 natives, who would have

the right, and the right could not then be denied them, of putting into this House men of their own race and colour."

155. Bill: "To provide for the apportionment and conditions of tenure of certain lands in the Colony," *Government Gazette* 8 (1930): AB 21, 1930.

156. For administrative conflict, see Steele, "Foundations of the Native Policy," 317–24. For local-level dissention between the old and the progressive, see the *Report of the Chief Native Commissioner* (1929), 1, who saw the countryside balanced between "the strength of immoral customs" and "the acute and not always well-directed attacks of modern thought and of the radically different concepts of civilisation." Yet by 1930, Jackson wrote the epitaph of the "traditional" leaders which the Native Affairs Act (1927) had been designed to reinforce, pointing out that "it is growing yearly more apparent that . . . they are slowly losing the little influence which remains to them. As mediums of communication between the Government and the native people, they continue to serve a useful purpose. As instruments by means of which to execute control or to inspire respect and blind obedience, their day is past." In the face of "definite steps forward by individuals," these leaders were finding it difficult to maintain their power. *CNC Report for 1930,* 1, 14.

157. C. L. Carbutt, *Report of the CNC for 1933,* 2.

158. "Natives near Towns," *Rhodesia Herald,* 3 May 1934, describes a special meeting of the Bulawayo Town Council which expressed dismay at the thought of urban Africans. "No encouragement at all should be given to any scheme to bring the natives closer to town. It is no use hoodwinking ourselves. . . . There are 360 coloured children in the coloured school in Bulawayo at present, a direct result of the proximity of the present location to the town," argued Councillor E. J. Davies.

159. A. S. Cripps, an outspoken missionary affiliated with the Church of England, weighed in early with support for segregation that would allow Africans to develop Africa "on its own African lines . . . to racial glory and . . . tribal honour," but complained that the proposed allocations were so inequitable as to be nonviable. "A segregation policy, if it be worth trying, is worth trying well," he argued. "The Land Report from the Native Standpoint," *Rhodesia Herald,* 6 May 1927. In January of 1929 Frank Noble told the Wesleyan Synod that Land Apportionment should be sympathetically, but carefully, watched. "Address to Wesleyan Synod," *Rhodesia Herald,* 14 January 1929. Other missionaries also became increasingly critical of Land Apportionment's implementation. The SRMC had objected as soon as it realized that far too much of the land allocated to Africans was poor quality or waterless. L. P. Hardaker (writing for the SRMC) to Editor, *Rhodesia Herald,* 8 May 1929.

160. Joblins, Legislative Assembly Debates (1929), 1186. And even Gann portrayed Frank Johnson as "a forceful, courageous, bullet-headed kind of man, an excellent speaker who could bewitch his audience by vigorous

argument and a flood of inaccurate statistics." Gann, *History of Southern Rhodesia,* 263.

161. Editorial, "Native Policy and Politics," *Rhodesia Herald,* 4 August 1933; editorial, "Competition and the Pyramid Policy," *Rhodesia Herald,* 15 August 1933. The Bulawayo newspaper was evidently even more critical. N. H. Wilson, the primary proponent of the "two pyramid policy" considered the *Rhodesia Herald's* reception to be positive in comparison to the *Bulawayo Chronicle's* labeling of it as "impossible, impracticable, rank hypocrisy and sheer eye-wash." "Reform Party Candidates on the Government," *Rhodesia Herald,* 24 September 1933.

162. Party platforms, "Reform Party Policy" and "The Rhodesia Party," *Rhodesia Herald,* 14 July 1933; and editorial, "Native Policy and Politics," *Rhodesia Herald,* 4 August 1933. The Rhodesia Party had been the governing party since the colony had received Responsible Government in 1923.

163. Rev. Frank Noble to Wesleyan Synod, "The Native Problem in the Colony," *Rhodesia Herald,* 20 January 1934.

164. Ibid.

165. "Missionaries Not Satisfied," *Rhodesia Herald,* 4 July 1930.

166. Noble, "The Native Problem in the Colony," *Rhodesia Herald,* 20 January 1934.

167. Ibid.

168. Samuel Gurney [American Methodists], presidential address, PSRMC (1924), 15–16. Gurney was, in part, responding to a speech by the governor (pp. 12–14), who had asserted that while complete segregation was undesirable, some measure of segregation was vital to the happiness of both Europeans and Africans.

169. Editorial, *Zambesi Mission Record* 9 (January 1930): 1–3. This was by no means a ringing endorsement of equality in the present. Rather, it evoked the French Revolution, and argued that current tendencies, with conflict between Protestant missionaries and segregationist, repressive settler policies, were moving in that direction.

170. Bishop Paget, sermon, Church of England Synod, *Rhodesia Herald,* 25 January 1927.

171. Canon E. W. Lloyd, "The Native Labour Problem," *Rhodesia Herald,* 25 February 1927. Lloyd, stationed at Rusape, and influenced strongly by A. S. Cripps, favored appropriate education, along separate African lines, and the Phelps-Stokes initiatives.

172. The SRMC had backed the Keigwin scheme as it was originally presented to them. But by the next biennial meeting, they saw the government schools at Domboshawa and Tjolotjo as competitors rather than complements, and the government's development agenda as dangerously secular. See *Proceedings of the Southern Rhodesian Missionary Conference* (1920), 6; (1922), 5–6, 13–20; (1928), 25.

173. Fr. E. Collingridge, Missionary Conference, 25–28 September 1934, JAH, box 65/2.

174. Ibid.

175. See the lists of speakers at the meetings of the Southern Rhodesian Missionary Conference from 1920 through 1928. The SRMC was addressed by Keigwin (1920), the governor, Peter Nielsen (NC Wankie, 1924), the Prime Minister, Hadfield (member of the Legislative Assembly), and Jowitt (1928). *Proceedings of the Southern Rhodesian Missionary Conference* 1920, 1924, 1928. At the 1935 Catholic conference, Fr. Rogers raised the question of the government's influence in education, and argued that the mission was, after passive compliance, now faced with "complete submission or cutting adrift." Fr. Daignault complained that "we are losing our grip on our schools, which are rapidly becoming government schools." Fr. Bick and Fr. Duffy both complained of government inspections that bullied them and interfered with religious work. Southern Rhodesia Missionary Conference, 1935, Minutes/Decisions, JAH, box 65/2.

176. See, for example, O'Hea [at Kutama] to Reverend Father, 10 March 1933, JAH, box 23, who found himself studying hard to remain in the vanguard. While he had his doubts about the ultimate wisdom of Jowitt's path, which he characterized as "really little better than Jesse Jones [of the Phelps-Stokes Foundation] at his best; and that is far from good," he found that "at any time, he is likely to impinge explosively when I cannot play to his tune."

177. Bishop Paget, "Bishop Praises Native Juvenile Bill," *Rhodesia Herald,* 24 January 1928.

178. Rev. John White to Editor, *Rhodesia Herald,* 8 July 1927.

179. Rev. Frank Noble, "Wesleyan Methodism's Part in the Development of the Colony," Wesleyan Synod, *Rhodesia Herald,* 14 January 1928.

180. The American Board and the Wesleyans may be the most notable examples. But the Catholic catechists also seem to have been fairly organized quite early on. And the LMS held meetings of Christian councils.

181. LMS, American Board, Wesleyans, etc.

182. The fourth biennial meeting of the Native Missionary Conference was held in 1934, and was attended by more than 200 African delegates, some European missionaries, and representatives of the Native Development Department. Delegates complained about the rudimentary standard of African education, advocating "a broader education commercially, socially and industrially" (B. J. Mnyanda, "Native Education in the Colony," *Rhodesia Herald,* 26 May 1934). They pointed out the problems and constraints inherent in the fact that NDD had control over "the ladder which every African hoped to climb to a better understanding and knowledge" (Mr. Tsolo, "Native Missionary Conference," *Rhodesia Herald,* 25 May 1934). And they echoed African elders in suggesting that the government should enact and enforce laws against interracial sex in order to prevent

the formation of a "coloured" class (Mnyanda, "Native Education"). Jowitt, the head of the NDD, was happy with none of these suggestions or critical observations. Yet the European missionaries saw such meetings as crucial parts of the emergence of an African church.

183. Sir Fraser Russell, Missionary Conference, 25–28 September 1934, JAH, box 65/2. See also Fr. J. Gillooly, Southern Rhodesia Missionary Conference on Education, 1934, JAH, box 65/2.

184. This demand continued despite the Depression. Even as he watched numbers of schools decline, Jowitt was impressed by Africans' hunger for education. "Even in times of difficulty," he noted in 1932, "the African parents are willing to make the necessary financial effort to keep their children at school. . . ." Jowitt, *Report of the Director of Native Development for 1932,* 21; J. Anderson (Hope Fountain) to LMS, 14 July 1936, CWM 99/J. Anderson.

185. Moffat, *Legislative Assembly Debates* (1929), 71–85, found the Land Apportionment Act opposed strongly by missionaries who demanded a larger share of land for the Africans and progressive African farmers than he or his government were prepared to provide.

186. For several of the most cutting complaints, see W. G. Brown to LMS, 29 April 1932; Brown to Jones, 15 April 1932, CWM 94/W. G. Brown; O'Hea to Brown, 11 September 1930, JAH, box 195/3.

187. For the optimistic view of this, see Noble, "Wesleyan Methodism's Part." For a more pessimistic version of the same sentiments, see Editorial, *Zambesi Mission Record* 9 (April 1932): 259–64. Instead of assimilating Africans to a European civilization, the Jesuits warn that European civilization must itself be Christianized before it is worth assimilating the two. Otherwise, either "the odour of our slums will penetrate into the native compound" or Africans' "nascent faith" would be "in danger of being smothered in a deluge of material blessings."

188. See, for example, statements by Mataluse, Meeting of the Native Board: Belingwe, 21 May 1935 and Chief Masuka, Meeting of the Native Board: Bikita, 6 May 1935, NAZ S1542/N2/B-D.

189. "Traditional" leaders were not all unalterably opposed to land purchases and market opportunities. Of the land purchases which occurred before 1925, one of the largest (6,350 acres) was made by Chief Makoni. Madhloli Kumalo, another leader with royal connections, was also a notable investor in land (6,417 acres). Palmer, *Land and Racial Domination in Rhodesia,* 281.

190. In 1929, NCs from Charter, Mazoe, and Umtali noted growing concern among older, male Africans about the "immorality" of young, frequently mission educated, women (*CNC Report for 1929,* 7). Meanwhile, some urban Africans, such as Walter Chipwaya, advocated restricting women's mobility in urban areas (Chipwaya to Editor, *Rhodesia Herald,* 16 May 1929). And when Africans got together, whether elders or edu-

cated, they advocated some type of control over women. For elders, see Schmidt, "Negotiated Spaces and Contested Terrain," 633. For the centrality of the issue to an educated group, see the account of the meeting of the Native Christian Conference, B. J. Mnyanda, "Native Education in the Colony," *Rhodesia Herald,* 26 May 1934.

191. See Ranger, *African Voice,* 110–37 and Palmer, *Land and Racial Domination,* 180–81.

192. Collingridge to Fr. Superior, 14 February 1930, JAH, box 124/3. Collingridge wanted tickets printed for outschools, so that a teacher would have a smaller, younger, class of students who paid sixpence a month. These efforts were supported by the Native Development Department.

193. In his first year, Jowitt had expressed his doubts about kraal schools, worrying that "one is in danger . . . of concentrating on the mass and forgetting the education." Jowitt, *Report of the Director of Native Education for 1928,* 16. In 1929 his inspectors reported that "many schools have been closed rather than replace poor teachers by more poor teachers." A. R. Mather, *Report of the Director of Native Development* for 1929, 55. In 1931 he continued to argue that the declining numbers of schools represented consolidation. Jowitt, *Report of the Director of Native Development* for 1931, 3. But by the next year, he acknowledged problems, noting that in the face of further declines in the number of kraal schools, and thus declines in the general accessibility of education: "It can no longer be claimed that this merely reflects desirable consolidation of effort. It also indicates that in many areas the educational effort of years has been rendered abortive. . . ." *Report of the Director of Native Development* for 1932, 4.

194. See, for example, P. H. Moyo, "Native Live in the Reserves," *NADA* (1925), 47. Moyo, a teacher at Tjolotjo, asserted that "the older men themselves only look forward to three things which are, namely, cattle, kaffir beer and polygamy." In 1925, when young men returned from school or town work, Moyo saw them as following the ways of their fathers. But with native development innovations in agriculture, and potentially industry, he expected this to change. In any case, he expected and hoped that sons would cease to follow their fathers' paths in the reserves.

195. Bradfield J. Mnyanda ("sometimes head teacher, Domboshawa Government School") to Editor, *NADA* 10 (1932): 108–11.

196. The literature on segregation in South Africa is far too large to discuss here. But my understanding of it has been heavily influenced by Saul Dubow, *Racial Segregation and the Origins of Apartheid in South Africa, 1919–1936* (New York: St. Martin's Press, 1989); Shula Marks, "Natal, the Zulu Royal Family and the Ideology of Segregation," *Journal of Southern African Studies* 4.2 (April 1978): 172–84; Shula Marks, *The Ambiguities of Dependence in South Africa* (Baltimore: Johns Hopkins University Press, 1986); Shula Marks, "Patriotism, Patriarchy and Purity: Natal and the Poli-

tics of Zulu Ethnic Consciousness," in *The Creation of Tribalism in Southern Africa,* Leroy Vail, ed. (Berkeley: University of California Press, 1989), 215-40; and John Cell, *The Highest Stage of White Supremacy* (Cambridge: Cambridge University Press, 1982), 1-81, 192-229.

197. After emancipation, according to this view, Americans "wholeheartedly deported the vast bulk of those slaves to the west coast of Africa," where they formed a republic, bypassing the racial problems that would otherwise have occurred. Malcolm, *Legislative Assembly Debates* (1929), 1193-94. For contrasts between the American South and South Africa, see Cell, *The Highest Stage of White Supremacy* and George M. Fredrickson, *White Supremacy* (Oxford: Oxford University Press, 1981)—both of which have enough difficulty finding similarities between two patterns of segregation without attempting to integrate Southern Rhodesia into a comparative analysis.

198. Frank Noble (MMS) to Methodist Synod, "The Native Problem in the Colony," *Rhodesia Herald,* 20 January 1934.

199. Governor Cecil Rodwell, "The Colony's Agricultural Outlook," *Rhodesia Herald,* 24 September 1930.

200. Moffat, *Legislative Assembly Debates* (1933), 987.

CONCLUSIONS

Southern Rhodesia's economic, social, and political systems did not just grow organically from economic realities. They were shaped not only by the social forces unleashed by conquest, mining, commercial farming, and industrial development, but also by the subjective knowledge, beliefs, and preconceptions of the people who participated in making the country's past—people whose vision was limited and shaped by their position within the region's society. Rather than a direct line from economic cause to social or political result, Southern Rhodesia was characterized by webs of knowledge and communication that transmitted the impact of economic events to the consciousness of historical actors, but left room for the actors themselves to work out significance and meaning.

This study has used reminiscences, official documents, missionary records, and newspapers to examine the struggles by the Africans, missionaries, officials, and settlers of Southern Rhodesia to comprehend their social environment and design and implement an ideal future through policies of violence, education, and controlled development. Between 1890 and 1934 both the social realities of Southern Rhodesia and the categories people used to perceive and understand those realities, changed radically. The settlers of Southern Rhodesia extended their efforts at domination from gold seeking to more ambitious efforts to restrict, constrain and use the African population and the land, and eventual projects to control social and economic change through "Native policy," "Native education," and ultimately "Native development." An initial European faith in violence as a strategy for extracting gold, cattle, and labor from the Africans of the region faltered only when Africans responded with their own acts of violence in the Risings of 1896–97, showing Europeans that violence was an expensive and ultimately uncertain way to rule for profit, and Africans that a military victory was unlikely. Afterward, Africans and European missionaries, officials, and settlers began to develop an ideological basis for the new society in a concept of "civilization," which meant the growth of individualism within the African community, a new understanding of and participation in European culture, and acceptance of the economic logic of capitalism. For all parties within Southern Rhodesia, ideas of civilization had both opportunities and costs. By 1910 the European community increasingly feared the social consequences of African education and mobility under the policy of civilization, and began to contemplate alternatives. At the end of the First World War, as the settler community took over the state, the European community abandoned the idea of a common civilization and sought a more nuanced notion of social change, in which 'progress' or 'development' could be pruned and shaped to provide an African community permanently removed from European culture and subservient to the European-dominated economy. Those efforts to promote divergence brought the triumph of a conservative, communalist logic that emphasized the cohesion of the community above the volition of the individual.

The rapid intellectual, social, and political changes that marked the early years of Southern Rhodesia grew out of an interaction between economic forces and ideas that was not merely a one-way exchange, or even a simple dialectic. Through their attempts to define their world, the people of the region built and rebuilt key concepts of change that structured both action and reaction and defined the terms of a multivocal conversation.

To write history is to ask questions. We constantly ask What happened, Why did it happen, and What did it mean for the region's future? But those questions alone are not enough. History does not emerge automatically in a comprehensible and meaningful form from a straightforward narrative of events, an analysis of social and economic development, or a denunciation of the many forms of domination and oppression. We must also ask how the people who lived through the events, developments, and domination experienced and understood their physical, social, and intellectual surroundings. Perceptions and experiences were, for the people of Southern Rhodesia, shaped through their prior knowledge, the language they had to express their experiences, and the social institutions available to facilitate the sharing of knowledge, perceptions, predictions, and fears. In examining the experience of the past, we must ask not merely about what happened, but also about the dynamics of knowledge—both how it moved, and what force it arrived with. What did the various individuals and groups of Southern Rhodesia know, accurately or inaccurately, about their surroundings, their neighbors, or their future, and when and how did that knowledge change?

Experiences in the environment of a rapidly changing colonial region were difficult to organize into comprehensible and useful knowledge. Africans, explorers, settlers, company and government officials, and missionaries struggled within Southern Rhodesia, as it grew from a frontier region to an economically depressed, settler-dominated colony, to develop concepts and ideas with which to understand their surroundings. Some of these, such as "civilization" or "segregation" had some external roots in various understandings of social change or "progress." Some, such as domination by conquest, or through the elaboration of discipline and deference, were substantially developed within the region. But all the key concepts that allowed the people of the region to communicate with each other were modified within Southern Rhodesia by various interest groups, and finally by the individual who was using the ideas to explain what he knew about work, or what she knew about families.

Knowledge, organized through key concepts of how society worked and what information fit together into a coherent whole, was a basic resource for the builders of Southern Rhodesia. Like economic resources, it provided a basis for contemporary perceptions of what was thinkable, possible, or likely. And accurate or inaccurate in reflecting empirical realities, the dynamics of knowledge were not abstract questions of interest only to students of discourse, or the province of an intellectual elite. The highly contested organization of knowledge was part of the organization of labor, and of production in general. It shaped the society by defining the terms for communal cohesion and intercommunal cleavage. And it guided the state, by channeling demands and directing the formulation of policy. Knowledge, frequently not reflecting empirical realities, was crucial to questions of physical and economic security during the 1890s, when Africans found themselves pressured by a poorly understood and definitely threatening Company, and settlers discovered that their ignorance of Africans could cost both profits and lives during the Risings of 1896–97. Knowledge of the uses of money was crucial to the basis of the region's economy during the early twentieth century, as it affected both the terms of labor recruitment for European-run enterprises, and the marketing of African-raised cattle and corn. Cultural knowledge and comprehension, furthermore, and the institutions that transmitted or controlled them, were crucial to the establishment of Southern Rhodesia's divided society through schools that taught children, neighbors who socialized newcomers, or the demands of a work relationship between a dominant European elite and its African workers.

Knowledge was not transmitted or controlled smoothly, and circumstances known and acted on by specific historical figures may have been substantially different from what historians, looking back, would reconstruct. Therefore, this study has used an examination of some of the issues that were vigorously debated during the period under discussion, and has attempted, through an examination of the terms of the debate, to understand the key concepts—such as civilization, discipline, development, and segregation—that structured contemporary understandings of the way the world worked. This is not an assertion of a hegemonic language or a closed discourse. Ideas such as civilization, discipline, or even segregation, permitted contemporaries to discuss many different concrete policy options, and to indulge in very different ideas of the futures than those the policies would ultimately produce. Southern Rhodesians used this language not merely to maintain a specific hierarchy and power structure within a static discourse, but to contemplate and plan for change. Yet those key images, even as they promoted or controlled change, and as one image took over from another, stated values and provided a set of terms and structures for knowledge. Through those statements of values and provision of some common language, key images facilitated certain types of communication between parts of a heterogeneous population within specific historical settings. Key images mediated both actors' knowledge and reactions to events or conditions, policy formation, and empirical, tangible outcomes.

In Southern Rhodesia the dynamics of knowledge, and therefore the construction of colonial society, were not predetermined by a dominant discourse or a hegemonic ideology. Neither was the shape of knowledge dictated through the inevitable course of economic development or class struggle. Southern Rhodesia's past, instead, was shaped by people navigating between hopes for prosperity and progress and fears of the degeneration and disintegration of their communities—struggling, debating, and worrying as they sought to prescribe and build a future.

BIBLIOGRAPHY

ARCHIVAL SOURCES

American Board of Commissioners for Foreign Missions (ABC) Archives, Houghton Library, Harvard University, Cambridge, Mass.
Council on World Missions (CWM) Archives, which include the records of the London Missionary Society (LMS), School of Oriental and African Studies, University of London.
International Missionary Congress and Council of British Missionary Societies (IMC/CBMS) Archives, School of Oriental and African Studies, University of London.
Jesuit Archives, Harare (JAH), Prestage House, Mount Pleasant, Harare, Zimbabwe.
National Archives, Zimbabwe (NAZ), Borrowdale, Harare, Zimbabwe.
Public Record Office at Kew, London.
United Society for the Propagation of the Gospel (USPG) Archives, Rhodes House Library, Oxford University, Oxford.
United States Department of Agriculture Library, Beltsville Md.
Wesleyan Methodist Missionary Society (MMS) Archives, School of Oriental and African Studies, University of London.

MAJOR OFFICIAL PUBLICATIONS

Company Documents

British South Africa Company, "Director's Report and Accounts" for the year ending 31 March 1904; 1906; 1907; 1908; 1910; 1911; 1912.
British South Africa Company "Report on the Company's Proceedings and the Condition of the Territories within the Sphere of Its Operations," 1889–92; 1892–94.

Imperial Documents

"Correspondence with the Anti-Slavery and Aborigines Protection Society Relating to the Native Reserves in Southern Rhodesia." London: HMSO [Cmd 547], 1920.

Coryndon, R. T., chair. "Papers Relating to the Southern Rhodesia Native Reserves Commission, 1915." London: HMSO, 1917.

Coryndon, R. T., chair. "Southern Rhodesian Native Reserves Commission, Interim Report, 1914"; "Southern Rhodesian Native Reserves Commission, Final Report, 1915." London: HMSO, 1914, 1915.

"First Report of Committee to Consider Certain Questions Relating to Rhodesia." London: HMSO [Cmd 1273], 1921.

Hilton-Young, E., chair. "Report of the Commission on Closer Union of the Dependencies in Eastern and Central Africa." London: HMSO, [Cmd 3234], 1929.

Martin, Sir R. E. R., ed. "Report on the Native Administration of the British South Africa Company." London: HMSO [C8547], 1897.

Ormsby-Gore, W. G. A., chair. "Education Policy in British Tropical Africa." Memorandum submitted to Secretary of State for the Colonies by Advisory Committee on Native Education in British Tropical African Dependencies. London: HMSO [Cmd 2374], 1925.

Southern Africa Native Affairs Commission (SANAC): Report (I), Minutes of Evidence (IV), and Written Submissions (V). Cape Town, 1904.

Southern Rhodesian Documents

Conference of Superintendants of Natives and Native Commissioners of the Colony of Southern Rhodesia (Conference held in December 1927). Salisbury: Government Printer, 1928.

Debates of the Legislative Council of Southern Rhodesia (to 1922).

Debates of the Legislative Assembly of Southern Rhodesia (1923–).

Decisions of the High Court of Southern Rhodesia (1911–1940).

Decisions of the Native Court of Appeal of Southern Rhodesia (1928–1940).

Government Gazette of Southern Rhodesia (useful primarily as a source of the text of bills set before the Legislative Council and Legislative Assembly).

Report of the Chief Native Commissioner for the years 1913–1938. Salisbury: Government Printer, 1914–1939.

Report of the Chief Native Commissioner of Mashonaland/Report of the Chief Native Commissioner of Matabeleland (to 1913).

Report of the Director of Agriculture/Report of the Secretary of the Department of Agriculture, 1904–1936.

Report of the Director of Education, 1899–1936.

Report of the Commission on Native Education in Southern Rhodesia, Salisbury: Government Printer [CSR20-1925], 1925.

Report of the Director of Native Education/Report of the Director of Native Development, 1928- .

Report of the Education Commission for Southern Rhodesia, Cape Town: Cape Times [CSR27-1929], 1929.

Report of the Education Committee for Southern Rhodesia, 1916, Salisbury, Rhodesia: Government Printer [A2-917], 1917.

Report of the Native Affairs Committee of Enquiry. Salisbury: Government Printer, 1911.

"Report on Employment of Native Female Domestic Labour in European Households in Southern Rhodesia" (C. L. Carbutt, chair, H. Jowitt, L. M. Foggin, and R. A. Askins). Salisbury: Government Printer, 1932.

Report on the British South Africa Police (published annually, 1915–1937, by the commissioner). Salisbury: Government Printer, 1915.

NEWSPAPERS AND PERIODICALS

Bulawayo Chronicle (newspaper, published in Bulawayo, Southern Rhodesia, for a settler audience).

Mashonaland Paper; Mashonaland Quarterly; Southern Rhodesian Quarterly (subsequent names for the Anglican diocesan periodical).

Native Affairs Department Annual (NADA, annual yearbook published by the Native Affairs Department with contributions from a variety of sources, though mostly officials, and intended for a general audience of settlers, officials, and missionaries).

Proceedings of the Southern Rhodesian Missionary Conference (formal record of the SRMC, published every two years, after a meeting).

Rhodesia Advertiser (newspaper published in Umtali [Mutare], Southern Rhodesia, for a settler audience).

Rhodesia Herald (newspaper published in Salisbury [Harare], Southern Rhodesia, for a settler audience).

Zambesi Mission Record (periodical published by the English branch of the Society of Jesus—the Jesuits—for a mission—supporting audience).

PRIMARY BOOKS AND ARTICLES

Alvord, E. D. "The Development of Native Agriculture and Land Tenure in Southern Rhodesia." Undated carbon typescript, U.S. Department of Agriculture Library, received 1959, 35.3ALS.

Baden-Powell, R. S. S. *The Matabele Campaign.* London: 1897. Reprint. West Port, Conn.: Negro Universities Press, 1970.

Brookes, E. H. *The History of Native Policy in South Africa* 2d ed. Pretoria: J. L. van Schaik, 1922, 1927.

Brookes, E. H. *Native Education in South Africa.* Pretoria: J. L. van Schaik, 1930.

Brown, W. H. *On the South African Frontier.* London, 1899. Reprint. New York: Negro Universities Press, 1970.

Chancellor, John [governor of SR], and Charles Coughlin. "Southern Rhodesia and Its Problems." *Journal of the African Society* 26 (October 1926): 1–9.

Coillard, Francois. *On the Threshhold of Central Africa,* 3d ed. London: Frank Cass, 1897, 1971.

Cripps, Arthur S. *An Africa for Africans: A plea on behalf of Territorial Segregation Areas and of Their Freedom in a South African Colony.* New York: Negro Universities Press, 1927, 1969.

Editorial. "Whither Africa." *African Observer* 1 (May 1934): 10–13.

Gilchrist, R. D. "Rhodesia's Place in the Native Problem." *Journal of the African Society* 32 (April 1933): 135–39.

Haggard, H. Rider. *King Solomon's Mines.* London, 1885.

Hemans, H. N. *The Log of a Native Commissioner,* London: H. F. and G. Witherby, 1935.

Hole, H. Marshall. *The Making of Rhodesia.* London: Macmillan, 1926.

————. *Old Rhodesian Days.* London: Frank Cass, 1928. Reprint 1968.

Huggins, G. M. "A Vital African Problem." *African Observer* 2 (February 1934): 18–25.

Jackson, H. M. G. "Native Education in Southern Rhodesia." *African Observer* 2 (December 1934): 28–30.

————. "The Natives of Southern Rhodesia: Their Position after Ten Years under Responsible Government." *African Observer* 1 (June 1934): 19–23.

Jowitt, Harold. *Principles of Education for African Teachers.* London: Longmans, Green, 1932.

Keigwin, H. S. "An Educational Experiment." *South African Journal of Science* 18 (December 1921): 172–82.

Knight-Bruce, G. W. H. *Journals of the Mashonaland Mission, 1888 to 1892.* London: United Society for the Propagation of the Gospel, 1892.

Loram, C. T. *The Education of the South African Native.* London: Longmans, Green, 1917.

Macmillan, W. M. "Southern Rhodesia and the Development of Africa." *Journal of the African Society* 32 (July 1933): 294–98.

Moffat, Robert. *Missionary Labours and Scenes in Southern Africa.* London: 1842.

Schreiner, Olive. *Trooper Peter Halket of Mashonaland.* London: J. Fisher Unwin, 1897.

Selous, F. C. *Travel and Adventure in Southeast Africa.* London: Rowland Ward, 1893. Reprint. New York: Arno Press, 1967.

Shropshire, Denys [Community of the Ressurection Mission, SR]. "Native Develpment in Southern Rhodesia." *Journal of the African Society* 32 (October 1933): 409-23.

Simons, H. J. "European Civilisation and African Crime." *African Observer* 2 (1934): 20-27.

Sykes, Frank W. *With Plumer in Matabeleland.* New York: Negro Universities Press, 1897, 1969.

Tawse-Jollie, Ethel. "Native Administration in Southern Rhodesia." *Journal of the Royal Society of Arts* 83 (30 August 1935): 973-85.

————. *The Real Rhodesia.* London: Hutchinson and Co., 1924.

Wills, W. A., and L. T. Collingridge, eds. *The Downfall of Lobengula.* London, New York: 1894, 1969.

Young, Cullen. "Our Ultimate Aim." *African Observer* 2 (February 1934): 26-34.

SECONDARY BOOKS, DISSERTATIONS, AND ARTICLES

Anderson, Benedict. *Imagined Communities.* London: Verso, 1983.

Anderson, James D. *The Education of Blacks in the South, 1860-1935.* Chapel Hill, N.C.: University of North Carolina Press, 1988.

Ashforth, Adam. *The Politics of Official Discourse in Twentieth-Century South Africa.* Oxford: Clarendon Press, 1990.

Barnes, Terri. "African Female Labour and the Urban Economy of Colonial Zimbabwe, with Special Reference to Harare, 1920-39." M.A. thesis, University of Zimbabwe, 1987.

Beach, D. N. *The Shona and Zimbabwe, 900-1850.* Gweru: Mambo Press, 1980.

————. *War and Politics in Zimbabwe, 1840-1900.* Gweru: Mambo Press, 1986.

Beinart, William. "Soil Erosion, Conservationism and Ideas about Development: A Southern African Exploration, 1900-1960." *Journal of Southern African Studies* 11.1 (October 1984): 52-83.

Berman, Bruce. *Control and Crisis in Colonial Kenya: The Dialectic of Domination.* London: James Currey, 1990.

Bhila, *Trade and Politics in a Shona Kingdom.* Harare: Longman, 1982.

Burke, Timothy. "Lifebuoy Men, Lux Women: Commodification, Consumption and Cleanliness in Colonial Zimbabwe." Ph.D. dissertation, Johns Hopkins University, 1992.

Cell, John W. *The Highest Stage of White Supremacy: The Origins of Segregation in South Africa and the American South.* Cambridge: Cambridge University Press, 1982.

Challiss, R. J. "The European Educational System in Southern Rhodesia, 1890 to 1930." *Zambezia* supplement, 1982.

————. "The Foundation of the Racially Segregated Educational System in Southern Rhodesia, 1890-1923, with Special Reference to the Education of Africans". Ph.D. thesis, University of Zimbabwe, 1982.

Chanock, *Law, Custom and Social Order: The Colonial Experience in Malawi and Zambia.* Cambridge: Cambridge University Press, 1985.

Cobbing, Julian R. D. "The Ndebele under the Khumalos, 1820-1900." Ph.D. thesis, History, University of Lancaster, 1976.

Colson, Elizabeth, and Thayer Scudder. *For Prayer and Profit: The Ritual, Economic, and Social Importance of Beer in Gwembe District, Zambia, 1950-1982.* Stanford: Stanford University Press, 1988.

Comarofff, Jean, and John Comaroff. *Of Revelation and Revolution: Christianity, Colonialism and Consciousness in South Africa.* Vol.. 1. Chicago: University of Chicago Press, 1991.

Cope, R. L. "C. W. de Kiewiet, the Imperial Factor, and South African 'Native Policy.'" *Journal of Southern African Studies* 15 (April 1989): 486-505.

Dachs, A. J., and W. F. Rea. *The Catholic Church and Zimbabwe, 1879-1979.* Gweru: Mambo Press, 1979.

Davis, Benjamin, and Wolfgang Doepcke. "Survival and Accumulation in Gutu: Class Formation and the Rise of the State in Colonial Zimbabwe, 1900-1939." *Journal of Southern African Studies* 14 (October 1987): 64-98.

Dubow, Saul. "Holding 'a Just Balance between White and Black': The Native Affairs Department in South Africa c. 1920-33." *Journal of Southern African Studies* 12:2 (April 1986): 217-39.

————. *Racial Segregation and the Origins of Apartheid in South Africa, 1919-1936.* New York: St. Martin's, 1989.

Eklof, Ben. *Russian Peasant Schools: Officialdom, Village Culture, and Popular Pedagogy, 1861-1914.* Berkeley: University of California Press, 1986.

Ferguson, James. "Mobile Workers, Modernist Narratives: A Critique of the Historiography of Transition on the Zambian Copperbelt." *Journal of Southern African Studies* 16:3 (September 1990): 385-412.

Fredrickson, George M. *White Supremacy: A Comparative Study in American and South African History.* Oxford: Oxford University Press, 1981.

Galbraith, John S. *Crown and Charter: The Early Years of the British South Africa Company.* Berkeley: University of California Press, 1974.

Gann, L. H. *A History of Southern Rhodesia: Early Days to 1934.* New York: Humanities Press, 1965.

Guy, Jeff. "The Destruction and Reconstruction of Zulu Society." In *Industrialisation and Social Change in South Africa: African Class Formation, Culture and Consciousness, 1870-1930,* edited by S. Marks and R. Rathbone, 167-194. London: Longman, 1982.

Horn, Pamela. *Education in Rural England, 1800–1914.* London: Gill and Macmillan, 1978.

Hurt, J. S. *Elementary Schooling and the Working Classes, 1860–1918.* London: Routledge and Kegan Paul, 1979.

Jeater, Diana. "Marriage, Perversion and Power: The Construction of Moral Discourse in Southern Rhodesia, 1890–1930". Ph.D. thesis, Oxford University, 1990; subsequently published as *Marriage, Perversion and Power: The Construction of Moral Discourse in Southern Rhodesia, 1890–1930.* Oxford: Oxford University Press, 1993.

Kallaway, Peter, ed. *Apartheid and Education: The Education of Black South Africans.* Johannesburg: Ravan Press, 1984.

Kennedy, Dane. *Islands of White.* Durham, N.C.: Duke University Press, 1987.

Keppel-Jones, Arthur. *Rhodes and Rhodesia: The White Conquest of Zimbabwe, 1884–1902.* Kingston, Ontario: Mcgill-Queen's University Press, 1983.

Leys, Colin. *European Politics in Southern Rhodesia.* Oxford: Clarendon Press, 1959.

Mandala, Elias C. *Work and Control in a Peasant Economy: A History of the Lower Tchiri Valley in Malawi.* Madison: University of Wisconsin Press, 1990.

Marks, Shula. *The Ambiguities of Dependence in South Africa: Class, Nationalism, and the State in Twentieth-Century Natal.* Baltimore: Johns Hopkins University Press, 1986.

––––––. "Natal, the Zulu Royal Family and the Ideology of Segregation," *Journal of Southern African Studies* 4.2 (April 1978): 172–94.

––––––. "Patriotism, Patriarchy and Purity: Natal and the Politics of Zulu Ethnic Consciousness." In *The Creation of Tribalism in Southern Africa,* edited by Leroy Vail, 215–240. Berkeley: University of California Press, 1989.

––––––. *Reluctant Rebellion: The 1906–8 Disturbances in Natal.* London: Oxford University Press, 1970.

Mason, Philip. *The Birth of a Dilemma.* London: Oxford University Press, 1958.

Miller, Joseph. *Way of Death: Merchant Capitalism and the Angloan Slave Trade.* Madison: University of Wisconsin Press, 1988.

Mosley, Paul. *The Settler Economies: Studies in the Economic History of Kenya and Southern Rhodesia, 1900–1963.* Cambridge: Cambridge University Press, 1983.

Mudenge, S. I. G. *A Political History of Munhumutapa.* Harare: Zimbabwe Publishing House, 1988.

Murray, Colin. *Families Divided: The Impact of Migrant Labour in Lesotho.* Cambridge: Cambridge University Press, 1981.

Murray, D. J. *The Governmental System in Southern Rhodesia.* Oxford: Clarendon Press, 1970.

Mutambirwa, J. A. C. *The Rise of Settler Power in Southern Rhodesia (Zimbabwe), 1898–1923.* Cranbury, N.J.: Associated Universities Presses, 1980.

Palley, Claire. *The Constitutional History and Law of Southern Rhodesia 1888–1965.* Oxford: Clarendon Press, 1966.

Palmer, Robin. *Land and Racial Domination in Rhodesia.* Berkeley: University of California Press, 1977.

Pape, John. "Black and White: The 'Perils of Sex' in Colonial Zimbabwe." *Journal of Southern African Studies* 16:4 (December 1990): 699–720.

Phimister, Ian R. *An Economic and Social History of Zimbabwe, 1890–1948.* London: Longman, 1988.

————. "Discourse and the Discipline of Historical Context" *Journal of Southern African Studies* 12:2 (April 1986) 263–275.

Ranger, Terence O. *The African Voice in Southern Rhodesia 1898–1930.* London: Heinemann, 1970.

————. "Literature and Political Economy: A. S. Cripps and the Makoni Labour Crisis of 1911," *Journal of Southern African Studies* 9:1 (October 1982) 33–53.

————. *Revolt in Southern Rhodesia, 1896–7: A Study in African Resistance.* Evanston: Northwestern University Press, 1967.

Schmidt, Elizabeth. "Farmers, Hunters and Gold Washers: A Reevaluation of Women's Roles in Precolonial and Colonial Zimbabwe." *African Economic History* 17 (1988): 45–80.

————. "Ideology, Economics, and the Role of Shona Women in Southern Rhodesia, 1850–1939." Ph.D. dissertation, History, University of Wisconsin, Madison, 1987.

————. "Negotiated Spaces and Contested Terrain: Men, Women and the Law in Colonial Zimbabwe, 1890–1939." *Journal of Southern African Studies* 16.4 (December 1990): 623–48.

————. *Peasants, Traders, and Wives: Shona Women in the History of Zimbabwe, 1870–1939.* Portsmouth, N.H.: Heinemann, 1992.

Schreuder, D. M. "The Cultural Factor in Victorian Imperialism: A Case-study of the British 'Civilising Mission.'" *Journal of Imperial and Commonwealth History* 4:3 (May 1976): 283–317.

————. *The Scramble for Southern Africa, 1877–1895.* Cambridge: Cambridge University Press, 1980.

Silver, Harold. *Education as History.* London: Methuen, 1983.

Silver, Pamela, and Harold Silver, *The Education of the Poor: The History of a National School, 1824–1974.* London: Routledge and Kegan Paul, 1974.

Smelser, Neil. *Social Paralysis and Social Change: British Working-Class*

Education in the Nineteenth Century. Berkeley: University of California Press, 1991.

Steele, Murray C. "The Foundations of a 'Native' Policy: Southern Rhodesia, 1923-33." Ph.D. thesis, Simon Fraser University, 1972.

Summers, Carol. "Demanding Education: African Educational Agendas in Southern Rhodesia, 1900-1934." Seminar paper, 1993.

————. "Educational Controversies: African Activism and Educational Strategies, 1920-34." Seminar paper, 1992.

Taylor, J. J. "The Emergence and Development of the Native Department in Southern Rhodesia, 1894-1914." Ph.D. thesis, University of London, 1979.

Vambe, Lawrence, *An Ill-Fated People: Zimbabwe before and after Rhodes.* London, Pittsburg: 1972.

van Onselen, Charles. *Chibaro: African Mine Labour in Southern Rhodesia, 1900-1933.* London: Pluto Press, 1976.

————. *Studies in the Social and Economic History of the Witwatersrand, 1886-1914.* New York: Longman, 1982.

Vincent, David. *Literacy and Popular Culture: England 1750-1914.* Cambridge: Cambridge University Press, 1989.

White, Landeg. *Magomero: Portrait of an African Village.* Cambridge: Cambridge University Press, 1987.

White, Luise. *The Comforts of Home: Prostitution in Colonial Nairobi.* Chicago: University of Chicago Press, 1990.

Yoshikune, Tsuneo. "Black Migrants in a White City: A History of African Harare, 1890-1925." Ph.D. thesis, University of Zimbabwe, 1990.

Zachrisson, Per. *An African Area in Change: Belingwe, 1894-1946.* Gothenburg: University of Gothenburg Press, 1978.

Index